'Ulama', Politics, and the Public Sphere

T0308820

UTAH SERIES IN TURKISH AND ISLAMIC STUDIES

M. Hakan Yavuz, Series Editor

A Religion, Not a State: Ali ʿAbd al-Raziq's Islamic Justification of Political Secularism
Souad T. Ali

Armenians and the Allies in Cilicia, 1914–1923
Yücel Güçlü

Debating Moderate Islam: The Geopolitics of Islam and the West
Edited by M. A. Muqtedar Khan

ʿUlamaʾ, Politics, and the Public Sphere: An Egyptian Perspective
Meir Hatina

The Armenian Massacres in Ottoman Turkey: A Disputed Genocide
Guenter Lewy

The Turk in America: The Creation of an Enduring Prejudice
Justin McCarthy

The Armenian Rebellion at Van
Justin McCarthy, Esat Arslan, Cemalettin Taşkıran, and Ömer Turan

Autobiographies of Orhan Pamuk: The Writer in His Novels
Michael McGaha

Sustainability of Microstates: The Case of North Cyprus
Ozay Mehmet

Turkish Foreign Policy, 1919–2006: Facts and Analysis with Documents
Edited by Baskin Oran
Translated by Mustafa Aksin

The Ottoman Army, 1914–1918: Disease and Death on the Battlefield
Hikmet Özdemir
Translated by Şaban Kardaş

The Search for God's Law: Islamic Jurisprudence in the Writings of Sayf al-Din al-Āmidī, Revised Edition
Bernard G. Weiss

The Emergence of a New Turkey: Democracy and the AK Parti
Edited by M. Hakan Yavuz

ʿUlamaʾ, Politics, and the Public Sphere

An Egyptian Perspective

MEIR HATINA

Utah Series in Turkish
and Islamic Studies

THE UNIVERSITY OF UTAH PRESS
Salt Lake City

Utah Series in Turkish and Islamic Studies
M. Hakan Yavuz, Series Editor

The Defiance House Man colophon is a registered trademark
of the University of Utah Press. It is based upon a four-foot-tall,
Ancient Puebloan pictograph (late PIII) near Glen Canyon, Utah.

14 13 12 11 10   1 2 3 4 5

LIBRARY OF CONGRESS CATALOGING-IN-PUBLICATION DATA

Hatina, Meir.
   ʿUlamaʾ, politics, and the public sphere : an Egyptian perspective /
Meir Hatina.
      p. cm.
   Includes bibliographical references and index.
   ISBN 978-1-60781-032-2 (cloth : alk. paper)
     1. Ulama—Egypt—History.   2. Islam—Egypt—History.
3. Egypt—Politics and government.   I. Title.
   BP64.E3H38 2010
   297.6′10962—dc22   2010024001

Photo courtesy of Travelers in the Middle East Archive (TIMEA)
Rice University, Houston, Texas

Printed and bound by Sheridan Books, Inc., Ann Arbor, Michigan.

For Ilana

Contents

A Note on Transliteration

The English transliteration of Arabic words follows standard academic rules as stipulated by the *International Journal of Middle East Studies*. Arabic names and terms used in the English-language literature appear in their English version.

Arabic terms are italicized, except for those that recur often, such as ʿulamaʾ, qadi, shaykh, and shariʿa. ʿ is used for the Arabic letter ʿayn and ʾ for hamza. No subscripts or superscripts are used.

The transliteration of Turkish words and names generally follows the system used in modern Turkish.

Preface

> The jurist is familiar with the art of politics and the way to reconcile men when they are fighting because of greed and temptations. The jurist serves as a mentor [*mu'allim*] and a guide [*murshid*] to the sultan in governing the people and regulating their affairs so as to ensure their following in the right path.
>
> —Abu Hamid al-Ghazali, *Ihya' 'ulum al-din*, vol. 1, p. 17

The status of the Sunni 'ulama' (religious scholars; sing. *'alim*) in modern times has attracted renewed academic interest over the last decade in light of their assertiveness regarding moral and sociopolitical issues on the Arab-Muslim agenda. Several works have reassessed the narrative of historians and social scientists that generally depicted the 'ulama' as marginal players—neither as activists nor as intellectual innovators—in comparison to the lay Islamists and certainly the Shi'ite 'ulama'. Notably, this reassessment has related the vitality of the 'ulama' to the Islamic resurgence from the 1970s onward, which forced the political elites to rely increasingly on the religious establishment, thereby allowing the 'ulama' greater freedom of activity.

The present study, however, returns to an earlier period in history and shows that such vitality is not new. Its roots go back to the second half of the nineteenth century and the early twentieth century, an accelerated period of state building and national cohesion, to which the 'ulama' reacted in diverse ways. An important prism is provided by the case of the 'ulama' of al-Azhar in Egypt.

Based on various primary Egyptian, Ottoman, and European sources, this study reveals a vibrant, multifaceted picture of Azharis who were involved in public and political affairs and who continued to serve as molders of culture following the collapse of the Islamic-Ottoman order and the formation of nation-states. A similar picture emerges from a comparative discussion of 'ulama' in other parts of the Arab Middle East, especially in the Fertile Crescent. Moreover, the sustained efforts of Sunni 'ulama' to restrain the nationalist/modernist impetus and to prevent the erosion of the Islamic ethos facilitated a more convenient climate for dissident Islamic movements to further their cause.

The research and writing of this book were made possible by the generous support of the Israel Science Foundation (ISF). My sincere appreciation goes to the following mentors and colleagues for their insights and critiques: Michael Winter, Emmanuel Sivan, John Voll, Rainer Brunner, Jakob Skovgaard-Petersen, Ami Ayalon, Meir Litvak, Sara Sviri, and Ron Shaham. I am also indebted to the two anonymous referees for their learned comments and advice about the manuscript. Thanks are due to Yoni Sheffer and Shai Zohar, who helped locate and collect important material, and to Judy Krausz, who skillfully edited the book. I am deeply grateful to Hakan Yavuz and the editorial staff at the University of Utah Press, especially Peter DeLafosse and Glenda Cotter, for their invaluable professional guidance. Finally, I embrace in gratitude my wife, Ilana, who sustained me through the last stages of the research with love and patience.

Meir Hatina
Jerusalem

INTRODUCTION
ʿUlamaʾ and Modernity: A Reappraisal

Western discourse on the status of clergy and religious functionaries in the three monotheistic creeds reflects a clear divide between their position in the premodern period and in modern times. As the custodians of learning and molders of communal identity in the premodern period, they were viewed as central to the functioning of society. In modern times, by contrast, in the face of the abandonment of religious conventions and norms by both the individual and the state, they were perceived as relegated to the margins of society. Terms such as "Promethean passion" and "metaphysical revolt" were widely used in research literature to express the religious upheaval in which the Kingdom of God was replaced by the human kingdom. The groundwork for this upheaval was attributed to the "triple revolution" in Christian Europe between 1600 and 1800: enlightenment, industrialism, and nationalism.[1]

In light of these developments, the clergy was often perceived in modern Western discourse as a group in crisis, caught in the tension between conservative institutions and radical forces of change. Sociologists, including Robert Towler and Paul M. Harrison, argued in the early 1970s that the clergy lacked manpower, its social status was in decline, and considerable uncertainty existed about its true role.[2] Addressing the modern predicament of the clerical professional, Harrison argued:

> In an age when the man on the street is oriented by a scientific culture that emphasizes empirical verification of any claims to truth, it is difficult to maintain the professional status of competing clerical groups. The ancient clerical assertion that the church possesses a universally valid and objectively received revelation has broken down.[3]

In the same vein, sociologist Steve Bruce, writing in the 1990s, spoke about the "the erosion of the supernatural" in modern times in terms of loss of members and authority by churches in Western Europe and the United States, while large numbers of people were beginning to experiment with a variety of new esoteric religions.[4] These analyses resulted in a relatively broad neglect of the clergy as a topic of study,[5] affecting research on the ʿulamaʾ in the Middle East context as well.

ʿULAMAʾ IN HISTORY

Historically, the ʿulamaʾ were in charge of interpreting and imparting the holy texts and were recognized as guardians of faith both by believers and by those in power. Their authority was neither abstract nor textual; rather, it was deeply entrenched in communal life. The study of the Qurʾan, the hadith (sayings attributed to the Prophet), and especially the presence of the holy law (shariʿa) in every aspect of life served as constant reminders of the implicit authority of religious knowledge and its earthly representatives. The imparting of knowledge was essential to guarantee the existence of the faith. But for its keepers, the ʿulamaʾ, it was also a source of livelihood and prestige and served as a vehicle for distinguishing their sectoral status from that of other groups in society. This process of the socialization of knowledge, which involved the coalescence of formal patterns of training and authorizing scholars, arbiters, and judges, perpetuated the public status of the ʿulamaʾ.

Religious knowledge constituted a kind of cultural capital that became a source of authority and a means to guide believers on the right path. Yet it was also an effective way to include or exclude individuals or groups from the exclusive pool of the learned.

Knowledge and religious authority endowed the ʿulamaʾ with effective control over entry into the academic and legal establishment and allowed the most senior clerics to create a kind of religious aristocracy of old, established families in places such as Cairo, Damascus, and Istanbul. The ongoing influence of these families had three main foundations: nepotism and guaranteed privileges for their descendants, patronage ties with those who sought support, and marriage ties with each other or with other families belonging to the elite.[6]

This impressive accomplishment of the ʿulamaʾ contrasted with the egalitarian basis of Islam, which lacked a clerical or priestly establishment as in the Catholic Church.

The religious authority of the ʿulamaʾ was not based solely on formal training in religious colleges (madrasas) and the ability to expound the shariʿa. An added source of their authority was charisma, acquired through pious and ethical conduct but mainly through the capacity to bestow a state of spiritual blessing (*baraka*) and perform miracles (*karamat*).[7] The most pronounced manifestations of such charismatic authority were sainthood and the ritual worship of saints, identified primarily with the Sufi movement, which gained a broad social base from the twelfth century onward.[8]

Charisma, according to Max Weber, is a personality attribute that enables individuals to stand out from ordinary people, who treat them as if they were endowed with supernatural qualities. Charismatic authority contrasts with traditional authority, which is based on formal institutions and relations. Moreover, it tends to rebel against normative institutions due to its inherent moral fervor and nonconformism. The contrast between charismatic virtues and organized social relationships in established contexts, however, is not so extreme or pronounced; it gives way to points of contact and interaction. In order to acquire recognition for his authority and disseminate his message, a charismatic leader must act within a concrete reality and on behalf of the community and display supernatural acts publicly in ceremonies, processions, and structures.[9] As Aviad Kleinberg writes, "without an audience there is no charisma": its existence is made possible only when some sort of group is prepared to attribute exceptional qualities to one of its members. Moreover, charisma is a force and a lever for the attainment of communal power, which obliges the religious and political authorities to turn it into a canonical discourse.[10] This methodological assumption is also borne out historically in Sunni Islam, in the reciprocal relationships between erudition and mysticism: scholars often follow Sufism as well.

Various studies have pointed to the links among learning, intercession with God, and divine grace, which diffused the inherent tension between formal and esoteric knowledge and ensured that it would not degenerate into extremism and confrontation. The connection between legalism and mysticism established the Sufi saints as part of a universal cultural model of worthy behavior by emphasizing the legal and moral aspect of their image while vesting the jurists with an additional, more attractive source of authority when learning alone was insufficient.[11]

Thus Sufism was presented as an option rather than an alternative in Sunni Islam. In this sense, the execution of the Persian Sufi preacher al-Husayn ibn Mansur al-Hallaj in Baghdad in the early tenth century and the anti-Sufi persecution by the puritanical Wahhabi movement in the Arabian Peninsula at the end of the eighteenth century were atypical episodes.[12]

The present volume, which deals with the mid-nineteenth and early twentieth centuries, provides additional indicators of the affinity between scholarship and Sufism. It also shows, however, that the mainstream ʿulamaʾ were essentially theologians and jurists (sing. *faqih*; pl. *fuqahaʾ*), as the biographical dictionaries indicate, and perceived themselves as such. They tended to be only mildly ascetic and were affiliated mainly with the more orthodox orders—the Naqshbandiyya, the Shadhiliyya, and the Khalwatiyya—rather than, for example, the Rifaʿiyya or the Saʿdiyya orders.

The religious authority of the ʿulamaʾ was a built-in component of the cosmic Islamic order, enabling them to become the focus of influence and privilege, especially under the Mamluk and Ottoman elites, whose ethnic and cultural foreignness prompted them to demonstrate superior loyalty to Islam and its spokesmen. The encounter with European colonialism and modernization at the start of the nineteenth century, however, led to a reorganization of local communal life and thus also a reshaping of the religious landscape.

ʿULAMAʾ AND MODERNITY
IN WESTERN HISTORIOGRAPHY

The historiography of modernization in the Middle East from the nineteenth century onward adopted two approaches that denigrated the status of the ʿulamaʾ in the context of the emergence of a new social and political order. One approach emphasized the intrusive nature of the modern state, under which the ʿulamaʾ were reduced to a bureaucratic branch left with jurisdiction only over family and personal status. The other emphasized the challenge presented by new social and intellectual forces that openly defied the religious authority of the ʿulamaʾ. These forces were molded in the milieu of the encounter with Western culture, the expansion of higher education, and growing social schisms, exemplified by Islamic reformism, modern nationalism, and the fundamentalism of the Muslim Brotherhood.[13]

All of these new movements claimed to speak in the name of Islam and for the Islamic cause, relying on their own interpretation of the scriptures and on new texts of their own. In this they were greatly assisted by emerging judicial systems other than the shariʿa, mass education, and the print and communication culture. These developments nurtured the processes of democratization and individualization of religious knowledge, making the Islamic discourse more pluralistic than ever, with a variety of spokesmen who vied for authority in the Muslim public arena.[14]

In Western historiography, the ʿulamaʾ emerged bruised and enervated from this array of challenges. Although the Islamic religion continued to provide a reservoir of symbols of protest, identity, and legitimation, its traditional spokesmen in the ʿulamaʾ community lagged behind in terms of influence. They tended to function as a rubber stamp for regime policy or as a tool to discredit local and foreign rivals. The rise of revolutionary regimes in the Middle East in the 1950s and 1960s and, after their demise, the appearance of waves of religious resurgence in the 1970s further constricted the relevance of the official ʿulamaʾ in the research of the period. Most of the standard-bearers of the religious resurgence came from the intelligentsia and, moreover, branded the ʿulamaʾ as traitors for their subservience to deviant regimes, which indicated that the Islamic protest was an essentially modern phenomenon.[15] It was the modern Muslim intellectual who placed activism and charisma before knowledge and was involved in politics that captured the imagination of Western observers.[16]

Two exceptions to the paradigm of the stagnation and decline of the ʿulamaʾ were the Shiʿi ʿulamaʾ (particularly in Iran) and the ʿulamaʾ of the semitribal milieu. The Shiʿi ʿulamaʾ had two assets at their disposal that ensured relative independence from the regime and served as a lever for active involvement in politics: (1) doctrinal and juridical power, as authorized by the "Hidden Imam," to guide the lives of the community until his return to the world to inaugurate the "Kingdom of Justice"; and (2) material power: control over commercial and economic sources and management of the assets of the religious trusts. According to Shahrough Akhavi, writing in 1995, "the Iranian Revolution of 1979 is but the latest example of the assertiveness of the Shiʿi ʿulamaʾ in the sociopolitical domain during the past two centuries."[17]

The semitribal ʿulamaʾ, especially in peripheral regions such as the Arabian Peninsula and North Africa, wielded great influence as a result of their geographic distance from the urban centers. They were revered for their saintly attributes and respected for their close relationship with local dynasties and the religious and judicial services they provided to the tribes, including religious instruction, mediation, and conflict resolution. These functions contributed to the integration of the tribes in the wider Muslim community. Examples include the revivalist movements of the Jazaʾiriyya in Algeria, the Sanusiyya in Libya, and the Mahdiyya in Sudan, all of which succeeded in establishing political entities in the name of re-generating a moral Islamic society. Elsewhere, as in Morocco, ʿulamaʾ led or backed the liberation movements aimed at attaining freedom from the yoke of European colonialism.[18]

The research depicted urban Sunni Islam quite differently, however: it was repeatedly portrayed as uniform in nature and as constituting a generally subservient element—or, at the very least, as introverted and on the defensive. The depiction of Sunni ʿulamaʾ as passive and intellectually noninnovative reflected the perception of historians and social scientists that they were traditional players unable to deal with the upheavals of modern times.[19] In Western historiography's obsessive search for significant milestones and turning points in the convoluted sociopolitical history of the Middle East, the ʿulamaʾ sector fell into obscurity.

This approach is best exemplified in observations by two leading scholars, Hamilton Gibb and Harold Bowen. In discussing the period toward the end of the eighteenth century in *Islamic Society and the West* (1957) they concluded that

> it is difficult to avoid the impression that in reality the position of the Ulema was gravely undermined. Though they still preserved the appearance of power, it was beginning to wear thin; their repeated compromise had shown that in the face of determined action, they would yield. The spectacle which the Şeyhs were to present during the nineteenth century was not solely the result of the rapid overthrow of the old social order. It was the sudden culmination of a long process that had gradually sapped their moral position.[20]

In P. M. Holt's view (writing in 1966), the modernizing reforms introduced by Sultan Mahmud II (1808–39), which included diverting religious endowments (*waqf*; pl. *awqaf*) for state purposes and establishing a new educational system, had the effect of "diminishing the status of the ʿulamaʾ." Bernard Lewis argued in 1973 that, following the Westernized reforms, "the ulema, already to some extent associated with political power, now became completely subservient to it, and lost touch with the people.... Ulema and dervishes alike were out of touch with the modern world, against which the new elites were struggling, and which at the same time they were striving to join." In the same vein, Ira M. Lapidus affirmed in 1988 that the Ottoman and Egyptian ʿulamaʾ had lost their influence on public policy. "The lack of an autonomous basis of power and a tradition of compliance operated in Egypt, as in the Ottoman Empire, to confine the 'ulama' to the defense of a narrow range of traditional pre-rogatives."[21] Iftikhar Zaman observed in 1995 that the colonial reorga-nization of society, along with the rise of new social, legal, and political structures, brought about discontinuity in the function of the 'ulama'. "Thus, during colonial rule the domain of operation of the 'ulama' be-came confined to the mosque and the *madrasa*."[22] This observation was reinforced by John L. Esposito and John Voll, who in 2001 referred to the decline of the 'ulama', and by Olivier Roy, who in 2002 pointed to their crisis of religious authority and transmission.[23]

These perceptions were even more pronounced in analyses of the micro-picture of the 'ulama' of al-Azhar, the venerated mosque-university in Egypt founded in 972. Afaf Lutfi al-Sayyid-Marsot wrote in 1968 that during the nineteenth century the 'ulama' lost their standing as the intel-lectual innovators in society, refused to have anything to do with reform, and "devoted themselves to the arduous task of survival. Change, to them, became a reprehensible innovation." Daniel Crecelius observed in 1972 that "modernization has meant for the 'ulama' an agonizing and constant retreat from political power and social preeminence." Another prominent scholar, Gabriel Baer, argued in 1983 that "the establishment of a stable dy-nasty and a centralized bureaucracy deprived them [the 'ulama'] of their former functions as legitimators and mediators. As a result, the 'ulama' lost the rest of their capability for any effective political activity."[24]

Similar conclusions have been drawn by more contemporary histori-ans, among them Carly Murphy, who described al-Azhar in terms of de-cline and submission,[25] supporting the paradigm that the guardians of the Islamic ethos were marginalized in the new cosmic order. More broadly, this assumption was intrinsic in the view that Muslim civilization and its fountainhead, the Ottoman Empire, were in decline in the face of the en-croachment of Western modernity.

As pointed out by scholars such as Lila Abu-Lughod, Walter Arm-brust, Timothy Mitchell, Gregory Starret, and Benjamin C. Fortna,[26] however, modernity was far from being a linear process of rationalism and emancipation in the Middle East. It was a much more complex process, in which Western cultural themes were contested while perceptions and traditions of the past survived or were even rejuvenated.

During the last two decades or so, various conventional percep-tions in the field of Middle Eastern studies that had been influenced by the paradigm of modernization have been challenged or revised. These premises include the absence of a dynamic Muslim public sphere;[27] the French conquest of Egypt in 1798 as heralding the start of the entry of local society into the modern era;[28] the decline of the Ottoman Empire from the eighteenth century onward and its ineffective reform policy;[29] the disharmony between Islam and nationalism; and the perception of nationalism as a new phenomenon in the Middle East with no historical or ethno-cultural antecedents.[30] Nevertheless, the denigrating narrative regarding the status of the religious establishment has been largely preserved and has continued to foster supportive research. Typically, a 1998 book by Anwar Alam about religion and state in Egypt, Iran, and Saudia Arabia holds that "throughout the nineteenth century, the development of modern educational, legal and commercial systems caused the increasing marginalization of the ʿulamaʾ."[31]

CONTESTING THE PARADIGM

The present work, which focuses on Egypt in the late nineteenth and early twentieth centuries, seeks to reassess the status of the Sunni ʿulamaʾ in an era of modernization and nation building. It shows that subservience to state authority did not necessarily mean submission in all aspects and that the loss of the monopoly over the judicial, educational, and intellectual realms did not mean marginalization. In this the study supports historical insights by Richard Antoun, Malika Zeghal, and Muhammad Qasim Zaman.

Antoun's book cites fieldwork that points to the sustained influence of preachers and their sermons as cultural agents in rural Jordan, as compared with other places in the Muslim world.[32] Zeghal's work about al-Azhar in Egypt focuses on the structural reform in that institution and the introduction of modern secular sciences in its curriculum from 1961 onward. These measures did not live up to the regime's expectations to integrate the ʿulamaʾ in the modernization process. On the contrary, they produced a new type of Azhari graduate: peripheral ʿulamaʾ who had received both a religious and a modern education but were attracted to the Islamists to an even greater extent than before, especially on the issue of implementing the shariʿa. Additionally, the regime's growing reliance on the religious establishment for public legitimization, side by side with the need to neutralize the Islamist opposition, heightened al-Azhar's power and paved the way to its greater involvement in public life during the 1980s.[33]

Zeghal's analyses are correct, but what should be emphasized is that—to the state's displeasure—religious assertiveness in the public arena was not solely the province of junior or peripheral ʿulamaʾ. It was also evident among senior 'ulama', including heads of al-Azhar such as 'Abd al-Halim Mahmud (1973–78) and Jadd al-Haqq 'Ali Jadd al-Haqq (1982–96). Moreover, the involvement of religious scholars in the public arena encompassed social and ethical issues as well. This aspect was clear even under the revolutionary regime. The most obvious example was the family-planning policy promoted by Gamal Abdel Nasser: it was only partially successful, not least because of the dissenting attitude of the 'ulama', especially in the rural areas. Another example was the determined struggle by Azharis against religious skepticism in intellectual discourse, which went back to the constitutional era (1923–52).[34]

Zeghal later broadened her historical perspective, taking into account the Azharis' active role in intellectual debates in the 1930s and 1940s while still adhering to her depiction of al-Azhar's position in the late twentieth century as one of "reemergence" in the political and intellectual scenes. Zeghal's assertion that al-Azhar in the last quarter of the twentieth century and beyond recentered its relevance in transnational debates in the context of competing with new religious agents is also problematic from a historical perspective. The Azharis' transnational cultural activity was evident long before; Mubarak's Egypt merely sustained previous official support for al-Azhar's positions, with the emergence of the new media giving further impetus to this outreach.[35]

Muhammad Qasim Zaman's book on the position of the 'ulama' in South Asia, mainly in Pakistan (with comparative notes referring to the Arab arena), supports Zeghal's basic analyses. Contrary to the anachronistic image assigned to the 'ulama', he argues that they in fact dealt with the challenge of modernity with varying degrees of success. They actually managed to widen their support and occasionally even dictated the parameters of the public discourse.[36]

The research by Antoun, Zeghal, and Zaman on the influence of the 'ulama' essentially spans the second half of the twentieth century. The present study goes further back in its comparative discussion, covering the second half of the nineteenth century to the start of the twentieth century. This adds historical depth and further insights that support the revisionist research on the status of the Sunni 'ulama' in modern times.[37]

Analysis of varied primary Egyptian, Ottoman, and European sources, including official documents, biographical dictionaries, compilations of fatwas (legal opinions), memoirs, and newspapers, evokes a more complex picture of al-Azhar. In a climate of dynamic change, Azharis found themselves on the defensive, yet deeply engaged in the public sphere in their determination to influence its course.

THE EGYPTIAN PUBLIC SPHERE
IN THE LATE NINETEENTH CENTURY

The concept of the public sphere, as developed by the sociologist Jürgen Habermas, refers to a third social space between the official and the private realms, in which issues of general interest are dealt with and public opinion is molded by means of persuasion, conflict, and contested meaning. The public sphere shifts the emphasis from the political authorities to society and is closely related to urban culture, both in the main centers and in provincial cities. Older socialization sites—such as salons, coffeehouses, theaters, museums, and lecture halls—were replaced in the later nineteenth century by a new infrastructure of communications and social integration. Foremost in this process were the print media (newspapers, periodicals, and books), joined in the twentieth century by the electronic media (radio, TV, satellite stations, and online media), facilitating the flow of knowledge and influencing target audiences. Habermas identified the public sphere historically with the growth of the European bourgeois state in the late eighteenth century against the background of the expansion of political participation and the coalescence of civil principles. It may be identified with the struggle to rein in governmental absolutism and with the demand for the establishment of a representative system and a liberal constitution.[38]

These attributes trickled into the Muslim milieu by means of colonial penetration, modernization, and cultural interaction. While they did not create a public sphere from naught, they did add modern features to it. Civil agents such as madrasas, Sufi orders (*turuq*), and professional guilds traditionally played an important role in maintaining the social order in Muslim society. They served as unofficial representatives of the population to the political authorities and as restraints on despotism.[39] In the Egyptian case, the focal points of the public sphere were in Cairo and Alexandria as well as in regional centers such as Tanta and Mansura. The public sphere was reinforced in the final quarter of the nineteenth century by the bureaucratization of the state under Muhammad ʿAli's dynasty, its integration in the capitalist world economy, and the rise of European influence—especially British—in various areas of Egyptian life. These developments also gave rise to a new class of Muslim intellectuals (the product of newly established governmental foreign schools), eager for Western knowledge and modern education. Their intellectual and ethical maturity embodied the Kantian concept of the use of personal wisdom, rather than reliance on a given authority, to create a qualitative basis for rational public debate.[40]

A major arena for this activity was the press, which gained momentum during the 1870s. In light of the reform of the educational system and the expanded student population, it produced and nurtured a literate audience within the middle class—the *effendiyya*. An additional contributing element was the presence of Syrian and Lebanese immigrant journalists who had fled Ottoman centralist control in their countries and viewed Egyptian journalism as fertile ground. Significantly, from 1880 to 1908 some 627 newspapers and periodicals were published in the two metropolitan centers of Cairo and Alexandria, with distribution continuously spiraling upward.[41]

The new intellectuals, by virtue of their occupations as writers, editors, and publishers, turned the press into a highly influential vehicle for disseminating "proper virtues,"[42] as part of a broader civil process as well as instigating lively debate over social and political issues. The public sphere thus became a contested arena for shaping collective values as well as the attitude toward the "other"—women, minorities, and non-Islamic cultures.

The new intellectuals became the central though not sole players in the public sphere. Others included landowners, army officers, and government officials as well as 'ulama', and Sufi shaykhs, who soon grasped the usefulness of the new media for disputation and for reaching new audiences.[43] The presence of religious jurists and mystics in the public sphere guaranteed that the public debate would be conducted not only according to rational parameters but according to metaphysical ones as well.

In some areas, al-Azhar's agenda overlapped with the goals of the Westernized political and intellectual elites—for example, in their common struggle against foreign conquest. Yet it also sought to rein in these elites when they discredited a deeply rooted religious ethos, such as the organic unity between Islam and the state or the authority of the shari'a in matters of personal status. Azharis thus continued to serve as historical actors in shaping the image of Islam and their own fate.

AN OUTLINE OF THE BOOK

Part I outlines the historical framework of the discussion. Chapter 1 sketches a historic profile of al-Azhar and its religious status in Egypt and the Muslim world. For centuries, political elites sought public legitimation from the venerated madrasa, while the common people relied on its voice to protest against fiscal and economic injustices perpetrated by the regime. Moreover, Azharis demonstrated political involvement, such as during the political crises and power struggles between the Ottomans and the Mamluks in the seventeenth and eighteenth centuries and during the French occupation of 1798–1801, when they led two major revolts. The religious primacy and communal prestige of the Azhar establishment, however, were eroded by the relentless policy of modernization instituted by Muhammad ʿAli and his successors (primarily Ismaʿil) during the nineteenth century, as discussed in chapter 2. Modernization equipped the Egyptian state with what Michel Foucault termed "disciplinary mechanisms"—modern strategies of control and supervision[44]—and gave rise to a modern intelligentsia. Yet these developments did not alter the essentially Islamic character of Egyptian society and thus did not marginalize the Azharis in their country's history.[45]

Some ʿulamaʾ were actively involved in protest and dissidence in the public arena. They served as committed agents seeking to mold new cultural and political contents in society's way of life. Their personal stories, like those of their more quietist colleagues, are constructed here, opening a window to the broader issue of the Egyptian ʿulamaʾ community and its involvement in major historical events. In effect, one of my goals is to examine the reciprocal relations between micro- and macro-history, between the personal and the collective story. This is clearly expressed in the account of the ʿUrabi revolt of 1881–82, which is the topic of part II.

The ʿUrabi revolt has been the subject of considerable research. The two most prominent works on the subject are Alexander Schölch's *Egypt for the Egyptians* (1981) and Juan R. Cole's *Colonialism and Revolution in the Middle East*.[46] Schölch's discussion is essentially political, while Cole's is sociological. Both works also make a pioneering albeit limited contribution to examination of the role of al-Azhar in the revolt. Schölch deals briefly with a small group of senior ʿulamaʾ, whereas Cole broadens this group to include mainly ʿulamaʾ who supported Ahmad ʿUrabi, as part of a broader discussion of the involvement of the intelligentsia in the protest movement. Both authors, however, take a generalized approach to the prosopographic and ideological aspects of the Azhari ʿulamaʾ. A closer historical exploration evokes a more diverse picture regarding al-Azhar and the revolt.

Al-Azhar's segmented character is revealed in the context of the revolt, as discussed in chapter 3. Side by side with religious fervor and political dissidence—to the extent of sanctioning the deposal of Khedive Tawfiq for religious deviation—political quietism and a continued devotion to scholasticism were also in evidence. Chapters 4 and 5 deepen the discussion of the self-identity of the Azharis, ranging from local Egyptian to Islamic-Ottoman, and point to close interaction between Azharis and their colleagues, especially in the Fertile Crescent. This interaction, reflected in mutual visits, encouraging local students to enroll in al-Azhar, and prolific correspondences, created a community of religious discourse that dealt with current issues, including the eroding status of faith and its spokesmen in a changing world. Azharis played a central part in this discourse.

The ʿUrabi movement came to an end with the British conquest of Egypt in 1882, but the role of the ʿulama' in the struggle over defining Egyptian self-identity continued. Part III analyzes the religious discourse of Azharis in a changing reality. Chapter 6 discusses the ideological confrontation between ʿulama' and reformist intellectuals, over the image of religious law; al-Azhar and Sufism; and the place of the "other"—women and religious minorities—in the community. This contest continued well into the twentieth century, conducted in the post-Ottoman context of the coalescence of an Egyptian national state, seeking to create a distinctive collective identity based on the Pharaonic heritage of the Nile Valley. Al-Azhar's reaction to this new national agenda is the subject of chapter 7. Finally, chapter 8 examines the encounter between Egyptian ʿulama' and the forces of modernity in a broader perspective. It offers a comparative analysis of the status of the guardians of the faith elsewhere in the Middle East during the crucial decades spanning the late nineteenth century and beginning of the twentieth century, primarily in the Fertile Crescent, with a glance at Shiʿi Iran.

This study focuses on the relationship between scholasticism and politics and between religion and state. Its findings provide new insights into the study of Sunni ʿulama' at the crucial juncture of the collapse of the Ottoman Empire and the formation of nation-states.

PART ONE

The 'Ulama' of Egypt

1 A Historical Sketch

Religious knowledge was perceived in the Islamic tradition as a sancti-fied value. The quest to attain it was analogous to an ascetic ritual act to appease Allah. To cease studying meant to become ignorant. Islamic lit-erature is filled with praise for the centrality of learning, as in the Qur'an: "Question the people of the Remembrance, if it should be that you do not know" (16:43) and "O my Lord, increase me in knowledge" (20:114) or the hadiths "Seek knowledge even in China," "Learned people are the heirs of the prophets," and "The ink of students is equal to the blood of martyrs on Judgment Day."[1]

Alongside the emphasis on the merits of religious knowledge was an emphasis on the elevated status of those who acquired it. In his monu-mental work *Ihya' 'ulum al-din* (Revitalization of the Religious Sci-ences), Abu Hamid al-Ghazali (d. 1111) asserted that learned people or the 'ulama' are preferable to the ordinary believer by seventy levels and are closest to the level of prophecy. On the day of the resurrection of the dead, the 'ulama', together with the prophets and the saints, will merit serving as advocates for the people before Allah.[2]

In the early history of the Muslim community, the mosque served as the focus of religious instruction, in addition to its basic function as a place of worship and assembly. The tenth century, however, witnessed the rise of another institution of higher education, the madrasa, which was devoted primarily to instruction in law (*fiqh*) in one of the four *mad-hahib*, the schools of Islamic jurisprudence (Hanafi, Shafi'i, Maliki, and Hanbali). The madrasa, an essentially urban institution, perpetuated the tradition of legal scholarship while also serving as a multifaceted adminis-trative system. Its graduates became jurisconsults (muftis), judges (qadis), teachers (*mudarrisun*), preachers (*khutaba'*), notaries (*shuhud*), govern-ment officials, and even ministers. Despite its formal structure, the ma-drasa curriculum was characterized by simple content based mainly on memorization and an impersonal relationship between scholar and student. Gradually the institution became an important channel for social mobility, a pillar of the Muslim communal order, and at times a springboard for political influence by its powerful and wealthy patrons.[3]

Madrasa shaykhs were more than experts in a body of knowledge. They served as a stabilizing and moderating force in society, functioning as intermediaries between ruler and subjects. In this, a key role was attributed to the *madhahib*, which were both legal bodies and communal networks, uniting their members through doctrinal, personal, familial, and social ties. These core affiliations enabled the *madhahib* and the ʿulamaʾ to reach out to the populace at large.[4] An additional channel for communal power was what Daniella Talmon-Heller terms *barakat al-ʿilm*: the authority to intercede and the ability to bestow a spiritual blessing.[5]

The manifold functions of the ʿulamaʾ turned them into "natural leaders of public opinion and informal representatives of the community," according to Miriam Hoexter and Nehemia Levtzion.[6] An idealized portrait of the *ʿalim* was provided by al-Ghazali, who wrote: "The jurist serves as a mentor and a guide to the sultan in governing the people and regulating their affairs so as to ensure their following in the right path."[7] But al-Ghazali's ideal did not accurately reflect Muslim history. With the main asset at the disposal of the ʿulamaʾ being religious knowledge, they were far from constituting an independent authority, such as the Christian church of the Middle Ages, which on occasion had sufficient power to crown or dethrone kings. This limitation evoked political quietism on the part of the ʿulamaʾ, justified theologically as abstinence from opposing a Muslim ruler, however tyrannical, lest civil war erupt, thereby endangering religious life and inviting external aggression.[8]

Even when political control passed from Arabs to Turks—the Seljuks, the Mamluks, and the Ottomans—from the eleventh century onward, the ʿulamaʾ chose to preserve their essentially quietist stance. Part of the explanation relates to the entrenchment of the status of the ʿulamaʾ over centuries as civil servants dependent on the good graces of the ruler. Another reason was the respect and esteem that the Turkish military ruling elites displayed toward Sunni Islam and their success in defending and even expanding its borders against the Shiʿi challenge and the invasions of the Crusaders, the Mongols, and the Byzantines.

The quest of the Turkish elites for religious legitimization to compensate for their ethnic and cultural foreignness created a give-and-take relationship with the ʿulamaʾ. This allowed the ʿulamaʾ to acquire influence in two important areas. The first was the application of public pressure on the rulers to correct social and economic injustices and establish a "moralistic" economy as a reflection of the perception of social justice in Islam. The second was preserving the inferior civil status of non-Muslims as "protected subjects" (*dhimmi*s) and restricting their presence in the governmental realm. Such influence was especially evident among the ʿulamaʾ associated with al-Azhar (the luminous) in Egypt, which for centuries served as the bastion of Islamic learning as well as a center of sociopolitical life.[9]

AL-AZHAR UNDER THE MAMLUKS AND THE OTTOMANS

Al-Azhar was founded in 972 CE by the Fatimids, conquerors of Egypt and Syria who migrated from northwest Africa in the early ninth century. As part of the Ismaʿiliyya sect, the Fatimids claimed direct descent from the Prophet's family through his daughter Fatima; debased the prestige and legitimacy of the ʿAbbasid dynasty in Baghdad; and used al-Azhar as a base to propagate anti-Sunni Shiʿism. They met with resistance from the Sunni majority in Egypt, however, and were unable to entrench their hold. Eventually routed by Salah al-Din al-Ayyubi (d. 1193), the military leader of Kurdish origin who later defeated the European Crusaders, Egypt returned to the Sunni fold. Al-Azhar became a center of Sunni orthodoxy, albeit of lesser status in comparison to other madrasas founded in the wake of suspicions of al-Azhar as a center of Shiʿi subversion. Its diminished status under the Ayyubids, however, was repaired under the Mamluk sultanate, established in Egypt in 1250, when al-Azhar once again became an important religious center.

The Mamluks themselves were former slaves brought to Egypt by the Ayyubid sultans to serve in their armies. After integrating into Egyptian life, they eventually emerged as the ruling elite, replacing the Ayyubids. Most were Kipchak Turks from the northern shore of the Black Sea, later joined by other ethnic groups (mainly Circassians from the Caucasus and Central Asia). The Mamluk sultanate, a military oligarchy that relied essentially on force and barely spoke Arabic, was careful to nurture Islamic scholarship as a political tool to gain legitimacy and keep rivals in check. Prestige and a desire to be fully integrated into the local Muslim culture (which attached a high value to religious knowledge and its dissemination) were also part of the Mamluk motivation to perpetuate the custom of patronage of religious institutions. This dictated cultivating close relationships with the ʿulamaʾ, who welcomed the Mamluks' strict control over the religious practices of the Sufi orders, outside mainstream orthodoxy, as well as their successful suppression of external enemies such as the Crusaders and the Mongols.[10]

The ʿulamaʾ, who were the literate elite of society, acquired their distinctive prestige not from their ethnic origins or by inheritance but from their intensive training in the various branches of religious scholarship. They did not constitute a hierarchical establishment, as did the Christian clergy, and their social and geographic profile was relatively heterogeneous, including non-Cairene and even non-Egyptian backgrounds. This ethnic and geographic diversity reflected the attraction of Cairo as a cosmopolitan focus of orthodox Islamic learning in that period.[11]

The ʿulamaʾ filled a wide range of influential posts, as muftis, judges, mosque preachers, and teachers. Senior scholars forged strong links with the ruling elites, including marital connections, and had access to the centers of power, which opened doors to them in the economic and commercial realms. This combination of moral authority, political ties, and economic backing also made them less vulnerable to pressure from the state authorities.[12]

The favored status of the ʿulamaʾ in society was preserved even during the regime change from the Mamluks to the Ottomans, who conquered Syria, Egypt, and the Muslim holy places of Arabia in 1516–17. The takeover of these strategically and religiously important regions in the heart of the Islamic world turned the Ottoman conquest into a watershed event in Muslim history. They heralded the completion of the transition of the Ottoman sultanate from a small emirate on the Byzantine border at the end of the thirteenth century to a vast empire, which posed a threat to Europe by the start of the sixteenth century.

An imperial center under the Mamluks, Egypt suffered a reduction to the status of a province under the Ottomans. This meant the subjection of Egypt to an administrative system that showed little interest in areas not deemed vital to the empire, such as education and culture. As a result, these realms did not undergo a deep process of Ottomanization. Consequently, the communal standing of the Egyptian ʿulamaʾ was maintained.

The Ottoman authorities did take care to sponsor religious institutions and bestow favors on eminent ʿulamaʾ (alongside leaders of Sufi orders), but their intervention in religious affairs was limited to the judicial realm: staffing the senior offices with Turkish ʿulamaʾ from the imperial capital, Istanbul. The other strata of religious scholarship, centered in al-Azhar, enjoyed a degree of independence from state intervention. Significantly, the prominent office of shaykh al-Azhar (rector), apparently established in the late seventeenth century, was held by local ʿulamaʾ from the Shafiʿi or the Maliki schools of law but not from the Hanafi school, which was the official rite in the Ottoman Empire. Moreover, al-Azhar completed two main processes under the Ottomans, who consistently showed respect for Islamic imperatives and punished anyone who strayed from them. It became a well-equipped and well-endowed learning institution and became totally identified with the religious establishment. The rest of the religious colleges in Cairo and the other cities served as its satellites, staffed mostly by al-Azhar graduates.[13] Al-Azhar's prestige also drew seekers of knowledge and religious opinions from outside Egypt, who streamed to it from Bilad al-Sham (Syria),[14] North Africa, and even farther reaches of the Muslim world.[15]

During the seventeenth and eighteenth centuries the intellectual quality of religious scholarship in al-Azhar acquired a narrower aspect, reflected mainly in the writing of commentaries on texts (*hawashiyya*), an age depicted by the historian Gamal El-Din El-Shayyal as "the age of commentaries." The natural and exact sciences were downgraded, used primarily for ritual needs such as calculating the lunar calendar, the Ramadan fast, or the correct direction of Mecca for prayer purposes. The study of philosophy was prohibited and was excluded from the curriculum.[16] This ban was reflected in the disappointment expressed by an Ottoman governor of Cairo in the mid-eighteenth century when he realized, after reviewing al-Azhar's curriculum, that Egypt's reputation as a "spring flowing with sciences" essentially related only to the religious legal sciences.[17] The nineteenth-century European observer Martin Hartmann aptly described Egypt as "the land of Islamic Science."[18]

Classes at al-Azhar, as described by ʿAli Pasha Mubarak, an important nineteenth-century educator and administrator, were conducted in the form of dictation. The students were seated around the lecturer in a circle (*halqa*), diligently recording his words and only occasionally permitted to ask questions. The lecturer was not responsible for the scholastic progress of the student (whether he made an effort or was lazy, whether he was present or absent). Most of the student's time was devoted to memorizing the material dictated in class in preparation for the next class. He was not required to pass monthly or even annual examinations. Memorizing the religious literature, which was perceived as the indisputable truth, and maintaining a slight connection with the centers of civilization in Western Europe dictated the topics of study and their extent.[19] Individual eminent ʿulamaʾ of the eighteenth century such as Hasan al-Jabarti, Murtada al-Zabidi, and Ramadan al-Khawanqi, however, did rejuvenate various traditional legal concepts. They displayed an interest in other fields of knowledge, including literature, poetry, history, medicine, astronomy, and geography.[20]

Criticism of the ideological insulation of al-Azhar by contemporary writers was accompanied by denunciations of the life of luxury led by senior ʿulamaʾ and their internal rivalries over honors, wealth, and position. Prominent critics were the poet Shaykh Hasan al-Badri al-Hijazi (d. 1718) and the Egyptian chronicler ʿAbd al-Rahman al-Jabarti (d. 1825). In a *qasida* (poem) al-Hijazi noted:

> Don't ask about the ʿulamaʾ of our time. Their condition is obvious to all. Nothing good or useful to you will emanate from them in this world or the next. Should they have a covetous urge, they will descend on the object [of it] like wild dogs [*kilab ʿaqira*]. Their enthusiasm for good deeds is weak. Stay away from them and you will have peace of mind, since being close to them will only cause you loss.[21]

Al-Jabarti also offered scathing criticism:

> The ʿulamaʾ were enticed by worldly pleasures and neglected their studies and their educational role. They did only the minimum required to preserve their religious status, and nothing more. Their homes became similar to those of the princes. They had servants, assistants, and property managers.... They were greedy, complaining and pleading, never satisfied. They busied themselves increasingly with immoral matters, to the point that they lost their authority as speakers of justice.[22]

In decrying the deterioration in the scholarly community of his day, however, al-Jabarti stressed that he was referring to only a small portion of the ʿulamaʾ, mainly the senior level. "Though there are many idlers, the age does not lack those who are righteous.... They are God's true elite among mankind."[23] In contrast to ʿulamaʾ such as Muhammad al-Sharqawi, Muhammad al-Mahdi, and Hasan al-Mahalli, who traded in their spiritual world for the material one, al-Jabarti cited puritanical ʿulamaʾ. These included Muhammad al-Hifni (d. 1767), who courageously defended the cause of justice against the powerful; and Muhammad ʿAbd al-Fattah al-Maliki (d. 1808), described by al-Jabarti as an honest man who refused gifts and rewards and whose judgments were well received by the people.[24] Moreover, al-Jabarti continued to sanctify the central role of the ʿulamaʾ in the Muslim community. In his discussion of the five levels of chosen persons that Allah distinguished from all others and appointed to disseminate justice, al-Jabarti ranked the ʿulamaʾ as second in importance after the prophets, before kings and rulers. He thereby substantiated the hadith "The ʿulamaʾ are the heirs of the prophets." Praising their religious knowledge, asceticism, and enforcement of religious law, he wrote:

> They continue to persevere diligently in strengthening the foundations of justice and in showing forth truth by lifting up the beacon of Divine Law, by establishing the guideposts to the way of Islam, and by perfecting the principles of piety. This they do by following that which is most cautious in issuing legal opinions and by disdaining permissiveness; for they are the stewards of God in the world and the elite of the human race.... They approach God with purity of heart, and fly to Him on the wings of learning and enlightenment. They are heroes in the fields of greatness, and melodious nightingales in the gardens of learning and discourse.[25]

Al-Jabarti's praise, while rhetorical and idealized,[26] reflected the sustained communal status of the ʿulamaʾ. Azharis served as cultural brokers and guardians of tradition, although, as Nelly Hanna points out, they did not monopolize all forms of learning or the transmission of knowledge. Other cultural agents and venues also played a role, including Sufi orders, private libraries, literary salons, and coffee shops.[27]

In blending cultural and social functions, the ʿulamaʾ also largely preserved their function as mediators between ruler and subjects. The appointment of the shaykh al-Azhar was largely the province of the ʿulamaʾ, and political intervention in the internal rivalries surrounding this process was minimal. This was the case during the power struggle between shaykhs Ahmad al-Nafrawi and ʿAbd al-Baqi al-Qalini in 1708 and between shaykhs ʿAbd al-Rahman al-ʿArishi and Ahmad al-ʿArusi in 1779.[28] This last episode revealed ethnic and scholastic factionalism. Al-ʿArishi, the Hanafi mufti and shaykh Riwaq al-Shuwam (the living quarters of the Syrian students), coveted the office of shaykh al-Azhar and gained the support of several of the Mamluk leaders. He was not of Egyptian origin, however, and belonged to the Hanafi school of law (the official rite in the Ottoman Empire), which constituted obstacles and provoked opposition among the Shafiʿis in al-Azhar. They contended that Egypt was Imam Muhammad ibn Idris al-Shafiʿi's homeland, in which the agreed practice was to appoint a Shafiʿi *ʿalim* as shaykh al-Azhar, since this was the school followed by the majority in Egypt. The struggle between the two camps, using their respective legal schools as a social and organizational base for their cause, eventually turned violent and involved force by the Ottoman authorities. Ultimately, the Shaficis emerged victorious and al-cArusi was appointed shaykh al-Azhar. Al-cArishi was dismissed from his position as mufti and was forced to take refuge in his home. He died shortly thereafter.[29]

Azharis at various levels of the hierarchy also played an active role in urban protests against economic exploitation by harsh taxation. The close association of some culama' with urban networks such as merchant associations, guilds, and Sufi orders provided them with an important lever for rallying the masses. From time to time, al-Azhar cooperated with the heads of the Sufi community from al-Bakri and al-Sadat families to champion economic grievances. But the leading shaykhs of al-Azhar took care not to go too far in opposing their political patrons and benefactors or in destabilizing the social order; they favored opposition without actual violence and compromise over frontal attack, a strategy that often proved productive.[30]

The influence of the culama' rose during periods of political turmoil and power struggles between the Mamluks and the Ottomans over political control and resources. Senior culama' were sent by the Mamluks as goodwill ambassadors to Istanbul, where they were treated with honor and esteem.[31] On occasion they also stood up to those in power. For example, when the heads of al-Azhar assembled to consider the request of the Ottoman governor to raise money for a military campaign against the Mamluks in Upper Egypt in 1785, Shaykh al-Azhar al-cArusi rejected it out of hand. He argued that the priority for him was solely the welfare of the Muslim subjects, not the victories of the Ottomans or the Mamluks. In another incident, a group of fellahin from the Sharqiyya region in the delta arrived in Cairo in 1794 to complain to Shaykh al-Azhar cAbdallah al-Sharqawi about tax exploitation by Muhammad Bey al-Alfi, a Mamluk dignitary. Al-Sharqawi assembled the culama', who decided to instruct the residents to close their shops and markets. The intensified waves of protest that resulted and the fear of lost income impelled the Mamluk leaders to enter into talks with the culama' and ultimately to accept their demand to rescind the edict.[32] These and other incidents illustrate the communal role played by the culama': far from shutting themselves away in the ivory towers of the mosques and madrasas, they often made these centers available as a starting point for demonstrations and protests. This was especially so in the case of culama' who were associated with Sufism and its orders, primarily the Khalwatiyya and the Shadhiliyya.

The Khalwatiyya order, named for cUmar al-Khalwati (d. 1397), established its center in Tabriz, Azerbaijan, in northeastern Iran. Offshoots sprang up rapidly in Southeast Asia, the Hijaz, North Africa, and Egypt, which witnessed an impressive spread of the Khalwatiyya during the eighteenth century, especially in the south. The Khalwatiyya order was distinguished from the Shadhiliyya in one essential way—the number of *maqamat* (the steps undertaken by a Sufi in order to attain spiritual wholeness): seven in the Khalwatiyya as compared to three in the Shadhiliyya.[33]

The Shadhiliyya order was named for Shaykh Abu al-Hasan al-Shadhili (d. 1258), one of the most prominent of the Maghreb Sufis. He arrived in Egypt in 1244 and settled in Alexandria, whereupon the Shadhiliyya began to spread throughout the country. His heir, ʿAbu al-ʿAbbas al-Mursi (d. 1287), played an important role in this proliferation. Broadly, the Shadhiliyya advocated the study and mastery of legal texts (*al-ʿulum al-zahira*) before adopting Sufism. This was also a condition for acceptance into the order.

Al-Shadhili viewed religious ignorance and satisfaction with this state as a grave sin. He never ceased his study of the shariʿa and its legal branches, even when he attained a distinguished Sufi status. Al-Shadhili preached humility and self-denial before Allah and was in the habit of introducing himself as Allah's slave rather than as a holy man (*qutb*). His basic approach was *tawhid* (the unity of God). He also called for active involvement in communal life and the eschewal of extreme asceticism, mortification of the soul, and begging. Sufism, al-Shadhili held, is not only ethics and ritual; it is also a social perception aimed at molding human behavior. Its actualization is made possible only through integration in the existing social order. He viewed worldly deeds as a form of ritual. Accordingly, he sanctioned a comfortable lifestyle and involvement in the fields of commerce, economics, and politics, so long as enslavement to the material world was avoided. Al-Shadhili also reinforced his activist agenda by aiding the needy and fighting against social exploitation. Furthermore, he took part in the jihad against the Crusaders in 1250, despite his failing eyesight.[34]

Al-Shadhili's attributes left their imprint on the character of many ʿulamaʾ, largely accounting for their communal involvement. Examples of such ʿulamaʾ include Muhammad Salim al-Hifnawi, ʿAli ibn Musa al-Husayni, ʿAli al-Saʿidi, and Ahmad ibn Muhammad al-Dardir. A large number of protests are associated with al-Dardir (d. 1786), a Maliki mufti and Khalwati Sufi. For example, he called for storming the Mamluks' residences in reaction to acts by Husayn Bey (a confidant of the Mamluk emir Ibrahim Bey), who confiscated property belonging to residents of the Husniyya quarter of Cairo, including the home of the head of the

Bayyumi order. "Either we die a martyr's death, or Allah will bring us victory," al-Dardir declared. The fear of riots prompted the Mamluk emirs to intervene and mediate in this matter. In another incident, al-Dardir was in Tanta for the festival of al-Sayyid Ahmad al-Badawi (d. 1276). When a government inspector circulated among the common people during the celebrations, demanding a tax from them, he was beaten by the shaykh's followers and forced to leave the area. Upon al-Dardir's return to Cairo, the city's dignitaries visited him to apologize for the event at Tanta.[35]

A laudatory description of the role of the Azharis in Ottoman Egypt was provided by the Egyptian scholar Mahmud al-Sharqawi in 1957: "Al-Azhar, beyond its educational institutions and its religious mission, served as a 'parliament' that expressed the feelings of the people—whether anger or satisfaction—toward the regime." In the same vein, ʿAbd al-ʿAziz Muhammad al-Shinnawi observed in 1971 that Azharis represented the popular leadership. He defined the greatest of al-Azhar's achievements as being the preservation of Egypt's Arab identity from Turkish influence despite the institution's recognition of the Islamic legitimacy of the Ottoman sultanate.[36] Some Egyptian commentators went even further and called the Azharis' stand against acts of regime injustice "the people's holy war [*jihad al-shaʿb*]."[37] Nevertheless, despite this activist image, a centuries-old tradition of political accommodation to the "men of the sword" and the absence of any military recruitment kept Azhari dissidence within the bounds of censure and mediation without sliding into a challenge to the political order.

This role changed under the French occupation (1798–1801), which confronted the ʿulamaʾ with the presence of a foreign Christian conqueror. The ʿulamaʾ rejected Napoleon Bonaparte's request that they serve as the new political elite of Egypt, a role that was outside their jurisdiction doctrinally and historically. Moreover, many of them retained their allegiance to the exiled Mamluk emirs and Ottoman officials, to whom they had patronage ties. But several senior Azharis, along with leading merchants and Christian notables, became members of the general advisory council (*diwan*) in Cairo, which represented the various provinces and advised the French administration. The presence of Azharis in the council was intended to ensure the welfare of the population and prevent any erosion of the Islamic character of the country. As it turned out, the council constituted more of an oppositionist presence than a cooperative one that aspired to governmental power, as demonstrated by the two insurrections that broke out in the capital in October 1798 and March 1800.[38] The harsh measures used to suppress these revolts widened the gap between the conquerors and the conquered.

Prominent in the uprisings was the role of the Riwaq al-Shuwam, one of the great dormitory quarters at al-Azhar and the recipient of many charitable trusts granted to it by the Mamluk beys. Its residents included both local students and students who came from Bilad al-Sham to acquire religious training at al-Azhar and earn an *ijaza* (license to teach and transmit religious knowledge). The Shuwam, under the leadership of Shaykh Badr al-Maqdisi, brother of Shaykh ʿAli ibn Musa al-Maqdisi, one of the most senior Hanafis in Egypt, were at the forefront of the struggle against the French. In retaliation, the French executed many of the rebels and mounted a hunt for al-Maqdisi. The Riwaq al-Shuwam was also the point of dispatch of Sulayman al-Halabi, the assassin of the French general Jean-Baptiste Kléber in June 1800. Al-Halabi became an Egyptian hero and was commemorated in books and plays. The French response to this act was not long in coming. Following widespread arrests and interrogations, four shaykhs, all from Gaza and all associated with the Riwaq al-Shuwam, were executed.[39]

Al-Azhar's struggle against the French conquest was not motivated by political aspirations. With the withdrawal of the French in 1801, the ʿulamaʾ refrained from challenging the renewal of Ottoman control over Egypt and ultimately expressed support for an external candidate, Muhammad ʿAli, as the new ruler. All they sought was the restoration of the former religio-political order, which in the past had allowed them to retain power and influence. Muhammad ʿAli, an army officer of Albanian origin motivated by dynastic ambitions and inclined toward large-scale centralization, disappointed these expectations, however. His repeated assaults on the economic power of religious dignitaries, such as taxing and confiscating lands endowed for religious purposes, engendered a revolt in July 1809 led by ʿUmar Makram, the *naqib al-ashraf* (leader of those who claimed to be descendants of the Prophet). The revolt was crushed, and Makram was exiled to Damietta.

2 Modernization and Protest

Under Muhammad ʿAli's rule (1805–48), which brought about the emergence of a centralized state with modern methods of control (such as the confinement, regulation, and supervision of the population), the ʿulamaʾ experienced what Daniel Crecelius has termed "the expulsion from Olympus."[1] Their privileged status was significantly curtailed in the wake of reforms in the realms of education, the judiciary, and the *waqf*. A similar erosion in status was experienced by the Sufi orders. The designation of Shaykh Muhammad al-Bakri as the official leader of the Sufis by governmental decree in 1812 enabled the state formally to supervise their internal affairs, including their religious ceremonies. As Frederick De Jong observed, the Sufi orders were transformed into "a fully fledged bureaucratic system."[2] An added liability inherent in the Azharis' troubled condition was the concentration of the vast majority of the population along the shores of the Nile, thereby facilitating a centralized regime.

These attributes contrasted with the position of the ʿulamaʾ in Syria. While they too came under the Ottoman government's reform program, they were selectively cooperative to the extent that their own interests were not harmed and major religious commandments were not violated. For example, they supported taxation and military conscription but opposed granting civic equality to non-Muslims—a stance that sometimes evoked massacres of Christians by Muslims in the cities of Syria and Lebanon. Their relative remoteness from Istanbul along with insufficient Ottoman resources to implement the reforms efficiently enabled the ʿulamaʾ and other local notables in Syria to preserve their political and economic assets and their mediatory function between the central government and the local population.[3]

Azharis found themselves on the defensive under Muhammad ʿAli's regime. Commenting cynically on their situation, ʿAbd al-Rahman al-Jabarti wrote that "the dog of tyranny had bared his teeth and howled, but

there was no one to stand up to him, or chase him away."[4] The Azharis' political weakness was evident from a regional perspective as well in terms of
the rise of revival movements such as the Wahhabiyya in the Arabian Peninsula, the Sanusiyya in Libya, and the Mahdiyya in Sudan, which actively
opposed the growing European penetration into the Islamic world and
the modernization processes in the Ottoman Empire. These movements
were led by charismatic figures, some endowed with a holy aura (*baraka*),
who cast themselves as the antithesis of the religious establishment and
denounced its ideological apathy and political submission. Similar assertiveness was evident on the part of ʿulamaʾ in areas more remote from the
Middle East, such as in Muslim communities in Central and Southeast
Asia, where the political system was more segmented and religious life
revolved around holy Sufis. These figures, combining legalism with mysticism, also played leading roles in the struggle against foreign invaders and
in shaping Muslim identity at the dawn of the modern age.[5]

The ʿulamaʾ corps in Egypt, however, remained an important element in society. The modernization process in Cairo—as in Istanbul—
involved secularization, although not in the sense of the separation of
religion and state. Rather, it took the form of the penetration of the state
into areas that traditionally had been under the control of the religious
establishment, such as the *waqf*, the educational system, and the judiciary. The Sunni ʿulamaʾ (in contrast, for example, to the Shiʿi ʿulamaʾ in
Iran) and especially their senior echelons were closely tied to the regime
through administrative and economic interdependence, which hampered
them from developing political or sectoral autonomy. They could only try
to limit the adoption of modern institutions and practices to the governmental level, where the ruler was supreme not only by force of the political reality but also in the Islamic functional distinction between "men of
the pen" and "men of the sword." The task of the ʿulamaʾ was to preserve,
interpret, and entrench holy law, while the state was expected to protect
this law and ensure its normative status.

Muhammad ʿAli focused on consolidating the power of the Egyptian
state by developing its military and administrative systems;[6] yet he also
nibbled away at al-Azhar's moral grip on society and its authority in the
areas of education and religious law. He himself declared his loyalty to the
ideal of unity between religion and state and was a patron of a group of
senior ʿulamaʾ who lent legitimacy to his rule and policies. Senior ʿulamaʾ
such as the *naqib al-ashraf*, the head of the Sufi orders, and the Maliki and
Hanafi muftis were co-opted as members of the advisory *diwan* that he
established, headed by his son Ibrahim, and were present when regime

edicts were announced. Others served as official historians and exponents of the regime policy. The politicization of Islam was also reflected
in religious appointments. For example, Muhammad ʿAli named Shaykh
Ahmad al-Tamimi of Hebron chief Hanafi mufti in 1835 with the intent
of gaining the loyalty of the dignitaries in Syria, then under Egyptian
control.[7]

Moreover, the technical character of modern higher education,
which Muhammad ʿAli encouraged with the intent of developing the
Egyptian war machine and improving the efficiency of the governmental administration, produced only small buds of an intellectual elite to
compete with the religious establishment. Reformist personalities such
as Hasan al-ʿAttar (shaykh al-Azhar, 1831–35); his pupil Rifaʿa Rafiʿ al-
Tahtawi (d. 1873), an important educational reformer during Muhammad
ʿAli's time; and ʿAli al-Qusi (d. 1877), a lecturer at al-Azhar, were isolated
figures in the ideological discourse of the period. Even they retained a
view of the ʿulamaʾ as heirs of the prophets, however, as did Jamal al-Din
al-Afghani and Muhammad ʿAbduh in the second half of the nineteenth
century. This stance signified recognition of the ongoing social standing
of the ʿulamaʾ and the need to enlist them as cultural arbiters in shaping the modern image of the Egyptian polity. In this vein, fatwas were
used by al-ʿAttar and by Muhammad al-ʿInabi (d. 1850/51), the mufti of
Alexandria, to promote the introduction of modern sciences into the official education system. Al-ʿInabi also defended the adoption of European
military technology as compatible with the shariʿa, on the basis of his research in early Islamic sources. But the moderating approach displayed
by al-ʿAttar, al-ʿInabi, and al-Tahtawi failed to influence the mainstream
ʿulamaʾ, who actively opposed their views.[8]

Indeed, the ʿulamaʾ were still perceived in the mid-nineteenth century and thereafter as defenders and propagators of Islam. According to
Lars Bjørneboe, the socio-religious system in which they operated still
functioned: state reforms did not alter its essential elements, mainly
"man's sense of dependence on God."[9] Moreover, despite a more pronounced formal separation between al-Azhar and the Sufi orders as part
of Muhammad ʿAli's divide-and-rule policy, the link between religious
scholarship and Sufism was preserved. Many of the Azharis continued to
be associated with *tasawwuf* (mysticism) and were active in Sufi orders.
Their activity not only embraced the urban milieu but extended to the
rural realm. As Haim Shaked has pointed out, most of the nineteenth-
century Azharis, including those who held the office of shaykh al-Azhar,
were raised and educated in villages, primarily in Lower Egypt or the

southern regions of Upper Egypt. Al-Azhar thus provided a main channel for social mobility. This constituted an incentive for many families
to send their sons to Cairo to study in so prestigious an institution. The
sustained affinity of many ʿulamaʾ for Sufi culture and for rural society
enabled them to broaden their popular influence. Prominent in this domain were senior figures both in Cairo and in the provinces, such as Muhammad al-Sharqawi, Muhammad ʿIllaysh, ʿAbd al-Hadi Naja al-Abyari,
Hasan al-ʿIdwi, Muhammad Khalil al-Hijrisi, and the brothers Muhammad and Ahmad al-Qayati.[10]

These figures represented the first, second, and even third generations of notable established ʿulamaʾ families, thereby inheriting offices
and positions of influence in both the judicial and Sufi realms. Thus, in
some cases their charisma emanated not only from personal, intellectual,
or spiritual attributes but also from their family genealogy and from the
offices they held—what Weber called the charisma of heredity (*erbcha-
risma*) and the "charisma of the office" (*amtcharisma*).[11]

Muhammad ʿAliʾs reformist program canceled out the political and
economic influence of the ʿulamaʾ, but it failed to weaken their status
as the country's intellectual elite and the attractiveness of al-Azhar as
an institution of religious learning. Thus Rifaʿa Rafiʿ al-Tahtawi, while
criticizing the Azharis' rigid mind-set and urging them to broaden their
knowledge in the modern sciences, did not deny their pivotal role in shaping the self-image of society and urged the political authorities to consult with them in affairs of state. Similarly, ʿAli Mubarak, al-Tahtawi's
prominent disciple in reforming Egypt's educational system, pointed to
al-Azhar's numerous academic and moral defects but nevertheless called
it a mosque and madrasa dedicated to "abolishing ignorance and granting eternal life to the world of knowledge."[12] Notably, large parts of his
monumental work *al-Khitat al-Tawfiqiyya al-jadida li-Misr al-Qahira*
(Tawfiq's Latest Projects in Egypt's Cairo, 1885–89, 20 vols.) are devoted
to biographies of Azharis.

These observations became more valid with the failure and eventual
closing of the new military schools and science-oriented schools after
Muhammad ʿAliʾs conquests ended in the mid-1830s. His successors,
ʿAbbas I (1848–54) and Saʿid (1854–63), adopted a more restrained
policy regarding the reform of al-Azhar, showing a greater interest in re-
pairing al-Azhar's building complex and augmenting its revenues. ʿAbbas
made a practice of visiting al-Azhar frequently to distribute coins to its
residents and sit in on lectures by the shaykh al-Azhar, Ibrahim al-Bayjuri
(d. 1860), who treated him as one of his students. ʿAbbas also initiated the

construction of dormitories for Bayjuri's disciples and students who came
to al-Azhar from his hometown. Saʿid, too, spread largesse among the
scholars and students at al-Azhar, and he instituted the practice of award-
ing robes of honor to eminent scholars as a symbol of status and prestige.
His patronage, however, did not yield especially important results in the
area of reform.[13]

Furthermore, not all the wishes of the Egyptian viceroy were accom-
modated by the "men of the pen." For example, a request by ʿAbbas to
the Hanafi grand mufti, Muhammad al-ʿAbbasi al-Mahdi, to issue a fatwa
announcing that not only the Ottoman sultan but the khedive had the
authority to revoke a death sentence was refused. Another confrontation
between the two occurred when ʿAbbas wanted to confiscate lands and
assets belonging to Muhammad ʿAli's descendants, on the grounds that
when Muhammad ʿAli came to Egypt he did not possess any property.
Thus what he left for his family was in fact public property that must be
returned through the offices of the viceroy's representative. Vigorously
opposing this claim despite warnings and threats against him, al-Mahdi
argued that it constituted a debasement of religious law. In response,
al-Mahdi was exiled to Abuqir. Ultimately, however, ʿAbbas was forced
to bring back the grand mufti in light of sharp protests by the ʿulamaʾ
in Cairo. Al-Mahdi was also involved in a confrontation with Ismaʿil, a
prince under Saʿid Pasha who tried to turn a family *waqf* into a public
waqf and use its income to cover its maintenance costs. Ismaʿil was forced
to relinquish this scheme due to the opposition of the mufti, who declared
that it would be easier for him to have his own property confiscated than
to live with the knowledge that one of his rulings was contrary to Allah's
commandments or that he favored a mortal creature over the Creator out
of fear of threats.[14]

The reign of Khedive Ismaʿil (1863–79) ushered in a significant
change in the status of the learned religious community in Egypt. This
change was palpable not only institutionally but also socially and cul-
turally. Al-Azhar began to lose its centrality as the focus of intellectual
life to a new intelligentsia of administrative officials, lawyers, journalists, and teachers, which produced leaders of protest movements target-
ing political and social ills. The varied leadership profiles of these protest
movements paralleled the nature of the protests themselves. Added to
traditional urban protests launched in mosques were new collectively organized demonstrations such as strikes and boycotts focused mainly in
colleges, schools, and factories.[15]

Processes of modernization were thus permeating the protests, bring-ing about a further erosion in the public status of the ʿulamaʾ. A major contributing element was the gradual emergence of the press in the Egyp-tian public space during the second half of the nineteenth century. The press undermined the monopoly of the ʿulamaʾ over the written word by allowing laypeople free access to the sacred texts; it also presented a fi-nancial threat to those ʿulamaʾ who engaged in copying compositions. While the ʿulamaʾ expressed reservations about and even hostility toward the modern press, however, they were unable to prevent its development. Newspapers served as an innovative conduit of modern knowledge for the limited literate segment of the population and the much wider illiter-ate sector, which crowded around readers in cafes and public bathhouses to hear the latest news being read aloud. Newspapers also contributed to the polarization of the public discourse and in times of political crisis, which were frequent in that period, functioned as a vehicle for mobilizing public opinion.[16]

The spirit of reform took root as well within the walls of al-Azhar, which was less insulated than in the past from external intervention in filling senior faculty positions and molding curricular content. Khedive Ismaʿil was particularly intrusive in his desire to "position Egypt in Eu-rope and not Africa" and turn its capital, Cairo, into a "Paris along the Nile."[17] With his encouragement Shaykh al-Azhar Mustafa al-ʿArusi (1864–70) consolidated a plan to improve the quality of instruction and administration and introduce modern subjects, thereby forcing the retire-ment of a group of ʿulamaʾ who did not meet the new criteria.[18] This did not please the heads of the *riwaq*s (student living quarters), whose fear of loss of status and factional rivalry prompted them to oppose the proposed reforms. Heading this opposition was Shaykh Muhammad ʿIllaysh.

ʿIllaysh (1802–82), born into a family of North African origin, was an outstanding Qurʾanic pupil in his childhood and at age fifteen entered al-Azhar, where he was considered a brilliant student. Upon receiving the *ijaza* in 1829, he began teaching at al-Azhar, primarily in the theological and legal sciences, and became known as a legalist with a strict interpreta-tion of the shariʿa commandments.[19] In one of his fatwas he ruled that knowledge of the shariʿa, to the extent of a person's mental capacity, is preferable to and more important than reading the Qurʾan: the shariʿa's purpose is broad and embraces the needs of both the individual and so-ciety, while the intent of the Qurʾan is private and limited to the reader alone. ʿIllaysh thus championed the concept of Islam as a religion that gives priority to shaping human conduct and a way of life. He also quoted Abu ʿAbdallah al-Maziri (d. 1141), who ruled that the duty of believers is to be familiar with all injunctions relating to their occupation or to what they are about to do (such as the money-trader who needs to know the rules of interest or the husband and wife who need to know their rights). Al-Maziri defined this duty as incumbent on the individual (*fard ʿayn*), while the requirement regarding the Qurʾan is that the individual must know only the opening sura (*al-Fatiha*).[20]

ʿIllaysh was also considered pious and ascetic. ʿAli Mubarak described him as tall and dignified in appearance and his sermons, usually delivered at the Friday service of the Husayni Mosque, as evoking a deeply emotional response in his audiences. ʿIllaysh never stooped to idle talk. His piety was typified by his habit of carrying his shoes in a bag to avoid defiling even the entrance to the mosque.[21] The preservation of the purity of the mosque as a place of worship and learning and scrupulous care in avoiding disrespect or damage to the Qurʾan were important themes in his rulings.[22] ʿIllaysh eschewed drinking coffee and sniffing tobacco. He dressed plainly and criticized the elegant attire and luxurious lifestyle of dignitaries and those in power. He ruled against the participation by ʿulamaʾ in nighttime celebrations and funeral ceremonies, for fear of exposure to behavior that was profane or forbidden by religion, such as dancing and shouting. When his son ʿAbdallah, who was a lecturer at al-Azhar, died of an illness in 1877, ʿIllaysh reportedly did not walk in the procession following the coffin but closed himself in his home, forbidding any eulogies or condolences.[23]

ʿIllaysh's puritanism led him to bitter clashes, at times violent, with ʿulamaʾ who disputed his views and rulings. One such incident involved Shaykh Hasan al-ʿIdwi (d. 1886), a scholar and Sufi who was linked to various branches of the Shadhiliyya order in Cairo, including the ʿAfifiyya. Having accumulated great wealth as the owner of large estates in Upper Egypt, he was a philanthropist who supported communal projects. He was also known for speaking plainly to Muslim rulers and urging them to show justice and mercy in dealing with their subjects.[24] In ʿIllaysh's judgment, al-ʿIdwi had issued a fatwa that was too liberal. In response, he and his Maghrebi disciples forcibly prevented al-ʿIdwi from delivering his lectures in al-Azhar and broke the chair on which he sat. State officials and senior ʿulamaʾ, angered by ʿIllaysh's conduct, investigated the matter and decided that al-ʿIdwi would return to his teaching post at al-Azhar, while ʿIllaysh would formally retain his position as the Maliki mufti but would be stripped of his powers. Unperturbed by this sanction, ʿIllaysh continued to teach and write, preserving his prestigious status within al-Azhar and among the populace. He later became involved in politics, both within the context of al-Azhar and in the broader Egyptian milieu. This involvement reached its peak during the ʿUrabi revolt of 1881–82. His colleague in these events was none other than al-ʿIdwi, with whom he had clashed thirty years earlier.[25]

ʿIllaysh's students included important ʿulamaʾ such as Mansur Kisab al-ʿIdwi, Muhammad al-Hadad, and Salim al-Bishri (later shaykh al-Azhar). ʿIllaysh's classes were attended by followers of other schools besides the Malikiyya, among them the Hanafi ʿAbd al-Rahman al-Bahrawi and the Shafiʿis Shams al-Din al-Inbabi and ʿAbd al-Rahman al-Sharbini, both of whom later served as shaykhs al-Azhar. At the same time, ʿIllaysh taught classes in hadith in the Husayni Mosque, attended by some 200 students. Appointed Maliki mufti in 1853, he thereby became a link in a distinguished chain of ʿulamaʾ who preceded him, such as ʿAli al-ʿAdawi al-Saʿidi (d. 1775), Ahmad ibn Muhammad al-Dardir (d. 1786), Muhammad al-ʿAmir al-Kabir (d. 1817), and his son Muhammad al-ʿAmir al-Shaghir (d. 1831). Al-Shaghir was also the head of the ʿArabiyya Shadhiliyya order and introduced ʿIllaysh to Sufism. ʿIllaysh eventually headed the order, but his Sufi involvement was less important than his work in the legal field.[26]

The office of Maliki mufti was considered secondary to that of shaykh al-Azhar. This reflected the power relationships between the legal schools in the institution and in Egyptian society: the Maliki school was lower than the Shafiʿis but well ahead of the Hanafis and the Hanbalis. Most of the student body, affiliated with the Maliki tradition, came from the provinces in Upper Egypt (Saʿid) and from North Africa. They were known for their puritanical beliefs and practices, fiery temperament, strict morality, and close affinity with the populace.[27]

Describing the Saʿidi students, ʿAli Mubarak noted that they survived on food provisions that they received only twice a year and money occasionally brought to them in Cairo by a father or brother. Some even poorer students received no monetary support at all and were confined to the *riwaq*, "spending their time in sadness." By contrast, the Maghrebi students, whose quarter was located on the western side of al-Azhar, had plentiful donations and *waqf* assets at their disposal. Most of them hailed from Tripoli, Tunis, and the interior regions of the Maghreb. Both Saʿidi and Maghrebi students are described in the biographical lexicons and chronicles as tough, fiery, and tending toward dissidence regarding both the Azhar authorities and the political authorities.[28] Their large numbers and rebellious nature provided their mentors, including ʿIllaysh, with an important source of popular power and a key lever for involvement in public and political life.

The firm opposition of ʿIllaysh and other Azharis to Shaykh al-Azhar al-ʿArusi's reform program ultimately led to his dismissal by Khedive Ismaʿil in 1870. A behind-the-scenes player in this development was Shaykh Hasan al-ʿIdwi, who was angling for the post of shaykh al-Azhar himself. He supported Ismaʿil's dismissal of al-ʿArusi in the face of possible opposition, arguing that the khedive functions as the Ottoman caliph's deputy (*wakil*) in Egypt and thus has the authority to dismiss the shaykh al-Azhar.[29] Ultimately, the office was filled not by al-ʿIdwi but by Muhammad al-ʿAbbasi al-Mahdi, who provided a renewed impetus to reformist efforts in al-Azhar.

Al-Mahdi (1827–97), scion of a noted family of scholars affiliated with the Hanafi school, was the son of Muhammad Amin al-Mahdi, a senior ʿalim during the period of the French conquest and the beginning of Muhammad ʿAli's era. The younger al-Mahdi was appointed Hanafi grand mufti of Egypt in 1848 (when he was only twenty-one) by Ibrahim Pasha, possibly as a result of the intervention of Shaykh al-Islam ʿArif Bey in Istanbul. His ties to the khedival family were strong despite a series of confrontations with its members (described above), as attested by his appointment to the two most senior posts in the religious establishment—grand mufti and shaykh al-Azhar.[30]

As shaykh al-Azhar, al-Mahdi used his good relations with the khedive's court as well as his office as grand mufti (which he continued to hold) to acquire generous grants to improve al-Azhar's financial situation. He also aspired to raise the level of instruction by ending the arbitrary practice of granting *ijaza*s and shifting to a formal system of official diplomas based on final examinations, thereby reducing nepotism in the ranks of the shaykhs. The highest level of diploma (*al-shahada al-ʿalimiyya*) required expertise in eleven religious subjects (primarily law, commentary, grammar, rhetoric, and logic) and passing tests by a panel headed by the shaykh al-Azhar and senior ʿulamaʾ from each school of law. This certificate constituted an entry ticket to judicial and teaching positions at al-Azhar, along with material benefits such as a monthly salary, annual allocations, and robes of honor from the khedive.[31] The system of examinations initiated by al-Mahdi led to a reduction in the number of graduates accredited as teachers to an average of six annually, despite a rise in the number of students. One reason for initiating the new system was to end the practice of many students who abandoned studies upon receiving the basic certificate, which exempted them from military service. Others, deciding that they had accrued sufficient religious expertise, returned to their places of birth without qualifying to become ʿulamaʾ.[32]

Al-Mahdi's appointment as shaykh al-Azhar reinforced the trend that emerged during the first half of the century toward strengthening the status of the Hanafiyya in Egypt's official religious institutions, especially in the shariʿa judicial system. The position of Hanafi grand mufti, which al-Mahdi held for over fifty years, reflected the elevated status of the Turco-Circassian elite. Under al-Mahdi it became the highest office in the country, also referred to as mufti of Egypt (*mufti al-diyar al-Misriyya*). His functions included advising the governmental authorities in religious matters,[33] resolving disputes between ʿulamaʾ, and, as the supreme judicial authority, monitoring the decisions of qadis.

Moreover, the seniority of the grand mufti reflected the ongoing process of the bureaucratization of the Egyptian state during the nineteenth century.[34] This development contributed to the greater efficiency of the judicial system, while also upgrading the influence of the Hanafiyya within it. ʿAli Mubarak notes in his book *al-Khitat* that many Egyptians shifted to this school to gain employment as judges.[35] Having acquired the additional office of shaykh al-Azhar, al-Mahdi aimed to expand the Hanafi influence within the scholarly community. The data available to him furnished an additional impetus. The 312 lecturers at al-Azhar in 1871–72 included 70 Hanafis, 143 Shafiʿis, 95 Malikis, and 4 Hanbalis. The 9,441 students included 1,131 Hanafis, 4,570 Shafiʿis, 3,710 Malikis, and 30 Hanbalis. Al-Mahdi set out to alter these figures by easing the access to al-Azhar's resources for Hanafi lecturers and students, to the detriment of the other legal schools.[36] Ultimately, he managed to change the balance only slightly. During his tenure (1871–86) and even beyond, the number of Hanafi lecturers did not exceed 80, while the other two major schools—the Shafiʿi and the Maliki—more or less retained their numerical strength. The number of Hanafi students grew during this period, however, from 1,131 in 1872 to 1,774 in 1892 out of a total student body of 8,259.[37]

The shift in seniority in the office of the shaykh al-Azhar to the Hanafis and the end of the traditional *ijaza* procedure in favor of formal examinations once again stirred waves of protest by the ʿulamaʾ. Here, too, the Malikis, under the leadership of Shaykh Muhammad ʿIllaysh, set the tone, while the Shafiʿis joined them with the aim of restoring the office of shaykh al-Azhar to themselves. Besmirching al-Mahdi, they charged that only someone who attached no importance to the religious sciences could behave as he did.[38] The Khedive Isma'il, in an attempt to soften the opposition to reforms in al-Azhar, tried to gain 'Illaysh's loyalty, granting him a monthly allocation of 800 pounds in 1863 and approving an allocation of abandoned state lands to him in 1871, but with little success.[39] The khedive's policy of Westernization as well as the heightened tax burden on the population following the integration of Egypt's economy into the world market and the implementation of ambitious domestic projects (for example, the Suez Canal) continued to draw harsh criticism from 'Illaysh and others.

Isma'il therefore turned his attention to the establishment of a higher school for the training of teachers in the modern sciences (Dar al-'Ulum, 1872), which he perceived as an easier mission than implementing an outright reform in al-Azhar.[40] Reformist 'ulama', such as the brothers Ahmad and Husayn al-Marsafi, soon found Dar al 'Ulum to be a more supportive environment than al-Azhar in advancing their views.[41]

Isma'il's politically motivated interest in gleaning support from the religious scholarly community was aimed at stabilizing his questionable status vis-à-vis his European creditors and gaining favor in the court of the Ottoman sultan, overshadowing his concern for administrative reform. This was clearly reflected in the events that preceded his deposal in 1879, when senior 'ulama', who enjoyed the many benefits he accorded them, backed Isma'il's efforts to incite local opposition against Governor Riyad Pasha's cabinet and his European ministers.[42]

The aversion to educational innovation of 'Illaysh and his colleagues also explains their opposition to Shaykh Jamal al-Din al-Afghani, who in his classes at al-Azhar during 1871–79 preached intellectual openness and a rejuvenation of Islamic teaching in the spirit of the modern era. Some of his disciples, such as 'Abdallah Wafi al-Fayyumi and Muhammad 'Abduh, encountered hostile treatment and were suspected of heresy.[43] 'Abduh was actually forced into a frontal confrontation with 'Illaysh. Reportedly, 'Illaysh was informed that the young student was delving deeply into the Mu'tazila philosophy. This early Islamic rationalist school taught that the Qur'an was created rather than eternal and preached human free will as a rational depiction of good and evil.[44] Studying it was therefore forbidden at al-Azhar. When 'Illaysh summoned 'Abduh and asked if this information was true, 'Abduh replied in the affirmative, challenged the doctrine of *taqlid* (adherence to the precedents set by earlier legal authorities), and defended the use of logic and evidence in studying religious literature. He also expressed readiness to debate any argument that 'Illaysh might present to him on the matter. 'Illaysh, viewing this reply as haughty and a challenge to his senior status, became angry and struck ʿAbduh, according to some reports. Other accounts held that he simply arranged to terminate the young man's studies at al-Azhar. It was only through the intervention of Shaykh al-Azhar al-Mahdi that ʿAbduh passed his teaching examination successfully and received his ʿalim certificate in 1876.[45]

ʿIllaysh was later sharply censured by ʿAbduh's followers, Rashid Rida and Ahmad Amin, who described him as narrow-minded and hot-tempered, quick to level the charge of heresy without justification.[46] By contrast, they praised al-Mahdi for his personal honesty and absence of favoritism. Nevertheless, they acknowledged that the demonization of ʿAbduh had become embedded in the consciousness of the Azhar community, preventing him from advancing the issue of reform in al-Azhar and sapping his efforts at ideological writing over a long period. Alienating ʿAbduh, as well as his mentor al-Afghani, had gravely affected the rehabilitation of the status of al-Azhar and of the Muslim nation as a whole, Rida observed.[47]

Ironically, the two rivals, the conservative ʿIllaysh and the reformist ʿAbduh, found themselves on the same side several years later in their vigorous support of the ʿUrabi movement's struggle against the growing European influence in Egypt and against Khedive Tawfiq's ineffective regime (1881–82).

PART TWO

Azharis and the ʿUrabi Revolt, 1881–1882

3 Islam and Dissidence

The ʿUrabi movement began as a military revolt initiated by embittered Egyptian army officers, which gradually metamorphosed into a popular proto–national liberation movement. It targeted both the Turco-Circassians, who controlled the army and the administration, and the Europeans, whose growing influence in Egyptian affairs overshadowed that of the Khedive Tawfiq. Various segments of the Egyptian civic intelligentsia played a role in the transformation of the ʿUrabi cause from a military movement to a mass protest movement, including governmental officials, professionals, students, and ʿulamaʾ, providing it with a broad logistic and propaganda base. A main channel for their activity was the print medium, which became increasingly politicized and contributed to the radicalization of political trends in Egypt.[1] Ahmad ʿUrabi himself embraced this medium with alacrity, calling it "the mouthpiece of the nation" (*lisan al-umma*).[2]

The rural sector was also represented, with village shaykhs and notables, fellahin, and even tribes joining the protest incidents. The human diversity of the movement, encompassing various and often conflicting layers, provided it with a multidimensional agenda (social, political, and anticolonial), which underscored ethnic, religious, and national emphases. It was this diverse profile that led Ignaz Goldziher to define the ʿUrabi movement in 1882 as a social movement.[3]

The episode may be divided into five main stages: the Riyad cabinet and dual control by the British and French (September 1879–February 1881); the incidents at Qasr al-Nil and ʿAbidin (February–September 1881); the Sharif cabinet and the revolutionary coalition (September 1881–February 1882); the revolutionary cabinet led by Mahmud Sami al-Barudi and Ahmad ʿUrabi (February 1882–June 1882); and the Alexandria riots, the British bombing, and the fall of Cairo (June 11–September 1882).[4]

Each of the stages, which were characterized by growing political insta-
bility, witnessed the consistent involvement of ʿulamaʾ of various ranks.
They proved to be a vital factor in mobilizing popular support for ʿUrabi,
having at their disposal not only the power of the word (sermons, *qasida*s,
and fatwas) but also communal influence through the public offices they
held, their associations, and their material assets, which swept along large
numbers of followers.

The professional and geographic reach of the ʿulamaʾ who supported
ʿUrabi was diverse, as reflected in the list of ʿulamaʾ who were imprisoned
after the suppression of the 1882 uprising. It included lecturers, muftis,
qadis, imams, *ashraf*, and heads of Sufi orders serving as religious min-
istrants in Cairo and Alexandria as well as in distant provinces such as
Minya, Asyut, Damietta, Rashid, Port Saʿid, Mansura, al-Bahira, and al-
ʿArish.[5] These supporters made maximal use of the communal network
at their disposal, including mosques, madrasas, and charitable societies.
Besides material resources, they provided psychological support through
their piety, moral influence, and appeal for unity, jihad, and self-sacrifice
in facing enemies, based on allegiance to both faith and homeland. This
cultural milieu was integral in the accepted cosmic structure of society,
thereby serving as a convenient medium for disseminating the messages
of the ʿUrabi movement.[6]

Lord Cromer (Evelyn Baring), appointed British consul general in
Egypt in 1883, noted that the most important and influential group in
molding public opinion during the revolt was the Azhar clergy, including the lower ranks of preachers and qadis in the provinces. Cromer's dis-
taste for them was part of his disdainful approach to Islam as a bankrupt
religion in the modern era. He called them the "Jacobins of the movement," who, like their counterparts in the French Revolution, sought to
destroy "whatever germs of civilization had been implanted into Egypt."[7]
He thus attempted to cast the ʿUrabi movement in a traditional, even fa-
natic Islamic mold, thereby also diminishing its stature as a progressive
movement demanding representative rule and social equality.[8] But the
important role of the scholarly religious community as a moral and social
force in the events of the revolt was confirmed by the historical record.

The influence of the ʿUrabist ʿulamaʾ in nationalist politics was
clearly evident in the capital, Cairo. They were appointed to the delegation of dignitaries from Cairo and Alexandria that conferred with Sharif
Pasha on the night of September 13, 1881, to persuade him to accept the
task of forming a new government after the resignation of the Riyad

cabinet as demanded by the army.[9] At the same time, they also led the campaign to dismiss Shaykh Muhammad al-ʿAbbasi al-Mahdi from the post of shaykh al-Azhar in light of his attempts to reform its teaching system and entrench the status of the Hanafi legal school there as well as his close identification with the khedive's court.[10]

In the view of both the military and the civilian sectors of the protest movement, who sought a radical transformation of the Egyptian entity, al-Mahdi represented the old Turco-Circassian regime and therefore needed to be removed. Moreover, ʿUrabi and his colleagues harbored suspicions that al-Mahdi, in his high religious office, was likely to issue a fatwa against them as rebels against the kingdom, which would provide Tawfiq with additional ammunition to delegitimize their movement.[11] In this sense, the micro-struggle over the religious leadership at al-Azhar was intertwined with the macro-struggle over Egypt's political hegemony. It dovetailed with the broader ʿUrabist thrust to install its followers in the state administrative and indoctrinational networks, including ʿulamaʾ such as Muhammad ʿAbduh as editor of the government newspaper *al-Waqaʾiʿ al-Misriyya* (Egyptian Events) and al-Sayyid ʿAli al-Bablawi as supreme supervisor of Dar al-Kutub (Khedival Library).[12]

The dismissal process of the shaykh al-Azhar began with the formation of an external investigative committee led by Ahmad Rashid Pasha to consider complaints by Azharis against al-Mahdi's management, his disbursement of salaries, and other contentious issues, including the examination system that he installed. While the investigative committee failed to find sufficient cause to take steps against al-Mahdi, in view of the unrest in the institution its members decided to hand over the shaykh al-Azhar's position to a scholar from the Shafiʿi school (in accordance with the older tradition), with al-Mahdi remaining in his post as grand mufti. The committee's recommendation was adopted by Prime Minister Sharif and Khedive Tawfiq, who stressed the need to restore harmony in al-Azhar. Their stance also reflected a desire to gain credit with the ʿulamaʾ community and thereby prevent the Azhar arena from becoming the province of the ʿUrabists. Tawfiq personally instructed the Azhar leadership to choose a new shaykh al-Azhar from the Shafiʿi school.[13]

The dismissal of al-Mahdi as shaykh al-Azhar in December 1881 was an important victory for the ʿUrabists. Although their demand to replace him with their ardent supporter Muhammad ʿIllaysh was rejected by Tawfiq, his choice of the Shafiʿi Shams al-Din al-Inbabi was acceptable to them, especially since a body appointed to assist him in the management

of the institution was composed of loyalists to the movement. They were
ʿIllaysh of the Malikiyya, ʿAbdallah al-Darsatami of the Hanafiyya, and
Yusuf al-Hanbali of the Hanbaliyya.

Al-Inbabi (d. 1895), scion of a prominent ʿulamaʾ family from Jiza,
was an expert in hadith scholarship, known mainly for his colophons (ha-
washi) and commentaries (shuruh or taqrirat) on earlier works by senior
ʿulamaʾ. A scholar with both religious and worldly interests, he was also
involved in the cotton trade.[14] In his role as shaykh al-Azhar, al-Inbabi
proved to be a convenient figure for the protest movement. Shortly after his appointment, he acceded to a request by ʿUrabi to call upon the
Muslim population to preserve tranquillity and act in accordance with
the religious command against scheming to acquire the property of Jews
or Christians or harming them.[15] For the Azharis, the appointment of the
new shaykh al-Azhar—who was less enthusiastic than al-Mahdi about
reshaping al-Azhar's educational system and displayed a disdain for the
scientific spirit of inquiry demanded by reformist critics—was a welcome
step.[16] For the Shafiʿis, specifically, al-Inbabi's appointment signaled
the institution's return to the right track: the resumption of Shafiʿiyya
leadership.

Azharis who supported the revolt were also involved in promoting
the notion of replacing Khedive Tawfiq with his uncle, Prince ʿAbd al-
Halim, who then resided in Constantinople. The primary instigators of
this scheme were Muhammad ʿIllaysh and Hasan al-ʿIdwi,[17] followers of
ʿUrabi who were known to have been in contact with Halim's retinue.
In principle, Halim did not reject the prospect of his appointment as
khedive if called for by circumstances. Moreover, the satirical antiregime
magazine Abu Naddara (The Bespectacled One), published by Yaʿqub
Sannuʿ in Paris and distributed clandestinely in Egyptian military circles,
was funded by Halim.[18] Tawfiq himself, fearful of the possibility of being deposed, sought the support of the foreign consuls in Egypt. He also
telegraphed Istanbul about his concern over reports that army circles were
planning to remove him in favor of Halim. Tawfiq noted in his message
that Halim was despised by the Egyptians and that ʿulamaʾ circles also
held him in low esteem, viewing him as godless—a position they had expressed in an open forum.[19]

The co-option of Islam for political purposes was a means also used by
the third party in the struggle for the khedival seat: the deposed Ismaʿil,
in exile in Istanbul, who made no secret of his ambition to resume his role
as ruler of Egypt. He too made efforts to establish links with Azharis in
order to promote his interests, aware of their important role in the protest
events.[20]

THE OTTOMAN DIMENSION

All the parties involved in the ʿUrabi episode viewed Istanbul, the nominal sovereign authority over Egypt, as an important lever in promoting their cause. They tried to obtain its support by using religion and religious spokesmen—a significant reflection of Azharis' influence in the political process. This influence and involvement became even greater as the domestic crisis intensified and the threat of external intervention grew, especially from the winter of 1881 to the summer of 1882.

Both rivals, Tawfiq and ʿUrabi, maintained ongoing ties with Istanbul, pledging loyalty to Sultan Abdülhamid II (1876–1908) while exchanging mutual barbs and accusations. Each managed to agitate the Ottomans by sparking fear of the loss of Ottoman sovereignty over Egypt as a result of the irresponsible acts of the other. Tawfiq claimed that foreign intervention would be unavoidable if the provocations of the ʿUrabists did not cease, adding that one of the movement's goals was to destroy the power of the Turco-Circassian elite.[21] On the opposing side, ʿUrabi contended that Tawfiq was interested in separating Egypt from the Ottoman Empire and the caliphate and subjugating it to the British, while casting himself as a defender of the rights of the sultan in Egypt. He stated in one of his letters to Istanbul in January 1882: "All our attention and energy is devoted to guarding the rights of our exalted [Ottoman] state and resisting those who wish to harm us and violate the rights of our lord—the commander of the faithful—so long as the Egyptians can breathe."[22] ʿUrabi's second in command, Mahmud Sami al-Barudi, who served as minister of war and later as prime minister, argued in a similar vein.[23]

Prominent ʿulamaʾ were enlisted to support ʿUrabi's point of view. Shaykh ʿIllaysh, in a letter to Istanbul describing the situation in Egypt, pointed to Tawfiq's lack of popularity with the public and his violation of the sultan's rights in the country:

> Since we could be deprived of Sublime Porte citizenship because of foreign intervention stemming from Khedive Tawfiq's incapacity and his violation of our law and order, the leaders of all the Egyptian people and myself have demanded the dismissal of the Khedive. If the sultan permits Prince Halim to replace Khedive Tawfiq, this will bring happiness to the Egyptian people forever. In such a case, permanent security can be implemented and we can remain safely under the sultan's patronage.[24]

The khedive, however, dismissed the letter as fabricated by ʿAbd al-Halim Pasha's supporters, who presumably had succeeded in deceiving an eighty-year-old scholar ('Illaysh) who had no interest in world affairs.[25] The very fact that the khedive addressed the Maliki mufti's letter, however, revealed his fear of an erosion of his public status if he was perceived as unfit to rule.

'Urabi also had mediation agents within the 'ulama' community at his disposal in Istanbul, who acted as close advisors and confidants to the sultan in matters concerning the Arab provinces. These included Muhammad Zafir al-Madani, Abu al-Huda al-Sayyadi, and Ahmad As'ad, who filled both a religious and a political function and were known to have extensive connections with religious circles—especially Sufi—in the Fertile Crescent and North Africa. They served as couriers in passing on 'Urabi's messages to Istanbul as well as advocates for him in the sultan's court, portraying him as loyal to the empire.[26]

Fearful of foreign intervention in Egypt, the Sublime Porte was forced to consolidate its position regarding its authority there. Abdülhamid harbored no great affection for Tawfiq as a descendant of Muhammad 'Ali, the ruler that the Ottomans perceived as having challenged their sovereignty over the Arab Middle East and de facto having separated Egypt from that authority. But the sultan was also no admirer of 'Urabi. On the contrary, in seeking to reinforce the boundaries of the empire against Christian penetration by promoting a pan-Islamic ideology and suppressing any nationalistic tendencies, Abdülhamid viewed the 'Urabists' rebelliousness and the constitutional agenda they promoted as a threat that was liable to spread to other regions in the empire. He was already concerned by signs of political dissent in the Arab provinces. A secret society had reportedly been established in Hijaz to promote the restoration of an Arab caliphate. Similar Pan-Arab ferment was evident in the Syrian and Lebanese cities, calling for rebellion against the Turks and the formation of an independent Arab entity. The sultan was also aware that the Anatolian Turkish population viewed Ahmad 'Urabi as a Muslim hero and had openly demonstrated in favor of his movement and instructed the Ottoman Interior Ministry to suppress subversive discourse and take any necessary steps in this regard.[27] Thus Tawfiq, weak as he was, was perceived as the sultan's representative in Egypt and as such merited sustained Ottoman support for his authority, which Abdülhamid believed would also prevent foreign intervention.[28]

Nevertheless, the Ottoman response was cautious, seeking to resolve the Egyptian question "noiselessly and peaceably" through mediation rather than by ostracizing 'Urabi entirely, given the public support for his cause. This was the mission assigned to two delegations that the Sublime Porte sent to Egypt.[29]

Upon the arrival of the first delegation, on October 2, 1881, the guest accommodations housing its members immediately became a pilgrimage destination for ʿulamaʾ who supported the ʿUrabi movement.[30] The head of the delegation, Nizami Pasha, listened politely as the shaykhs praised ʿUrabi and the activity undertaken by al-Barudi (his loyal supporter in the war office) but did not conceal his support for Tawfiq, who was awarded insignia of honor and merit conferred by the sultan. Nizami carefully balanced his meeting with ʿUrabi ʿulamaʾ with a parallel meeting with pro-khedive ʿulamaʾ led by Shaykh al-Azhar al-Mahdi; the supreme head of the official Sufi orders, ʿAbd al-Baqi al-Bakri; and Shaykh ʿAbd al-Khaliq al-Sadat, another prominent Sufi leader. Moreover, the emphasis on their commitment to preserving public order conveyed by ʿUrabi army officers to Nizami and their protestations of loyalty to the Ottoman state as "the focus of our hopes and the home of the Islamic caliphate" did not have the intended effect.[31]

The primary theme of Nizami's address to the officers at the army headquarters at Qasr al-Nil, delivered with al-Barudi as minister of war at his side, was their duty to obey the ruler. He emphasized that the khedive, as the authorized representative of the sultan, was endowed with the sultan's esteem and love; whoever crossed the khedive crossed the sultan. Nizami pointedly quoted a verse from the Qurʾan: "O believers, obey God, and obey the Messenger and those in authority among you" (4:59). This was true sevenfold, he declared, for the military, who were required to carry out the orders of the ruler in every situation without hesitation or qualification for the sake of elevating the word of Islam and defending the homeland.[32]

A pointed personal message by Nizami to ʿUrabi to obey the khedive elicited no response. On the contrary, the crisis of confidence in the khedive intensified, as ʿUrabi's strength continued to grow after the departure of the sultan's delegation. The ʿUrabi movement's public display of noncompliance with the legal authority of the khedive, exacerbated by an open besmirching of his name, heightened Ottoman sensitivity regarding the political repercussions of the Egyptian crisis in the other Arab provinces of the empire. This concern mounted with growing European pressure on Istanbul to intervene in the events in Egypt (including sending military forces) and the eruption of the Mahdi revolt in Sudan in February 1882. These developments impelled the Sublime Porte to harden its position against the ʿUrabists, reflected explicitly in the dispatch of a second Ottoman delegation to Egypt, which arrived on June 7, 1882.

This time the goal was to distance ʿUrabi from the Egyptian arena by summoning him to Istanbul and by demonstrating unqualified support for the khedive, who was depicted as a figure of morality and piety and far worthier to rule than his uncle, ʿAbd al-Halim.[33] On this occasion, too, ʿulamaʾ who supported the revolt (led by ʿIllaysh, al-ʿIdwi, and Muhammad al-Khadr) tried to influence the Ottoman position. But they were given a cool and impatient reception by the head of the delegation, Darwish Pasha, reflecting Ottoman distress with the arrival of British warships off the coast of Alexandria in the summer of 1882 and the presentation of an Anglo-French memorandum demanding the exile of ʿUrabi and his key colleagues.

Reports of the two encounters between Darwish and the ʿulamaʾ delegation referred to a strained atmosphere. In the first, on June 7, the ʿulamaʾ attempted to focus on the political situation: the need to reach an understanding with ʿUrabi and defuse British aggression toward Egypt. But Darwish, impatient to meet with the foreign consuls, ended the meeting quickly. In the second encounter, a day later, the ʿulamaʾ reiterated the need for a firm stand vis-à-vis Europe. They also quoted hadiths and religious arguments obligating the dismissal of a ruler (Tawfiq) who sides with the enemies of religion and the homeland. ʿIllaysh warned against turning Tawfiq into another Tunisian bey, functioning as a puppet ruler under the French, while al-ʿIdwi and others voiced their concern about the need to evict the British Navy ships. Darwish, cutting them off sharply, informed them that the Jiza palace, his guest accommodation, was not a coffeehouse for rowdy politicians and that he had come to implement the sultan's instructions, not to get advice. He ordered the ʿulamaʾ to cut their remarks short and leave.

Darwish's intention was to dampen the enthusiasm of the ʿUrabist ʿulamaʾ and clarify that his goal was to stabilize the situation, not exacerbate it. As a veteran military figure, he apparently viewed his task as dictating a rigid model of religious-state relations that did not allow the intervention of religious figures in governmental politics. Reverberations of this humiliating event evoked agitation in the Azhar community, however, with masses of students gathering in the courtyard of the Azhar Mosque during prayer time to protest the insult to their shaykhs. One of the speakers at the protest was ʿAbdallah Nadim, a leading orator of the revolt, who used his rhetorical talents and the religious setting to attack both Darwish and the khedive. Darwish, in consultation with the Sublime Porte, promptly issued an official denial of the reports about the humiliation of the ʿulamaʾ and, softening his approach to ʿUrabi, agreed to receive him for a discussion.[34]

Pro-khedive ʿulamaʾ also sought to influence Darwish's position.

Telegrams sent to him by ʿulamaʾ and notables from Alexandria and other provinces, such as Asyut, Manfalut, and al-Duwayr, welcomed the dispatch of the Ottoman delegation to Egypt to put an end to the public disorder and riots. They also pledged absolute loyalty to the khedive and his government as the authorities acting for the welfare and security of the country.[35]

The Darwish delegation left Egypt on July 7, 1882, empty-handed. Signs of war were apparent by then. Several days later, British Navy ships shelled Alexandria, a prologue to the conquest of the interior of Egypt two months afterward, thereby reinforcing Ottoman reservations regarding ʿUrabi.

The Istanbul press, which systematically denied reports circulating in England and France that the sultan intended to replace Tawfiq with Prince ʿAbd al-Halim, described Egypt as "an Islamic land that constitutes the beating heart in the body of the Ottoman sultanate."[36] Frantic messages dispatched by ʿUrabi and al-Barudi to Istanbul warning of the growing foreign influence in Egypt and the transformation of the country into a second Tunisia (which was captured by the French in April 1881) failed to turn the tide toward their cause.[37] Some of their frustration was vented by planting rumors and reports in the pro-ʿUrabi press to the effect that the Ottomans would join with the Europeans in destroying Egypt or that they intended to send forces of their own to Egypt—a move that would encounter strong resistance, these reports warned. Istanbul, responding in a formal message delivered to ʿUrabi, accused him of aspiring to the post of khedive of Egypt all along and of having no authority to rebel in the name of the Prophet or of the sultan in his capacity as the Commander of the Faithful. ʿUrabi avoided publicizing this reply, which could have reduced public support for him by revealing that the sultan had turned against him.

The rift between the ʿUrabi camp and the sultan's court obliged ʿUrabi's supporters in Istanbul, led by Shaykh Ahmad Asʿad (who had been a member of Darwish Pasha's delegation to Egypt), to reconcile their differences with their superiors. In discussions with ʿUrabi, Asʿad explained that ʿUrabi's position was unacceptable to the sultan and he must therefore abandon it. Asʿad stressed the need for tranquillity, warning that the loss of Egypt would eventually lead to the loss of the Ottoman Empire itself.[38]

The involvement of ʿulamaʾ such as ʿIllaysh and al-ʿIdwi in the ʿUrabi camp and Asʿad and Zafir on the Ottoman side, acting as mediators and couriers on the Cairo-Istanbul axis, signified the relevance of the ʿulamaʾ

in both Egyptian and Ottoman politics. More broadly, Istanbul's involvement in the ʿUrabi episode demonstrates that the ties between the Ottoman Empire and Egypt were closer and more intensive than reflected in the extant research, as can be learned from abundant documents located in the Yildiz Archive, now part of the Başbakanlık Arşivi (Prime Minister's Archives) in Istanbul.[39]

DEFYING A MUSLIM RULER

The involvement of ʿulamaʾ in Egyptian politics peaked in two large general assemblies (jamʿiyyat ʾumumiyya) convened by the leaders of the ʿUrabi movement at the Ministry of the Interior in Cairo in July 1882. The movement's emergency situation was evident in both gatherings. The first, held on July 17, was prompted by a military escalation in the wake of British shelling of the embankments and fortifications erected by the ʿUrabi army along the Alexandria shore and the fear of a British invasion into the interior of the country. The khedive, residing in Alexandria, was said to have placed himself under the protection of the British forces, a move that ʿUrabi depicted as "an insult to Egyptians, Muslims and Copts alike."[40]

Some seventy people attended the conference, consisting of leading Cairo governmental officials, prominent merchants, ʿulamaʾ, and representatives of other religious communities. The tone was set by the senior ʿulamaʾ, ʿIllaysh and al-ʿIdwi, who denounced Tawfiq as a traitor and called for jihad against the British. The assembly was held during the Ramadan fast, associated in Muslim collective memory with the impressive victories by the Prophet during the formative period of Islam, which served to enhance the rousing religious rhetoric of ʿIllaysh and al-ʿIdwi. But this rhetoric also exposed the interethnic dissonance between Muslims and Copts in Egypt. The Coptic representatives asserted that their community would have difficulty joining a religious war in the name of Islam, in contrast to a patriotic war of self-defense. They also warned against hasty decisions so long as it was unclear whether the khedive and his ministers in Alexandria had actually put themselves at the disposal of the British forces.[41]

Ultimately, the decisions passed at the assembly did not exclude the prospect of further dialogue with the khedive. They were limited to persuading Tawfiq and the cabinet ministers to return from Alexandria to Cairo and carry on with military preparations so long as English forces remained in Alexandria with their ships anchored in the harbor. Acting on a proposal by the former minister of public works, ʿAli Mubarak, a khedival loyalist, the conference body authorized the formation of a mediation delegation of six to travel to Alexandria and present the conclusions of the assembly to the khedive. Its members were Mubarak himself; Raʾuf Pasha, a former governor of Sudan; Ahmad al-Suyufi, a member of the Chamber of Delegates; Saʿid al-Shamakhi, representing the state of Marakesh in Egypt; and two ʿulamaʾ: ʿAli al-Nayil and Ahmad Kabwa, a Maliki who served as shaykh Riwaq al-Saʿidiyya at al-Azhar.[42]

ʿUrabi, conferring with the delegation at Kafr al-Dawwar, outside Alexandria, retained his insistence on Tawfiq's deposal. From there, the delegation went on to Alexandria to persuade the khedive to reach a compromise.[43] Refusing, the khedive issued a proclamation on July 20, dismissing ʿUrabi from his post as minister of war and charging him with responsibility for the shelling of Alexandria, the paralysis of the transportation, mail, and telegraph systems, and the continuation of military preparations contrary to the khedive's instructions. Religion was also brought into the proclamation in defaming the ʿUrabists' for being a deviant Shiʿi sect, showing disobedience to a legitimate ruler, and causing anarchy. At the same time, Tawfiq warned the Egyptian population against joining the ʿUrabi movement, emphasizing that the British were allies and not aggressors against Egypt or the Sublime Porte. Any person displaying opposition to the British troops, he stated, would be treated as a rebel. The khedive singled out the ʿulamaʾ and other notables as responsible for public order and for ensuring the obedience of the people to the state authorities.[44]

ʿUrabi had defied the khedive's authority for some time, and the successes he accrued served to reinforce his political ambitions. The formal dismissal provided him with an opportunity to elevate his status as the sole guardian of Egypt's homeland, faith, and honor and to recruit the support of the populace for a defensive war in the wake of Tawfiq's abandonment of them.[45] Seeking to acquire official sanction from the representatives of civil society, he convened a second assembly on July 29, 1882, this time attended by 393 people from Cairo and other regions in Lower and Middle Egypt. They represented a sectoral cross section of the ʿUrabi movement, as Alexander Schölch and Juan R. Cole point out, including the elite, urban and rural dignitaries, and the intelligentsia, thereby providing the movement with a broader civil rather than military base. The last segment—composed of government officials, army officers, members of the free professions, and religious figures—constituted a dominant proportion of the assembly numerically: 160 (41 percent). It is interesting that half were religious personalities, primarily ʿulamaʾ from al-Azhar and provincial qadis, along with a number of Christian priests. Several muftis and qadis from the provinces of Damietta and Rusta were specially invited to flesh out the list of signatories, to the satisfaction of the organizers.[46] The prominent presence of ʿulamaʾ lent an Islamic tone to the assembly decisions, however, once again exposing dissonance between Muslims and Copts.

Underlying the decisions made by the assembly was a disregard for the khedive's decision to dismiss ʿUrabi from the Ministry of War and a rejection of the khedive's authority now that he was under the patronage of the British. ʿUrabi was authorized to continue military preparations to block the arrival of the British in Cairo, and the country was put under a military regime.[47] In light of these decisions, ʿUrabi was acknowledged as the "Defender of the Land of Egypt" (*Hami al-Diyar al-Misriyya*). Moreover, a report of the assembly with the list of signatories was sent to Istanbul as part of ʿUrabi's ongoing attempt to display unity and compatibility with the Sublime Porte and to highlight the popular rather than military character of his movement.[48]

Religious legitimation to deviate from the Sunni taboo of rebellion against a Muslim ruler was provided by the senior ʿulamaʾ, headed by ʿIllaysh. He was joined by al-ʿIdwi and Abu al-ʿAlaʾ al-Khalfawi. Al-Khalfawi, a Hanafi scholar from the province of Minufiyya, was a lecturer at al-Azhar and mufti of the Judicial Council (Majlis al-Ahkam) in Cairo, established in 1848–49. Al-Khalfawi had been a loyal follower of Khedive Ismaʿil and, like al-ʿIdwi, was involved in the events that preceded Ismaʿil's deposition in 1879. He was also a close associate of the mufti of Egypt, al-Mahdi, and influenced ʿAbbas Pasha to end al-Mahdi's exile for refusing to issue a fatwa favorable to ʿAbbas and reinstate him in Cairo. In return, al-Mahdi bestowed positions and other benefits on al-Khalfawi.[49] During the events of the uprising, al-Khalfawi crossed to the other side of the fence and stood together with his colleagues, advocating Tawfiq's deposition.

A declaration by ʿIllaysh, al-ʿIdwi, and al-Khalfawi at ʿUrabi's request, which carried the weight of a fatwa, called for Tawfiq to be deposed for transgressing two Qurʾanic prohibitions: nonimplementation of Allah's laws, which turns the culprit into a heretic, a rebel, and an exploiter (5:44–46); and the inclusion of Jews and Christians as allies (5:51). If Tawfiq was denounced as having strayed from the faith (*mariq*) and subjecting himself to the patronage of heretics, against whom a jihad must be mounted without delay, ʿUrabi was hailed as a defender of the rights of the Commander of the Faithful (the sultan) and for demonstrating the power of Allah in this world.[50] Following the declaration of the fatwa, a petition signed by 10,000 notables, including ʿulamaʾ, was submitted to the Ottoman representatives in Cairo in demand of backing the deposition of the khedive.[51]

The demand for Tawfiq's removal, hinted at even in the first assembly, reflected a heightened level of political dissidence on the part of ʿIllaysh. Notably, in several of his essays ʿIllaysh had warned against reckless charges of heresy against other believers and cautioned that the deposition of an imam or a ruler would lead to a grave split among Muslims and widespread bloodshed. He sanctified the *bayʿa* (oath of allegiance) to an established authority and denounced rebellion against it (*baghy*) by quoting from the hadith "He who dies without the oath of allegiance [to the ruler] dies the death of a pagan." In other writings, however, he enumerated the duties of the ruler toward Islam and its believers, explaining that any deviation from these duties releases the bonds of loyalty toward him. The duties included the capacity to lead and be resourceful in times of crisis and disaster, uphold justice, apply the shariʿa, "prohibit wrong," and carry out jihad against heretics.[52] The critical reality in which the Egyptian community and the ʿUrabi movement itself found themselves prompted ʿIllaysh to emphasize the obligations of the ruler—which Tawfiq had failed to carry out—over the loyalty owed to him.

ʿIllaysh's theologically based judgment of Tawfiq in 1882 did not differ substantively from his judgment of the Moroccan sultan ʿAbd al-Rahman ibn Hisham thirty-five years earlier in a lengthy fatwa published in connection with the Algerian uprising against the French (1830–48). That fatwa was compiled in 1847 at the request of Emir ʿAbd al-Qadir al-Jazaʾiri (d. 1883), leader of the rebellion against the French, who criticized the Muslim states for failing to stand up to the heretics with determination, thereby shirking the duty of jihad. Al-Jazaʾiri specifically named the sultan of Morocco, ʿAbd al-Rahman, as a traitor to Islam for supplying the French forces with food, clothing, guns, and pack animals while withholding such assistance from the jihad fighters. The sultan, submitting to a French dictate, demanded that al-Jazaʾiri and his men lay down their arms. The emir's refusal, claiming that the sultan did not have legal authority and that he was not obliged to submit to him, exposed him to persecution. With this in mind, al-Jazaʾiri asked, did he not have the right to bear arms against the sultan of Morocco? ʿIllaysh, expressing regret over the submissive stance of the Moroccan ruler, issued a definitive and immutable judgment that al-Jazaʾiri was acting in self-defense against an unjust ruler who deviated from mandatory Islamic conduct. A Muslim who aids heretics or calls for a truce with them, ʿIllaysh maintained, is an enemy of Islam, and a war against him is a holy war in which the casualties are martyrs.[53]

The announcement of Tawfiq's deposition met with the approval of other ʿulamaʾ present at the second assembly, including Yusuf al-Hanbali, Muhammad al-ʿAshmuni, and Muhammad al-Qalamawi, all lecturers at al-Azhar; Zayn al-Marsafi, a lecturer at Dar al-ʿUlum; ʿAbd al-Qadir al-Dilbishani and ʿAbd al-Rahman al-Suwaysi, members of the Supreme Shariʿa Court; ʿAbdallah al-Darsatawi, the Zabatiyya mufti of Egypt; Masʿud al-Nabulsi, the awqaf mufti; Ahmad al-Khashab, qadi of the province of Jiza; Salim ʿUmar al-Qalʿawi; and ʿUthman Madukh, imam and preacher of the Sultan Shams al-Din Muhammad Mosque in Cairo.[54] By contrast, several senior ʿulamaʾ who were present at the announcement of the deposition or were informed of it later refused to sign or opposed the declaration. These included Grand Mufti al-Mahdi, who argued that only the Ottoman sultan had the right to depose the khedive;[55] the heads of the official Sufi orders, ʿAbd al-Baqi al-Bakri and ʿAbd al-Khaliq al-Sadat; ʿAbd al-Rahman al-Bahrawi (the imam of the khedive's court) and ʿAbd al-Qadir al-Rafiʿi, both members of the Supreme Shariʿa Court;[56] and ʿAbd al-Hadi Naja al-Abyari, the imam of the khedive's court.[57] Al-Abyari (d. 1887), a Shafiʿi scholar and a Sufi known for his extensive writing in the fields of literature and language,[58] laid out his position in essays and fatwas, warning that religious arbiters must be exceedingly cautious in leveling the charge of heresy against Muslims, and all the more so against Muslim rulers, except in unequivocal cases such as idol worship.[59]

Another nonsignatory was Shaykh al-Azhar Shams al-Din al-Inbabi, who wished to preserve his neutrality. His initial support for the ʿUrabi movement after his appointment to his position in late 1881 had been less than resolute, and he did not attend the second assembly, claiming illness.[60] Several of the signatories later alleged that their signatures were coerced. Other names were transposed onto the list of signatories of the deposition declaration by followers of ʿUrabi in later declarations and in memoirs, with the aim of reinforcing the religious position justifying the denial of the khedive's sovereignty.[61]

Although the conflict in the ʿulamaʾ ranks over this issue involved political affiliations and power struggles over posts and honors, it was also ideological, revolving around the duty to obey a Muslim ruler. ʿUrabi's supporters viewed Tawfiq as being under the patronage of the Christian powers and as having abandoned his faith, thereby meriting deposition.

Identifying him with heretic forces was a prerequisite for denouncing him, while also constituting an additional incentive for glorifying ʿUrabi's name. This message was embedded in sermons and *qasida*s delivered in a popular emotional style, mainly in mosques. The mosques repeatedly proved their viability as intermediary agencies, whether as organizational bases for street protests or as recruitment sites for raising money to support the war effort. The sermons and *qasida*s were also covered extensively in the ʿUrabi press—for example, in ʿAbduh's *al-Waqaʾiʿ al-Misriyya*, Nadim's *al-Tankit waʾl-Tabkit* (Mockery and Reproach) and *al-Taʾif* (The Rover), and Hasan al-Shamsi's *al-Mufid* (The Informer).[62] Oral communication thus meshed with the printed press in conveying the religious rhetoric of the ʿUrabist cause.

In sermons preached in Asyut, Shaykhs ʿAli al-Maliji and Mahmud Ibrahim likened Tawfiq to rulers who abandoned the defense of Islam in favor of attending to their personal affairs, thereby causing great suffering to believers. By contrast, the shaykhs asserted, ʿUrabi devoted himself and his army to Allah, thereby revealing the greatness and power of the Muslims while acting to eliminate deviance and perversion. The Shafiʿi mufti of al-Azhar, Mustafa ʿIzz, attributed the political upheavals in Egypt to the country's exposure to Western modernization and the imitation of the culture and laws of foreigners, which had upset the natural order of things and subjected Muslims to the authority of non-Muslims. According to ʿIzz: "This went so far that unbelievers would ride horses and carriages with Muslims running in front of them, or that the cursed [unbelievers] would extend their feet with their black shoes to Muslims in order to have them polished by them."[63]

While Tawfiq was identified with darkness, deviation, and exploitation, ʿUrabi was identified with the rejuvenation of the Islamic religion (*mujaddid*) and adherence to its commandments. His victory therefore was guaranteed by Allah, declared Shaykhs Ahmad Sayf al-Bari and Zayn al-Marsafi in their *qasida*s.[64]

The contrast between Tawfiq and ʿUrabi was heightened by the demonization of the British. Historic memory was evoked: the British danger was depicted as a modern version of the Tatar and Crusader aggression of the twelfth and thirteenth centuries. Preachers, among them Muhammad Abu al-Fadl in Cairo and Hamidu al-Damanhuri in Damanhur, denounced the behavior of the British as hypocritical and provocative, aimed at turning Egypt from a domain of peace into a domain of war. Other preachers in Asyut and Mansura raised the banner of self-sacrifice for Allah as the duty of every Muslim sound in body and mind, by which to acquire prestige in this world and eternal life in the next. In a *qasida*, the preacher Ahmad ʿAbd al-Ghani called the present era a time of seriousness, loyalty, determination, and the fervor of youth. "In God's name! This is not the time for mischief-making or for listening to music or dancing under the influence alcohol," ʿAbd al-Ghani exhorted. The content of the *qasida*s, and even more so the sermons, was imbued with fervor and determination. They appealed for enlistment in support of faith and justice but also for forbearance and tenacity until Allah's promised victory, hinting at an awareness of the military might of the enemy.[65]

In contrast to the dissident narrative, the khedive's supporters projected a quietist stance highlighting his attributes as the sole legitimate authority, the representative of the Ottoman sultan, and the barrier against anarchy and bloodshed. The religious debate conducted against the ʿUrabi movement was similarly waged in the mosques, in the press, and in fatwas. Its intent was to provide viability and moral support for the campaign of delegitimation conducted by Tawfiq against ʿUrabi, portraying him as a rebel against the kingdom. The essence of the royalist narrative was provided in articles written by Shaykh Hamza Fathallah (d. 1918) for *al-Burhan* (The Proof) and *al-Iʿtidal* (Moderation), two newspapers published in Alexandria.[66] The title a*l-Iʿtidal* reflected its ideological approach, calling on the ʿUrabi movement to show obedience and submission to heads of state. In his articles, Fathallah projected an ecumenical version of Islam as a moral religion with universal attributes, requiring worthy conduct of its believers and friendship toward their non-Muslim neighbors. This narrative was intended as an antithesis to ʿUrabi's aggressive position, which was portrayed as nothing more than a cover-up for "satanic temptations, self-love, and personal interests."[67]

The main argument that Fathallah used to delegitimize the ʿUrabi movement as "rebellious" (*ʿasi*) was its pretension to mount a religious war against foreigners. He thus drew on two central themes in Islamic theology. The first was his depiction of a declaration of religious war as the sole prerogative of the caliph or his representative, the khedive; anyone who usurped this privilege was considered a rebel. Significantly, Fathallah did not address the possibility of a defensive war in which Muslims were the target of attack, which legally obliges a general mobilization even without the approval of the ruler. In Fathallah's view, this was never the situation from the start, since the British were not considered enemies but rather legal protectors present in Islamic territory by agreement or permission (*mustaʿminun* or *muʿahidun*). Moreover, using their assistance to restore order was no sin, Fathallah emphasized, and was sometimes required by the circumstances of reality, as could be learned from the behavior of well-known leaders in Muslim history.

The second Islamic theme that Fathallah used was the concept of *maslaha* (public welfare). 'Urabi's muscular agenda vis-à-vis the British was depicted as irrational, foolish, and rash, serving only to intensify the crisis while failing to weigh the relative military strength of the sides, thus exposing the faith and its believers to the actual danger of conquest and enslavement. The age of superhuman attributes and miracles ended with the death of the Prophet, Fathallah observed cynically. What was happening at present, he concluded, was suicide—a loaded concept in Islam, punishable by eternal affliction in hell, as written in the Qur'an: "And cast not yourselves by your hands into destruction, but be good-doers; God loves the good-doers" (2:195).[68]

'Urabi himself belittled Fathallah's accusations, observing that the shaykh wanted to hand over the country to its enemies without a battle and, moreover, that his religious knowledge was shallow and misleading.[69] Conscious of the power of Islam as a religious lever, the Barudi-'Urabi revolutionary cabinet formed in February 1882 launched a campaign to neutralize the oppositionist press, especially the press identified with the khedive. *Al-Burhan* was forced to dismiss Fathallah from the post of editor-in-chief as a condition of continuing to publish. A formal closure order was issued against Fathallah's other platform, *al-I'tidal*, shortly after it was launched (apparently in July 1882).[70]

A quietist Islam was favored by most of the senior 'ulama' who supported the khedive, but their voice was drowned out by the religious fervor of dissident Islam, fanned by the presence of the British forces in Alexandria. This presence played into the hands of the dissident spokesmen, who called up Islamic faith as a symbol of group identification and solidarity, turning it into the primary language of opposition to the khedive's regime and the presence of the foreigners. Sufi orders played a significant role in this trend.

SUFISM AND POLITICS

Sufi orders, especially the Shadhiliyya and Khalwatiyya, provided popular backing for the steps taken by some of the 'Urabist 'ulama' in Cairo. The activist worldview of these orders, which preached involvement in communal and political life and an avoidance of extreme asceticism, provided an ideological incentive for their participation in the events of the revolt. This perception emphasized the close link between the duty to

Allah (*wajib Allah*) and the duty to humankind (*wajib al-nas*).[71] Moreover, these orders did not accept the authority of Shaykh ʿAbd al-Baqi
al-Bakri, the head of the official Sufi orders, who was loyal to the khedive. This allowed them wide latitude in organizing demonstrations and
commemorations and in raising money for the ʿUrabi army. Like internal
disputes in al-Azhar over orientation and posts, internal differences in the
Sufi network, especially regarding al-Bakri's thrust toward centralization
and reform, were entwined in the proto-national struggle.[72]

The ʿArabiyya Shadhiliyya order of the ʿIllaysh family and the Shadhiliyya order of the ʿIdwi family played key roles in guiding Sufi protest activity in the Cairene milieu and its environs. Other orders, led by Azharis
such as Khalil al-ʿAzzazi, Muhammad Khalil al-Hijrisi, and Muhammad
Abu ʿUlyan, were also involved in the protest movement.[73]

Al-ʿAzzazi was descended from an ʿulamaʾ family in the village of al-
ʿAzzazi in the Sharqiyya province, which was a Sufi base centered at the
grave of Sidi al-Majdhub. Many members of his family had held key religious and governmental positions in the region under Muhammad ʿAli
and his dynasty. Notwithstanding his religious training, al-ʿAzzazi also
displayed an interest in the more temporal fields of study, such as mathematics, astronomy, geography, and engineering.[74] Al-Hijrisi, in addition
to being a Khalwati Sufi, was a prominent Shafiʿi lecturer at al-Azhar who
also dealt in commerce. According to Wilfrid Scawen Blunt, a Victorian
poet and an admirer of the ʿUrabi movement, al-Hijrisi had a close relationship with the ʿUrabist officers in Cairo and was also in contact with
dissidents in Mecca who called for reforms in the Ottoman Empire.[75] Abu
ʿUlyan, born in Aswan to a family that traced its lineage to the Prophet's
family, was a student of both ʿIllaysh and al-ʿIdwi and became the head
of the Muhammadiyya Shadhiliyya order. Renowned for his piety, he
refused honors and lands offered him by Khedive Ismaʿil in an effort to
enhance his own popularity and criticized colleagues who succumbed to
such temptations. He was also known as a harsh critic of al-Bakri's reform
policy for the Sufi system. The ʿUrabi events further exacerbated the tension between them, with the two figures aligned on opposite sides.[76]

Outside Cairo, primarily in Upper Egypt, several of the Khalwatiyya
sects provided additional support for the ʿUrabi movement, most prominently the Qayatiyya order in Minya. Its leaders, the brothers Muhammad
(d. 1902) and Ahmad (d. 1890) al-Qayati, were deeply involved in religious scholarship, Sufism, and politics. They were born in the village of al-
Qayat into a family of religious dignitaries identified with the Shafiʿi legal
school. Their grandfather, Shaykh ʿAbd al-Latif (d. 1842), was trained at

al-Azhar by prominent ʿulamaʾ such as ʿAbd al-ʿAlim al-Sanhuri, who also instructed him in the mysteries of Sufism. The relatively minimal presence of ʿulamaʾ in the villages of Upper Egypt as well as the population's strong affinity with holy men reinforced ʿAbd al-Latif's status in the Minya province. His close relationship with the Sufi saint Ibrahim al-Shalqani al-ʿImrani, in a nearby village, allowed ʿAbd al-Latif to acquire knowledge of the hidden and the attributes of holiness, which enabled him to establish a separate sect—the Qayatiyya. ʿAbd al-Latif viewed himself as carrying on a distinguished Sufi lineage (*silsila*) whose roots went back to Sidi, father of Harira, one of the Prophet's companions. ʿAli Mubarak describes him in his book *al-Khitat* as exemplary in his honesty, devotion to justice, and tolerance, attributes that earned him respect among the *dhimmi*s as well.[77]

ʿAbd al-Latif's son, ʿAbd al-Jawwad (d. 1870), also attained the status of a holy man with magical powers. He was renowned for his generosity to the needy and for inspiring the population to acquire religious knowledge and uphold social justice. The aura of holiness that surrounded him was reflected in numerous stories about his hidden attributes. Following his burial alongside his father, a large *mawlid* (saint's day commemoration) was held annually in honor of both, with the participation of ʿulamaʾ, dignitaries, prominent merchants, and ordinary pilgrims who came to pray and seek grace. Beyond its religious, social, and economic functions, the *mawlid* also served as a convenient forum for recruiting followers into the ranks of the Qayatiyya order.[78]

ʿAbd al-Jawwad's sons Muhammad and Ahmad perpetuated their father's scholarly and Sufi traditions. Educated in al-Qayat, both moved to Cairo, studying at al-Azhar under the patronage of Shaykh Khalifa al-Safti, a prominent follower of their grandfather. Other ʿulamaʾ whose classes they attended were Muhammad al-ʿAshmuni, Shams al-Din al-Inbabi, Muhammad ʿIllaysh, and Muhammad al-Khusri. Upon ʿAbd al-Jawwad's death, his son Muhammad inherited his role as head of the Qayatiyya order, choosing to return permanently to his village, al-Qayat. His brother Ahmad, remaining in Cairo, taught at al-Azhar after receiving the *ijaza*, specializing in the fields of rhetoric (*bayan*) and language (*nahw*). With the death of his patron, Shaykh Safti, Ahmad was appointed shaykh Riwaq al-Fashniyya in his place in 1876.[79] The life courses of both brothers, like those of other religious figures, were deeply affected by the ʿUrabi revolt.

The influence of the Qayatiyya order on the events of the revolt was evident. The order's organizational infrastructure and membership (some

4,000 persons) were mobilized to support the military effort. With the approach of the decisive confrontation with the British, the Qayati brothers, together with other ʿulamaʾ, appeared at the soldiers' assembly points (for example, at Tall al-Kabir and at Kafr al-Dawwar) to inspire them with sermons and verses read from the Qurʾan and hadith. Similarly, *dhikr* (remembrance of God) ceremonies and ritual repetitions of names of Sufi saints were held to ensure military success.[80] The participation of the Qayatiyya order in the protest movement was described by the local authorities and by the British as one of "the most serious cases."[81]

In Frederick De Jong's view, the motives of the Khalwatiyya sects in Upper Egypt who supported the revolt differed from those of the ʿUrabi movement proper. Their active participation in the insurrection "was basically a continuation of their struggle to improve their living conditions. When this improvement came, the state of rebelliousness in Upper Egypt came to an end."[82]

De Jong's socioeconomic analysis centers on the rebellious spirit that typified the social history of Upper Egypt, as shown by Gabriel Baer in his research.[83] Although this analysis is important, it ignores several factors. First, Sufi orders constituted both a social and a religious framework based on the image of a charismatic, dominant leader who generally emanated from the Azhar community—a widespread phenomenon in the Egyptian religious landscape through the nineteenth century. The religious motivation of such shaykhs and their close followers therefore cannot be ignored; no line can be drawn between their religious and social realms, because Sufi orders in essence constituted a blend of both. Notably, Baer himself did not exclude religious motives for the peasants' revolts, observing that "many of the leaders apparently succeeded in arousing the fellahs because of their claim to holiness."[84]

Second, while the ʿUrabi revolt had a pronounced national character, it was also conducted along religious and ethnic lines. This enabled it to rally sympathy and support among the population in Upper Egypt, given their intense religiosity and strong affinity with holy men. Another factor was the large number of estates in the region owned by Turco-Circassians,[85] an ethnic component that the ʿUrabist agenda marked for elimination. Curiously, De Jong singles out only the Qayatiyya order as "possibly" motivated by nationalistic or religious sentiments,[86] ignoring other dissident Sufi orders that were also active in the insurrection.

4 In Defense of Religion and Homeland

The book *Nafhat al-basham fi rihlat al-Sham* (The Scent of Balsam in the Journey of Sham, 1901), written by the leader of the order, Muhammad al-Qayati, gives an instructive explanation of the motives of the Qayatiyya order in joining the ʿUrabi movement. In an introduction, al-Qayati notes that the revolt began in the wake of demands by Egyptian army officers led by Ahmad ʿUrabi to root out discrimination and despotism in the army ranks. Ignored by the government, the officers gradually escalated their demands until Britain felt impelled to intervene. Presuming to be the world's champion of freedom, Britain went to war against Egypt.

This external threat prompted the Egyptians to come to their country's defense, even to the point of self-sacrifice, in accordance with the Qurʾanic imperative "Make ready for them whatever force and strings of horses you can, to terrify thereby the enemy of God and your enemy" (8:60). In al-Qayati's view, "Self-defense is the duty of every nation that is forced into war by another nation. Indeed, defense of the motherland is the first and the last thing that must be done and is a duty incumbent on all honorable persons, without regard to differences of religion, language, faith, or customs."[1] This also explains the recruitment of ʿulamaʾ and Sufi shaykhs, who, al-Qayati stressed, would help dispel the curse hanging over the homeland by their prayers and sermons. He thus sought to deflect criticism of these sectors by the Egyptian authorities, who claimed that their role was the study and propagation of religious knowledge, not intervention in politics. Al-Qayati confirmed that this was indeed the traditional role of the "holy vessels"; but, he contended, that role was limited to ordinary times. It was not applicable in times of emergency, such as in the Egyptian case: "when we were convinced that the foreigners were expropriating the land, settling and breeding in it, and that the war was a religious war to defend faith, homeland, honor, and all that is sanctified."[2]

The essence of al-Qayati's narrative regarding his order's motives for joining the ʿUrabi cause was the defense of religion and the homeland. Defending religion against an infidel aggressor supported the raison d'être of Islam as the ultimate and most perfect godly revelation, while defending the homeland provided local territorial identification and applied to all its inhabitants. Muhammad al-Qayati's discourse on identity was harmonious in conception, revealing a multifaceted cultural world that recognized territorial pluralism in the context of a universal faith. No wonder he portrayed Egypt as "the precious homeland" (*al-watan al-ʿaziz*) and the Ottoman Empire as "the most exalted Islamic state" (*aʿzam al-duwal al-Islamiyya*) and "the house of the great caliphate" (*dar al-khilafa al-ʿuzmaʾ*).[3]

Allegiance to one's native polity was not unusual in Islamic discourse in view of the reality of territorial divisions in the Muslim world, especially following the decline of the caliphate in the tenth century. This segmented reality also gained theological and judicial approval by leading and pragmatic medieval scholars such as Abu Hamid al-Ghazali and Taqi al-Din ibn Taymiyya, who stressed that the unity of the Muslim community is essentially one of belief, not of political form. Thus it is permissible to have several political centers that are part of Dar al-Islam (the House of Islam)—so long, of course, as the shariʿa is implemented and observed. This reality was reinforced under the Ottoman Empire (established in the fifteenth century), which allowed for a large measure of local administrative autonomy in return for the maintenance of public order and the remittance of taxes to Istanbul. As historians such as James Piscatori, Sami Zubaida, and Haim Gerber have pointed out, the "Asiatic" or "Oriental" model of political unity and centralized government portrayed by Western scholars is inconsistent with the historical record. Rather, the political structure in the Muslim Middle East was segmented. The direct control of the ruling dynasty extended no farther than the capital and its adjacent areas. Beyond these areas, political influence was exercised through networks of patronage and alliances with local power bases composed of notables, army officers, heads of Sufi orders, and tribal shaykhs.[4]

In essence, Islamic imperial rule remained external to the communal and social structures of the provinces, contenting itself with maintaining public order and a steady flow of taxes to Istanbul and guided by a divide-and-rule strategy. Many of the ʿulamaʾ during the nineteenth and early twentieth centuries had been born into semiautonomous entities and perceived them as both natural and legitimate. Their local orientation was reinforced in the face of the disruptive political and economic reality into which these entities were plunged during their lifetimes, exacerbated by the growing threat of foreign occupation. Pan-Islamism in its political and unitarian sense was more an ethos and a theological exercise. Otherwise it is impossible to understand, for example, the insignificant response by ʿulamaʾ to the pan-Islamic call of Sultan Abdülhamid II in the late nineteenth century. This appeal failed to arrest the collapse of the Islamic order embodied in the Ottoman Empire and the formation of nation-states following World War I.[5]

The pluralistic system of geographical divisions as a given in the Muslim world was particularly evident in Egypt, acquiring local political and cultural emphases during the Mamluk period and evolving into political autonomy under Muhammad ʿAli's dynasty. The discrete existence of Egypt was also reflected in important literary genres, such as chronicles and bibliographical dictionaries.[6] Al-Qayati, like many ʿulamaʾ of his era, was born into the Nilotic political entity molded by Muhammad ʿAli and viewed it as natural and legitimate. Moreover, he did not conceal his pride in the Arabic language spoken by its inhabitants and praised those Ottomans who could speak it.[7] His loyalty to the Egyptian entity was heightened all the more in the wake of the distressing situation of foreign aggression.

Al-Qayati's senior colleague and mentor, Shaykh Muhammad ʿIllaysh, also displayed his allegiance to the Nile Valley during the ʿUrabist events when he deviated from a fatwa he himself had published in 1840, following the French invasion of Algeria, in which he had sanctioned the duty of Muslims to emigrate from territory conquered by infidels with superior military power. His argument then, based on historic episodes of Muslim withdrawal from Sicily and Spain, was that the emotional affinity to a country is not a sufficient argument to avoid the duty of emigration. This duty was a religious imperative aimed at ensuring survival and refuge, because the situation was a matter of life and death for men and slavery for women and children. But in a similar situation—the British encroachment into Egypt—forty-two years later, in 1882, ʿIllaysh did not preach in favor of emigration. On the contrary, he called for uncompromising jihad.[8]

Hasan al-ʿIdwi, too, during his interrogation after the suppression of the ʿUrabi movement, declared that the defense of the homeland was both a religious and a political duty. Lending practical content to his opinion, he appeared on the battlefield in August 1882 at the village of al-Dawwar together with two other shaykhs, Ahmad al-Basri and Ahmad Marwan, and inspired the soldiers with readings of hadiths by al-Bukhari.[9] The meshing of defense of religion with defense of the homeland by al-Qayati, ʿIllaysh, and al-ʿIdwi instilled this perception in their followers in the two closely related circles in which they were active and influential: al-Azhar and the Sufi orders. Their sermons in mosques and in public forums also trickled down to the wider public.

An interesting work by Shaykh Husayn al-Marsafi, *Risalat al-kalim al-thaman* (An Essay on Eight Words, 1881), written during the events of the ʿUrabi revolution, provides another glimpse of the Azharis' multiple identities in the nineteenth century. Its author, while adopting a neutral stance, nevertheless hints at sympathy for the ʿUrabist cause.[10]

Al-Marsafi (d. 1890), from the province of Qaluba, came from a prominent family of religious and literary personalities and was described as one of the revivers of the ancient Arabic heritage. Rather than continuing as an instructor at al-Azhar, he, along with his brother Zayn, joined the faculty of Dar al-ʿUlum upon its founding in 1872, taught Arabic language and literature, and, together with Muhammad ʿAbduh, became part of a circle of reformist ʿulamaʾ there.[11] Al-Marsafi, influenced by exposure to Western (especially French) culture, aimed in his essay to forge an ideological basis for the existence of a modern Muslim society through a discussion of the concepts of nation, homeland, government, justice, tyranny, politics, freedom, and education. Notably, several members of the reformist circle who were ʿUrabi followers adopted these concepts in their demand to inaugurate an enlightened constitutional system.

Al-Marsafi begins his essay with a discussion of the concepts of nation and homeland, thereby signaling their importance in his worldview. His definition of nation is broad and diverges from the traditional meaning. He depicts it not only in Islamic terms but in linguistic terms as well. Moreover, he views language as "the most worthy identity for a nation."[12] This is because a common language fosters social integration, encouraging solidarity and preventing alienation and wickedness. Al-Marsafi defines the second concept, homeland, as a designated landmass in which the nation lives and whose name is known and is differentiated from that of its neighbors, such as Egypt and Hijaz, or the "Egyptian nation" and "Hijazi nation." He identifies group territoriality with a private home and emphasizes the importance of defending it against any harm. Entry into it may be permitted only to those who approach it with a worthy purpose: to assist, to be hosted, or to live there, all in compliance with the certified local authorities. Clearly, al-Marsafi was influenced in these observations not only by the notion of the nation-state in Europe but also by the Egyptian reality in which he lived, in the face of growing foreign penetration.

This is the way a nation must behave, he asserts, and in this respect its instincts are no different from those of animals who defend their living space.[13]

Territory and language take precedence over al-Marsafi's discussion of religion, which raises the issue of the role of religion in the life of the nation. Al-Marsafi himself does not dwell on the subject and is satisfied with the laconic comment that "a nation which is defined by religion is one that follows a prophet and his judgement."[14] He does, however, expand on the boundaries that the faithful of that religion may not exceed. He posits the model of an ethical and ecumenical faith that does not slip into blind fanaticism, repression, and threat regarding others who hold a different creed; otherwise, the result is not a nation of religion but an unruly mob driven by base instincts and caprice. Apparently, al-Marsafi's aim was to depoliticize Islam as a guarantee of social and intercultural harmony. Evidence of this is the warning that he directs at ʿulamaʾ and preachers who ignore the responsibility they bear for their words when addressing the ignorant masses and introducing alien elements into religion.[15] This stance marked the line separating the reformist group led by Muhammad ʿAbduh and ʿAbdallah Nadim, to which al-Marsafi belonged, from the group of more conservative ʿulamaʾ led by ʿIllaysh and al-ʿIdwi.

The involvement of the more conservative group in the ʿUrabi events of the uprising demonstrated that an Islamic ideology, as Zubaida and Cole have pointed out, can integrate well in a broad proto-national movement.[16] This is what occurred in the ʿUrabi episode. Nevertheless, the pro-ʿUrabi conservative ʿulamaʾ did not give their blessing to sweeping changes in the existing order of Egyptian society. Wilfrid Blunt, a strong advocate of the ʿUrabist cause, tried to create the opposite impression, declaring in 1881 that the ideas of the liberal ʿulamaʾ in al-Azhar, headed by ʿAbduh, had actually become a living reality and that the Azharis had joined the social and political reform movement in Islam, heart and soul.[17] In the same vein, the Egyptian historian Latifa Muhammad Salim, in a book written a century later (1981), asserted that the entire religious community that joined ʿUrabi was committed to the reforms put forward by ʿAbduh.[18]

In reality, ʿAbduh and his reformist colleagues were a minority group, both numerically and ideologically, in comparison with the more conservative majority led by personalities such as ʿIllaysh, al-ʿIdwi, the Qayati brothers, Abu al-ʿAlaʾ al-Khalfawi, and Khalil al-ʿAzzazi. The published work and statements of these mainstream religious leaders before, during, and after the events of the revolt reveal a strong puritanical stance regarding the Muslim public arena (see chapter 6 on this point). Here it is sufficient to consider the differences in approach between the two camps regarding the status of the Copts in the community, an issue that emerged during the events of the ʿUrabi uprising.

The brand of Islam that the more conservative ʿulamaʾ introduced to propel the ʿUrabi movement forward provided the communal solidarity, or ethnic marker, that distinguished Muslims from the followers of other religions after the European aggression against Egypt.[19] The heightened emphasis on the superiority of Islam over other cultures also meant an affirmation of the inferior civil status of the Copts, then a population of some 500,000 out of approximately 10 million at the end of the nineteenth century. Not surprisingly, the wide use of Islamic terminology, and especially the call for jihad, elicited an equivocal response from the heads of the Coptic Church, who claimed that only the Ottoman sultan was authorized to declare a holy war and that they, as Christians, would have difficulty identifying with the prospect of a religious war to be waged against the British.

ʿAbduh and Nadim of the reformist wing of the ʿUrabi camp, who advocated a humanist approach, attempted to neutralize the term "jihad" by describing the struggle as a patriotic campaign in which all people living in the homeland were partners.[20] Nadim declared in his newspaper *al-Tankit waʾl-Tabkit* that love of the homeland, concern for its welfare, development of its natural resources, and preservation of its language and customs were the duties of both Muslims and Copts equally. ʿAbduh and Nadim also infused their statements with practical content through their involvement in the Islamic Welfare Association (founded in Alexandria in 1879), which preached national unity among other things. They also maintained close relations with reformists from the Coptic community, such as Butrus Ghali, assisting them in promoting charitable and welfare activities.[21]

By contrast, the more conservative ʿulamaʾ, led by ʿIllaysh and al-ʿIdwi, ignored the sensitivity of the Coptic presence. As scions of old families in the Nile Valley, they had a strong physical and emotional affinity with Egyptian territory, heightened by the crisis situation in Egypt at the end of the nineteenth century. Yet their cultural heritage also assigned a central role to the universal values of Islam. In this respect, they and their writings were part of a discursive Islamic orbit—what Carl F. Petry called "the consciously international judiciary"—in which geographical borders are blurred, while texts and ideas are shared by both scholars and the lay public in different, even distant parts of the Islamic world.

This transregional discourse was supported by a shared print market and regional Islamic networks.[22] Thus loyalty to a universal Islamic corpus, which, inter alia, defined the normative status of non-Muslims as protected minorities (*dhimmis*), dictated the view of the Copts as having a subordinate status in the Egyptian polity.

ʿUrabi himself promised the Copts judicial and political equality with Muslims. He took care to maintain close relations with the Coptic dignitaries, headed by Patriarch Cyril V, and even received material support from them.[23] The National Party (the base of the opposition movement) also defined itself as a political and not a religious party, open to all and advocating equal rights and equality before the law. When incidents of incitement and violence against Copts were reported in several regions during that unstable time, ʿUrabi denounced them sharply, and some local Muslim dignitaries made efforts to defuse intercommunal tensions.[24] Yet ʿUrabi, who had spent four years studying at al-Azhar before embarking on a military career,[25] also understood the potential in using Islamic rhetoric and calling for jihad to rally mass support against the British and gave it his blessing.[26]

In his memoirs ʿUrabi extolled the vigorous recruitment for the defensive war he led, describing it as "a vibrancy that was unprecedented in the history of Islam in modern times." But ʿUrabi's attempt to detach jihad from its specific Islamic context and present it as a war by the Egyptian nation—with all its ethnicities—for homeland, justice, and equality proved too artificial and failed to attain its goal.[27] The traditional perception of a holy war against heretics, as Schölch pointed out, was the one that constituted the main ideological basis of the protest movement.[28] The Islamic undertones of the ʿUrabist revolt also evoked dissent on the part of many Syrian Christian journalists, who used their growing influence in the Egyptian press to enhance the negative and regressive image of the revolt in Egyptian historiography well into the twentieth century.[29]

Differing perceptions of the status of non-Muslims and other issues such as the right of *ijtihad* (human reasoning) and matters of personal status exposed the ideological divisions among ʿUrabi's supporters, essentially between the ʿIllaysh and the ʿAbduh camps. But the crisis in which the rebel movement found itself forced them to present a united front. Significantly, the conquest of Cairo by the British in September 1882 found the leaders of both camps behind bars. Shortly before, ʿIllaysh had managed to fulfill ʿUrabi's request to issue a fatwa ordering the removal of several statues mounted a decade earlier in two European neighborhoods of Cairo: a statue of Ibrahim Pasha in the Uzbeqiyya quarter and

four statues of lions at the Qasr al-Nil Bridge at the edge of the Ismaʿiliyya
neighborhood. Beyond the religious prohibition against displaying images of humans or animals and denunciation of it as a *jahili* (pagan) practice and an imitation of the ways of heretics, the fatwa was also prompted
by political motives. Its intention was not only to demolish the overt
symbols of Muhammad ʿAli's dynasty in the public sphere but no less importantly to assail Western modernization in Egypt and thereby heighten
religious fervor at the critical moment of military confrontation with the
British.

ʿIllaysh's ruling was accepted by ʿulamaʾ belonging to the other legal
schools. It was also supported in a separate fatwa by the mufti of Egypt,
Muhammad al-ʿAbbasi al-Mahdi, a loyal follower of Khedive Tawfiq. Al-
Mahdi, who was bound by the commandments of Islam and the requirements of his high religious office, ratified the obligation of both the authorities and their subjects to forbid the display of any kind of drawing or
sculpture by recourse to the imperative to "forbid wrong." He also emphasized, however, that the necessity for Muslim rulers to prevent the exploitation and suffering of their subjects, usurious practices, and the opening
of places of entertainment was more urgent than removing the statues.[30]
Al-Mahdi thus sought to delegitimize ʿUrabi as unworthy of the title "defender of the faith," inasmuch as he had not prevented these unsuitable
manifestations in society. The statues episode once again revealed the
close affinity between religious learning and politics—an integral aspect
of the revolt—while also indicating the significant role of fatwas in the
Egyptian public discourse.

SUPPRESSION: REWARDS AND PUNISHMENTS

The ʿUrabi movement failed to develop to the point of consolidating
its political structures or removing the foreign presence from Egypt. Its
diffuse political agenda was a serious obstacle, as was the fragile internal
cohesion of the social groups who supported it. More important was its
military inferiority vis-à-vis the British, which was reflected in the sting-
ing defeat at Tall al-Kabir on September 13, 1882.[31] Furthermore, the Ottoman Empire dismissed the ʿUrabists' declarations of loyalty, while also
ignoring and even suppressing domestic sympathy for their cause.[32] In
several dispatches to Istanbul ʿUrabi noted that Tawfiq had joined forces
with the British in order to detach the Egyptians from the Ottoman Empire and that it was "our obligation" to defend the country and protect the
rights of the sultan.[33] These declarations of loyalty were repeated during

ʿUrabi's trial, when he argued in his defense that he had acted in the name of a higher legitimate authority: Sultan Abdülhamid, "who appointed me to defend the homeland." The names of ʿulamaʾ who were close advisors to the sultan appeared in ʿUrabi's defense plea in the form of letters that they had sent to him, expressing the sultan's satisfaction with his role and depicting the ʿUrabists as his "loyal servants."[34]

The emphasis on ʿUrabi's subservience to Abdülhamid in his capacity as the Commander of the Faithful prompted Wilfrid Blunt to argue that it was in no way an infraction even if ʿUrabi's behavior had not been authorized, since during the war months he acted according to an Islamic imperative to defend Egypt against Christianity.[35]

The Ottomans' abandonment of ʿUrabi stemmed from European pressure and the fear of further foreign involvement in Egypt as well as from a concern that the dissidence in Egypt would spread to other Muslim areas of the empire. Low-key rumblings were already discernible in Syria in response to the centralized policy adopted by Istanbul. Open insurrection against the authority of the sultan had been displayed in the Mahdi revolt in Sudan, whose leader, Muhammad Ahmad ibn ʿAbdallah, declared himself the "heir of the Prophet" and defamed the Ottoman regime as having "killed the religion of Allah" by its deviance from the shariʿa in implementing foreign laws and granting non-Muslims a preferential status.[36]

Ultimately, the ʿUrabi episode was perceived by the Sublime Porte as disobedience of legitimate authority. Khedive Tawfiq, after all, was still identified as the representative of the sultan in Egypt. This status was officially ratified in a proclamation issued by the sultan in August 1882, to the satisfaction of both Tawfiq and the British, who promptly circulated copies of it in India in order to suppress signs of support there for the dissident movement in Egypt.[37]

The content of the proclamation revolved around the duty to obey the khedive as the figure who derives his authority from the sultan and ʿUrabi's blatant violation of this duty. It played upon the centuries-old Muslim impetus to maintain public order and close ranks in the face of foreign aggression.

ʿUrabi Pasha's moves reveal that his underlying intention was to thrust the Ottoman Empire into contention and disorder and to foment disputes between the subjects in order to fulfill his illegal personal goals. Had he not harbored this hope, he would not have created—or expressed readiness for—situations that could plunge Alexandria into harsh clashes with the British Navy. Had he listened to the orders and advice instructing him to avoid such disasters…he would have avoided shedding the blood of many people, bringing about the involvement of a foreign army in Egypt, and leading the Sublime Porte into the current problematic situation.… The Ottoman state was honorable enough to send a delegation with the aim of bringing ʿUrabi to Istanbul to warn him and explain to him in the strongest terms the need to abandon the deviant course he had taken and to resolve the Egyptian crisis in a cordial manner.… But ʿUrabi continued in his illegal, diseased, and licentious ways, thereby evoking a judgment against him as a rebel against the kingdom. He should have known that the Khedive is one of the foundations of the sublime Ottoman state and one of the loyal and magnificent governors of the exalted sultanate; thus the preservation of his influence and honor is paramount.[38]

The terms "insurgents" (Ottoman *usat*/Arabic *ʿusat*) and "rebels" (Ottoman *bugat*/Arabic *bugha*) used by Sultan Abdülhamid were clearly intended to emphasize the gravity of ʿUrabi's acts from a religious point of view and thereby prepare Muslim public opinion for his denunciation. Yet in the proclamation ʿUrabi and his followers were labeled merely "rebels," who, according to Sunni law, are still considered to be part of the community of believers and are not to be treated as infidels or apostates. The initial aim therefore was to return the rebels to the fold and to obedience to the established order, not to execute them.[39]

The pro-Ottoman press in the Arabic-speaking provinces was recruited to disseminate the condemnatory proclamation. The Beirut-based *al-Jawaʾib* (Circulating News) and *al-Janna* (Paradise) published the text in Arabic. Copies were sent to Egypt, where it was distributed by the official paper *al-Ahram*. Another newspaper, *Abu Lisan* (Mouthpiece), carried out the task of distributing the proclamation among the soldiers in ʿUrabi's army, with the aim of causing rifts and defections.[40]

The Ottoman proclamation was a grave moral and political blow to ʿUrabi, who had based his claim of loyalty to Egypt largely on support by the sultan. Moreover, he attributed the discouragement and defeatism that overtook his soldiers and supporters on the eve of the confrontation with the British at Tall al-Kabir to the proclamation, which was issued shortly beforehand. Some of his followers immediately shifted their support back to the khedive, in the belief that ʿUrabi was indeed leading a rebellion. Venting his bitterness during his trial, ʿUrabi declared that the proclamation was nothing more than an effort to pacify the British. Moreover, he claimed, it actually contradicted Islam, for the issue was a war against the enemies of Allah who sought to take control of Muslim land. In this context he reiterated that the protest movement he led did not behave rashly or violently. All it sought was to restore a peaceful existence to Egyptian society, to spare it the tragedy of humiliation, and to defend its honor. Therefore it was not surprising that the movement elicited great empathy among the people.[41]

In his memoirs (written in 1910) ʿUrabi did not blame the sultan himself but directed his criticism at the sultan's retinue, who "received bribes" from the British. Leaving this issue open to public debate, however, he stated that if the sultan actually was involved in this affair "it is the duty of the Muslims to depose him for violating a religious injunction."[42]

In the wake of the British conquest, a system of cooperation with the occupiers and European patronage was established by force. The khedival institution survived the events of the uprising, though at a high price: the loss of power and legitimacy. Tawfiq's return to Cairo on September 25, 1882, to resume governmental control was accompanied by the demonstrative presence of the new masters—the British. The event was marked by an elaborate reception. Among the many persons who received the khedive were senior ʿulamaʾ, including Shaykh al-Azhar al-Inbabi, all of whom intoned a short prayer in honor of his return and bowed before him. The following day, in a reception held in his palace, Tawfiq told a delegation of ʿulamaʾ who came to greet him: "You are men of letters and not politicians. The first to be guilty again of interfering with politics will be punished severely." In response they pledged absolute loyalty to the khedive.[43] By his remark Tawfiq sought to redefine the boundaries of the authority of the ʿulamaʾ community, some of whom had turned against him during the revolutionary events.

The same message of deterrence was conveyed by the country's official newspaper, *al-Ahram*, which reported in detail on the arrest and trial of various rebellious ʿulamaʾ. The paper also mocked several of them for having displayed foolishness and ignorance during the uprising—for example, Hasan al-ʿIdwi, who habitually praised ʿUrabi lavishly and adopted obsequious mannerisms when in his presence; or shaykhs who had presumed to draw up plans for a military attack against the British naval armada off Alexandria.[44] Clearly, *al-Ahram*'s criticism was aimed at the involvement of ʿulamaʾ in politics, which was depicted as outside their professional realm and field of expertise. Nevertheless, the focus on them pointed to their importance in the protest events. By contrast, the newspaper lavished praise on ʿulamaʾ who preached the need to preserve public order and even granted refuge and protection to Christian subjects whose lives were endangered by the ʿUrabist events, as in Minya and Suez.[45]

Establishment ʿulamaʾ also took part in deconstructing the link between religious scholarship and politics. Shaykh Muhi al-Din al-Nabahani, in a sermon delivered at the madrasa in Alexandria in the presence of ʿulamaʾ and dignitaries in early October 1882, spoke of the need for calm, worthy preaching and cooperation for the sake of the welfare of the country. Whoever fails to act in the spirit of true faith and worthy preaching, the shaykh warned, "has no religion." He called upon the ʿulamaʾ—"the lights that illuminate the way"—to unite for the sake of promoting peace and justice and banishing evil and animosity. Similar messages were conveyed by ʿulamaʾ in festive assemblies organized in Cairo and Tanta upon the return of the khedive to Cairo to celebrate the rescue of Egypt from the disaster that had threatened it.[46] The narrative promoted by the khedival court and its spokesmen from the ʿulamaʾ community was one of a quietist Islam. Those senior ʿulamaʾ who adhered to this narrative and demonstrated loyalty to Khedive Tawfiq were also suitably rewarded.

In a khedival order of October 3, 1882, the mufti of Egypt, Muhammad al-ʿAbassi al-Mahdi, was restored to his other position as shaykh al-Azhar, after having been removed from it by the ʿUrabists. One of his first acts was to restart the process of modernizing al-Azhar by issuing a new regulation code, which, like the 1872 code, was aimed at regulating the licensing of graduates for teaching positions at al-Azhar. Several years later (in 1887), however, he requested to be released from both of his high offices, claiming that they were too heavy a burden. Underlying this step was al-Mahdi's displeasure with Tawfiq's overly docile stance toward the British and his reluctance to endorse new laws passed by the government to widen the powers of the national courts (*mahakim ahliya*).[47] The post of shaykh al-Azhar was filled once again by Shams al-Din al-Inbabi (1887–96), yet another indication that the khedive viewed him as untainted by excessive involvement in the events of the uprising. Tawfiq's successor, ʿAbbas Hilmi II (1892–1914), continued to shower praise and honors on al-Inbabi.[48] The post of mufti was granted to Shaykh Muhammad al-Banna, but only for a short period; al-Mahdi then resumed it and held it until his death in 1897.

Tawfiq loyalists among the leaders of the Sufi official network, ʿAbd al-Baqi al-Bakri and ʿAbd al-Khaliq al-Sadat, continued to serve as members of the khedival advisory council and the general council, which convened for the first time in November 1883. Al-Bakri's support for the khedive and his public acceptance of the British presence—demonstrated by a large banquet he held for the commander of the British forces, Sir Grant Wellesley—did not detract from his authority over the orders under his supervision. This reflected not only his personal charisma but also the start of a process of centralization of the Sufi network. Another figure who was well rewarded was Shaykh Hamza Fathallah, an anti-ʿUrabist propagandist, who was appointed as the first supervisor of Arabic in the Ministry of Education.[49]

By contrast, the pro-ʿUrabi ʿulamaʾ camp was in distress. Once the military defeat became known, some of these ʿulamaʾ crossed over and swore allegiance anew to the khedive, as the army officers and dignitaries had done. A particularly prominent figure was Shaykh ʿAli al-Laythi (d. 1896). He had begun his career as a Sufi identified with the Sanusiyya order in Libya and later became court poet (*nadim*) for Khedive Ismaʿil and his son Tawfiq.[50] Al-Laythi joined the ʿUrabi revolt in its later stages, devoting himself to strengthening the morale of the soldiers at Kafr al-Dawwar on the eve of the British invasion by reading out *qasida*s he wrote, calling for ʿUrabi's victory over the band of enemies whose memory must be erased in Egypt.[51] Following the defeat, ʿUrabi and his supporters accused al-Laythi of using the same weapon—the *qasida*—to regain Khedive Tawfiq's trust. He had read the khedive a long *qasida* disassociating himself from the distressing sedition (*fitna*) and describing life as peaceful under Tawfiq's just rule. Other facets of al-Laythi's personality, such as moral corruption in financial matters and in the dispensation of honors, were also targeted for criticism by the pro-ʿUrabi camp.[52]

Muhammad ʿAbduh came to al-Laythi's defense in an article published after the poet's death in 1896, pointing out that al-Laythi was not one of the hypocrites who had begged for mercy from Tawfiq. Such behavior was contemptible to him. On the contrary, al-Laythi's first remarks to the khedive constituted worthy advice: to act with wisdom and compassion toward those involved in the uprising. "This is better than entrenching hostility in their hearts by punishing them."[53]

Shaykh ʿAbd al-Hadi Naja al-Abyari and Shaykh ʿAbd al-Qadir al-Rafiʿi were also denounced by the ʿUrabists, for trading the cause of the just revolution for "love of life and fear of punishment by the victors." ʿUrabi castigated al-Abyari (d. 1887), the imam of the khedive's court, for leading the proceedings at the reception in Tawfiq's honor upon his return to Cairo following the defeat, after he had encouraged the masses by reading the well-known *qasida* written by Ibrahim Durayd during the Tatar invasion of Baghdad. The rest of the ʿulamaʾ at the reception had followed him with cries of "Long live the sublime ruler, victorious and distinguished."[54]

ʿAbd al-Qadir al-Rafiʿi (d. 1905), scion of a well-known ʿulamaʾ family from Tripoli, Lebanon, was a member of the Supreme Shariʿa Court in Cairo and was known for his expertise in Hanafi law but also for his affinity for Khalwatiyya Sufism.[55] His relative the historian ʿAbd al-Rahman al-Rafiʿi mentioned him as one of the signatories of the decision at the assembly of July 1882 to depose Tawfiq. This involvement was denied by ʿAbd al-Qadir's son, who claimed that his father was careful to avoid disputes and refrained from interceding in any way. Moreover, his son asserted, ʿAbd al-Qadir had expressed dissatisfaction with the ʿUrabi revolt and had thought it was destined to end in failure; he had not signed any statement issued by the ʿUrabists, even though he was courted by them; and he was among the first, alongside al-Mahdi, to go to Alexandria to back Tawfiq, thereby evoking ʿUrabi's anger.[56] Other sources also substantiate ʿAbd al-Qadir al-Rafiʿi's noninvolvement in the ʿUrabist cause, which was apparently true for al-Abyari as well. The accusations of defection signaled frustration and distress among the ʿUrabists in light of the failure of their movement and reflected their desperate struggle to win over public opinion and show that the protest movement had attained wide support among senior ʿulamaʾ.

ʿUlamaʾ who did play an active role in the revolution paid the bitter price of dissidence. ʿIllaysh, eighty years old and ailing, was taken from his home and imprisoned. He was charged with religious incitement and delegitimizing the right of the khedive to govern.[57] He died in the prison infirmary before his trial in October 1882. The authorities promptly claimed that ʿIllaysh had died of a long illness, thereby deflecting accusations by his associates that the cause was poisoning. His family's request to conduct his funeral at home was denied.[58] With ʿIllaysh's death, the post of Maliki mufti was also abolished, though it was reinstated five years later by Shaykh Salim al-Bishri, one of ʿIllaysh's students, who was to serve as shaykh al-Azhar (1916–19).[59]

ʿIllaysh's senior colleague al-ʿIdwi was also arrested and interrogated. When questioned about why he did not concentrate his activity on teaching religious studies instead of choosing to join up with the ʿUrabist army at Kafr al-Dawwar, al-ʿIdwi responded bitingly: in order "to read al-Bukhari's hadith collections and pray for the victory of Allah." While he denied the existence of a fatwa deposing Tawfiq, he declared that if he had been consulted on whether to publish such a legal opinion he would have responded in the affirmative and would have signed it unhesitatingly. Challenging his interrogators, he demanded: "And can you Muslims deny that the khedive deserves to be deposed for straying from his loyalty to religion and homeland?"[60] Nevertheless, al-ʿIdwi was released after a few days of questioning on condition that he return to his village in Minya.[61]

Not all the ʿulamaʾ who were arrested shared al-ʿIdwi's self-assurance and defiant tone. Some denied any involvement in the protest movement or stated that they were compelled to back it for fear of their lives. Thus Abu al-ʿAlaʾ al-Khalfawi, mufti of the Majlis al-Ahkam in Cairo, argued during his interrogation that he had mediated in the khedival court to restore ʿUrabi to his post as minister of war for the sake of public order; after the open revolt against the khedive, however, he had discontinued his support for ʿUrabi. He also denied that he had criticized the khedive in the ʿulamaʾ meeting with the Ottoman delegation headed by Darwish Pasha. It was only fear of the army officers, he said, that had induced him to sign the resolutions of the two general assemblies in July 1882, rejecting the khedive's orders to cease military preparations for resisting the British invasion and to depose ʿUrabi from his post. As for his name being cited along with ʿIllaysh's and al-ʿIdwi's in a fatwa declaring Tawfiq unfit to rule, al-Khalfawi called it a deliberate scheme by the officers to convince Shaykh al-Azhar al-Inbabi to sign the fatwa.[62]

Another Azhari scholar, Ahmad al-Mansur, stressed that animosity had developed between him and the ʿUrabists following the removal of al-Mahdi from the rectorship of al-Azhar in December 1881 and that he had remained largely aloof from the events. Admitting his willingness to sign the decision that opposed the removal of ʿUrabi as minister of war, Mansur explained that he did so only after many of his eminent colleagues had signed.[63]

Al-Khalfawi's and Mansur's denials did not help them very much. As far as their interrogators were concerned, they failed to provide satisfactory answers to the essential charge directed against them and other accused clergy: their very presence in the political sphere, which constituted an absolute deviation from their official duties as scholars, whose task was "to disseminate the religious sciences and preserve the peace of mind of the people."[64]

One Azhari who did provide a direct response was Ahmad al-Basri, as shown in the dialogue between him and his interrogators (on December 7, 1882):

Q: What is your name?
A: Ahmad al-Basri, from Abu al-Shaykh in the province of Asyut.
Q: In what field did you work until recently?
A: As a teacher at al-Azhar.

Q: Since you are a teacher at al-Azhar, and your role is to disseminate the religious sciences, what was your reason for joining the rebels and assisting them?

A: I did not join them and I did not assist them.

Q: Didn't you, together with several of your colleagues, go to see Darwish Pasha, the representative of the Sublime Porte, when he arrived in Egypt?

A: Yes, I went.

Q: Didn't you say to him out loud that disquiet and concern are widespread in the land because of the English ships in the port of Alexandria?

A: Yes, I said that.

Q: This shows that you joined the rebels and assisted them, for if not, you would not have intervened in political matters that are outside your jurisdiction but are in the jurisdiction of governmental officials, such as ministers and the like, who were appointed by the Khedive to examine these matters and deal with them.

A: I intervened in this issue only because I understood that it relates to religion.

Q: How did you understand that it relates to religion?

A: I understood this because the warships arrived together and because I heard from people that they arrived with the aim of taking control of the country.

Q: Your argument that this issue is connected to religion is baseless. That day, the important imams were with the above-mentioned pasha [Darwish], yet they did not speak about this matter.

A: The fact that these imams did not speak does not mean that I too must be silent over an issue connected to religion.

Q: In what way is the issue related to religion?

A: In the way that we understand that a foreigner has taken control over the country.

Q: If this issue had a connection to religion, the legitimate authority, appointed legally, would have assembled you and asked you about this. It is unreasonable to accept that the moment you heard about this matter from the crowd—an educated person like yourself—you have determined this to be correct without discussing this in the presence of elevated persons such as statesmen.

A: I did not meet with anyone, and no one came to me, but, rather, in the meeting referred to [with Darwish Pasha] I said what I said based on what I understood.[65]

Al-Basri's honest reply, like the denials of his colleagues al-Khalfawi and al-Mansur regarding their participation in the revolutionary events, did not convince the tribunal. All three were removed from their posts, and their homes and property were confiscated.

Other ʿulamaʾ were also dismissed from their positions and stripped of their rights. Some were exiled from the country for several years. Those who were dismissed included faculty members at al-Azhar in Cairo and qadis from various districts, such as Ahmad al-ʿIdwi, Ahmad al-Mansur, Muhammad al-Basri, Muhammad al-Samaluti, Ahmad Marwan, ʿAli al-Jamil, ʿAbd al-Wahhab ʿAbd al-Munʿim, Muhammad Jabbar, ʿAbd al-Barr al-Raml, and Muhammad Ghazal. Among the deported ʿulamaʾ were ʿAbd al-Rahman ʿIllaysh,[66] Muhammad Khalil al-Hijrisi, and Yusuf Sharaba, who were exiled to Istanbul, Gaza, and Mecca, respectively. Others were exiled to Beirut, including Muhammad ʿAbduh, ʿAmin Abu Yusuf, and Muhammad and Ahmad al-Qayati. A request by the Qayati brothers to be allowed to be sent to the Hijaz in order to be close to the holy places, which would ease their distress, was rejected. They were taken to Alexandria and put on a ship bound for Beirut.[67]

5 Exile as a Prism for Cultural Interaction

The sentences of exile meted out to pro-ʿUrabist ʿulamaʾ following the suppression of the revolt did not necessarily mean that they became strangers in alien lands or detached from productive intellectual endeavor. On the contrary, exile became a second home to them as a result of inter-cultural and personal ties maintained with colleagues in the scholarly world throughout the Middle East, stemming primarily from their shared experience at al-Azhar, which drew scholars and students from all parts of the Ottoman Empire. The Egyptian exiles were welcomed warmly by ʿulamaʾ in the Arabian Peninsula and Fertile Crescent, were given posts as preachers and educators, and devoted themselves to writing and mold-ing the Islamic discourse of the time. Some even became involved in local politics. It is instructive to trace the activities of several such exiles, includ-ing Muhammad Khalil al-Hijrisi, ʿAbd al-Rahman ʿIllaysh, Muhammad ʿAbduh, and the brothers Muhammad and Ahmad al-Qayati.

Soon after arriving in Mecca—the destination of his exile—Muham-mad Khalil al-Hijrisi began teaching there, became acquainted with the Idrisiyya Sufi order, and recorded his observations about the order's ide-ology and rituals.[1] ʿAbd al-Rahman ʿIllaysh, whose exile from Egypt ap-parently prevented him from assuming the leadership of the ʿArabiyya Shadhiliyya order after the death of his father,[2] was transported to Istan-bul but was soon suspected of political subversion by the authorities there. According to Shaykh ʿAbd al-Halim Mahmud, a Sufi Shadhili and shaykh al-Azhar (d. 1978), the accusation against ʿAbd al-Rahman was that he supported the Moroccan sultan's ambition to claim the caliphate. He was subsequently imprisoned for two years in harsh conditions. Upon his release, he was exiled to the island of Rhodes and after some time was permitted to settle in Damascus. There ʿAbd al-Rahman was hosted by Emir ʿAbd al-Qadir al-Jazaʾiri, who heaped honors on him, inter alia, for the support of the Algerian struggle against the French and their ally, the sultan of Morocco, by his father (Muhammad ʿIllaysh). Upon the death of the emir in 1887, ʿAbd al-Rahman eulogized him at his massive funeral, in which the emir was buried next to the revered Sufi master Ibn ʿArabi (d. 1240).[3]

ʿIllaysh's colleague in the ʿUrabi revolt Muhammad ʿAbduh, who was exiled to Beirut, eventually reached Paris, where he joined his mentor Jamal al-Din al-Afghani in editing the pan-Islamist and anticolonialist newspaper *al-ʿUrwa al-Wuthqa* (The Firm Bond). Although short-lived (1884), the paper reverberated in the Muslim world and was circulated among large numbers of ʿulamaʾ and other dignitaries in the Fertile Crescent.[4] It also reached the exiled Qayati brothers, Muhammad and Ahmad, who had settled in Beirut. Muhammad al-Qayati praised the newspaper as being innovative and for exposing the evil face of British policy in Egypt, which promised reform and construction but instead brought about corruption and destruction. A biography of ʿAbduh written by his pupil Rashid Rida describes al-Qayati as being in the habit of reading the paper aloud in public, in the style of a sermon delivered in a mosque, and interjecting expressions of commendation and appreciation at intervals during the reading.[5]

How much influence the reformist spirit of *al-ʿUrwa al-Wuthqa* had on al-Qayati is difficult to assess. Clearly, his closeness to ʿAbduh did not turn him into a blind advocate of ʿAbduh's progressive views (see the discussion below). Conceivably, what made the greatest impact on al-Qayati was the paper's militant stance—its anti-British and pan-Islamic line, which was in fact dictated by al-Afghani. The newspaper was also unrestrained in its denunciation of Khedive Tawfiq, who was despised by al-Qayati and his colleagues. The paper demanded that he shed his submissiveness to the British and show a readiness to die as a martyr for his faith and country if need be, as evidence of being a true believer; otherwise the Egyptian people must take their fate into their own hands and act according to Islamic teaching by resisting the British occupation.[6]

Although not a modernist in his outlook, Muhammad al-Qayati held ʿAbduh in high esteem. The contact between them intensified upon ʿAbduh's return to Beirut in 1885. He remained there for three years, teaching at the Sultaniyya school. The Qayati brothers also introduced him to local Salafi circles close to ʿAbd al-Qadir al-Jazaʾiri, most notably ʿAbd al-Razzaq al-Bitar (d. 1917), scion of a renowned ʿulamaʾ family from Damascus prominent in the nineteenth century.[7]

MUSLIMS IN THE AGE OF MODERNITY:
MUHAMMAD AL-QAYATI'S ACCOUNT

For the Qayati brothers, Beirut was a jumping-off point in gaining familiarity with the countries of the Fertile Crescent. In his book *Nafhat al-basham fi rihlat al-Sham* (1901), Muhammad al-Qayati describes their travels through Damascus, Beirut, Tripoli, Sidon, Jerusalem, Hebron, and Nablus in detail, providing a fascinating portrait of the religious landscape and social composition of these cities.[8] Weaving in personal judgments, based on his intimate knowledge of the Egyptian experience, al-Qayati provides an additional perspective for comparing Egypt with Syria in the age of modernization and tracing the cultural interaction between these two regions.

Al-Qayati's book focuses on two main topics: the local elites and social norms and customs. In describing the local elites, he highlights their diversity, ranging from government officials and merchants to 'ulama' and Sufi shaykhs. He analyzes the two latter groups, who filled key posts in religious and cultural life, in depth. Most of these figures, as biographical dictionaries also reveal, were educated in al-Azhar as members of the influential Riwaq al-Shuwam and retained a strong tie with the Azhar community after returning to their birthplaces throughout Syria.[9] This bond was reflected in their correspondence with Azharis about theological and legal issues as well as the roles of mysticism, grammar, literature, and poetry. They also recommended and encouraged local students to become candidates for study there. Indeed, many of the 'ulama' who hosted the Qayati brothers during their travels were acquaintances from their years as students together at al-Azhar. Several came from affluent families and were involved in commerce, thereby reinforcing the economic ties between Egypt and Syria.[10] These cross-regional Islamic networks were undoubtedly facilitated by developments in the second half of the nineteenth century, such as improved roads, newly constructed railroads, the opening of the Suez Canal, and advances in mass printing, which contributed to the proliferation of ideas in the Ottoman Middle East and beyond.[11]

During the encounters between the Qayati brothers and their acquaintances they discussed not only religious and cultural matters but politics as well. They reviewed the condition of Islam and of the Muslims, expressing resentment at the "age of the traitors" (*dahr al-khuwwan*), as exemplified by the Egyptian leaders who were "struck with blindness" during the events of the 'Urabi revolt.[12] The Qayati brothers, in their struggle against foreign aggression, found much in common with notables who had played a similar role in other countries and who also made their home in the Syrian domain after their defeat. These figures included ʿAbd al-Qadir al-Jazaʾiri of Algeria, ʿAbdallah al-Kurdi of Iraq, and Ghulam Muhammad Sirdar Akram of Afghanistan.[13]

In surveying local social customs, al-Qayati focused primarily on two cities: Beirut and Damascus. He described Beirut as an Islamic city in character but with a government, army, and infrastructure based on the European model. He was particularly impressed by the high level of security and low level of crime in the city, which he explained as being the product of well-organized governing systems and observance of the law both by those in power and by ordinary people. The situation was different in Egypt, he pointed out, which was led by exploitative, despotic rulers who turned the law into a fraud and believed that they were immune from deposition or dismissal.[14] Regarding the ethnography of Beirut, al-Qayati noted that despite good neighborly relations with the Christian population, who constituted the majority and were linked with various European powers through commercial and patronage relationships, the Muslims displayed zeal for their religion and did not imitate the Christians. Their behavior showed no suggestion of rebelliousness, such as drinking wine or operating cafes that sold alcoholic drinks or drugs.[15] Al-Qayati sketched a similar picture in this respect for other cities he visited, such as Damascus, Sidon, Tripoli, and Jerusalem. In his view, loyalty to an Islamic lifestyle was a source of pride to the Muslim inhabitants.[16]

Al-Qayati's empathy for the Muslims in Beirut and their moral lifestyle was nevertheless interwoven with a certain disdain for their conduct during religious festivals and rites of celebration and mourning. For example, he noted that their reservoir of poems and songs marking the Prophet's birthday was limited and out of date and that their reading of the Qurʾan lacked precision and fluency. "The people of Beirut, and in effect of Syria generally, badly need precise, qualitative, and tuneful Qurʾan readers," he declared, hinting at the rightful address to remedy these shortcomings: al-Azhar. He described the wedding ceremonies as lacking careful planning. This applied as well to funeral services, in which the women did not cry out or shout, the men displayed no sorrow in their facial expressions, and the refreshments were mostly sweet, "in contrast to what is customary among the inhabitants of Egypt."[17]

Commenting on the attire of the Muslims of Beirut, al-Qayati noted that some of the men wore a Western-style brimmed hat, jacket, and trousers and others wore an Eastern robe, as was customary in Egypt.

The women's attire was varied and colorful but revealed nothing of their
bodies. This distinguished them from the Christian women, whose permissive and revealing manner of dress drew his criticism. In al-Qayati's
view, they emulated European women in every way except language.
He described the Christian women of Beirut as offering their charms to
wealthy and foolish men. Refuting the Christian premise that such behavior is a hallmark of civilized society, al-Qayati, revealing his opinion
of the values of modernity, argued that such thinking strips religion of
its moral content and violates the shariʿa, one of whose foundations is
decency. "Those who seek prostitution define the attributes of religion
as something blemished," he asserted, quoting a comment by a member
of a notable family of dignitaries in Beirut, Hasan Effendi Bayyuham,
who also observed that "modernity is nothing but a diminishment of
religion."[18]

While acknowledging that norms had been breached to a certain
extent in Egypt too, al-Qayati stressed that most women there wore traditional attire, although they had added adornments and decorations.[19]
In his view, however, rejecting modernity did not mean disqualifying
the modern sciences, such as engineering, mathematics, geography, and
even some knowledge of Western languages. He praised schools for girls,
which imparted knowledge of mathematics, reading, and sewing to their
pupils.[20] This stance revealed openness and an acknowledgment of the
right of women to acquire education, although it was conditional on the
preservation of the institution of the family and the avoidance of any challenge to male social supremacy.[21] Such conservative views are apparent,
inter alia, in al-Qayati's sharp attack on a widely debated book by Qasim
Amin, *Tahrir al-marʾa* (Woman's Emancipation, 1899).[22]

Damascus, al-Qayati observed in his book, was less exposed to modernity than Beirut. Most of its buildings were constructed of mud and
wood, except for the mosques, the graves of the saints, and the old madrasas, which "are among the most beautiful in the landscapes of this world."
The manners of its residents were exceedingly pleasing, to the point that
the inhabitants tended to exaggerate their politeness and the welcome
they extended, in comparison to the norm in Egypt. The women were
typified by quiet and modest behavior, which was also the case for Christian women, who did not generally adorn themselves in the *jahili* style,
as in Beirut. Still, al-Qayati observed, the tendency to imitate European
women was growing. He also emphasized the Damascene affinity for
sweets and for clothing that is adorned and glittery.[23]

In describing the attributes of the Muslims in the Fertile Crescent cities that he visited, particularly their careful observance of religion and the preservation of social morality, al-Qayati drew an analogy with the Egyptian reality, injecting blunt criticism of the social and political system there:

> In effect, Syria is the best Islamic land at this time, even though expertise in the Qur'an and in religious knowledge is greater in Egypt. Still, indecent things are not visible in public as in Egypt, for abhorrent deeds are well hidden, and one does not see special places for prostitutes as in the Land of Egypt. One also does not see the smoking of hashish or the condition of addiction, etc., in public. You will find only coffee and tobacco in all the coffeehouses in Syria, whether in Beirut or elsewhere, with patrons sitting there in a state of total composure. Therefore, a prince or a common man or an *'alim* will not hesitate to sit down there, for there is nothing in these coffee houses to damage virtue, such as using drugs, drinking alcohol, or uttering vulgarities or obscenities, as mentally ill and crazed persons do.[24]

Al-Qayati was pessimistic about the prospect that the Egyptian rulers would take any steps to end such immoral manifestations and restore the dignity of Islam and its laws:

> If you question any one of the rulers of Egypt about this, he would reply: "This period is a period of freedom, and the European states would not want to relinquish this freedom." How can we use distant nations as an excuse—since they have no connection with what is happening in our countries and in our religious practices—to justify the abandonment of religious ritual, humanism, virtues, and [religious] law. We do not believe that if we forbid our women and men to engage in abhorrent acts and behave wantonly and lawlessly in public they [the Europeans] will attack us for preventing this corruption, from which neither they nor we will derive any national or religious benefit whatsoever.
>
> Ultimately, the rulers and inhabitants of Egypt are still in love with the people of Europe and their ethics and customs, mimicking them to such an extent that they exceed them in these respects.... May Allah have mercy in the face of the acts of this generation. What would have happened if the Egyptian rulers forbade their fellow inhabitants—who are under their firm control—from performing indecent acts that are contrary to Islam, which is their religion and the religion of their fathers and

forefathers for 1,300 years? Would any of the foreigners force them to abandon the laws of their true religion? Absolutely not.[25]

The behavior of the Egyptian rulers, al-Qayati concluded, is even worse than that of the Christians in Europe:

> Some of the Europeans are not entirely devoted to religion or do not ob-serve all its requirements, but they do not break its rules, belittle its cer-emonies, or scorn its believers, as do the leaders of the Muslims now. If only these leaders could imitate the Christians in this, too, as they imitate them in their other customs. What a pity for the [Islamic] religion, for its believers, and for its loss in the eyes of these emirs who think that imita-tion requires scorning it and its believers completely. We pray to Allah to inspire their understanding and banish their sick thoughts and indecent opinion of this true religion, the path of righteousness.[26]

While al-Qayati's narrative also reflected personal bitterness over the degradation and exile that he and others involved in the ʿUrabi events experienced, its strongest message was a religious scholar's censure of the eroding status of Islam in the encounter with modernity. Notably, his unfamiliarity with the West, which he never visited, contributed to his disdain for modernity—in contrast, for example, to Shaykh Rifaʿa Rafiʿ al-Tahtawi a half-century earlier. As an imam of one of Muhammad ʿAli's student missions to Europe, al-Tahtawi soon became an enthusiastic ad-mirer of the new modern civilization and described it in his writings.[27]

The extensive social documentation in Muhammad al-Qayati's book illuminates the multifaceted religio-cultural links that existed between Egypt and the Syrian provinces in the second half of the nineteenth cen-tury. Against this background, al-Azhar stands out as a Middle Eastern beacon that attracted large numbers of scholars despite the erosion of its status domestically as a result of Egyptian governmental reforms and the rivalry of other religious centers such as Damascus and Istanbul.[28] Arab historians, including the Egyptian ʿAbd al-ʿAziz Muhammad al-Shinnawi and the Syrian Mustafa Ramadan, defined the institution as second only to the hajj to Mecca in serving to unite the diverse areas of the Muslim world. In al-Shinnawi's metaphoric depiction, "while the Kaʿba in Mecca served as the religious *qibla* [the prayer direction], al-Azhar in Cairo pro-vided the scientific learning *qibla*."[29]

Al-Azhar's distinguished position as the focus of religious learn-ing in the Muslim orbit was reflected not only in biographies by its non-Egyptian graduates but also in religious guidance and fatwas. One such fatwa was issued by senior Azharis in early 1899 in the wake of a dispute that broke out in Egypt and throughout Syria over holding the hajj in Mecca due to fear of an outbreak of smallpox that could be spread by pilgrims from India, where the disease had broken out. The fatwa ruled that since none of the legal schools had ever conditioned the holding of the hajj on the possibility of a plague, this was not an obstacle to fulfilling the commandment of the hajj.[30]

Locating al-Azhar within a broader network of scholarship serves as a basis for widening the scope of research regarding the extent of the ties between the ʿulamaʾ and their colleagues in Syria and elsewhere. Various studies have centered on Muhammad ʿAbduh's sojourn in Beirut and his interaction with members of the Salafi reform movement.[31] ʿAbduh represented a minority viewpoint in al-Azhar in his time, however, and therefore exerted only a limited ideological influence outside Egypt. As shown by Mona Abaza and Giora Eliraz, his reformist impact was actually more palpable in Southeast Asia, where it attracted a vast audience due to its inclusive message.[32] By contrast, Azharis with a more puritanical mind-set became models for their colleagues in the Middle Eastern domain.

Some of these Azharis were identified not only with Islamic legal studies but also with Sufi culture, which was extremely popular in Syrian society, as indicated in Muhammad al-Qayati's volume. He and his brother Ahmad were received with honor and esteem wherever they visited, in no small measure because of their affinity for Sufism.[33] This held true as well for ʿAbd al-Rahman ʿIllaysh when he resided in Damascus under al-Jazaʾiri's patronage and for Muhammad Khalil al-Hijrisi when he resided in Mecca under the patronage of the Idrisi order.[34] Notably, Sufism and its practices were a primary target for criticism by ʿAbduh in Egypt and his Salafi colleagues in the Fertile Crescent, particularly Jamal al-Din al-Qasimi, Rashid Rida, ʿAbd al-Rahman Kawakibi, and ʿAbd al-Hamid al-Zahrawi. Yet in their struggle against its controversial practices, such as the worship of saints, they found themselves in a minority, whether in Egypt or in Syria. Their aim to modernize Islamic traditions and weaken the power relationships within the ʿulamaʾ corps in favor of the lower ranks, to which they belonged, exposed them to denunciation and excommunication by their more senior and orthodox rivals in Cairo and Damascus. These powerful ʿulamaʾ had the advantage of an efficient infrastructure, social prestige, and, no less important, the backing of the political authorities.[35]

A COUNTERAPPROACH
TO MODERNITY

Al-Qayati's account constituted a defiant manifesto highlighting the negative impact of modernity, and the notion of cultural rapprochement between East and West, on the Muslim community. In contrast, al-Qayati's
contemporary ʿAbd al-Rahman Sami, an Egyptian-born merchant, provided a narrative more positive and open to modernity. Sami, too, spent
time in Syria at the end of the nineteenth century, recording his impres-
sions in a book titled *al-Qawl al-haqq fi Bayrut wa-Dimashq* (The Truth
about Beirut and Damascus).[36]

Sami described Beirut in a variety of complimentary ways—"the
shining star of Syria," "the city of knowledge and medicine"—and depicted its streets, houses, municipal institutions, hospitals, and public
gardens as built along the European model. He placed special emphasis
on the city's well-developed print and journalism culture as well as its
schools and colleges, most of them Christian. These institutions were intended for boys and girls alike and attracted a large number of students
from Syria, who thereby acquired useful vocational knowledge. Sami observed that the modern educational approach of these schools fomented
a "cultural revival" and pointed to the presence of sectors in the Levant
that utilized every opportunity for progress and prosperity offered by the
modern age. Sami apparently was not particularly troubled that missionary groups generally sponsored such educational activity—a sensitive issue with those Muslim observers of the period who viewed missionaries
as an additional arm of European colonialism in the destruction of local
self-identity. From his point of view, this educational thrust was welcome
altruistic activity, as the acquisition of knowledge was one of the attributes of modern times.[37]

Moving from the institutional and educational realm to the population itself, Sami described Beirut society as industrious, productive, and
harmonious, with different classes intermingling (for example, during
holidays and celebrations) without distinction between rich and poor.[38]
He also showed an empathetic and inclusive attitude toward the Christian inhabitants, with no mention of interethnic tension between them
and the Muslim population. He praised Christian women in particular
as mannerly, modest, educated, and knowledgeable in foreign languages.
Additionally, he lauded the literary and intellectual accomplishments of
Christian writers such as Nasif al-Yaziji and Butrus al-Bustani.[39]

Sami sketched a similarly pleasant picture of Damascus, which he called the "paradise of the East" and "the pride of its cities."[40] Damascus was distinctive for its spectacular parks and the cleanliness of its neighborhoods and roads, due in large measure to the abundance of water that reached every home and byway in the city and its environs. Its inhabitants were endowed with high morals and virtues, solidarity, and a warm attitude toward strangers who visited the city. It was also known as a center of knowledge and education, although the tone was set primarily by the Christians, who were more intent than Muslims on promoting modern sciences and foreign languages. By contrast, Sami described the Muslim schools as mainly devoted to religious and legal studies, training their students for positions in education and as mosque officials, side by side with government schools, which offered training for the bureaucracy and other managerial fields. Sami depicted the social and ethnic mosaic of Damascus as multifaceted and impressive: religious differences never constituted an obstacle to harmony and brotherhood between Muslims and non-Muslims.[41]

Although this harmony was upset in the wake of the anti-Christian riots of 1860, which constituted a "black mark" in the city's history, Sami noted that the situation reverted to its former orderly state as part of a general effort to preserve the unity of the homeland and attend to its welfare. Quoting the inhabitants, he wrote: "We are separate in our faiths but love unites us."[42] He attributed these fraternal ties between the denominational sectors of the city to material factors, including economic well-being, employment opportunities, social support and welfare networks, well-developed commerce, and facilities for leisure-time activities and excursions.[43]

The books of al-Qayati and Sami provide two different perspectives on the relationship between tradition and modernity on the threshold of the twentieth century. For al-Qayati, the religious scholar, the values of science and modern culture embodied a threat to Islam and its superiority over other cultures; for the Western-oriented Sami, they were welcome attributes of society. The different cultural orientations of the two writers also dictated a different conception of the ʿulamaʾ and their role in the polity. Al-Qayati viewed them exclusively as men of religious learning within the Muslim community. Sami, by contrast, had a broader view of them as primarily men of learning equipped with Western knowledge— whether Muslims or Christians—who were the harbingers of renewal in local Middle Eastern society.[44] These differing concepts reflected the contest over the cultural and intellectual guidance of society during this period.

RETURNING TO THE HOMELAND

During their exile, the Qayati brothers and others attempted to gain support through the influence of local dignitaries to obtain a pardon from the khedive, but these efforts were unsuccessful.[45] The Ottoman authorities were suspicious of the Egyptian exiles from the moment they reached Beirut, their first stop, in late 1882. They were immediately put under surveillance, and in January 1883 the sultan ordered them to leave not only Syria but the entire territory of the Ottoman Empire without delay. This order agitated both the exiles and the local Muslim notables, who tried to have it annulled.[46]

In an attempt to ward off their bitter fate, Muhammad al-Qayati and his colleagues obtained an audience with the governor of Syria, Ahmad Pasha Hamdi, expressing their fear that relocation in Europe would make their life harsher, because they were unfamiliar with the languages and the habits there and their means of subsistence were meager. They also pointed out the dishonor that would result for the Sublime Porte if Muslims who sought refuge under the protection of the caliph, Commander of the Faithful, were expelled from its sovereign territory. Pressure exerted by local dignitaries and warnings sent to Istanbul regarding the damage to the status of the sultan in the Arab provinces in the event of the expulsion resulted in the retraction of the order and the granting of permission to the Egyptian exiles to remain where they were.[47]

Conceivably, the background to the restrictive policy adopted by the Ottomans toward the ʿUrabist exiles lay in the Ottoman historic memory of Egypt's occupation of Syria (1832–39) as well as fear of the spread of the dissident mood in the Muslim population. In Tufan Buzpiner's view, the Ottomans were concerned about the exiles' nationalistic ideology in light of their involvement in the ʿUrabi movement. Whether the movement was actually nationalist or not was irrelevant: what was salient was how the Ottoman government perceived it.[48] Another, no less important consideration (discussed above) apparently prompted the Ottomans to behave as they did in this episode: the disobedience shown in Egypt toward the established order as embodied in Khedive Tawfiq, who functioned as the de jure representative of the sultan in Egypt. The Ottomans viewed the very presence of the Egyptian exiles—and the ʿulamaʾ among them who had legitimized Tawfiq's deposal—as a danger portending the defiance of legitimate authority in Syria as well. A constant reminder of this defiance was the continued use of the defamatory term "insurgents" (ʿusat) in the pro-Ottoman local papers when referring to the ʿUrabi episode and the repeated assertion of its harmful ramifications.[49]

With the completion of their sentences of exile (during the years 1886–88), most of the exiled ʿulamaʾ returned to Egypt. The Qayati brothers, ʿAbd al-Rahman ʿIllaysh, ʿAbduh, and other returning ʿulamaʾ then adopted a politically conciliatory stance and resumed the primary roles of scholars and communal leaders that they had held before their involvement in dissident politics during the ʿUrabi events.

The Qayati brothers were received with great honor by ʿulamaʾ and dignitaries in Tanta and Cairo, where they disembarked en route to their home in Minya. Upon the deaths of Ahmad al-Qayati in 1890 and his brother Muhammad in 1902, their graves in the village of al-Qayat became a popular pilgrimage site, as was also the case for their father and grandfather.[50] ʿAbd al-Rahman ʿIllaysh (d. 1921) returned to Cairo and resumed his involvement in the ʿArabiyya Shadhiliyya order, claiming the role of leader. As it turned out, he neglected the demands of the position and was lax in entrenching the order, with the result that it had lost its status by the beginning of the twentieth century.[51] Nevertheless, ʿAbd al-Rahman's role as a link in a spiritual genealogy (*silsila*) of Sufi saints (going back to the Prophet's family) earned him great prestige. He was described as scrupulous in avoiding mundane matters, honored both by the highborn and by the masses, and esteemed and consulted by locals as well as by European Christians.[52] Upon returning to Egypt in 1888, Muhammad ʿAbduh set about rejuvenating the image of Islam in the modernist spirit within the parameters of the legal channels open to him, primarily in his roles as a member of the directorate of al-Azhar and as supreme mufti until his death in 1905.

Other returnees, however, had a different attitude. Muhammad Khalil al-Hijrisi, for example, agreed to return to Egypt at the conclusion of his exile in Mecca only if Ahmad ʿUrabi was released from his exile in Ceylon and not before the death or abdication of Tawfiq. Al-Hijrisi kept up a long correspondence with ʿUrabi. In one of his letters he asked ʿUrabi to break off all relations with Amin al-Shamsi al-Zaqaziqi, one of ʿUrabi's followers, whom al-Hijrisi had encountered at the hajj. Al-Zaqaziqi had complained about the loss of his property and social standing as a result of his involvement in the uprising, instead of expressing sorrow at the great loss endured by the homeland. "He is one of those people whose primary interest is in this world alone," al-Hijrisi observed.[53]

ʿUrabi himself, after returning to Egypt in 1901 in the wake of a pardon granted by Khedive ʿAbbas Hilmi II, kept a low profile. He remained in his village, occupied by prayer and maintaining an ascetic way of life until his death in 1911.[54] Although his political struggle was far behind him, his struggle to clear his name in the annals of Egyptian history was not. His detractors included not only the writers of the country's official historiography, sponsored by Muhammad ʿAli's dynasty, but the compilers of the country's national-liberal historiography, then in the process of coalescence.

The radical wing of the Egyptian nationalist movement, headed by the leader of the National Party, Mustafa Kamil, declared that ʿUrabi should not have been allowed to return to Egypt at all in view of the grave damage that he had caused the country—its loss of national sovereignty. According to Kamil, instead of leaving the country as Egyptian and Ottoman officials had advised him to do on several occasions, ʿUrabi had played into the hands of the British, who made no secret of their ambition to control Egypt. Moreover, Kamil charged, ʿUrabi's name was unfit to be entered in the pantheon of Egypt's national heroes because he chose humiliating submission rather than an honorable death on the battlefield.[55] Less aggressive criticism was voiced by the more moderate Egyptian nationalist wing led by Ahmad Lutfi al-Sayyid, head of the Umma Party. Al-Sayyid praised the intention of the revolutionaries to form a constitution but criticized their extremist methods, which he attributed to the military background of ʿUrabi and his colleagues.[56]

ʿUrabi's negative image in national-liberal circles, as Thomas Mayer has shown, played into the hands of those compiling the country's official historiography, who sought to reinforce the status of the ruling dynasty and besmirch the ʿUrabi movement in the annals of Egyptian history.[57] They portrayed Ismaʿil as a wise reformist ruler who invested maximal efforts to benefit his country and his successor, Tawfiq, as just and patriotic, acting to save Egypt from foreign conquest. ʿUrabi, by contrast, was depicted as impulsive and treacherous.[58] The renowned poet and khedival protégé Ahmad Shawqi (d. 1932) described ʿUrabi and his colleagues as those "who left and returned to Egypt as insignificant persons."[59]

In rebutting his detractors, ʿUrabi relied heavily on Islamic rhetoric as he had done in the past, emphasizing that his leadership of the insurrection movement reflected the will of Allah. Moreover, he chose to delegitimize the khedival regime specifically in the religious context. He called upon Egyptians to divest themselves of Western modernity, which he defined as false; distance themselves from indecency; and cleave to their religion. "There is no greatness or honor without religion," he stressed.[60]

PART THREE

Confronting a Changing World

6 Debating Islam

The essence of the struggle between supporters and opponents of the ʿUrabi movement within the ʿulamaʾ community centered on the issue of the duty to obey a Muslim ruler. While supporters among the ʿulamaʾ viewed the khedive as a puppet of the Christian powers and therefore as having relinquished faith—thus evoking the duty to depose him—opponents of the movement viewed him as a legitimate authority figure and the lawful representative of the Ottoman sultan. The dispute between the two camps, conducted through fatwas and the press, pointed to the multifaceted nature of Islamic thought, which provided a considerable reservoir of arguments both pro and con, reflected in creative interpretations. The debate also revealed the dilemma of the ʿulamaʾ over adherence to the religious ideal of just and meritorious rule, on the one hand, and the legitimation of the existing political order no matter how flawed out of fear of anarchy, on the other.

Yet, alongside the divide in the Azharis' political thought between supporters and opponents of the revolt, a conservative common ground was discernible in all that concerned family, society, and morality. The Islamic discourse revealed a scholarly community in transition, subject to growing intervention by the modern state and operating in the shadow of ongoing European penetration. Simultaneously, the community's vocation itself was being challenged by the expansion of education and the emergence of new educational systems, the rise of public literacy, a growing bureaucracy, and a proliferating print culture. In the final quarter of the nineteenth century these developments contributed to an expanded public sphere in Egypt and to the growing impact of public opinion. Such developments sprang mainly from the educated urban middle class, which was gaining influence, and relied on a relatively well developed civil society made up of professional unions, political clubs, welfare societies, literary salons, open public lectures, and, especially, the press.

Newspapers, periodicals, and publishing houses (mostly privately owned)—with valuable input by Christian intellectuals who had migrated to Egypt from the Fertile Crescent—constituted a primary medium for the cultivation of public opinion and an important channel for political activity. The press became a vital hothouse for a new, educated generation concerned with issues about the essence of Egypt's social and political culture. This undermined the status of the religious scholar, who was no longer perceived as immune from criticism but was even depicted as self-centered and lacking curiosity about the world.[1] In the view of these modern intellectuals, the ideal religious functionary would not only preach devotion to the faith and to religious learning but would also have expertise in current affairs and be able to disseminate practical and contemporary knowledge to promote progress, economic prosperity, social unity, and loyalty to the homeland. Such a figure therefore did not have to be a graduate of a madrasa but could come from any academic or professional educational environment relevant to the needs of society and the times.[2]

Overshadowed by these developments, the pillars of arbitration and monopoly over religious knowledge that had supported the traditional ʿulamaʾ crumbled, challenged by a minority of reformist ʿulamaʾ together with a larger number of lay intellectuals. They called for the unmediated reading of the holy text and the mass dissemination of its principles to the public. These reformists, widely viewed in the research literature as bearing a message of renewal, openness, and constitutionalism, functioned as primary agents of change.[3] By contrast, the extensive intellectual corpus produced by their ideological rivals in the Azhar community at that time was only marginally explored by historians, reflecting the deprecating historiographic narrative regarding the religious establishment in modern times.

The polarization of Islamic thought—or, in the words of Dale Eickelman and James Piscatori, "the fragmentation of authority"[4]—indeed challenged the traditional guardians of the faith. A careful historical reading, however, reveals that they reacted assertively and polemically. Responding to the need to deal effectively with their reformist rivals, they overcame their distrust of the print medium and, moving beyond the traditional pedagogical modes (sermons in mosques, copying texts, and issuing fatwas), adopted the modern medium of rapid mass printing to promote their views and reach wide audiences. Like their reformist rivals, the conservative ʿulamaʾ also were aware of the sense of confusion and crisis in Muslim society in light of the European colonial and cultural penetration, and they too pressed for reform. But the model they offered focused on the moral purification of the believer in the face of cultural corruption and on raising the barriers between Islam and foreign cultures. In their perception, the study and adoption of a European lifestyle or Western thought was analogous to an expression of no confidence in Islamic teaching and constituted a danger to the social order.[5]

In tracing the struggle over the image of Islam and its believers, the discussion in this chapter reveals a nuanced and segmented picture of a religious discourse at a crossroads between the decline of the traditional Islamic order and the emergence of modern national states. Contemporary written materials of various kinds, especially compilations of fatwas, offer an important prism through which to examine this struggle.

FATWAS AND THE PUBLIC SPHERE

Fatwas were issued by muftis in response to questions posed by private individuals or official institutions (*mustaftis*). They were written in accordance with the *madhhab* (legal school) to which the mufti adhered and usually cited the sources upon which he had drawn. As a norm, fatwas were issued only in response to actual problems and not in regard to abstract matters, although the possibility of inventing questions in order to advance a doctrinal premise or political cause could not be ruled out.[6]

Unlike the ruling of a qadi, which dealt only with issues of human relations (*mu'amalat*), a fatwa could also deal with issues of worship (*'ibadat*), theology, and religious customs. It was meant to apply to the public at large and was not confined to a specific person or place. Furthermore, a fatwa was not a judicial decision that had to be executed; it was authoritative legal advice. Theoretically, however, fatwas could not be ignored by qadis, especially if issued by a mufti of high rank, such as the şeyhülislâm (chief jurist) in Istanbul, the shaykh al-Azhar in Cairo, or the head of one of the four schools of Sunni Islam (Hanafi, Shafi'i, Maliki, and Hanbali). Fatwas became an integral part of court proceedings in the core regions of the Ottoman Empire, especially in Istanbul, Ankara, Bursa, and Kayseri.[7] They played an important role in Islamic jurisprudence, constituting the link between normative legal theory and the real world.

In the early centuries of Islam, fatwas functioned as a vehicle for the development of the shari'a. After the coalescence of the schools of law in the ninth century, fatwas helped accommodate the shari'a to changing sociopolitical circumstances by perpetuating the use of *ijtihad* (judicial reasoning), albeit within limits.[8] Beyond religious guidance, fatwas also functioned as a bridge between the ʿulamaʾ and the common people, thereby positing the ʿulamaʾ as a stabilizing factor in society, mediating between ruler and subjects. Fatwas reflected the public mood but also sought to shape it.[9] In echoing the voice of the populace, fatwas could be classified as "popular literature," in Haim Gerber's phraseology.[10]

Major social, economic, and cultural shifts in the nineteenth century heightened the importance of fatwas as a religious and moral guide. Most fatwas were issued in handwriting and later published in compilations. A few were simply read out in mosques or public gatherings and later quoted in court rulings, religious literature, and archival records. Increasingly, fatwas were used as a lever in political affairs and became a component in the broad struggle over the status of Islam in the polity. This trend was accelerated by the expanding use of the printing press and the growth of a literate community, who constituted an important constituency for political mobilization in support of or opposition to government policies.[11] Thus fatwas came to address the larger Muslim public.

Fatwas played a vital role in the context of the ʿUrabi revolt in Egypt (1881–82). They reveal that the stance of the ʿulamaʾ regarding the revolt ranged from political quietism to political dissidence, yet they were all essentially on the same side in their display of social conservatism within the schools of law that they represented. By way of example, the two key religious figures during the period were Muhammad ʿIllaysh, a Maliki, who supported ʿUrabi and ruled in favor of deposing Khedive Tawfiq; and Muhammad al-ʿAbbasi al-Mahdi, the Hanafi mufti of Egypt and shaykh al-Azhar, who supported the khedive and denounced his opponents. The legal outlook of both these figures on a variety of issues is clearly articulated in compilations of the fatwas that they published: ʿIllaysh's *Fath al-ʿali al-malik fiʾl-fatwa ʿala madhhab al-Imam Malik* (The Revelation of the Sublime Ruler [God] in Issuing Legal Opinions according to the School of Imam Malik, 1883, 2 vols.) and al-Mahdi's *al-Fatawa al-Mahdiyya fiʾl-waqaʾiʿ al-Misriyya* (al-Mahdi's Legal Opinions on Egyptian Events, 1887, 7 vols.).[12] The title of the second compilation explicitly indicates the contextual relevance of the fatwas in reflecting both the changing Egyptian reality and the public's need for religious guidance.[13] In the case of al-Mahdi, the fatwas gained additional credence by virtue of his official status as head of the judicial system.

A survey of these and other religious opinions reveals that few fatwas dealt with political topics, and those that did were issued at the request of persons in power who had specific interests. This constitutes a further indication that the political sphere continued to be outside the realm of activity or interest of the Azhar community as in the past, except during times of crisis. At such times they were called upon for support and even intervention in political matters, as was the case during the Mamluk and the Ottoman periods, the French occupation, and the ʿUrabi revolt. By contrast, theology, law, society, and morality were the major topics of the usual fatwas. They were typified by a generally puritanical approach in terms of providing moral guidance, discouraging frivolity, and preserving the superior status of Islam and Muslims over all other religions. At the same time, they adopted a sectoral agenda, such as emphasizing the authority of the ʿulamaʾ in combating the reformist challenge.

TAQLID AND IJTIHAD

Muslim reformists pressed for an ambitious agenda: the deconstruction of the existing legal order. As such they challenged the age-old religious authority of the *sahaba* (the Prophet's companions), as reflected in hadith literature, and sought liberation from the burden of *taqlid* (the adherence to the teaching of a certain legal school), which the reformists viewed as the main cause of the stagnation of Islam. This perception also accounted for their aim to weaken the validity of *ijmaʿ* (consensus among the jurists). In its place they posited the *maslaha* (the public good) as an independent judicial principle, turning it into a lever for reform in a range of national, social, and gender issues. These legal principles, espoused by the reformists, were based on the unmediated interpretation of divine revelation through reasoning, in the spirit of the Muʿtazila movement dating back to the eighth century[14]—or, as Judith Tucker defined it, the mental power of analysis.[15]

The reformists' arguments became a topic of debate, response, and dispute with their rivals in the Azhar community. In the Azharis' view, *taqlid* was the foundation stone of the legal and social system of the Sunni community and served to enhance its cohesion. Questioning the validity of the *taqlid* would inevitably mean not only the shattering of both the traditional frame of reference and social stability but also the disintegration of the authority of the ʿulamaʾ. This accounted for the Azharis' vigorous defense of the concept.

The Maliki mufti Muhammad ʿIllaysh was an important and influential voice in the ideological debate over the issue of reform during the late nineteenth century. In his writing, and especially in his legal rulings, he provided the earliest systematic defense of the institution of *taqlid* in

combating the reformist effort to undermine it and expand the boundaries of *ijtihad*. While the reformist orientation viewed *taqlid* as destructive and as a recipe for social degeneration, the traditionalist community
(and its primary spokesman, ʿIllaysh) viewed it as a judicial system devoted to preventing anarchy, preserving the integrity of each legal rite,
and barring the influence of personal caprice in handing down a fatwa.

ʿIllaysh adopted an uncompromising position on the question of
the *sahaba* and the imams who founded the legal schools, whom he pronounced to be infallible in their interpretation of the Qurʾan. In a long
fatwa apparently published in the early 1850s, ʿIllaysh ruled that the
sahaba were among the giants of Islam, who received messages directly
from the Prophet and were attentive to his views. Casting doubt on their
credibility or disregarding them bordered on violating the Sunna and
being an act of deviation (*fusuq*).[16] Similarly, ʿIllaysh's junior colleague
Muhammad al-Qayati declared categorically that the *sahaba* were among
the best people created by God after the prophets. They were like "stars
who illuminate the straight path," with expertise in Islam and its ways.
Casting aspersions on them was tantamount to undermining religion
and automatically excluded such detractors from the community of
believers.[17]

ʿIllaysh defined *ijtihad* as the province of the heads of the four schools
of law, who acquired their knowledge through many years of delving into
the study of Islam. To abandon their canonic texts and approach the holy
writings directly therefore would signify a deviation from the rightful
path and constitute incitement and rebelliousness that should be rooted
out by force.

ʿIllaysh was not content with a dry historic and legal explanation
alone. As a Sufi master, he introduced an added mystical theme: the
founders of the schools of law were directly inspired by Allah and His
Prophet (*ahl al-kashf*). Quoting the Sufi mystic ʿAbd al-Wahhab al-
Shaʿrani (d. 1565), he pointed out that the opinions of the four imams
could not possibly deviate from the shariʿa. This was because they had
established the foundations of the legal schools on the basis of *haqiqa*
(esoteric truth), the elevated state that tied their souls to the soul of the
Prophet in a way that enabled them to consult with him about every subject in the Qurʾan and the hadith before committing it to writing. Such
a meeting of souls was one of the miracles of the saints; and if the imams
were not saints, then "there is no saint on the face of the earth." This additional attribute of sanctity put the imams in a category separate from
that of ordinary scholars: they were friends of God (*awliyaʾ*), in essence

making them infallible (*ma'sumin*) and their rulings obligatory. This was also the reason for the closure of the gates of *ijtihad* upon the coalescence of the schools of law in the ninth century, 'Illaysh contended. Anyone who denied the status of the imams as friends of Allah should be renounced as an enemy of Islam.[18]

'Illaysh's fatwa revealed his legalistic mind-set despite his affinity with Sufism. It was originally directed at the Sanusi order in Cyrenaica, Libya, whose leader, Muhammad al-Sanusi (d. 1859), claimed to have superhuman powers and assumed the right of *ijtihad* in light of his genealogical kinship to the Prophet, while also granting this right to others. He thus bypassed the schools of law, relying directly on the holy text and thereby undermining the normative legal system. 'Illaysh's fatwa constituted a continuum of an earlier anti-Sanusi fatwa issued by his teacher Mustafa al-Bulaqi in the early 1840s, which called for eschewing *ijtihad* and urged emulating only the imams of the legal schools, because they belonged to an earlier generation and thus were closer to the period of the Prophet. Al-Bulaqi warned that anyone who imagined himself to be above the imams' level of *ijtihad* was deluding himself, for "Satan is toying with his soul." Followers of such a person would be judged as if they had accepted medicine from someone who is not a doctor.[19]

The anti-Sanusi context of the fatwas by al-Bulaqi and 'Illaysh reflected a widespread legal tradition that disqualified any critical approach toward the corpus of religious knowledge, positing an authoritarian approach instead.[20] The traditional corpus, 'Illaysh held, had been developed during generations of debate and scholarly research and was supported by the consensus of the 'ulama' (*ijma'*). Anyone who undermined it undermined the unity of the community and was to be considered a heretic, according to Sunni parameters.

As a jurist, however, 'Illaysh also posited an internal division of the concept of *ijtihad*, breaking it down into several degrees. He considered the highest degree to be that of the independent mufti (*mutlaq*), who is an expert on the sources of the law—the Qur'an, the hadith, and the disputes between the scholars. He is not subject to *taqlid* or to any legal school. But, quoting the Shafi'i jurist Abu Zakariyya Muhyi al-Din al-Nawawi (d. 1277) and relying on medieval Maliki jurists such as al-Qasim ibn Firruh al-Shatibi (d. 1194) and Shihab al-Din al-Qarafi (d. 1285), 'Illaysh held that this degree was an ideal that did not exist in reality once the period of the imams ended or was found only in a select group of jurists. Apart from them, all those qualified to hand down judicial rulings belonged to the accepted legal schools and applied *ijtihad* in the context of strict internal

rules laid down by their school (*ijtihad muntasib liʾl-madhhab*). They
were called "fettered" (*muqayyad*) muftis.[21]

ʿIllaysh's defense of the legal schools took various forms. He ruled
that a person who curses a colleague's legal school is considered to be an
apostate who must repent or else be executed, for "defaming a legal school
is the practice of an infidel only."[22] He also sharply criticized what he
termed the current fashion of crossing over from school to school, which
he perceived as demeaning to the stature of the schools. He forbade study
at or ruling according to a given school of law without affiliating with it
as well as accepting the authority of a person who was untrained or who
was ordained by an unrecognized scholar. Such a person violated a serious
prohibition and must be punished harshly. ʿIllaysh thus sought indirectly
to reinforce the stature of the scholar and the mufti in society, ensure a
direct and personal link between scholar and students, and avoid a loss of
control over teaching and legal rulings, especially in an age of print culture—another threat to the power of Islam, of which he was well aware.[23]

Stabilizing the judicial system of the schools of law also meant stabilizing the moral authority of the ʿulamaʾ as teachers and guides. This
goal was clearly reflected in other fatwas in which ʿIllaysh ruled—relying on Maliki scholars—that knowledge is not passed on by inheritance
but must be acquired, and not by reading texts alone. Any leniency on
this issue incurs the danger of distorting the dictates of religion. Consequently, he asserted, the legal and state authorities must vigorously prevent unqualified persons from handing down rulings and from misleading the masses.[24]

Muhammad al-ʿAbbasi al-Mahdi, the Hanafi mufti of Egypt and
shaykh al-Azhar (1870–97), was also a defender of the institution of
taqlid. While ʿIllaysh, in his day, dealt with the Sanusi challenge in Libya,
al-Mahdi contended with the Mahdi challenge in Sudan, which, under
the leadership of Muhammad Ahmad ibn ʿAbdallah (the "Mahdi"), took
the form of an open rebellion against the Egyptian-Ottoman regime in
1881. The Sudanese Mahdi's judicial methodology in effect annulled the
authority of the legal schools, replacing it with divine inspiration (*ilham*)
as a supreme legal source derived from the direct revelation of the Prophet
to him through a dream.[25] Such authority, claimed as a supreme judicial
source and as immune to error, exposed the Mahdi to sharp denunciation
from the ʿulamaʾ community and especially from the Azharis.

In 1883, at the request of Khedive Tawfiq, Shaykh al-Azhar al-Mahdi
published a denunciatory fatwa aimed at restoring the faded honor of
the textual sources and the shariʿa and refuting the Sudanese leader's

declaration that he was the "anticipated Mahdi" who must be obeyed by all. The fatwa asserted that after his death the Prophet's contact with people (whether in their sleep or awake) could not alter the rules of the shariʿa. One of these rules was that the caliph may be appointed either by an oath (*bayʿa*) taken by the chosen representatives of the people or by appointment by his predecessor in office. Furthermore, when a legitimate caliph is in place, any *bayʿa* taken thereafter is null and void. Beyond its theological and judicial importance, the fatwa was significant politically. It ratified the duty of obedience to the Ottoman sultan and his deputy, the Egyptian khedive, as the legitimate rulers of the Muslims, in disregard of the British occupation of Egypt. The Sudanese Mahdi, for his part, tended to avoid disputation with his Azhari rivals, contenting himself with accusing them of submission and pandering to rulers whom he labeled deviants from the shariʿa in ruling over Muslims by force of secular laws and granting equal rights to non-Muslims.[26]

Muhammad al-ʿAbbasi al-Mahdi elucidated his puritanical approach to *taqlid* and *ijtihad* in other fatwas as well. He forbade any deviation from the Hanafi authoritative texts or reliance on other legal schools that were more convenient for certain rulings or even on a synthesis between them (*talfiq*). To illustrate, according to Hanafi law, a woman whose husband has disappeared and does not pay for her support (*nafaqa*) cannot obtain a divorce or claim payment from her absent husband. By contrast, Maliki law holds that failure to provide financial support undermines the essence of the marriage and therefore constitutes a basis for a suit for divorce in court. In light of an increasing number of women in nineteenth-century Egypt who sought Maliki muftis, al-Mahdi ruled that their fatwas were null and void, because only Hanafi law was valid. He also initiated sanctions and punishments against Maliki muftis. In another example, a series of fatwas issued by a mufti by the name of ʿAmr Abu Zayd from the village of ʿUqaba, which promoted progressive interpretations of the law of repudiation (*talaq*), evoked a ruling by al-Mahdi that the mufti should be punished and prevented from issuing any further legal opinions.[27]

The grand mufti's approach, as noted by Rudolph Peters, was part of a broader legal thrust to make all Egyptian law Hanafi. It also revealed al-Mahdi's orthodox mind-set, reflected in his determination to implement the shariʿa and his consistent opposition to the Westernization of the Nile Valley, the notion of monetary interest, and the opening of places of entertainment.[28]

Beyond disputes over legal interpretation, the contention between conservatives and reformists was no less acute over broader social and moral issues, testifying to the measures of change and reform that were taking root in Egypt and throughout the Ottoman Empire in the late nineteenth century. Three issues were at the heart of this dispute, evoking sharp polemics and rivalry: non-Muslims, women, and Sufis.

NON-MUSLIMS

The status of non-Muslims (mainly Christians, Jews, and Zoroastrians) in classical Islam was legally defined by the term *dhimmi*. *Dhimmi*s were "protected subjects" entitled to freedom of worship and security of life and property in exchange for recognition of the superiority of Islam and compliance with various political and social restrictions. These included paying a poll tax (*jizya*), wearing distinctive clothing, and prohibitions against supervising Muslims, riding saddled animals, bearing arms, building houses higher than those of Muslims, and publicly celebrating their own religious ceremonies.[29]

Just as non-Muslims were required to conform to the regulations imposed on them, Muslims were obliged to protect non-Muslims from exploitation and harmful acts. The *dhimma* arrangement was thus a binding contract between two sides. It was prompted by the ethnic and cultural diversity of the Muslim world during the early centuries of Islam, creating an environment that promoted a degree of tolerance toward religious minorities.

Nevertheless, the inherent tensions among the three monotheistic creeds, each claiming a monopoly over religious and historical truth,[30] served periodically as a source of friction between Muslims and non-Muslims. Christians suffered more during periods of conflict with European countries and other instigations of intercommunal friction, being more numerous and more visible. Jews, by contrast, constituted a far smaller population and kept a low profile.[31]

The legally inferior status of non-Muslim communities was retained under the Ottoman Empire as an Islamic polity whose historic roots were embedded in holy wars against infidels. The Ottoman treatment of non-Muslims was relatively fair, however, at least in the urban centers. As shown by Islamic court records (*sijill*) in the sixteenth and seventieth centuries, non-Muslims in some regions, in particular Jews, were involved prominently in commercial life and held public posts. Additionally, they could petition the Ottoman authorities in cases of harassment or violation of their granted rights by Muslim individuals or officials.[32]

The nineteenth century witnessed a gradual legal process of releasing

non-Muslims from their inferior status in society. Reformist govern-
ments, especially in Cairo and Istanbul, exempted religious minorities
from the traditional *jizya*, allowed them to enlist in the army, and granted
them civic and economic liberties. Such emancipation, embodied in the
Ottoman reforms known as the Tanzimat (1839–76), resulted not from
ideological conviction but from political considerations on the part of
the Muslim elites: enhancing internal cohesion and neutralizing separat-
ist tendencies (especially in the Balkans) in order to block the European
encroachment into Muslim lands more effectively.

The tone was set by Sultan ʿAbd al-Majid (1839–63), who in 1854 declared: "My heart knows no difference between the subjects of my empire;
all rights and privileges will be given to all subjects without any distinction."[33] This emphasis on the Western notion of civic equality as the new
basis for the Ottoman state was followed by practical steps. Christians
and Jews were accepted in governmental schools on an equal basis and
were allowed to hold administrative posts; the traditional clothing regulations differentiating them from their Muslim neighbors were abolished;
and restrictions on the construction of places of worship were removed.
The judicial system also underwent a transformation with the introduction of Western-inspired civil codes, leaving the shariʿa to cover matters of
personal status only, such as marriage, divorce, child custody, inheritance,
and *waqf*.[34] These reforms brought about a substantial improvement in
the status of religious minorities, while further eroding the hold of Islam
on social life, especially in urban centers.

The emancipation of non-Muslims from their inferior social status as
dhimmis during the nineteenth century engendered an intense polemic
within the Muslim scholarly community, reflected in a large body of fatwas and counter-fatwas. This juridical discourse, while providing legal
solutions to specific problems, also reflected broader ethical considerations. If the exponents of emancipation tried to lower the legal and social
barriers between Muslims and non-Muslims, their opponents resolutely
sought to preserve these barriers and thereby enhance sectoral cohesion
in an era of change and dislocation.

Voices of Openness

Reformist ʿulamaʾ in Cairo such as Muhammad ʿAbduh, Hamza Fathallah, Husayn al-Marsafi, and Rashid Rida adopted a humanistic or civic
attitude toward the Copts as equal partners in the Egyptian homeland
and advocated an ecumenical approach toward Western Christian culture.[35] ʿAbduh referred to Christians and Jews in his treatises as "people

of the Book" (*ahl al-kitab*), thereby highlighting their monotheistic and honorable status, rather than applying the term *dhimmi*s, with its inferior connotation. He had a vision of Islam as a "social religion," embodying a spirit of community and concern for human welfare.[36] ʿAbduh also translated this ecumenical orientation into deeds. While living in exile in Beirut (1884–88), he initiated an interreligious dialogue and fostered rapprochement, turning his house into a cosmopolitan intellectual center.[37] During his tenure as mufti of Egypt (1899–1905), he issued a large number of fatwas in response to questions arising from daily contact between Muslims and non-Muslims as well as from the demands of modern life. These fatwas, disseminated by modern means of communications, earned him fame throughout the Muslim world but also exposed him to denunciation in orthodox circles.

In a 1903 responsum to a Muslim living in the Transvaal in South Africa (known as the "Transvaal fatwa") ʿAbduh allowed Muslims to wear the Christian (i.e., European) hat (*burnita*) and implicitly other styles of dress, as dictated by necessity (such as protection from the sun), so long as this did not lead to abandoning Islam. Moreover, he boldly ruled that it is lawful for Muslims to eat the flesh of animals slaughtered by Jews and Christians, based on the Qurʾanic verse: "The food of those who were given the Book is permitted to you" (5:5). As an advocate of an eclectic approach to the Islamic legal tradition, ʿAbduh supported this argument by resorting to renowned jurists of the Maliki school who adopted a more liberal stance on this issue, as compared to the Hanafi school with which he was formally identified as grand mufti of Egypt.[38]

ʿAbduh's Transvaal fatwa was reinforced and expanded by his disciple, Shaykh Rashid Rida (d. 1935). In regard to wearing European dress, such as hats and trousers, Rida argued that the Qurʾan and the Sunna, and consequently Islamic jurisprudence as a whole, did not specify any particular kind of Islamic dress. On the contrary, the Prophet and his companions themselves wore the style of dress of both the polytheists and the "people of the Book." Pointing to the triviality of the issue, Rida concluded that "any sensible nation that posits dress as a pillar of its faith or daily conduct makes a mockery of religion." He applied the same rationale to the issue of using European perfumes while carrying out Islamic rituals such as praying in a mosque.[39] But he adopted a more sophisticated approach with regard to the prohibition of eating meat if any name other than Allah was uttered in the blessing prior to the slaughter of the animal (5:3, 6:121), which thereby violated the sacred unity of Allah (*tawhid*).[40] Using *ijtihad*, he mitigated this prohibition with a double-edged argument:

first, he pointed to disagreement among earlier jurists in cases where it was clear that non-Muslim slaughterers had uttered a name other than Allah; second, he emphasized the consensus over the permissibility of meat for Muslim consumption in cases of uncertainty (which was the more common situation), as demonstrated in the Sunna when the Prophet and his companions ate meat offered to them by Jews.[41]

Rida's argument was part of a broader outline that he adopted for intercommunal rapprochement based on the imperative "no compulsion is there in religion" (2:256) and the teaching of the Prophet that he who harms a *dhimmi* will be judged on the day of resurrection. Hence Rida approved of paying visits to non-Muslims during their holidays, illnesses, and funerals, although without taking an active part in their religious activities or indulging in forbidden acts such as drinking wine, which would make the transgressor an apostate.[42] He also sanctioned testimony by non-Muslims in a shariʿa court in certain matters related to Muslims, such as wills or medical circumstances, especially in the absence of Muslim eyewitnesses or when other evidence supported such testimony. In Rida's view, equality rather than religious affiliation should be the guideline regarding the acceptability of court testimony.[43]

A group of Azharis backed another of ʿAbduh's fatwas, on the sensitive issue of accepting financial assistance from non-Muslims for worthy Islamic communal purposes such as providing education and food to orphans and the poor or aiding the Muslim community during periods of turmoil, all of which he advocated. Moreover, these ʿulamaʾ approved using the expertise of non-Muslims for ritual needs such as the construction of pulpits (*minbar*, pl. *manabir*) or prayer niches (*mihrab*, pl. *maharib*) in mosques. They held that such assistance did not violate the prohibition against Muslim subordination to non-Muslims and denounced any Muslim who rejected such services or defamed those who used them,[44] basing their ruling on the verse "Help one another toward piety and godfearing; do not help each other toward sin and enmity" (5:2).

ʿAbduh's fatwas evoked intense debate between reformists and conservatives, putting the broader issue of social intermingling and the assimilation of religious minorities on the Muslim public agenda. Counterfatwas and statements by conservative ʿulamaʾ attacked ʿAbduh for distorting the Qurʾan and the time-honored legal tradition and urged Khedive ʿAbbas Hilmi to dismiss him from his post. The position of one who carries out *iftaʾ* (the practice of issuing fatwas), they argued, should be occupied by a jurist who follows the rulings of his legal school, not an innovator.[45]

Voices of Dissent

While the reformists promoted an inclusive outlook in the name of the utilitarian-ethical concept of *maslaha*—posited as an unconditional source of law and becoming the driving force for social reform[46]—their adversaries promoted an exclusive outlook based on the Qurʾanic injunction "forbidding wrong" (3:104). This injunction, inter alia, prohibits domination or humiliation of Muslims by non-Muslims.[47] The dissident stance of Azharis was intended to reestablish the social boundaries separating Muslims and non-Muslims and to reassert Islam's moral superiority as an entrenched ethos in the Muslim collective memory. These aims were closely related to the Azharis' desire to curb the modernization policy of the state. They feared that it would encourage interaction between Muslims and infidels, thereby endangering the very existence of Islam and with it the moral authority of the religious establishment.[48]

In an undated fatwa, the Maliki mufti Muhammad ʿIllaysh ruled that Muslims and their leaders must prevent *dhimmi*s from engaging in any activity or public display that imbues them with eminence or superiority over Muslims, because they are the enemies of Allah and His Prophet, Muhammad. Accordingly, *dhimmi*s should not be allowed to display their faith or even be seen in public during their holidays, celebrations, funerals, or other deviant religious observances. Moreover, they are forbidden to ride a horse or walk in the middle of the street. Anyone who deviates from these restrictions, ʿIllaysh held, is considered to be

a violator of a contract, giving the Muslim ruler the right to choose between death and imprisonment as a punishment. It is the duty of the ruler to avoid acts that would enhance the social status of *dhimmi*s. Any Muslim who allows such violations by non-Muslims due to material gain is a sinner [*fasiq*] and must repent immediately. If he allowed such violations in order to glorify their faith he is to be considered an infidel [*mariq*] and must be warned three times to repent. Otherwise he will be executed.[49]

Another fatwa issued by ʿIllaysh was a responsum to a question about whether *dhimmi*s should be prevented from joining a Muslim funeral procession. ʿIllaysh responded in the affirmative, arguing that the purpose of walking in a funeral procession is to recommend the deceased to paradise. Since the infidels are impure (*anjas*) and enemies of Allah, they do not deserve to fill this role. Furthermore, he argued, one of the first acts of the deceased is to plead with Allah to forgive all those who took part in his funeral; yet the infidels are not entitled to be forgiven, ʿIllaysh ruled, quoting the Qurʾan: "God forgives not that aught should be with Him associated.... Whoso associates with God anything has indeed forged a mighty sin" (4:48). Rather than allowing the infidel to join the procession, which signifies displaying affinity for him, the duty of Muslims is to humiliate him in order to emphasize Islam's superiority. In effect, the issue in ʿIllaysh's view was not the participation of *dhimmis* in the funerals of Muslims but rather the rationale for the very existence of Islam. This may also explain his ruling forbidding the execution of a Muslim, even a slave, who kills a *dhimmi* freeman, because "the nobility of Islam is higher than the nobility of freedom."[50] Not surprisingly, he frequently relied on Qurʾanic verses that leave no room for maneuver or compromise regarding infidels, portraying a life or death struggle against them in the context of both the religion and the nation.[51]

In this puritanical stance toward non-Muslims, ʿIllaysh followed Ahmad ibn Muhammad al-Dardir, the renowned late-eighteenth-century Maliki mufti of Egypt. Al-Dardir was a critic of what he perceived as "the better treatment by the political elite of non-Muslims over Muslims," to the extent, he observed cynically, that the Muslims wished to change places with the *dhimmis*.[52]

The Shafiʿi Muhammad al-Qayati, ʿIllaysh's disciple and colleague who resided in Syria following his exile from Egypt after the suppression of the ʿUrabi movement (see chapter 5), perpetuated this puritanical point of view. He issued fatwas and treatises criticizing the elegant clothes and permissive habits of Christian subjects in Beirut and Damascus following their civic emancipation, which, he claimed, threatened the moral behavior of Muslims. What the Christians considered to be the aesthetic face of modernity, he contended, was nothing more than stripping religion of its moral essence and following the ways of the *jahiliyya* (the pre-Islamic age of ignorance).[53]

In a similar vein, al-Qayati expressed disdain for Christian religious ceremonies such as the processions on Easter in which the image of the crucified Jesus, punctured by nails and dripping with blood, was carried aloft or artifacts such as pictures and statues in churches. All these practices distorted monotheism and would not serve any useful purpose on doomsday, he declared.[54] Imbued with an elitist view of Islam as superior to all other cultures, al-Qayati also attacked Christian intellectuals in Beirut who were involved in the revival of Arabic (for example, Nasif al-Yaziji) for having distanced themselves from their Muslim teachers and dishonoring the ancient Islamic heritage in the realms of literature and poetry. In this context, the saying "They buy from us and sell to us" was applicable, in al-Qayati's view.[55]

The Hanafi grand mufti of Egypt and shaykh al-Azhar Muhammad al-ʿAbbasi al-Mahdi, who was a main adversary of ʿUrabist ʿulamaʾ such as ʿIllaysh, al-Qayati, al-ʿIdwi, and al-Khalfawi, also tended to display a restrictive approach toward any change in the status of non-Muslims. In a fatwa issued in 1849, al-Mahdi approved the prevention of a Copt from buying a house in a village inhabited by Muslims, forcing the owner to sell it to a Muslim. He instructed the provincial qadis to enforce this restriction and deter Muslims from such misconduct. *Dhimmi*s, al-Mahdi argued in a ruling that replicated ʿIllaysh's (see above), must be prevented from acts or acquisitions that caused damage or inconvenience to Muslims or accrued power or respect to themselves, because they belonged to an inferior category of people (*ahl al-saghar*). He based his ruling on a much earlier fatwa by Ebu Suud al-ʿImadi, *şeyhülislâm* of the Ottoman state (1545–74), obliging Muslims to buy up all *dhimmi* houses that surround a mosque even if compulsory measures were required to carry this out. In another fatwa, dated 1874, al-Mahdi reemphasized the legal superiority of Muslims over non-Muslims by ruling that only testimony by coreligionists was valid in a Muslim court in cases in which the defendant was a Muslim.[56] He also set boundaries for Muslims regarding visits to non-Muslims during their religious holidays or copying certain habits of their dress, to avoid violating the religious prohibition against resembling the infidel (*tashabbuh*).[57]

Similar limits were laid down by al-Mahdi's colleague Shaykh ʿAbd al-Hadi Naja al-Abyari. He ruled that a *dhimmi*, although not bound by the commandments of Islam, nevertheless was not permitted to challenge those commandments by inappropriate acts such as entering a mosque, listening to the Qurʾan, drinking wine in public, using or receiving services from Muslim offices or institutions, or building a house higher than the homes of his Muslim neighbors. Moreover, he was prohibited from holding governmental office or serving on local Muslim councils. In cases of conviction for theft or adultery, a *dhimmi* had to be judged in the same way as a Muslim: the amputation of a hand for theft and stoning (in the case of a married man) or whipping (in the case of an unmarried man) for adultery.[58]

Additionally, al-Abyari, ʿIllaysh, and al-Mahdi were determined to reinforce efforts to convert *dhimmi*s to Islam and to prevent the possibility of reversion to their former religion (*ridda*) by applying economic and criminal sanctions as deterrents. Thus, while conversion to Islam presented no difficulties, reconversion to a previous faith or conversion to some other creed and abandoning the Muslim community was perceived as a legal violation and carried penalties.

A similarly harsh approach in the matter of religious conversion was adopted by Ottoman legalists, despite the Tanzimat reforms (1839–76) and to the displeasure of the British. Stratford Canning, their ambassador in Istanbul (1842–58), viewed this issue as fundamental to the attainment of religious equality throughout the Ottoman Empire.[59] Indeed, the debate over religious conversion in the centers of reform in Istanbul and Cairo touched on the essence of the entrenched perception of Islam as a belief system superior to any other. Not surprisingly, this imperative evoked wide debate in the fatwas of the time. Al-Abyari detailed the punishments that could be imposed on a person who converted from Islam (*murtadd*) and did not repent. Punishments ranged from a prohibition against eating meat slaughtered by the hand of the convert to forced divorce, the confiscation of all property and its transfer to a *waqf*, and, ultimately, execution. "Such a person cannot be left in a state of departure from Islam," al-Abyari ruled.[60]

Dealing with other aspects of the conversion issue, in a fatwa ʿIllaysh approved the action of a qadi in denying the right of a Christian woman to return her two young daughters to Christianity after they had been converted to Islam by their father, who had since died. Should a *dhimmi* object to this judgment, ʿIllaysh ruled that the ruler or his deputy had the choice of execution or enslavement as a punishment.[61] In another fatwa he ruled that a Christian woman who continued to refuse her Muslim husband's request to be instructed in the principles of Islam for half a year, in addition to violating the laws of women's purity, was a *murtadd* and had to be divorced, inasmuch as she was living in an Islamic land, heard the muezzin five times a day, and had a husband well versed in religion.[62]

In a fatwa issued in 1854 al-Mahdi ruled, in accordance with the Hanafi position, that a Coptic woman who had converted to Islam but reverted to her past creed under pressure from her family must be imprisoned until she accepted Islam once again or else must remain in prison until her dying day.[63] He ruled further that even children who were at an age when they could distinguish between good and evil automatically became Muslims when one parent converted to Islam, because their dependence on their parents would continue until they reached adulthood. In another fatwa (dated 1879) al-Mahdi referred to a case in which a Christian man converted to Islam, married a Muslim woman and had children, but then renounced Islam and died in this state. The man also had a Christian wife and children. Al-Mahdi ruled that his Christian family was not entitled to a share in the inheritance, regardless of whether the assets were accumulated before or after his apostasy.[64]

ʿIllaysh and (even more so) al-Mahdi, however, were careful to emphasize the monotheistic status of non-Muslims and the preservation of their rights as granted by the institution of *dhimma*. In one example, al-Mahdi cited the equal status of *dhimmi* women and Muslim women in Islamic marital law, albeit with the exception of inheritance and several other conditions.[65]

Islamic assertiveness regarding the issue of freedom of religious belief may be illuminated by two cases of conversion from Islam to Christianity during the period under discussion. The first involved a certain Ahmad Fahuri of Cairo, whose act of conversion to Christianity in 1878 evoked the wrath of his family and his community to the point that he feared for his life. He sought refuge in the American missionary school in Cairo, with the aid of British missionaries, despite a promise by Egyptian officials that no harm would befall him if he returned home. The second case involved a certain Muhammad Habib, also of Cairo, whose conversion from Islam led to his arrest and trial in a shariʿa court in 1883 for the crime of apostasy. Upon the intervention of the British consulate and the Egyptian government, he was placed under the protection of the police. An arrangement was made for him to be transported to Cyprus until the atmosphere calmed down, while his property would be protected until his return to Egypt. This arrangement did not prevent the forcible divorce of his wife, according to Islamic law, and the status of his property remained uncertain. General Edward Malet, the British consul (1879–83), in describing the affair, commented regretfully that "in the present day it has been found necessary in Egypt to resort to such an expedient [banishment] in order to protect a convert from Islam." He noted that religious freedom throughout the Ottoman lands had been established by the Hatt-ı Hümayun, known as the Edict of Tolerance (1856), and the expectation was that this would be carried out in Egypt.[66]

Several conclusions may be drawn from these fatwas of the conservative-oriented ʿulamaʾ regarding the status of non-Muslims in the nineteenth century. Although moral assertiveness on the issue of the inferiority of non-Muslims was manifested at that time mainly by low-ranking ʿulamaʾ or those residing in remote provinces, it was also advocated by senior ʿulamaʾ in Cairo. In promoting this issue, Islam was used as an ethical marker in defining the social and cultural boundaries between Muslims and their non-Muslim neighbors. Despite their rigid attitude regarding the second-class civic position of non-Muslims, how-ever, these ʿulamaʾ were in essence demanding the implementation of traditional regulations that were being ignored by the political authori-ties. In this sense, the ʿulamaʾ adhered to the tenets of the Pact of ʿUmar and took care not to deviate from them: *dhimmi*s were to be classified as infidels and discriminated against, but they were not to be persecuted and were clearly preferable to polytheists.

Viewed historically, the assertiveness of the ʿulamaʾ did not arrest the process of co-opting non-Muslims into Egyptian society following the collapse of the Ottoman Empire and the formation of nation-states on its ruins in the post–World War I period. Normative rulings embodied in fatwas on the issue of non-Muslims mostly failed to dictate the agenda of the political elite or even the actual behavior of the society. Fatwas were part of an Islamic legal discourse that was on the defensive, marginalized in the wake of state building and the reshaping of the collective iden-tity based on modern Western premises of nationalism and egalitarian citizenship. In this context, former *dhimmi*s became formal citizens of nation-states. Nevertheless, the dissent of the ʿulamaʾ on this issue made the co-optive process of non-Muslims more difficult, given the continued importance of the affinity for religion in the social milieu of the modern Middle East.

Additionally, the preservation of the legal ideal of the *dhimma* insti-tution in fatwas and other published materials in a growing literate com-munity, and in the context of the anticolonial and anti-Zionist struggle, kept the issue of religious minorities on the Arab agenda. It also provided modern Islamists with a political lever with which to attack existing re-gimes for "deviating from Islam." In contrast to the Islamic modernism of Muhammad ʿAbduh, Islamists tended to sharpen rather than blur the line that separated Islam from other cultures,[67] with fewer apologetics in relation to the implementation of the shariʿa or the status of minorities under Islamic rule.

WOMEN

Toward the end of the nineteenth century the debate over women's rights in the family and in society (including marriage and divorce, child cus-tody, education, confinement to the home, and wearing the veil) occupied a significant part of Egyptian discourse. It was fueled to a great extent by the overall process of modernization, the shift toward capitalism, the inte-gration into the European economy, the abolishment of the institution of slavery, the British occupation, and the rise of nationalism. Significantly, the state itself issued laws that encouraged the education of girls, and in 1873 Khedive Isma'il inaugurated the first girls' school. Two years later, the education of girls in elementary schools was declared mandatory.

Nevertheless, despite the transformations in various aspects of the economic, social, and political realms in Egypt, change in the status of women was slight, a reflection of entrenched family and societal norms and insufficient initiative by the state. Although the gender issue was widely discussed in public forums and in intellectual circles, it did not evoke significant practical change. Its major spokespersons were Westernized writers; modernist 'ulama' such as Muhammad 'Abduh, the mufti of Egypt; and feminist women. These feminists, most famously Malak Hifni Nasif, came from the upper- or middle-class sectors, which looked to Paris and London rather than Cairo and Istanbul as models for political and social reform.[68]

The debate over gender intensified with the appearance of two books by Qasim Amin (d. 1904), *Tahrir al-mar'a* (Woman's Emancipation, 1899) and *al-Mar'a al-jadida* (The New Woman, 1900). Amin, a French-trained jurist and an avid reformist in the 'Abduh camp, became the spokesman for the emancipation of women. In his published work he advocated the abolition of polygamy and arranged marriages, the expansion of education for women, and the removal of the veil. His intellectual defiance stemmed not only from personal conviction, as someone who had experienced Western culture and viewed it as a source of inspiration in solving social problems, but also from pragmatic political considerations. In his view, the image of the woman defined the image of the nation: the intellectual and social development of women, who constituted half the population, was closely bound up with the development of the nation.[69]

Amin's books, which were an important source of inspiration for the women's movement that emerged in Egypt at the start of the twentieth century, propelled him into the eye of the storm. Religious figures and conservative thinkers denounced his views as fomenting the collapse of the local value system and societal norms of dignity and decency and demanded that the gender status quo be preserved. Even nationalist circles, especially those associated with the National Party headed by Mustafa Kamil, disagreed with the extent of Amin's proposed reforms. While they supported the notion of women's education, they opposed the removal of the veil and the cessation of social separation between women and men. The concept they favored was a "domestic ideology" that sought to moderate the traditional gender role division by highlighting the values of partnership and love in the family and expanding the role of the woman in the education of the children. This approach reflected the religious leanings of the National Party as well as the fear of its adherents, who belonged to the lower middle class, that their social status and their employability might be weakened by gender egalitarianism. The women's issue thus served as an additional component in the cultural and social contest over the image of the Egyptian political community.[70]

The topic was given additional impetus by the growing struggle for Egyptian independence from the British during the first two decades of the twentieth century, which opened up a legitimate avenue of activity by women on behalf of the shared national goal while allowing them to lay the groundwork for feminist activity. The movement remained an urban phenomenon of the upper and middle class, however, thereby failing to challenge the prevailing social order. Its restrained demands to limit male privileges in family matters and to broaden women's civil and political rights elicited only a partial response from the government.[71]

Yet, despite its relatively limited success, the women's issue (like the issue of non-Muslims) evoked an unequivocal response from puritanical Azharis in light of its religious and social sensitivity. Opposing the emancipatory ideology of the reformist circles, which supported the entry of women into the public space, these Azharis posited theological and social barriers. In their view, the place of the woman was at home, where she would fulfill her biological obligations as a wife and mother and be protected from the outside world with its dangers and temptations. While the private sphere was perceived as safe, decent, and moral, the public sphere was seen as dissolute and corrupting.

Indeed, the question of women leaving the confines of the home and appearing in the public domain was a central theme in fatwas and other materials published by ʿulamaʾ in the late nineteenth and early twentieth centuries. A typical case was brought to ʿIllaysh, the Maliki mufti. A husband forbade his wife to leave the house except with his permission but later permitted her to leave for a specific chore, such as buying food or clothing in the marketplace. She left the house for a different reason, however, without requesting permission from her husband. The question was whether she could rely on the permission he gave her for specific chores or whether her husband must divorce her for what she did on her own recognizance. ʿIllaysh ruled that the specific permission was insufficient in such a case, and divorce was mandated because she went out for another reason. But ʿIllaysh stipulated, quoting al-Shafiʿi, that divorce is not applicable for a woman who enters a place that her husband forbade out of forgetfulness or necessity (such as giving birth).[72] In another fatwa he reaffirmed the inferior status of a woman's testimony as insufficient in court; it must be backed by that of an upstanding male witness and another woman.[73] If a woman is accused of fornication but claims she is still a virgin and four midwives provide expert testimony that she is speaking the truth, however, their testimony is no different than the testimony of four men, and the punishment for adultery is not to be applied. Even if it is agreed that the testimony of women is weaker, a doubt exists, and that doubt defers the application of the punishment.[74]

Elsewhere ʿIllaysh illuminated his position regarding modesty for women by likening a drawing slate to a veiled woman: if the veil is removed, the picture on the slate is revealed. "The veil is the linchpin and the heart of this world," and the essence of this issue is that going without a veil arouses the senses, ʿIllaysh explained. Feelings and desires are always present, but if they are repressed by sleep or by a struggle against desire, then the moral deviation or corruption inherent in socializing between the sexes will be avoided.[75]

The gender issue also preoccupied al-Mahdi, the mufti of Egypt. He too entrusted the woman's right to leave the house and enter the public space to her husband, who could divorce her if she disobeyed. He also forbade the qadi to rule on divorce for nonpayment of alimony, or for any other reason, in the absence of the husband.[76] Other rulings by al-Mahdi related to prohibiting mothers from arranging the marriages of their daughters, especially minors (under age nine), because only fathers and grandfathers have the authority to do so. Nevertheless, he ruled that the father does not have the right to force marriage on a daughter who has reached the age of intellectual maturity. If she does not consent, such a marriage is nullified.[77] Thus, operating within a legal discourse that essentially did not contest male supremacy or prerogatives, al-Mahdi worked to secure certain female rights from abuse.

The role of the woman in the family and the community was a cardinal issue for Egyptian Islamic jurists. It was linked as well to the topic of education and the acquisition of knowledge. A dispute that broke out between reformists and conservatives in the late 1890s over the issue of the right of a woman to acquire literacy is revealing. While reformist sectors declared that the right to literacy is the foundation of the acquisition of knowledge and clear evidence of enlightenment and progress, conservative circles defined it as a dangerous source of moral degeneration that must be prohibited. These circles not only reinforced their stance with textual sources from the Qurʾan, the hadith, and *fiqh* but also used their rivals' starting point—permitting literacy for women based on the absence of a specific prohibition against it by the Prophet in his time—as a lever to forbid it. For example, some conservatives ruled that literacy for women might have been permitted during the pure Salafi period but is absolutely forbidden in the present time, which is tainted from all sides by a climate of corruption.[78]

Fatwas served as an important but not exclusive vehicle in the attempt to redefine gender relationships in Egyptian society. Essays and editorial commentary on the topic of gender written by religious authorities in a polemical mode also contributed to this discourse. These sources, too, serve as a valuable barometer and an informative basis for tracing changes in the Egyptian gender reality. A good example is to be found in the Islamic newspaper *Makarim al-Akhlaq al-Islamiyya* (Elevated Islamic Ethics), which in its November 1900 issue published an eyewitness report of a wedding party in Cairo by one of its writers. The open windows of the house in which the party was held, the report pointed out, allowed any passerby to see women mingling with men openly and unashamedly, as if they were their wives, competing with each other for the men's attention by their adornments. Even when vulgar language was used, the women showed no sign of embarrassment and the men did not seem to feel that anything was wrong with this behavior. On the contrary, they appeared quite content. In the view of the newspaper, this display reflected a general climate of licentiousness and adultery.[79]

Sharply critical, the newspaper went on to describe the moral breakdown caused by the emergence of women in the public sphere, attributing the decline of the Muslim nation from its position of greatness to this development. In the paper's view, women's decency had become a thing of the past. Women now left home with their faces and hands exposed, perfumed, adorned with jangling necklaces, and walking with a swaying, seductive gait. All the traditional legal prohibitions have thus been breached, and lawlessness reigns everywhere. A young woman who walks in marketplaces acts like a prostitute among lovers; women in luxurious attire and heavy makeup who visit graves at the appointed times and on holidays "show lawlessness in their eyes," while the eyes of the men who gaze at them "jump out of their sockets." Carriages fill the streets, carrying women without a head covering, who laugh loudly and wink at people they know. Similarly, the brothels have become visible to all.[80]

Makarim al-Akhlaq al-Islamiyya placed the responsibility for the phenomenon of permissiveness first and foremost on the husbands, for having displayed feebleness and poor judgment in "rescinding tradition and granting space to their wives." In so doing, they have damaged their manliness and brought shame on themselves. In an article published in

July 1900, 'Abd al-Rahman al-Hut, one of the correspondents, pointed out that it is the husband's duty to prevent his wife from acting in any way that conflicts with the legal tradition. If he acquiesces to her wishes and allows her to appear in public in a provocative way, he thereby harms himself and sins before Allah. "A religious person with a sense of honor will not consent to such a situation." Relying on verses in the Qur'an, al-Hut defined a husband as a guardian and shepherd who is responsible for his family. His rights therefore are sanctified and must be protected from any harm. "Allah entrusted the matter of your wives to your hands only because He knows they are afflicted with feebleness of the mind and of determination when they struggle against lust," al-Hut explained. On the basis of a hadith attributed to 'Ali ibn Abi Talib, he warned that women must be prohibited from doing as they wish lest they cause devastation. Care must be taken that a woman who leaves the house does so only for an urgent reason and with the consent of her husband or father, and if possible in a carriage. She should cover her face and be dressed in plain, modest clothes that cover any jewelry, with her gaze downcast, avoiding the proximity of men. Another writer, taking a more aggressive stand, exhorted that a husband who has even a remnant of zeal for Islam must immediately rip up his wife's thin scarf and replace it with a thicker veil of pure silk.[81]

Makarim al-Akhlaq al-Islamiyya's frontal attack on the passivity of the husband in acceding to his wife's wishes constituted a veiled censure of the government for insufficiently clarifying the concept of personal freedom that it granted to its citizens or demarcating its boundaries. The public believed that this concept was self-evident and that people were free to do as they wished, the paper argued. It is therefore no surprise that "under the auspices of freedom, the woman abdicates submission to her husband and behaves as she pleases." The newspaper thus expressed its negative position regarding Western modernity generally, which in its view had caused the gender reality in the Nile Valley to become dissolute, with no moral restrictions.[82]

SUFISM

Sufism or Islamic mysticism, which by the twelfth century had developed into a broad social stratum (often referred to as orders or fraternities), faced periodic criticism throughout Islamic history. Viewing itself as the living spirit of the Muslim tradition, it emphasized the spiritual over the legal and closeness to rather than remoteness from Allah.[83] This mind-set resonated with the masses but evoked bitter criticism from certain me-dieval jurists,[84] who denounced such Sufi rites as extreme asceticism, the veneration of saints, and the *dhikr* ceremonies. Nevertheless, the anti-Sufi polemic, which emanated mainly from the puritanical Hanbali school, did not develop into a blanket condemnation of Sufism as such, attesting to the entrenched position of Sufi culture in Muslim society. Only in the late eighteenth century did it face unambiguous opposition, mounted by the neo-Hanbalist Wahhabiyya movement in the Arabian Peninsula. The Wahhabis' obsessive concern with guarding the unity of Allah precluded any compromise with Sufism and resulted in a campaign of destruction of the tombs and shrines of venerated Muslim saints.[85]

With the entrance of Muslim society into the modern era in the nine-teenth century, opposition to Sufism intensified. Modernization in the Middle East affected governmental and economic institutions as well as lifestyles and culture. It had a negative impact on the status of the Sufi orders (as on the orthodox establishment), especially in the large cities. State supervision of the activities of the orders was reinforced, and most of the orders were incorporated in an official hierarchical system headed by the Bakri family. Increasingly, entrenched Sufi beliefs and rituals that enriched the spiritual experience in Muslim life were viewed with disdain by both foreign and local observers.[86]

To many foreign observers, whether travelers or diplomats, Sufism reflected a backward culture that had no place in an era of enlightenment. It was also portrayed as a symptom of the more general phenomenon of superstition that dominated the East.[87] According to the nineteenth-century English traveler John Gadsby, "The Easterns are proverbially the most superstitious people in existence. With almost every event that takes place, every movement they make, every dream that occupies their thoughts in their beds, they connect some supernatural agency." In Gadsby's perception, superstition was far worse than political suppression or military despotism.[88]

The ideals of progress and enlightenment served as a moral weapon for the Islamic reformists in Cairo, as for their Salafi colleagues in Da-mascus, but were mainly used to counter Eurocentric criticism and reaf-firm the purity of Islam. The reformists promoted a polemical narrative that presented the Sufi orders as at best irrelevant to the processes of social change and at worst responsible for the backwardness of Muslim society.[89] This stance was especially prominent in the modernistic dis-course in Egypt, where the reformist polemic against Sufism intensified and spread during the last quarter of the nineteenth century. Its main spokesmen were Muhammad ʿAbduh, Husayn al-Marsafi, ʿAbdallah Nadim, Muhammad ʿUmar, ʿAbd al-ʿAziz Shawish, ʿAli Yusuf, and Rashid Rida—scholars and writers who had been affiliated with Sufism in their youth. Notably, they praised the Sufi concept as embodying the realm of ethics (ʿilm al-akhlaq), aimed at purifying the soul and nurturing the attributes of modesty, honesty, and patience. They acknowledged the important historic role played by the Sufi orders in spreading the Islamic faith. But they vehemently condemned the corrupt practices that, they argued, had contaminated Sufism over the centuries, such as exaggerated ecstasy, withdrawal from everyday affairs, the compulsive veneration of saints, and dhikr rituals involving obsessive shouting, singing, and dancing. These practices were denounced as "devil worship."[90]

The criticism of popular Islam and its ceremonies, labeled a deviation from the true faith, also had nationalist or proto-nationalist overtones. Such rituals were delegitimized for presenting Islam in a ridiculous light in the eyes of strangers and, moreover, for encouraging submissiveness and blocking any real attempt to face the challenges of modernity in the Muslim world. Religious reform was thus interwoven with the quest for national pride and viability.[91]

The reformist discourse regarding Sufi culture was shaped primarily by ʿAbduh in the official gazette al-Waqaʾiʿ al-Misriyya and in fatwas. His main focus was on the central theme of sainthood. ʿAbduh sought to refute the Sufi claim that the cult of saints, embodied mainly in the mawlid ceremonies, has dual immunity: religiously, in that the saintly attributes are passed from each shaykh to his successors, and historically, in that the cult was entrenched in local culture with the consent of prominent ʿulamaʾ and state officials. ʿAbduh argued, first, that sainthood is individual. Even if a particular miracle is accepted, it is confined to that saint alone. One of the characteristics of sainthood is that it cannot be imitated, inherited, or passed on. Otherwise it is a deception. Second, the legitimation of any custom must be based on its conformity with religious injunctions and not on its historical scope.[92]

Still, ʿAbduh avoided openly criticizing the ʿulamaʾ, the gatekeepers of the faith and of public morality, for failing to prohibit deviant Sufi practices. The importance of conducting an effective campaign against such rites compelled him to adopt a conciliatory attitude toward the silence of the ʿulamaʾ, who, he noted, were trapped between the ignorance of the masses and the tyranny of the rulers.[93]

ʿAbduh linked the deviant cult of saints to the decline of Muslim political and cultural viability in modern times. "Troubles did not reach us and distortion did not enter our home until Muslims began to conduct their religious life from the outset without delving into the authentic in religious law."[94] While sainthood constituted the main polemical focus of ʿAbduh and his disciples, it was not the sole issue. Other practices were also denounced, especially some related to the Saʿdiyya and Qadiriyya orders. In an article dated November 1880, ʿAbduh quoted a report sent by the supervising shaykh of the al-Husayn Mosque to the Ministry of Public Endowments, complaining that during the *dhikr* ceremonies conducted by Saʿdis every Thursday at the mosque the name of Allah was drowned out by their loud drumming. Repeated requests by the shaykh to the Saʿdiyya officials to end this custom were rejected. Similarly, ʿAbduh denounced the mingling of men and women, the ritual practices of eating snakes and broken glass, and self-flagellation with sharp implements.[95]

ʿAbduh's scriptural imperative for uprooting these practices was "forbidding wrong." This imperative, which, he explained, applies to the public space of Muslim society and requires moral action against religious misconduct, was central to his anti-Sufi polemic. It was the public space that provided the primary stage for the colorful Sufi ceremonies. In emphasizing the centrality of "forbidding wrong" in Islamic law, ʿAbduh urged the government to enforce its authority by whatever means necessary.[96] Ironically, this was the same injunction used by ʿAbduh's rivals, who in turn urged the government to protect public morality from the deviant views put forward by the reformists.

Sufi shaykhs, some of whom were affiliated with the Azhari community as lecturers and muftis and also took part in the ʿUrabi movement, were aware of the growing reformist criticism of the Sufi outlook and practices. They defended the Sufi ethos through a combination of ideological conviction, apologetics, and delegitimation of their critics. The tone was set by Muhammad ʿIllaysh, who was first and foremost a theologian and jurist and whose starting point was the *ʿilm* (revealed formalistic knowledge). Yet he also had a Sufi affinity, which he did not deny, expounding it in a series of fatwas and commentaries. As a devoted follower of Ibn ʿArabi, ʿIllaysh defended the doctrine of the unity of the universe, which joins Allah with creation (*wahdat al-wujud*), defining divine inspiration (*kashf*) and contact with the Prophet through dreams as authentic. He viewed seclusion (*khalwa*) as worthy (*mustahabba*) and even obligatory, in that it largely formed the basis for religious purity, spiritual striving, and the banishment of lust. He also sanctioned wearing the turban (*taj*) and the robe (*khirqa*) to mark the conclusion of the training of the follower, as firmly embedded in the Sunna.[97]

In ʿIllaysh's view, the issue regarding this style of dress did not merely involve a visual aspect but had religious, social, and organizational significance. It was the Prophet himself who wrapped a turban around the head of one of his friends and placed the flag of command in his hand to serve as a symbol to the people before going out to a war of jihad, in order to heighten the sense of unity, identity, and belonging in the camp of the believers. If the Prophet behaved thus, how can one criticize the Sufi orders, whose robes and flags are the symbol with which their followers identify, while eschewing any demonstrations of hostility toward other orders? Therefore, ʿIllaysh concluded, anyone who questions the practice of seclusion or the wearing of the *taj* and the *khirqa* is to be viewed as holding heretical and ignorant views and, in light of the harm he does to religion, must be forcibly educated.[98] In various fatwas ʿIllaysh confirmed popular beliefs closely identified with Sufism in regard to torture by fire undergone by deceased sinners in their graves, cautioning that anyone who denies this is a heretic destined to be severely tortured in hell.[99] Similarly, he gave credibility to the existence of prophets and martyrs who fell in battlefield but are alive in their graves, eating, drinking, praying, fasting, and making pilgrimages, and topics such as the fate of the soul of the departed, paradise and hell, and ghosts and devils.[100]

ʿIllaysh did advocate restraint regarding Sufi behavior, however, and sought to restrict its visible manifestations, thereby revealing his inherent conviction regarding the importance of avoiding exaggeration and extremism (*ghuluww*) in Sufism, alongside a desire to neutralize criticism of the movement and to position it in the mainstream Islamic tradition. In ʿIllaysh's view, esoteric knowledge does not replace formal legal knowledge but supplements it and is supported by it. Nonadherence to the Sunna and the shariʿa drains Sufism of its authentic content and turns it into fiction, he argued. "The further a scholar distances himself from the shariʿa, the weaker the light of his teachings," ʿIllaysh observed.[101] He ruled, accordingly, that the ability to see visions in dreams or to speak in the name of deceased saints through séances (*tahdir al-arwah*) is the province of those who possess the "perfect soul," with exceptional sanctity and divine inspiration (*al-karamat al-khariqa*). They are also the ones authorized to envision Allah, although no human image may be attributed to Him.[102] Anyone outside this group who claims to be able to envision Allah is a deviant who engages in witchcraft aimed at fulfilling earthly, material goals and will have no place in paradise.

ʿIllaysh was also careful to display reverence toward the Prophet. He denied the claim that the Prophet was no different from others in regard to his dreams: this assertion was ignorant and insulting, because the Prophet's dreams, like those of the prophets who preceded him, embodied the revelation of the Divine Presence itself.[103]

Addressing the subject of pilgrimages to the graves of saints (*ziyara*), ʿIllaysh stated explicitly that the practices of self-purification by anointment with oil and dust at these graves have no spiritual benefit or significance; rather, they are abominable fabrications (*ʿbida shaniʿa*). The true blessing (*baraka*) is to be found in pondering the acts of the saints and adopting them as an example and a model. ʿIllaysh acknowledged that other deviations were still practiced in his time, including circling around the grave of a saint, rubbing the monument, kissing it, and tying scarves or items of clothing to it with the aim of attaining *baraka*. He likened this to idol worship (*ʿibadat al-asnam*) during the pre-Islamic period in its empowerment and elevation of objects and structures. If this prohibition applies to the graves of saints, it is all the more applicable to the Kaʿba, the mosque, or the Qurʾan, he stated.[104]

Similarly, relying on the consensus of all the schools of religious law, ʿIllaysh condemned the practices of singing, playing drums and flutes, dancing, and clapping that had become part of the *dhikr* and *samaʿ* ceremonies. These practices, he said, do not reflect true Sufism and in fact endanger its very existence. Moreover, they constitute heresy or atheism (*zandaqa*) and *ʿibadat al-ʿijl* (calf worship), which lead the masses away from the path of Islam. All who believe in Allah and the next world are forbidden to take part in or be present at such practices, he warned. The state authorities, for their part, must perform their duty by preventing deviants from entering mosques and other sacred places.[105]

Prohibitions in the Sufi context were also specified by ʿIllaysh's son and successor as head of the ʿArabiyya Shadhiliyya order, ʿAbd al-Rahman, who ruled in a 1900 fatwa that the commandments of Islam were explicit and deviants were accursed. He defined the *dhikr* ceremony as authentic and fitting only if conducted according to the rules of the shariʿa. Ecstatic dancing, shouting, and vulgar talk were indecent innovations and conflicted with the path of Allah, whose essence is good manners and moral behavior. Those who exhibited such indecent behavior were crazed and accursed and deserved to be executed even if they repented.[106]

Other shaykhs of the period who likewise bridged scholarship and Sufism followed a course that balanced the revealed law (shariʿa) with esoteric truth (*haqiqa*). Such shaykhs included ʿAbd al-Hadi Naja al-Abyari, Hasan al-ʿIdwi, Muhammad al-Qayati, and Muhammad Khalil al-Hijrisi. They held that the path to knowing Allah consisted of both the shari‘a and the *haqiqa*. The shari‘a was analogous to a tree and the *haqiqa* to its fruit. Without devotion and adherence to the shari‘a, the *haqiqa* has no value. While glorifying the study of Sufism as "the kernel" (*al-lubb*) in striving for a strong love of Allah, these shaykhs denounced ignorant Sufis who degraded legal scholarship by mockingly describing it as "the husk" (*al-qishra*). Those who behave thus demean legal scholarship, al-Abyari ruled, and will not be spared from hell.

Al-Abyari and his colleagues thereby sanctified the principle of the unity of Allah, placing belief in the law before belief of the heart. They asserted that a person who boasts of his closeness to Allah and absolves himself from prayer or from shari‘a prohibitions such the one against drinking wine should be executed and doomed to eternal damnation. Executing such a person is preferable to the execution of a hundred heretics, for the damage he causes to religion and to its believers is greater.

These shaykhs also posited appropriate rules of conduct during visits to the graves of kinfolk or pilgrimages to the graves of saints (*adab al-ziyara*). Such rules required the believers to display dignity and awe, avoid raising their voices, and pray at length for the soul of the departed and for life and comfort in paradise—all this while facing in the direction of the *qibla*, with their backs to the grave. The rules were to be followed all the more punctiliously when making a pilgrimage to the Prophet's grave in Medina, al-‘Idwi emphasized: encircling the grave, kissing the monument, and such practices were forbidden, and the prayers in the mosque there must be recited in a hushed voice. Any violation of these rules would be judged as severely as adopting Christian practices and their icons.

Al-‘Idwi and his colleagues stressed that the believer's restrained behavior, in accordance with the commands of the shari‘a, does not lessen the importance of the *haqiqa*. On the contrary, they held, it was only by means of the *haqiqa*, depicted as the cream (*zibda*), that an enriched religious life, steadfast faith, and a high level of knowledge of Allah can be attained. The *haqiqa*, defined by al-Qayati as "the path of communication and knowledge" (*tariq al-wisal wa'l-ta‘aruf*), embodies basic principles such as empowerment through Allah (*taqwa*), seclusion (*halwa*), and fear of God (*wara’*). Al-Abyari, challenging critics of Sufism, argued that a generations-old consensus had coalesced in the ‘ulama’ community regarding the hidden world (*‘ilm al-batin*) and that any effort to present it as permitting what is forbidden, or forbidding what is permitted, is a reflection of ignorance. Al-Abyari quoted Abu Hamid al-Ghazali and even Ibn ‘Arabi, who defined esoteric knowledge as the study of infusing the heart with a holy spirit and placing this knowledge at the pinnacle of scholarship; its scholars had the strongest faith, the closest proximity to Allah, and the greatest expertise in His wisdom. Thus whoever claims that hidden knowledge contradicts revealed legal knowledge is closer to heresy than to belief.[107]

The umbrella of religious legal consensus acquired by Sufism extended as well to several of its specific components, especially the miraculous attributes of the shaykhs (*karamat al-awliya'*), both deceased and living. According to al-ʿIdwi and al-Hijrisi, the belief in saints was unequivocally obligatory; whoever questioned this was to be regarded as one of the "lowly and ignorant *muʿtazili*." Al-ʿIdwi pointed out that the religious training of the saints was deeply rooted in the Qurʾan, the Sunna, and the legal literature. Al-Hijrisi added that the saintly attributes of miracle making and healing remained part of the Jewish and Christian religions and should not therefore be denied in Islam, which is the superior religion and whose believers are the best of all peoples.[108] These and other spokesmen acquired the support of Shams al-Din al-Inbabi, the Shaykh al-Azhar in 1882–96, who had links to the Ahmadiyya order. He held that Sufism without the shariʿa was a delusion, while the shariʿa without Sufism was paralyzed. Using human anatomy as an analogy, al-Inbabi likened the shariʿa to the outer skin and the *haqiqa* to the hidden heart.[109]

The reformists, airing their views in local newspapers and in modern educational institutions such as Dar al-ʿUlum, mounted a comprehensive campaign to purify Islam from false innovations both in Sufism and in scholastic teachings. ʿAbduh attributed these false innovations to the methods adopted both by the Sufi orders and by the official ʿulamaʾ: the former sought Allah only in their heart, thereby becoming too emotional, while the latter sought Him in their books, thereby becoming too formalistic. ʿAbduh had great expectations of Muhammad al-ʿAbbasi al-Mahdi (the chief mufti of Egypt and Shaykh al-Azhar, d. 1897) and of ʿAbd al-Baqi al-Bakri (the head of the Sufi orders, d. 1891).[110] They were the leading religious figures in the Nile Valley and as such held the key to promoting the desired theological reforms. ʿAbduh was to be disappointed, however.

Al-Mahdi, a puritan and a moralist in matters of worship, did indeed denounce certain Sufi concepts and rituals as distorting Islam. In a fatwa dated 1876 he ruled that any person claiming to have knowledge of the hidden world who was followed with excessive zeal and who evoked public unrest should be subject to criminal sanctions determined by the ruler (*taʿzir*). In an 1880 fatwa al-Mahdi prohibited drumming, raised voices, and mingling between men and women in the mosque during the *dhikr* ceremonies.[111] This fatwa was praised by ʿAbduh, who presented it as a comprehensive prohibition of anything that distorted religion, whether within the mosque or beyond. The fatwa, he said, signified the victory of the army of the righteous over false and misleading brigades and cleared the way for a blessed movement that would spread outward from Cairo to the countryside.[112] In other religious matters on the reformist agenda, however, such as employing *ijtihad* more extensively, improving the social status of women and religious minorities, and promoting cultural rapprochement between Islam and the West, al-Mahdi's stance was more restrictive (see the discussion above).

ʿAbd al-Baqi al-Bakri provided even less cause for optimism. Although his ordinance of 1881, issued under pressure from Khedive Tawfiq, included various restrictions on Sufi public activity during religious festivals, the ultimate significance was that the ordinance simply enhanced his own status vis-à-vis the individual heads of the Sufi orders. Thereafter their administrative and judicial autonomy was eroded by al-Bakri's official representatives. As a result many Sufi shaykhs detached themselves from the formal Sufi system.[113] While al-Bakri was committed in principle to introducing reforms in Sufi culture, he ultimately did little that was substantive and thus could not be considered a reformist in the full sense of the word. One indication of his failure was ongoing reformist criticism of ongoing Sufi practices in the late nineteenth and early twentieth centuries, such as dancing, singing, drumming, self-flagellation, and ritual starvation. The reformist critics in this period were ʿAbduh's followers ʿAbdallah Nadim and Rashid Rida, while the target of their criticism was ʿAbd al-Baqi's successor, Muhammad Tawfiq al-Bakri (d. 1932).

Nadim's and Rida's criticism of Sufism was sharper than ʿAbduh's, reflecting mounting frustration with the indecisive stance of the al-Bakri dynasty. In Rida's biting words, "When the head of the household beats a drum, it is no surprise that the young ones in the house dance."[114] Nadim cited examples from the past as evidence of Sufi conduct that was more restrained. He argued that the writings of earlier Sufis, some of whom were commemorated by orders named after them (such as ʿAbd al-Qadir al-Jilani and ʿAbd al-ʿAziz al-Dabbagh), revealed that they attributed great importance to scholastic legal teaching and warned against neglecting it. Nadim, who was the orator of the proto-national ʿUrabi movement, also emphasized the damage to the image of the Egyptian nation caused by Sufi excesses. Their religious deviations, he charged, provided foreign observers with ammunition to ridicule Islam. These observers depicted

Sufi ceremonies as shows, carnivals, and foolery. As a consequence, the Egyptian nation was perceived as an irrational and backward society. Commenting sarcastically on the growing number of *mawlid*s in Egypt, Nadim observed that "while the Europeans have a carnival each year, we have a carnival each day."[115]

Nadim's colleague Rida, who at the beginning of the twentieth century was influenced by the puritanical Hanbali doctrine, devoted many of his fatwas and articles in the Salafi newspaper *al-Manar* (Minaret) to an attack on the Sufi mind-set. He compared the Sufis to the Shiʿis as advocates of exaggeration (*ghuluww*) in that they attributed supernatural powers to their leaders, obeying them unquestioningly. He also charged that by focusing on the inner meaning of Qurʾanic verses and by delving too deeply into their hidden philosophic aspects the Sufis distorted the plain meaning of the Qurʾan. In Rida's view, in bringing people together from all parts of the country, the various *mawlid*s did offer material and cultural benefits for the Muslim community, but the negative aspects of these festivals outweighed the positive ones. The tomb of each saint, he charged, had become a kind of second Kaʿba, with the saint's status elevated to that of the Prophet. All this, he emphasized, took place under state patronage and with state funding. Furthermore, Rida pointed out, some of the prominent scholars to whom *mawlid*s were dedicated, such as al-Shafiʿi (d. 820) and al-Ghazali (d. 1111), were important defenders of the Sunna and critics of deviant innovations. Al-Shafiʿi, for example, divided the night into three equal parts: for study, for worship, and for sleep: the first two parts were devoted to the other world, and the last to the believer's health. In Rida's view, this division was far worthier than spending the night dancing and chanting.[116]

Muhammad Tawfiq al-Bakri, whom Nadim and Rida charged with responsibility for this situation, sought to neutralize these attacks by publicly emphasizing the importance of formal religious knowledge, the enforcement of public morality, and restrained Sufi activity. But he continued to laud the positive role played by the Sufi orders in spreading Islam and retaining its viability, a role also acknowledged by European observers in their writings. For al-Bakri, the contemporary importance of Sufism was equal to that of the first Muslim conquests in the seventh century, especially in the spread of Islam's influence in Africa, China, India, and Central Asia.[117]

Nadim's and Rida's disappointment with al-Bakri's halfhearted efforts to reform Sufi culture was accompanied by sharp attacks against the ʿulamaʾ who, by their silence concerning deviant religious rituals, acquiesced to the practices of the Sufi orders in misleading the people. Nevertheless, like ʿAbduh, Nadim and Rida were careful not to go too far in denouncing either the Bakri family or the ʿulamaʾ, being aware of their prestigious status in Egyptian society. Rather, both writers recommended various measures to prevent deviant practices. Nadim suggested assigning the public the role of watchdog of religious morality: anyone who heard heretical statements or witnessed deviations in the Sufi community could report them to Shaykh al-Bakri so that those responsible would be punished. Nadim also offered his satirical journal, *al-Ustadh* (The Master), as a platform for exposing deviations from Islam. Clearly, Nadim sought to expose al-Bakri to public pressure in order to impel him to fulfill his commitment to Sufi reform, embodied in official ordinances that he issued in 1895 and 1905.[118]

Rida's suggestions, by contrast, were more practical. He recommended enforcing the rule of law, tightening government supervision over the *mawlid*s, and forming a committee headed by the grand mufti and shaykh al-Azhar to monitor the mosque network, including posting guards at mosque entrances. Still, Rida pointed out, in the long run the major reform had to be enacted through preaching and through guidance of the Sufi orders and the public regarding the authentic essence of Sufism.[119]

Ultimately, promoting genuine reform in Sufism depended on the goodwill of both the state authorities and the Sufi shaykhs. From the state's point of view, interaction with the masses, especially in light of the ongoing struggle for independence from the British occupation, required a sustained display of tolerance toward Sufism and its customs. Notably, the political parties, attempting to gain public support, formed alliances with various Sufi orders, often helping them attain state recognition.[120] Sufi shaykhs, for their part, faced with the emergence of new nationalist and Islamist elements who expropriated their social and intellectual functions, were anxious to protect their moral authority in society and obstruct the path of advocates of religious reform in Egypt.[121]

SUMMARY

The debate between reformists and conservatives over issues such as *ijtihad* vs. *taqlid*, non-Muslims, women, and Sufism was intertwined with rivalry over recognition as the sole arbiter of faith and cultural orientation in society. The two camps based their arguments on a different reading of the sacred texts, thereby reflecting the diverse nature of Islamic discourse and its close interaction with the exigencies of reality. The tone of the debate, however, was set by the conservative-oriented ʿulamaʾ, reflecting the reaction of an Islamic system threatened by Western encroachment. Some of these ʿulamaʾ were political dissidents in their advocacy of the ʿUrabi cause, while most of the others were quietists, acknowledging the legitimate authority of the khedival regime.

Both dissident and quietist ʿulamaʾ displayed resilience in social and moral matters. Their ideological compass was the Qurʾanic imperative "forbidding wrong" with regard to defending the faith against religious skepticism, preventing immoral conduct, and protecting Muslims from the possibility of domination or humiliation by non-Muslims.[122] This imperative related first and foremost to the public space in Muslim society and was addressed mainly to those in authority: religious scholars and state officials.

It was the renowned medieval scholar al-Ghazali who highlighted the importance of "forbidding wrong," as follows:

> It is the most prominent pillar of religion and the most important thing that Allah revealed to all the Prophets. If its tenets are eliminated and its ordinances ignored, then revelation will cease; darkness will cover the era; confusion, ignorance, and corruption will spread; the country will be ruined; worship will perish; and the people will not know such a loss of direction except on doomsday.... The person who strives to correct this weakness and remove these defects is to be considered a renewer [*mujaddid*] of the Sunna.[123]

Al-Ghazali explained that preventing Muslims from doing wrong means supervising or controlling them.[124] He went so far as to sanction the formation of armed bands to enforce the duty of forbidding wrong, even without the permission of the ruler—a ruling that evoked reservations. Many other aspects of al-Ghazali's commentary on forbidding wrong, however, including his legal stance on excluding non-Muslims from performing this duty (thereby restricting their sociopolitical integration), were cited affirmatively by various scholars of his time and thereafter.[125]

Azharis' normative rulings embodied mainly in fatwas and tracts on judicial, sectarian, gender, and Sufi issues revealed an assertive state of mind in encountering a changing sociopolitical reality. Viewed from a historical perspective, these rulings and tracts mostly failed to dictate the agenda of the political elite or even the actual behavior of society. Fatwas were part of an Islamic legal discourse that was on the defensive, marginalized in the wake of state building and the reshaping of the collective identity based on modern Western premises of progress, nationalism, and legal citizenship. In this context, for example, former *dhimmi*s became formal citizens, while women eventually gained access to education and entry into social and professional life. Azhari dissent on these loaded issues, however, triggered a contentious Egyptian discourse and placed obstacles in the way of the reformist-national agenda to establish a more inclusive political community.[126]

Thus, contrary to Bernard Lewis's observation in 1973, theology was not viewed as "old-fashioned and irrelevant"; nor had the ʿulamaʾ "lost touch with the people" in the face of Westernization.[127] Rather, the ʿulamaʾ continued to play a significant role in transmitting and disseminating the communal memory, although they were forced to contend with the "new priesthood," to use Anthony Smith's phrase: the growing stratum of the professional intelligentsia, nurtured by secular learning and committed to rational, critical discourse.[128]

7   Al-Azhar and the Egyptian Nation-State

Egypt's contentious encounter with the West, marked by confrontation and challenge that led to the ʿUrabi revolt, culminated in the British conquest in 1882. Typical of their colonial style of rule, the British refrained from comprehensive reform in local society, with the exception of the economic and administrative realms essential to stabilize the functioning of the Egyptian polity. Underlying this rule, however, was a Victorian and ethnocentric outlook that viewed Muslim culture patronizingly. Lord Cromer, the British consul general in Cairo (1883–1906) who exerted a formative influence on the Anglo-Egyptian relationship and was known as the "molder of modern Egypt," did not conceal his aversion to Islam. He defined it as an intolerant, repressive, and hypocritical political and social system, blindly obeyed by its subjects and constituting an obstacle to reform. In his view, "the true Easterner is a loyal conservative," an attribute that in his mind precluded any possibility of a substantive change in values or lifestyle.[1]

Cromer's skeptical and disapproving attitude, reflected above all in a meager budgetary allocation for the development of the education system, largely determined the nonintervention of the British administration in local religious affairs. This played into the hands of al-Azhar, which boasted that "freedom of religion and its independence from foreign influence have become an embedded foundation and a sanctified value in the souls of the Egyptians."[2] British policy thus had the effect of nurturing the survivability of that venerable institution and actually encumbering reformist efforts initiated at the close of the nineteenth and beginning of the twentieth centuries by the mufti of Egypt, Muhammad ʿAbduh, who developed cordial relations with the British. The negative image of ʿAbduh in the halls of al-Azhar as undermining the foundations of the faith and as an agent of the British branded him as a dissident reformer.[3] A telling indicator of reformist frustration was the ongoing disputation carried on by ʿAbduh and his followers, most prominently Rashid Rida, against the rigidity of the Azharis, who "removed themselves from the spirit of the times" and dealt with politics more than with religion.[4] British indifference to the realms of culture and society also constituted an obstacle for advocates of liberal nationalism embraced by the Umma Party, under the leadership of Ahmad Lutfi al-Sayyid, who aimed to establish an Egyptian collective identity based on its distinctive geography (the Nile Valley) and culture (the Pharaonic heritage) while excluding religion from the public space.[5]

Al-Azhar ultimately gained the upper hand in its struggle against Islamic modernism and liberal nationalism, but the debate over the status of religion and its official spokesmen in the Egyptian state continued and intensified at the start of the twentieth century.

While the medium of pure politics was not the strong suit of the reformist trend in advancing its agenda for change, the print medium was. Print organs with a direct or indirect link to the reformist circle led by Jamal al-Din al-Afghani and Muhammad ʿAbduh were numerous, espousing the goal of challenging public opinion and putting pressure on decision makers. The ideology of "publicness," in Michael Gasper's depiction, was the primary vehicle used to bring the reformist issue to the attention of the public.[6] The reformists' main accusation was aimed at the rigidity of the ʿulamaʾ. They demanded the rejuvenation of Islamic thought by adopting a broad approach to the concept of knowledge as including all the types of knowledge that could be useful in helping revitalize the community. Prominent newspapers in this effort were *al-Ustadh,* edited by ʿAbdallah Nadim; *al-Manar,* edited by Rashid Rida; and *al-Muʾayyad* (Victorious), edited by ʿAli Yusuf. By contrast, the strength of their Azhari rivals lay mainly in the polemical and institutional infrastructure at their disposal, including an annual governmental budget that grew over the years as well as access and ties to the elite circles, especially in the khedival court.[7] As shown in preceding chapters, they did not neglect the journalistic arena. Although an official al-Azhar organ appeared only in 1931, ʿulamaʾ made their opinions known in the extant press, both Islamic and general.[8]

A review of the Islamic organs reveals that Azhari scholars did not adhere to a strategy of "opposition and withdrawal," attributed to them by various researchers.[9] Furthermore, they were not necessarily conservative in every area or issue: the boundaries separating them from the reformists were neither sharply defined nor systematic. They were also attentive to events in the wider Arab-Muslim world and found common ground with ʿulamaʾ in other places who, despite different sociopolitical contexts and specific cultures, shared the acute experience of a crisis in the Islamic world. In this sense, an "intellectual village" may be said to have existed, in which ʿulamaʾ from various geographical locations discussed and elucidated issues revolving around the charged encounter between tradition and modernity and ways of resolving it. Such encounters also touched on their own functioning and how they dealt with the challenge posed by other cultural agents. This was reflected within al-Azhar itself, where an internal debate, sometimes piercing, was conducted over the management of the institution and the role of its members in society.

Some Azharis expressed disappointment with the passive image of the conformist ʿalim, positing instead an activist ʿalim uncloistered in an academic ivory tower and constituting a presence in the public space. For example, Muhammad al-Ahmadi al-Zawahiri, later shaykh al-Azhar (1929–35), who showered the ʿulamaʾ with an assortment of complimentary attributes (kings of Islam, successors of the prophets, ministers of the state, princes) in *al-ʿIlm waʾl-ʿulamaʾ* (1904), nevertheless cautioned:

> The role of the ʿulamaʾ is not limited to teaching students religious sciences in madrasas as occurs at present. Their role is more important, comprehensive, and productive and relates to all realms of endeavor. It is tied to the affairs of this world and the next world, for the ʿalim is the one who lays the groundwork for the principles by which man conducts himself and runs his daily life. The ʿalim also formulates the guidelines by which the nation conducts its material, cultural, and other affairs.... It is the ʿalim who should lead the way to spiritual happiness, mental enhancement, and the secrets of legislation and encourage perfection of attributes and deeds and dedication to the worship of Allah. It is the ʿalim who should show the way to the benefits of traveling around the world, borrowing from contemporary cultures, exploring Europe, and attending medical and professional academic schools.[10]

Other Azharis were less critical and more apologetic in lauding their historic and contemporary functioning, especially as "the heirs of the prophets" by virtue of their adherence to the prohibition of "forbidding wrong" and their determined stand against political tyranny.[11] Thus ʿulamaʾ responded to a changing social reality, ranging from constructive criticism to justification, and fashioned ways of adjusting to it.

RESTORING THE MORAL COMMUNITY

The encounter of Azharis and other ʿulamaʾ in the Arab Middle East with modernity was less traumatic than has been gauged by some observers, especially in the realm of judicial legislation. Throughout Muslim history the ʿulamaʾ had adjusted to legislation by rulers and proceedings by non-shariʿa courts. Such accommodation was perceived as part of *siyasa* (public policy), a realm supplementing that of the shariʿa, in which the state is free to legislate and to formulate its policy so long as this does not violate the instructions of the shariʿa. As Ron Shaham has shown, modern developments therefore did not necessarily constitute a total disconnect from the past; they also included elements of continuity.[12]

Moreover, some of the reformist programs initiated by the political elites were consolidated through a process of debate within ʿulamaʾ circles, thereby ensuring a measure of control over their implementation that would prevent radical deviation from religious norms. When state reform policy or the public discourse of liberal-nationalist circles strayed from matters of public law to matters of ritual, education, the laws of personal status, and public morality, however, the ʿulamaʾ reacted assertively through protest and opposition. Such issues essentially touched on the moral image of the community. The consistent assertiveness of the ʿulamaʾ in this area thus cannot be attributed solely to sectoral or material considerations (namely, a desire to retain social status and economic power), as, for example, Crecelius claimed in the case of Egypt.[13]

Clearly, modernization was perceived by the Egyptian ʿulamaʾ as destructive not only to their status but to the status of the faith as a whole. In the Islamic perception, the existence of a morally healthy and committed community is an a priori condition for the preservation of the faith from corruption. Humans beings are sociable creatures, prone to a complex of urges and appetites that must be forcibly controlled by the state and the law. Obedience to the law is a social imperative and a guarantee of the preservation of collective order as well as constituting a metaphysical act of faith that satisfies the will of Allah, the supreme legislator on earth. It was not for naught that jurists granted the ruler—even a tyrannical ruler—immunity from deposition or rebellion so long as he enforced the religious commandments. The ultimate aim was to prevent social anarchy. Thus an ideological raison d'être impelled the Azharis to reinforce the moral fabric of society in order to guarantee that society would conduct itself according to the commandments of Allah. Achievements in this realm, of course, could also preserve the status of the religious establishment.

Indeed, a survey of Islamic periodicals linked to the Azhari discourse published in the late nineteenth and early twentieth centuries shows a pronounced focus on the ratification and clarification of religious and moral obligations (especially those dealing with the public space), reflecting concern and determination to halt the exposure of local society to the secular Western ethical code. The repeated use of pejorative phraseology such as "conspiracy," "granting patronage to Christian cultural activity," and "brainwashing local Muslims" reveals a religious world acutely on the defensive against well-endowed rivals seeking to "extinguish the light of Allah" and "erase Islam" from the face of the earth, reviving the historic memory of the twelfth-century Crusades.[14]

While recognizing the need for religious and educational reform,[15] the Islamic press sought to channel it to restoring Islamic ethics rather than compromising with them. Two periodicals are relevant in this context, although they have received little attention in the research literature on the dispute over the status of religion in the Egyptian state during the period under discussion. The first is *Makarim al-Akhlaq al-Islamiyya* (1900–?), founded by the Society for Islamic Values, whose first secretary general was Shaykh ʿAbd al-Wahhab al-Najjar. Its members included a large number of ʿulamaʾ and dignitaries, some of them serving as officials in the Ministry of Endowments. This affiliation exemplified the blend of communal and journalistic activity by some Azharis. The second periodical was *al-Islam* (1894–1913), edited by Ahmad al-Shadhili al-Azhari, an Azhari scholar.

In its very first issue (in January 1900) *Makarim al-Akhlaq al-Islamiyya* raised the alarm concerning the moral decline of the Muslim community in light of the encounter with modernity as a clamorous antithesis to its sublime historic past:

> In the past, the hearts of the believers were pure, brothers clasping each other's hand, friends assisting one another, heroes displaying mercy, soulmates closely tied, distancing themselves from evil, turning away from the nonfulfillment of religious injunctions, avoiding disputes, observing women's morality, recoiling from profanity…eschewing any possibility of wine running like water, neglect of prayer, removal of the veil, gossip in encounters, spoken vulgarities or lecherous glances at a woman. Taking interest was forbidden, gambling was beyond the pale, and the *hudud* [Qurʾanic punishments] were imposed....
>
> Indeed, Islam was upheld by its believers, who viewed death for the sake of elevating the word of Allah as a sublime and profitable act and the

partial fulfillment of the religious commandments as a betrayal of Allah,
the Prophet, and the community of believers.... Islam flourished when its
commandments were observed and faith was the law of the nation, the
primary source.... However, the current reality stands in sharp contrast to
Islamic teachings, and yet we endorse it: drinking wine, fornicating, neglecting prayer, taking interest, going bankrupt by gambling, surrendering
to lust and corruption, abandoning the Qurʾan, emulating other cultures,
distorting education, encouraging permissiveness in women, holding the
ʿulamaʾ in contempt, and imitating the West. We have violated every commandment of religious law and permitted all that it prohibited. The house
of the judge and the house of prayer have remained standing, but both are
on the verge of expiring.[16]

The contrast between the sublime past and the gloomy present not only
leads to nostalgia and remorse, the newspaper pointed out, but also constitutes an incentive to take action and correct the distortion that has reduced religion to an empty shell without content or essence. This is all
the more so in Egypt, the ancient dwelling place of the Prophet's family,
the reservoir of age-old knowledge, the hothouse that nurtures religious
figures zealous in their belief, and, no less important, the beloved and precious homeland. This country, now overshadowed by a corrupting occupation and waves of Westernization, has passed from an "Islamic phase"
to a "Western phase," with the attendant range of negative manifestations
in the private and especially the public space.[17]

The deputy secretary of the Society for Islamic Values, Muhammad
Rushdi, pointed out in a lengthy article that a group of the righteous
(taʾifat al-salihin) still guards the flame. In preserving the image of Islam,
however, they are forced to contend with other groups: the common
people (taʾifat al-ʿawamm), who are unenlightened and fulfill only a few
of the religious obligations or neglect religion entirely; and the Westernizers (taʾifat al-mutafarnijin), who view observance of the Islamic faith as
shameful and the shariʿa as a disgrace and an antithesis to progress, while
disparaging the ʿulamaʾ before strangers. Rushdi found it ironic that the
Westernizers are educated but so locked into their viewpoint that conducting a rational discussion with them is impossible.[18]

What is the root of this evil, the newspaper asked. Its reply was the neglect of the Qurʾanic obligation to "forbid wrong," which is one of the pillars of the faith, the most elevated form of jihad, and the code that guides
the behavior of the believer in this world. It implies the moral superiority
of Islam over other cultures, which is the secret of its success. In the words

of the verse: "You are the best nation ever brought forth to men, bidding to honour, and forbidding dishonour, and believing in God" (3:110). No wonder that both subjects and rulers have shown reverence for this imperative and that it has served as a barrier to political tyranny. The non-enforcement of the imperative in previous centuries, however, and even more so in the present era, is the primary cause of arousing Allah's wrath and has left Muslims confused and backward.[19]

Although *Makarim al-Akhlaq al-Islamiyya* emphasized its apolitical character and an absence of affiliation with any particular party, it did not conceal its frustration with the government's conduct in regard to reinforcing the religious foundations of the Egyptian state. The state is tasked with implementing the obligation to "forbid wrong" by means of its educational, judicial, and enforcement systems. The government and the nation are linked to each other, the paper pointed out, but the absence of determination and activism on the part of the government has exacerbated the degenerative situation of the nation, obligating bodies such as the Society for Islamic Values to enter the picture.[20]

This diagnosis dictates the prognosis, which is in the hands of Muslims alone and is not a metaphysical force, the paper concluded, quoting the Qur'anic verse "Allah will not change a thing in His nation until it brings about change itself" (13:11). The Muslims' urgent task, the paper stressed, is to confront the European corruption of society with the weapon of religious activism, for those who hesitate to defend their religion are heretics.[21]

Makarim al-Akhlaq al-Islamiyya gave special emphasis to the pedagogic importance of holidays and festivals—sanctified times distinct from everyday life when people rest from their daily burdens and make time for family, social ties, acts of charity, and reflection. These are the times to heighten religious fervor through sermons in the mosques and marketplaces, to warn against sinfulness, and to plant new faith in the people's hearts.[22] The paper also published sermons delivered in mosques and devoted a column to fatwas for religious guidance.

Some of the fatwas dealt with specific issues in a broader perspective, aimed at promoting a purifying agenda. In answering a question about whether it is permissible to listen to Qur'anic verses read by a woman, the paper quoted a fatwa replying in the affirmative but used the opportunity to express aversion to the freedom gained by women in modern times. For example, when a man hears a woman's voice he immediately desires her and feels a temptation to stroke her body. When from afar a man identifies a woman walking in the street, with her shoulders and hips swaying,

he quickens his step to reach her. When a man arrives at his friend's home
and hears a soft voice and bracelets jangling, he glances in that direction
and his ears perk up, the paper wrote.[23] A specific question about the
meaning of sinfulness or moral depravity (*fisq*) elicited a broad reply in
another fatwa that spanned the gamut of manifestations, constituting a
"plague" (*blaaʾ*) that has swept over Muslim society, including adultery,
drinking wine, and gambling.[24] Other fatwas forbade the use of modern
technical equipment for religious rituals, such as a phonograph for listening to Qurʾanic verses, to avoid cheapening Allah's words and turning
the Qurʾan into a music box to be found in the marketplaces or used as
entertainment for the young in private houses. Displaying the likeness of
animals or of any living figures is defined as idol worship, which is punished by mortification in hell.[25]

Through fatwas, printed sermons, and letters to the editor the paper
in effect maintained a lively dialogue with its readers and managed to
elicit positive feedback from them regarding religious activity in various
parts of Egypt that could instill a sense of optimism and hope that re-
demption was at hand.[26]

The paper defined restoring a moral society as a complex pedagogical
project that must be placed entirely in the hands of the ʿulamaʾ (despite
historic blemishes in the conduct of some), in light of their expertise in
the religious sources and their moral authority. The paper commended
these jurists and scholars as "the people of the resurrection" (*ahl al-
nahda*), thereby censuring the polarization in the Islamic discourse and
the ignorant pretension of the intelligentsia in pressing for the unmediated interpretation of the scriptures. The layman, in the words of the
paper,

> bursts into a reading of a long or short theological text, which he learns by
> heart without understanding any of its content, like a parrot. He spends
> a great deal of time studying it, but without benefit. And if he is lucky
> and he learns this with the commentaries in the margins of the page, he
> will be confounded and confused by the complexity of the explanations,
> introductions, results, and terminology.... The truth is, he does not see
> the fruit of his efforts and is "as the likeness of an ass carrying books."
> [Qurʾan 62:5][27]

Makarim al-Akhlaq al-Islamiyya also demanded that reformist newspaper editors halt their unbridled attacks against the ʿulamaʾ and their
rulings. There is nothing wrong with criticizing the ʿulamaʾ, the paper

explained, but this must be done with dignity and good intentions, as is the practice toward priests in Christian Europe. Ultimately the ʿulamaʾ are the successors to the prophets, and the nation's link with them is in effect the link with religion itself.[28]

The issue of rejuvenating religious morality was also a primary concern of the periodical *al-Islam,* edited by Shaykh Ahmad al-Shadhili al-Azhari, which first appeared in 1894. In the view of the paper, virtue is the most qualitative moral value and best expresses the purpose of humankind. A virtuous person is someone who utilizes the human potential granted by Allah to the fullest and develops immunity to passions and lust. Doing good deeds is not only a guarantee against hell in the next world but also a qualitative formula for a life of harmony and kinship among believers in this world. Guided by this concept, the paper emphasized the importance of carrying out ritual injunctions such as prayer, fasting, and pilgrimage and enumerated a list of good as well as bad attributes.[29] Good attributes include sincerity (*sidq*), justness (*ʿadl*), integrity (*birr*), purity of spirit (*taharat al-nafs*), discretion (*kitman al-sir*), modesty (*tawaduʾ*), and loyalty (*wafaʾ*). Bad elements include gambling (*maysir*), lying (*kizb*), jealousy (*hasad*), hypocrisy (*riyaʾ*), exploitation (*jawr*), slander (*ghiba*), haughtiness (*kubr*), bragging (*fakhr*), and betrayal (*ghadr*). A person's transition from one category to the other represents a decline from loftiness to baseness or vice versa.[30]

This emphasis on the distinction between good and bad or between worthy and invalid reflected a growing anxiety about the fate of the Islamic faith and an impetus to stop its further erosion:

> A nation that worships idols and has no faith is like someone who is drowning in the sea, buffeted at one time by strong waves and at another time thrown against rocks helplessly. In either case he has no chance of survival. This nation also resembles a blind she-camel stumbling about in complete darkness and most probably finding death.... Such a nation deserves contempt and mockery since it has no divine law, no divine order to guide it toward truth and away from falsehood. In the words of Allah, its people "are but as the cattle; nay, they are further astray from the way" [Qurʾan 25:44].[31]

The growing apprehension regarding the fate of Islam evoked heightened censure aimed primarily at the Westernized sector of society. In the name of rationalism this sector had abandoned religion entirely, according to *al-Islam,* in the mistaken belief that religion was backward and propagated this message to the local population and to foreigners alike. While the paper recognized the importance of rational thinking as differentiating humans from beasts, it sought to place metaphysical limits on it. Accordingly, it created a distinction between science (ʿilm), which is universal and aims to enhance human welfare, and culture (thaqafa), which is unique to each nation. In the case of Muslims, Islam constitutes the foundation of their culture. Nevertheless, taking part in the internal discourse in the ʿulamaʾ community, the paper also criticized the Azhari establishment. Some of whose members, it charged, forbade the study of modern sciences or Western languages a priori, although these could assist in improving the position of the nation.[32] Anti-Sufi criticism also appeared in al-Islam, but it was more subdued. The paper urged Shaykh al-Baqi al-Bakri, head of the Sufi orders, to guide the common people on the path of righteousness and to recognize only those Sufi shaykhs who adhered to the Qurʾan and the Sunna, showed integrity, and were capable of imparting proper religious guidance.[33]

Alongside its religious concern with the erosion of faith, al-Islam also reflected political anxiety over the crumbling of the community of believers, as exemplified by the Ottoman Empire itself. The periodical referred to the weakening of the empire's power, reflected in the French conquest of Algeria (1881) and the British conquest of Egypt (1882), which had become permanent facts by then; the encroaching European colonialism, which expanded to include the Italian conquest of Libya in 1911; and the anti-Ottoman rebellions in the Balkans in 1913. These events exacerbated the sense of crisis in the Islamic discourse community, as seen in al-Islam.

In contrast to Makarim al-Akhlaq al-Islamiyya, which declared itself to be apolitical and devoted itself to preaching and education, al-Islam went a step further. It dealt with the political sphere, connecting the religious breakdown to the political one: the government's abandonment of Islamic values. As its issue of October 1911 observed, "The Muslims became factionalized and abandoned the instructions of religion and therefore declined from their greatness and lordliness to lowliness, from superiority to inferiority, from power to weakness."[34] In this vein the paper decried the failure of Muslim rulers such as those in Morocco and Afghanistan to support the Ottoman sultan during the war with Italy. It also censured the political parties in Egypt, especially the National Party and the Umma Party, for failing to put aside their rivalry in order to unite in support of the Ottoman state. This concern was voiced again a year later, during the events in the Balkans. In al-Islam's view, dynastic interests, power struggles, and personal considerations outweighed religious considerations and sapped the resilience of the Muslims in facing their European rivals.[35]

While the Italian conquest of Libya revealed the internal feebleness of the Muslim nation, it also exposed the ugly, predatory character of Christian Europe in its blatant attempt to wipe out the Ottoman Empire, *al-Islam* declared. It charged that this attempt was intertwined with intensive missionary activity throughout the Middle East, especially by Britain and Ireland, under the guise of establishing educational institutions and hospitals.[36] In light of these acute circumstances, the paper exhorted, every believer has a duty to assist the Sublime Porte to the extent possible, including choosing death over life for the sake of preserving the Muslim community and its rights, for "life in the shadow of humiliation and misery is analogous to death." This duty is nurtured primarily by the religious bond, which is deeply implanted in the hearts of believers and overshadows other identities--territorial, ethnic, or linguistic.[37]

The paper was effusive in its praise for the Ottoman Empire, pointing out that Islam had reached the pinnacle of its geographic expansion and its cultural blossoming there and under its patronage Muslims acquired protection and prosperity, while non-Muslims enjoyed tolerance and justice. The empire therefore merited vigorous recruitment by its subjects. "Without the Ottoman Empire, Muslims will be left with no state," the paper warned.[38]

The appeal for the defense of Istanbul reflected the importance of the pan-Islamic identity in the discourse of the Azharis, although a place of honor was always reserved for the local Egyptian element. This last aspect was reinforced with the loss of Ottoman identity in the wake of the events of World War I.

AL-AZHAR AND THE 1919 REVOLT

The end of World War I in 1918, which also brought about the end of the Ottoman Empire, marked the beginning of a new, more accelerated stage in the process of Egypt's national coalescence. A watershed event in this context was the anti-British revolt in 1919, under the leadership of Sa'd Zaghlul and the Wafd Party, which led to the establishment of a constitutional monarchy in 1923.[39]

The influence of al-Azhar on Egyptian politics at that time and on Egypt's relations with the British occupation was minimal. In contrast to the central role played by the 'ulama' in the leadership of urban protests during the Mamluk and Ottoman periods and their active participation in the anticolonialist opposition during the French conquest and the ʿUrabi rebellion, the ʿulamaʾ no longer served as primary spokesmen in the events of the 1919 revolt. They were unrepresented in the political leadership of the independence movement, which consisted of various sectors of the Westernized elite: landowners, members of the professions (especially lawyers), bureaucrats, and journalists. The changed composition of the country's leadership also dictated a changed ideological outlook, which was more concertedly nationalistic in light of the collapse of the Ottoman state and the entrenchment of the British occupation. This shift may explain the greater presence of Copts in the events of the revolt. Moreover, modernization also produced new patterns of protest in the cities. The mosque as the focal point of assembly was replaced by high schools, colleges, and factories, where protest activity was collective and organized and included strikes and boycotts.[40]

These developments clearly resulted in an additional erosion of the status of the Azharis, whose role in guiding the revolt and molding its political aims became secondary. They did not replicate their leadership position that had been so evident during the French conquest, as ʿAbd al-Rahman al-Rafiʿi points out.[41] Nevertheless, their contribution in instilling a religious element in the rhetoric of resistance to the British occupation, and in turning this into an important resource in the mobilization of the masses, should not be ignored.

The religious symbolism of the revolt and the role played in it by Azharis were also affirmed in the memoirs of Islamists who were al-Azhar rivals, especially Hasan al-Banna (d. 1949), the founder of the Muslim Brotherhood, and Sayyid Qutb (d. 1966), the ideologist of Sunni radicalism. As a child of thirteen during the events of the revolt, al-Banna had been struck by the stream of demonstrations and riots, bearing slogans such as "Love of the homeland from faith," "The spirit of Allah will guide us," and "If not independence, then paradise." Qutb, a child in the same period, praised the fiery sermons delivered in mosques and schools in support of the rebellion, embedding it in the hearts of adults and children alike.[42]

Indeed, al-Azhar served as one of the meeting points of the revolutionaries, and its community (both scholars and students) was to be found in the first ranks of the riots against the British in the streets of Cairo, Alexandria, and the provincial cities. Azharis also led fellahin riots in village communities such as in the Southern Delta and the Bani Suwaif regions. Sermons in the mosques were widely attended, and the

homes of prominent ʿulamaʾ served as meeting places, venues for decision making, and pilgrimage sites for students and demonstrators. These
ʿulamaʾ, some of whom were arrested several times and placed in deten-
tion camps, included Mahmud ʿAbu al-ʿUyun, Muhammad Yussuf, ʿAbd
Rabbihi Muftah, ʿAli Surur al-Zankaluni, ʿAbd al-Baqi Surur, Mustafa
al-Qayati, and Muhammad ʿAbd al-Latif Daraz.[43] Al-Qayati and Daraz
were given considerable attention in biographical dictionaries and in essays by the well-known Egyptian historian al-Rahman al-Rafiʿi. They are
described in these sources as playing an active role in the Egyptian nationalist movement from its beginnings and as being among the senior
Azharis who took part in the 1919 revolt. This involvement also paved the
way for their subsequent involvement in the political sphere.[44] Al-Qayati
(d. 1926) was one of Saʿd Zaghlul's closest advisors and became a member
of parliament, representing the Wafd Party as a delegate from the Minya
district during the first half of the 1920s.[45] Daraz (d. 1977) also was closely
associated with the Wafd Party, and especially with Mahmud Fahmi al-
Nuqarashi, who served as prime minister (1946–48). Notably, the link
between both these figures and the Wafd estranged them from the royal
court and its allies.[46]

Azhari protest activity and its influence on the events of the rebellion were also regularly documented in reports to London by British officials.[47] While the British were careful to display respect for al-Azhar,
even though they never gained its cooperation, they worked at neutralizing its role in the events of the revolt by closing off the streets leading
to the institution and stationing soldiers at key points around it. In one
incident a British patrol reportedly broke into the al-Azhar compound,
eliciting a furious reaction by the senior ʿulamaʾ, led by Shaykh al-Azhar
Muhammad ʿAbu al-Fadl al-Jizawi. The ʿulamaʾ promptly sent a petition
to the British high commissioner, demanding complete independence
for Egypt as the only way to restore order and prevent continued riot-
ing. The petition emphasized that no nation has the right to usurp the
independence of another, no matter how weak it might be in resources
or population size, for "Allah created nations to be free." The demand was
joined by ʿulamaʾ from nearby cities such as Alexandria, Tanta, Dusuq,
and Damietta.[48]

The declared nationalist and secular aims of the revolt therefore were
blended with religious fervor. The presence of Islam as a component of
Egyptian nationalism, alongside its geographic, linguistic, and historical foundations, granted its spokesmen the status of legitimizers (as well
as delegitimizers) of the political elite. Azharis backed the processes of

Egyptian state building but also posed difficulties for these processes whenever religious institutions or an entrenched Islamic ethos such as the organic unity of religion and state or the supremacy of the shariʿa in matters of personal status were threatened.

THE ISSUE OF REFORMING AL-AZHAR

As in the past, al-Azhar served as a central focus of contention, this time facing efforts at reforming its institutions and its curricula initiated by Shaykh al-Azhar Mustafa al-Maraghi in the late 1920s. The reformist program that he proposed centered on including modern fields of knowledge in the curriculum, such as foreign languages, psychology, and the history of religions.[49] It evoked intense opposition among the ʿulamaʾ, once again exposing the ideological divisions as well as the political affiliations of the various parties involved. Al-Maraghi, known for his modernist leanings, did not conceal his political affinity for the Constitutional Liberal Party, a confirmed opponent of the royal court. The historical and political aspects of his reform program have been widely covered in the research literature, especially by Daniel Crecelius.[50] But its ideological aspects, as reflected in the controversy conducted in the press against al-Maraghi by Muhammad Hamza ʿIllaysh (a lecturer at al-Azhar and a scion of the noted ʿIllaysh family) and the response by Shaykh ʿAbd al-Mutaʿal al-Saʿidi (a lecturer in al-Azhar's Arabic faculty), merit further study.

As the starting point for his opposition to al-Maraghi's reform program, Muhammad Hamza ʿIllaysh claimed that Islam does not require its believers to have a knowledge of everything in life: astronomy and philosophy, for example, can undermine divine revelation and the story of creation and will only provide effective ammunition for use by the enemies of Islam. He accused al-Maraghi of opening the gates of *ijtihad* and thereby endangering the faith, because by doing so he enabled access by any ignoramus who does not follow the Qurʾan or understand the hadith. In ʿIllaysh's view, which supported the puritanical stance of his illustrious nineteenth-century forebear, the Maliki mufti Muhammad ʿIllaysh, no contemporary scholars met the requirements of *ijtihad.* The four schools of Islamic law were complete and established, having made optimal use of the hadith literature to broaden their foundations. A supplementary source sanctioned by ʿIllaysh consisted of the commentaries of the later ʿulamaʾ in the margins of the works of early ʿulamaʾ (*taqrirat* or *shuruh*). Similarly, ʿIllaysh censured al-Maraghi's support for the comparative study of various religions and creeds. In his view, this would only heighten the hostility of Muslims toward people of other religions, in that those religions are inferior to Islam and filled with deviations and distortions.[51]

ʿIllaysh's position evoked sharp condemnation by ʿAbd al-Mutaʿal al-Saʿidi, who held reformist views and backed al-Maraghi's initiative. Al-Saʿidi disparaged ʿIllaysh's Sufi pedigree by implying that clinging to old thinking encourages people to disconnect themselves from the nation and the world and to lead ascetic and meaningless lives. He pointed out sarcastically that while "ʿIllaysh the great" (Muhammad ʿIllaysh) had been one of the opponents of a previous generation of reformists, including al-Afghani and ʿAbduh, "the small ʿIllaysh" (Muhammad Hamza ʿIllaysh) was among the opponents of al-Maraghi.

Al-Saʿidi laid out a broad array of arguments to counter the opposition to reform. He perceived two central issues, however, as the key to any reform in religious life: *ijtihad* and teaching the practical sciences. In al-Saʿidi's view, not every scriptural commentator came from the ʿulamaʾ community when the gates of *ijtihad* were open until the tenth century, so that ʿIllaysh's fear regarding access to the scriptures by the ignorant applies to the early period as well. ʿIllaysh's claim that no one in the present day fulfills the requirements of *ijtihad* is also baseless, al-Saʿidi argued. Such claims reflect a disregard for Allah's ability to create people of the status of Abu Hanifa or al-Shafiʿi. Moreover, the wide dissemination of the major schools of law does not mean that they are finite and are the sole arbiters of human conduct, as shown by the existence of the Zaydiyya school in Yemen, the Zahariyya in the Maghreb, and the Jaʿfariyya in Persia. Generally, al-Saʿidi concluded, there should be no fear of opening the gates of *ijtihad,* which is meant to deal with the many legal problems that arise in the modern era and can remove the label of backwardness that has been unjustly attached to the schools of law.

Al-Saʿidi pointed out that Islam makes no distinctions among types or fields of knowledge, so that the practical sciences (such as the natural and exact sciences) are an integral part of the history of Islamic knowledge. They were studied by leading ʿulamaʾ such as Abu Hamid al-Ghazali and Ibn Rushd and attracted many followers within al-Azhar. In citing both the distant and the recent past, al-Saʿidi sought to impart historic depth to a discourse of flexibility and openness regarding the religious study curriculum, thereby presenting the reforms proposed by Shaykh al-Azhar al-Maraghi as correcting a historical distortion and ʿIllaysh's opposition to them as baseless as well as harmful to Islam.[52]

Despite scattered gains, the stance of ʿIllaysh and his colleagues in the struggle against reform in al-Azhar and in the fields of religious law and education lost out in an era of national coalescence, state building, and the expansion of education, which also nurtured a new educated class pressing for a constitution and mass participation in the political system. These processes brought about further erosion in the power of the religious establishment and eventually changed al-Azhar from a medieval madrasa to a relatively modern university. The Sufi orders, too, whose members were closely tied to the Azhari system,[53] experienced a further decline in status in light of inner divisions and functional weakness along with the usurpation of their traditional social functions by other agents—mainly the state and civil bodies such as the Muslim Brotherhood. Nevertheless, the role of guardians of the faith was sustained by al-Azhar and the Sufi orders in the struggle over the moral image of the Egyptian polity, a carryover that was assisted by the turbulent political reality of the late 1920s and early 1930s.

The state constitution inaugurated in 1923 served as a basis for the parliamentary system adopted in Egypt and as a foundation for the intellectuals' expectations of a national revival. Its implementation was problematic, however, in light of a tenacious power struggle between the royal court, on the one hand, and the government and parliament (which were controlled by the Wafd Party), on the other, with the British pulling the strings behind the scenes. In these struggles Islam served as a political lever, used especially by the king with vigorous support from al-Azhar, both representing the old order. Moreover, the Wafdist political elite tended to show caution on topics touching on religious law, aware of the entrenched status of Islam in a society whose population now constituted an electoral constituency with the establishment of a representative political system. This reality, which was reinforced by the government's need for political legitimation under the British colonial occupation, left room for the involvement of al-Azhar in key issues on the public agenda.[54]

AL-AZHAR'S ASSERTIVENESS

The research literature has fully documented the involvement of Azharis, with the full backing of King Fuad, in the issue of the restoration of the caliphate in the period 1923–26, after its abolition by Mustafa Kemal (Atatürk) in Turkey.[55] Although this involvement failed, producing poor results in the Islamic Congress in Cairo in 1926, it did attest to Azhari resilience. Such resilience was also evident in concerted polemical campaigns conducted against modernist writers, who tended to interpret Islam as an ethical code and were perceived as undermining the principles of the faith, as exemplified by the well-known cases of Ahmad Lutfi al-Sayyid (1924), ʿAli ʿAbd al-Raziq (1925), and Taha Hussein (1926). In these affairs, al-Azhar served not only as challenger and accuser for the sin of besmirching the religion but also as punisher and excommunicator, based on its ancient authority as the interpreter of tradition. Notably, al-Azhar did not succeed in attaining all that it wished in these cases, for the intellectuals involved continued to mold a challenging reformist discourse, supported by a democratic constitutional climate and a well-developed print culture.[56] But it did contribute to defining the boundaries of the discourse on faith more precisely.

Echoes of the impression made by the bitter confrontations between al-Azhar and the modernist writers over the role of religion in the state and society are clearly discernible in the essays and press interviews of ʿAli ʿAbd al-Raziq in the late 1920s. ʿAbd al-Raziq (d. 1966), a qadi in the shariʿa court in Mansura, was dismissed from his position and expelled from the al-Azhar community in the wake of the publication of a book in which he called for the separation of religion and state.[57] ʿAbd al-Raziq continued writing in defense of democratic values and also involved himself in political activity. He made no secret of the humiliation he had endured at the hands of al-Azhar. ʿAbd al-Raziq bitterly denounced the arrogance and repressiveness of the religious establishment, despite its constitutional status as subject to the executive branch of government, and called for the establishment of a "determined regime" that would advance true religious reform and guarantee freedom of thought to every citizen. He charged that al-Azhar, as a religious university that produced talented ʿulamaʾ, was only "a cipher with no benefit whatsoever" in its present state and expressed his aspiration to see men trained in religion graduate from modern—even European—colleges rather than from madrasas.[58]

Taha Hussein's semiautobiographical book *al-Ayyam* (The Days, 1940) contains a similar denunciation. Hussein (d. 1973), one of the great writers of modern Egypt, personally experienced the coerciveness of al-Azhar when, as a student there, he called for a critical approach in researching the history and literature of Islam. He was dismissed from al-Azhar before he had secured the final certificate. Moreover, his book *Fiʾl al-shiʿr al-jahili* (On Pre-Islamic Poetry, 1926), which argued that what is called pre-Islamic literature was actually forged only after the appearance of Islam, aroused protest at al-Azhar and was suppressed. The distribution of the book was later allowed only after the writer had expunged several of his controversial assertions from the original version. Hussein revealed

his aversion for the traditional system of learning in *al-Ayyam,* pointing
to the poor teaching skills of the official ʿulamaʾ in Cairo and, by contrast, praising the magnetism of mystics and laymen who in fact were ignorant of the legal tradition, especially in the provinces and in rural areas.
He described the gap in status between the two groups and his personal
preference:

> Whereas in Cairo the ulema come and go and no one takes much notice
> of them…in the provinces you see the "learned" and sheikhs of the towns
> and villages coming and going in an atmosphere of majesty and respect.
> When they speak, people listen to them with an esteem that fascinates
> and attracts. Our friend [i.e., Taha Hussein] came under the influence of
> this country spirit…. When he used to listen to them [the "learned" in the
> provinces] speaking, admiration and wonder seized him, of which he tried
> to find the like in Cairo in the presence of the great ulemas and the major-
> ity of the sheikhs, but in vain.[59]

Despite Taha Husseinʾs disdain for al-Azhar, the institution remained
a stronghold of orthodoxy even in the constitutional era. Additional
evidence of this reality is provided by an episode involving Shaykh Muhammad ʿAbu Zayd in 1930. ʿAbu Zayd had published an edition of the
Qurʾan with critical commentary on the traditional interpretations that
had accepted supernatural phenomena described therein as self-evident.
The book was banned, and its author was forbidden to deliver sermons in
mosques or hold religious conclaves.[60]

Azhari attacks against these and other intellectuals elicited public
debate on the topic of freedom of thought (*hurriyat al-raʾy*), which was
guaranteed in the 1923 constitution. The issue became an integral component of the democratic discourse in Egypt in the interwar period. Al-
Azhar, for its part, actively attempted to subsume the concept of freedom
of thought and opinion under the aegis of Islam and thereby expropri-
ate the sole right to represent it from critics. Azhari spokesmen emphasized that freedom of thought is embedded in the scriptures, is protected
by the institution of the *shura* (consultation), and constitutes the basis
for understanding the faith. It is the element that imbues human life
with dynamism and historically has nurtured a thriving, proliferating
nation while preventing despotic rule. This distinguishes Islam from the
religions that preceded it, which showed a disdainful attitude toward the
human capacity to comprehend the secret of the universe and the human
role in it. Every science and field has its experts, the venerable institution

declared in 1936, and the science of the shariʿa cannot be wantonly accessible to just anyone or the result will be anarchy.[61]

In its thrust to enforce its moral authority in society, al-Azhar frequently relied on vigorous support from the king. King Fuad nurtured al-Azhar as an important source of legitimization and reinforcement vis-à-vis his sworn enemy, the Wafd Party, thereby hampering all the more the goal of reforming that religious institution. Al-Azhar, for its part, made a point of displaying loyalty to the king, who "defends the sanctity of religion against derision by the frivolous and protects the honor of the ʿulamaʾ."[62]

Article 153 of the constitution, which granted the king the authority to supervise, appoint officials, and budget for religious institutions, became an important judicial and political prop for al-Azhar, enabling it to enhance its presence in the Egyptian public arena.[63] More traditional venues such as religious institutes and mosques throughout the country also served the Azharis' cause, along with modern tools—primarily the print medium.[64] The most prominent publication in this context was *Nur al-Islam* (Light of Islam), an official organ launched in 1931, renamed *Majallat al-Azhar* (Azhar Journal) in 1935. Its editors forged an unbreakable link between the message of Islam and the message of al-Azhar,[65] defining the journal's main goal as the struggle against the "enemies of the correct faith" and emphasizing the contribution of al-Azhar to Islamic studies and the religious guidance of Muslims. While labeling the press one of the most dangerous vehicles, enabling the enemies to "spread their wicked ideas over every hill" and "corrupt the hearts of the believers," the editors nevertheless acknowledged its effectiveness.[66]

Establishment ʿulamaʾ attacked foreign cultural activity vociferously in *Majallat al-Azhar,* describing it as missionizing and neo-Crusader, supported by the British authorities, and far more dangerous than any physical injury to Muslim life or property. None other than Shaykh al-Maraghi, initiator of the rejuvenation of al-Azhar, established the Association for the Defense of Islam (al-Jamʿiyya li-Himayat al-Islam) in 1928 with the goal of uprooting all missionary activity in Egypt.[67] The Azhari polemic also included the denunciation of other religions, such as Judaism, and of sects that split off from Islam, such as the Bahaʾi and the Ahmadiyya.

The struggle over the soul of the believer was also reinforced on the front of ritual, personal status, and social morality. The discourse in this realm was characterized mainly by a puritanical worldview. The fatwa column published in *Majallat al-Azhar* by the Committee of Legal

Opinions (Lajnat al-Fatawa) at al-Azhar, which covered a wide range of topics in response to questions submitted by a varied audience, provided an important source of guidance. It constituted a kind of response to the fatwa column in the nonofficial *al-Manar* and its editor, Rashid Rida, the founder of the fundamentalist neo-Salafiyya (adhering to the fore-fathers), who positioned himself as an intellectual and political rival of al-Azhar.

The vast majority of questions in *Majallat al-Azhar*'s fatwa column were submitted by functionaries in the Egyptian religious and educa-tion systems as well as government officials, with questions also received from other Arab and Muslim countries. A significant number of the fat-was were devoted to issues pertaining to theology, ritual, and personal status. Others related to practical daily issues such as the economy, health, autopsies, birth control, smoking, art, the education of children, and pub-lic morality. The public arena was clearly the focus of the fatwa column, reflecting the traditional perception that the image of the community must radiate religious ideals and the divine presence. It also pointed to the desire to renew the moral values of the community in light of its expo-sure to the hedonistic and permissive cultural codes that had penetrated the Muslim space in the encounter with Western modernity. Not surpris-ingly, the notion of the superiority of Islam as a value and a social system surpassing all other ideologies underlay many of the fatwas, thereby ex-posing the growing fear of a sweeping erosion of the faith.

The ideological underpinning of al-Azhar's efforts to put an end to the manifestation of religious doubt and moral corruption was the Qur'anic commandment to "forbid wrong," later defined as "one of the weapons of the absolute and powerful truth" to prevent cultural corruption.[68] Such determination was applauded even by Rashid Rida, a sharp critic of the Azhari establishment,[69] who nevertheless praised the devotion of many ʿulamaʾ to eliminating heresy and moral corruption in society. He attrib-uted the successes of the ʿulamaʾ in this area to the designation of Islam as the state religion (section 2 of the 1923 constitution).[70]

Al-Azhar nevertheless found itself waging a defensive battle on two fronts by the end of the 1920s: against the nationalist government over its mounting efforts to advance reform in the country's religious and educa-tional institutions and against the Muslim Brotherhood, a newly emer-gent populist movement based primarily in the new *effendiyya* (the urban middle-class intelligentsia).[71] The Brotherhood nurtured an activist per-ception of Islam and challenged the authority of the ʿulamaʾ, holding them responsible for the moral corruption of Egyptian society because of their dogmatic thinking and their submission to the political elite. This dual challenge by both the government and the Brotherhood weakened al-Azhar's status, though it did not neutralize it.

The progress of state-sponsored reform in al-Azhar was slow and subject to setbacks, especially as it was linked to the political struggle between the monarchy and the government. The thrust toward reform was supported by a small group of open-minded ʿulamaʾ, but its focus was more on organizational structure than on curricular content.[72] ʿAbd al-Mutaʿal al-Saʿidi, the reformist scholar who faced hostility from the leaders of al-Azhar in 1926 after sharply criticizing the teaching methods at the religious colleges, charged that the reforms at al-Azhar failed to mold a uniform approach among the ʿulamaʾ regarding the need to show openness toward the modern era. Boldly summing up the situation, he observed that "the majority are instructed in preserving the old as a religious duty, while a minority recoil from the old and loathe the freeze." These internal power struggles, al-Saʿidi stressed, also reflected badly on the Azhari student. "If he does not cleave to the old, he will have difficulty in completing his studies, and in the absence of substantive reform in al-Azhar he will eventually fail in his examinations and be expelled from the institution."[73]

The second challenge to the status of al-Azhar, embodied in the Muslim Brotherhood, nevertheless did not reach the point of overt confrontation and was contained. The leader of the Brotherhood, Hasan al-Banna, did denounce al-Azhar for its unwillingness to condemn foreign imperialism and its submission to a deviant local government, in contrast to its glorious past as defender of justice and the welfare of the people and as "the bearer of weapons against tyranny and oppression." This failure in its duty to defend Islam also led to the corruption of communal life, he charged. Yet, despite this criticism, al-Banna was careful to maintain cordial relations with Azharis on all levels. The most prominent of these was Mustafa al-Maraghi, shaykh al-Azhar for two terms (1928–29, 1935–45), who was perceived by the Brotherhood as a model scholar truly working for the renewal of Islam. Al-Maraghi's systematic endeavors to reform al-Azhar and his demands to monitor the activities of Sufi orders closely were warmly received by the Brotherhood.[74]

Other prominent ʿulamaʾ, including Muhammad al-Hadar Husayn, Muhammad ʿAbd al-Latif Daraz, and ʿAbd al-Wahhab al-Najjar, preached in Muslim Brotherhood mosques and wrote for its organs. Al-Azhar's control of a broad network of religious institutions throughout Egypt constituted another reason for al-Banna's conciliatory approach to it.

Other leaders of the Brotherhood, such as Salah al-ʿAshmawi and Mu-hammad al-Ghazali, held a more alienated position toward the Azharis, but their stance remained marginal in light of al-Banna's undisputed leadership.[75]

Despite power struggles and ideological dissonance, especially over the issues of the duty to obey a Muslim ruler and the authority to represent religion, al-Azhar and the Muslim Brotherhood shared a common view of Islam as a comprehensive framework for molding faith and conduct alike. Each body functioned in its own field and to the extent of its resources to halt the tide of erosion of the faith and contributed to heightening religious awareness: al-Azhar by fostering worship and the Brotherhood by fostering the political dimension of Islam. Both also cooperated on occasion to eradicate immoral social conduct, such as prostitution and gambling, as well as dissident views that were perceived as heresy.

Widely publicized examples of the heresy issue were the cases of Muhammad Khalaf Allah (1947), a doctoral candidate in the faculty of Arabic Literature at the University of Cairo, who questioned the authenticity of certain episodes in the Qurʾan, and Shaykh Khalid Muhammad Khalid (1950), who published a book calling for the separation of religion and state. Khalid also denounced the ʿulamaʾ as traitors to the Islamic religion because of their corruption and for preaching a fatalistic belief in the acceptance of a life of poverty in this world in anticipation of reward in the next one.

Khalaf Allah's punishment was the disqualification of his dissertation, while his doctoral advisor was forced to leave his post as lecturer. In an official manifesto addressed to the king and the state authorities, al-Azhar asserted that what Khalaf Allah defined as legitimate *ijtihad* was actually a mockery of one of the foundations of religion, which demanded a purification of the university and the schools in Egypt from "every manifestation of heresy."[76] In Khalid's case, the punishment was the banning of his book by order of the state prosecutor general, at the request of both al-Azhar and the Brotherhood, for its unrestrained attack on Islam and its spokesmen. A court ruling eventually annulled the ban and allowed the circulation of the book, based, significantly, on Islamic arguments to support its decision. This pattern was in line with the regime's cautious approach to the issue of religion and state—promoting the rationalization of the Egyptian legal system according to Western codes while integrating, rather than excluding, Islamic tenets.[77]

The relative erosion in the status of al-Azhar as a result of the dual challenge it faced from the government and Islamists was also experienced by the Sufi network. Sufism offered the masses a temporary reprieve from their everyday worries and provided comfort and refuge from the political and social upheavals of the time. Governmental supervision of the public activity of the Sufi orders focused on the urban centers: Cairo and the surrounding towns. In the provincial towns and rural areas, however, especially in Upper Egypt, the orders were able to retain their strong public presence in light of their widespread communal networks and the relative conservatism of the population. The Sufi presence has been the subject of considerable research in Egypt's nationalistic literature, focusing on the tension between tradition and modernity, emotions and rationalism.[78] This aspect was highlighted as well by historians such as Hamilton Gibb and Michael Gilsenan, who also pointed to the popularity of the veneration and the *mawlid*s of saints.[79]

In many cases, the popular influence of the Sufi orders prompted the state to utilize the orders to enhance its authority in the provinces. For example, the constitutional regime sought to enlist the Sufi shaykhs as educational agents in reinforcing national identity, moral values, and social solidarity.[80] The bitter rivals of Sufism within the Islamist spectrum—the Muslim Brotherhood and, from the 1960s, the militant groups as well—constituted an essentially urban phenomenon, with only a few of their members being of agrarian origin.[81] This also contributed to the endurance of the Sufi status in the rural community. Not surprisingly, controversial rituals denounced by Islamist circles and repressed in the urban centers by the government continued to be practiced in the provinces.

EPILOGUE

The July 1952 revolution marked a new era in al-Azhar's long history. The new regime under the leadership of Gamal Abdel Nasser appropriated the Azharis' religious authority by abolishing the shariʿa courts (1956) and transforming al-Azhar into a modern state university (1961). These steps were designed not necessarily to exclude Islam from the political discourse but to motivate it to endorse the government's revolutionary policy: the suppression of the Muslim Brotherhood domestically and the delegitimation of rival Arab regimes by branding them as atheistic (Iraq under ʿAbd al-Karim Qasim, 1958–63) or reactionary (the Saudi, Yemeni, and Jordanian monarchies). The revolutionary regime also intensified the incorporation of Sufi orders into the state system. Their popular networks in the countryside provided the regime with easy access to rural populations, while their close ties with other orders in the Arab world, especially in North Africa, were helpful in disseminating the official Pan-Arab ideology.[82]

The Islamic content that Azharis (as well as Sufi shaykhs) imparted to the revolution's messages helped the ʿulamaʾ curtail the drift of Nasserist policy toward sweeping secularism. Thus, for example, Shaykh al-Azhar Mahmud Shaltut (1958–63) endorsed Arab socialism as deriving its legitimacy from Islam while censuring Western socialism as a hedonistic philosophy of materialistic gain, thereby reinforcing the Islamic hue of Nasserist Egypt.[83] Employing such a tactic of damage control was the best the ʿulamaʾ could do, given the loss of their quasi-autonomy over time. They kept a low profile in domestic political affairs and foreign policy, while focusing on preserving al-Azhar's central role in molding the self-image of society. This was reflected in sharp Azhari attacks against harmful social manifestations such as theft, licentiousness, and the co-education of boys and girls, which were attributed to the corrupting influence of Westernization.

In emphasizing the linkage of Egyptian society, Islam, and al-Azhar, the ʿulamaʾ sought to convey that any attempt by the regime to detach society from the Islamic heritage was doomed to failure while at the same time retaining their own status as the stronghold of religious life in the country. Rejecting the Muslim Brotherhood's brand of dissident Islam and backing the regime's repressive measures against the movement, Azharis advanced their own version of a quietist yet orthodox official Islam.

This religious resilience was best exemplified by the resignations of three shaykhs al-Azhar between 1952 and 1958 in protest against growing state interference in the internal affairs of the institution. In response, the government appointed military figures to fill key positions in the Azhar administration, but they failed to gain sufficient cooperation from the ʿulamaʾ. Significantly, the profile of many Azharis was provincial and agrarian, nurturing a more conservative orientation on issues such as education, family life, and social morality as compared to their academic counterparts at the University of Cairo. Furthermore, the introduction of the secular sciences (ʿulum al-dunya) into al-Azhar's curriculum under the law of 1961 failed to weaken the preeminent status of the theological studies.[84] Rejecting demands by modernists to transform al-Azhar into a faculty of theology within a modern university, the regime decided to preserve the separate status of the religious institution and turn it into a symbol in the struggle for national renewal. This objective was reflected in an impressive expansion of al-Azhar's budget, which in 1966 reached £E 7 million, as compared to £E 900,502 in 1948.[85]

Although the religious dimension was secondary to Nasserite political loyalties, as James Jankowski has argued,[86] it was nevertheless an essential component of the regime's political legitimacy. Nasser was able to dismiss the concept of the caliphate as irrelevant to modern times,[87] but he could not publicly deny the organic unity between religion and state. In fact, he used religion for political ends at two crucial stages of his Pan-Arabist drive: in announcing the nationalization of the Suez Canal from the Azhar Mosque in 1956 and in depicting the Arab military defeat by Israel in 1967 as a warning from Allah to the nation to purify itself from sin. The ensuing struggle against Israel was similarly portrayed in Islamic terms by Azhari fatwas denouncing the treachery of the Jews dating back to the dawn of Muslim history and sermons calling for jihad against Israel as the duty of every Muslim believer.[88]

In addition to continuing to provide a moral base for state authority, Islam also served as an institutional framework for social transactions. Two proposed legislative bills aimed at improving the status of women in the family and society (1960, 1967) were shelved as a result of political considerations and mounting pressure by al-Azhar.[89] Shaykh al-Azhar Shaltut himself revealed his perception of the role of Islam in the state by declaring: "He who expresses loyalty to the faith but denies the shariʿa… is not a Muslim in the eyes of Allah."[90]

Ideological piety was even more strongly emphasized by Shaltut's successors and other senior ʿulamaʾ, who, for example, endorsed bigamy as a religious obligation and a human need—a stance that discomfited those governmental officials who advanced the cause of individual liberty and equality in Egyptian society.[91] The very fact that the ancient bastion of orthodox Islam was systematically singled out for attack by politicians and modernist thinkers both before and during the revolutionary period was a further indication of its abiding position in the Nile Valley.[92]

8 'Ulama' in the Middle East: A Comparative Perspective

Egyptian history experienced modernization alongside colonialism and nationalist (or proto-nationalist) resistance at the end of the nineteenth century and beginning of the twentieth century. While this phase in its history was largely molded by Westernized elites and modernist intellectuals, the role of the 'ulama' was also palpable. Drawing on moral as well as material resources, 'ulama' channeled these assets toward reinforcing or, alternatively, challenging the political agenda of the time. The high point of their involvement in these agitated Egyptian politics came during the 'Urabi episode—the rebellion against the khedive and the anti-colonialist struggle against the British. The main thrust of the 'ulama' was to halt the erosion in the status of Islam in the public arena and, by default, to preserve their sectoral status in the face of the social and ideological challenge posed by reformists and nationalists alike.

Religious and political assertiveness was not limited to al-Azhar, the ancient bastion of Islamic learning in Egypt. It was also evident in other urban centers of the Ottoman Middle East that were undergoing similar political and socioeconomic changes. The assertiveness of Sunni 'ulama' in these centers did not reach the level of influence of the Shi'i clerics in Iran or even in Iraq, but it was of historic importance. An interesting case is Istanbul, where 'ulama' were actively involved in dissident politics against the regime of Sultan Abdülhamid II (1876–1908), which also paved the way for their tactical rapprochement with the sultan's main rivals, the Young Turks and the Committee of Union and Progress (CUP). Under the CUP (1908–18), Ottoman-Turkish 'ulama' even entered formal politics as party leaders and members of parliament in an effort to counter the secular encroachment upon their society.[1] Religious assertiveness was even more pronounced in the Arab lands, especially in Bilad al-Sham (Syria).

THE SYRIAN ORBIT

The 'ulama' in the Syrian urban milieu were an organic part of both the local elite and the provincial Ottoman administration. They controlled a wide range of religious, legal, and educational institutions as well as the economically influential *awqaf*. Some 'ulama' were members of wealthy families with assets in commerce and land. Others were affiliated with Sufi orders and with the *ashraf* (heads of prestigious religious families), whose claims of descent from the Prophet were accepted locally.[2] Involved in the "politics of notables," in Albert Hourani's terminology, the 'ulama' became key players in shaping communal priorities during the nineteenth century.[3]

Reforms in Syria instituted by Istanbul in the nineteenth century, culminating in the progressive legislation known as the Tanzimat (1839–76), created a new judicial and political reality and paved the way for secular influences. Nevertheless, the status of the 'ulama' was not drastically affected. They preserved their standing as a group, mainly through cooperation with the local Ottoman authorities and by establishing contacts with Istanbul, and continued to enjoy communal influence (as shown, for example, by Moshe Ma'oz, Ruth Roded, Linda Schilcher, Mahmoud Yazbak, Elizabeth Sirriyeh, and Jakob Skovgaard-Petersen).[4] The 'ulama' gave their blessing to most of the administrative and military reforms and actively promoted them in some cases, such as compulsory military service and broader taxation.[5] They rejected reforms that they viewed as undermining the religious ethos, however, best exemplified by the issue of granting equal rights to non-Muslims.

The Christian community in Syria had no qualms about displaying its achievements in public (in contrast to the Jewish community, which kept a low profile)—sometimes with the encouragement of foreign consuls and missionary orders. This support by the colonial powers and missionaries was depicted in local Islamic discourse as a coordinated conspiracy to uproot the Islamic faith.[6] As a result, Islamic-Christian discord spread from the theological to the socioeconomic realm. By the late Ottoman era the tolerance and social exchange characteristic of intercommunal relations in earlier periods gave way to heightened sectarian tension and dissonance.[7]

Often the 'ulama' took steps to counteract the legalized rights of Christians and Jews by perpetuating discrimination against them in Muslim and civil courts of law or by excluding them from participation in local councils. In some cases 'ulama' played a role in incitement against

Christians, which occasionally deteriorated into violence (as in the urban
centers of Syria and Lebanon in 1850 and 1860, respectively).[8]

Such was the case in the city of Nablus in November 1853, when a
Muslim crowd gathered in front of the office of the local mufti, demanding the closure of Christian churches or at the very least the reduction of
their privileges as well as lowering the height of their doors and windows.
The mufti of the city issued a fatwa stating that the honor of Islam does
not permit the construction of new churches and that only those that existed prior to the Muslim occupation in the seventh century would be
tolerated. Singling out the Protestants, who intensified their missionary
activity in Nablus and other cities in Syria during the reformist period, the
mufti declared that they should not be allowed to worship in any meeting
place. Three years later, in April 1856, shortly after the appearance of the
sultanic Hatt-ı Hümayun, known as the Edict of Tolerance, the ʿulamaʾ
of Nablus convened to discuss what they termed Christian provocations:
processions, celebrations, and firing guns in the air to mark their new civic
status. The ʿulamaʾ accused the Hatt-ı Hümayun of engendering the death
of Muhammad's faith and of violating a divine decree in the Qurʾan.[9]

In Damascus the Shafiʿi mufti ʿUmar bin Muhammad al-ʿUmari
(d. 1860) assembled all the dignitaries in the city council (*majlis*) and de-
monstratively threw the reformist Ottoman edicts into a waste bin, pro-
nouncing them invalid on the grounds that they contained anti-Islamic
clauses. Responding to reports of Muslims attending Protestant ritual
gatherings, a prominent qadi in Nazareth declared that "the sultan eats
melons," a derogatory expression signifying that the sultan was talking
nonsense when he issued a *firman* granting liberty of conscience to all
subjects. According to the qadi, the sultan's officials and subjects were
duty bound to obey him only so long as his orders were in conformity
with the law.[10]

European consuls criticized the Ottoman authorities' refusal to arrest
and punish such ʿulamaʾ for fear of undermining public order.[11] The authorities did adopt measures against some dissident religious dignitaries,
however, including arrest, banishment, and reducing their influence in
the educational and *waqf* systems, along with appointing qadis of Turkish rather than local origin.[12] Not surprisingly, the death of the reformist
Sultan ʿAbd al-Majid in 1861 elicited relief among the ʿulamaʾ in Syria that
"Islam was saved."[13]

The Syrian ʿulamaʾ also adopted an assertive stand against their
ideological adversaries within the Islamic orbit—first and foremost, the
Salafiyya movement. The Salafiyya, assimilating the reformist ideas of

al-Afghani and even more so of 'Abduh,[14] aimed at a more flexible and adaptive Islam, thereby resolving the dilemma of how to be both Muslim and modern. The Salafis criticized the 'ulama' for rigidly following established interpretations and entrenching the normative status of the legal schools codified in the tenth century.[15] Salafi criticism was also directed at Sufi shaykhs for endorsing rituals such as the cult of saints, which were seen as distorting the spirit and purity of Islam.[16] Intellectually, the Salafiyya became linked to Arabism when it emerged as a social and political force in the early twentieth century.

Taking on the task of theological reform, the Salafiyya positioned itself as an Islamic scholastic elite that challenged the existing traditional one. It included scholars such as Tahir al-Jazahiri, 'Abd al-Razzaq al-Bitar, Salim al-Qasimi, 'Abd al-Rahman al-Kawakibi, Rashid Rida, and 'Abd al-Hamid al-Zahrawi.[17] These scholars were newcomers to the 'ulama' community and held lower-level positions in it, which colored their reformist appeal with social criticism directed at the privileged status of the highly placed 'ulama'. While the specifics of the ideological and social struggle between the two camps varied from place to place, the traditional 'ulama' retained the upper hand and eventually marginalized the Salafis.[18] They managed to do so by drawing on their communal assets as well as their intimate ties with the Ottoman authorities, who were appreciative of the loyalty displayed by the 'ulama' in their confrontation with the militant Wahhabiyya and its aim to overpower the empire.[19] A significant factor that reinforced the stance of the traditionalist 'ulama' against the reformist agenda of the Salafiyya was that many of the 'ulama' had acquired their religious education in al-Azhar and maintained close contact with its scholars, another indication of the Azhari influence on Syrian religious discourse.[20]

Sultan Abdülhamid, stressing the empire's pan-Islamic character and supporting the country's religious establishment and Sufi orders, subjected Salafiyya spokesmen, including 'ulama', to harassment, arrest, and in some cases exile. The Young Turks, who overthrew the sultan in 1908 and championed the ideal of progress, withdrew the government's support for the anti-Salafiyya campaign; but the campaign continued, especially in the press.[21]

The other dimension of the Salafi platform—the cultivation of a distinct Arab identity—was also largely rejected by the traditionalist 'ulama'. The Pan-Arab concept began gaining momentum in Syria in the early twentieth century in light of the continuing decline of the Ottoman Empire and, more particularly, the centralization policy of the Young

Turks. This policy resulted in the marginalization of the Arabic language
in favor of Turkish in the realms of education and administration.[22] With
the emergence of Pan-Arab secret societies in Syria from 1908 to 1914,
Arabism gained political backing. Two leading Salafi ʿulamaʾ, Rida and
al-Zahrawi, played a key role in this development. Both held influential
positions in Arab politics in Syria and were vocal spokesmen in promoting Arab demands vis-à-vis the government in Istanbul. These demands
shifted from a call for Arab autonomy in the late nineteenth century to
the more focused goal of a single Arab state with a representative government and the protection of minority rights on the eve of World War I.[23]

Few ʿulamaʾ other than Rida and al-Zahrawi, however, were to be
found in the leadership of the Arab secret societies.[24] Clearly, Arabism
posed a political and social challenge to the traditional notables, with
whom the ʿulamaʾ were intertwined. Moreover, many ʿulamaʾ felt a
sustained loyalty to the Ottoman Empire as the embodiment of the traditional Islamic order. Perhaps the primary reason for the low represen-
tation of ʿulamaʾ in Arab politics, however, was the cultural agenda of
Arabism, which embraced a Western political model and promoted unity
and friendship between Muslims and non-Muslims as full and equal partners in the enterprise of the Arab national awakening.[25]

The interaction between ʿulamaʾ and the Arab national movement
in Syria on the eve of World War I was thus minimal. In contrast to their
Sunni colleagues in Egypt, who had played an important role in the
ʿUrabi revolt, the ʿulamaʾ in Syria remained largely disengaged from the
emerging Arab movement. Furthermore, they attempted to delegitimize
its spokesmen both from the Salafi wing and from the secular intelligentsia. A further contrast between the Syrian ʿulamaʾ and their Egyptian
colleagues was their rejection of Arabism: they not only opposed its Westernized concepts but opposed the territorial implications of Pan-Arabism
as well. Several ʿulamaʾ were part of a thirty-member delegation to Istanbul in September 1915 to express the allegiance of the Arabs to the Ottoman caliphate and government.[26] Their anti-Arabist impetus stemmed
from the geopolitical attributes of Syria (its distinctive geographical diversity) along with the absence of a colonial presence. By contrast, the
lack of these two features in Egypt facilitated a more harmonious interaction between religious and national identities in the Nile Valley.

The stance of Syrian ʿulamaʾ toward Arab nationalism raises the
broader issue of the role of ʿulamaʾ in national liberation movements of
the time and the extent of their contribution or opposition to the agenda
of these movements.

ʿULAMAʾ AND NATIONALISM

The literature on the emerging national discourse in the Middle East in the late nineteenth and early twentieth centuries has focused mainly on the perceptions of the new intelligentsia of government officials, army officers, and writers. This sector, whose ideological outlook was formed during a period of accelerated modernization, state building, and expanded literacy, displayed openness to Western culture and advocated religious reform, national independence, and constitutionalism. Little attention has been paid to the ʿulamaʾ sector, also present at the birth of national movements in the period cited. This inattention to the ʿulamaʾ is not surprising, since they were generally identified as adherents to the traditional order, embodying the community of believers and the institution of the caliphate, and not as intellectual innovators or dissidents. They were thus considered marginal in the national discourse in the Middle East, in comparison to the Westernized elites and modernist intellectuals.

Indeed, modern nationalism contained an important component of structural and ethical secularization and advocated more rational and civic forms of society. It aspired to position itself as the primary focus of individual loyalty and as the principal agent in defining the cultural milieu of the collective. The nationalist narrative claimed possession of the community's historical memory, cultivating a sense of joint origin (a myth of descent) and shared destiny based on ethnolinguistic affinities and historical experiences. In this process of national coalescence, and the redefinition of the "self" and the "other," religion shifted from being viewed as a concept of a sacred cosmic order to being viewed as one element among many in the collective identity, such as territory, ethnicity, kinship, history, and language. Against this background, conflicts between political elites and religious spokesmen were ignited.[27]

The political milieu of the ʿulamaʾ in the post–World War I period was focused on the polity of which they formed a part, leaving the pan-Islamic premise of the community of believers largely at the level of a theological exercise. Although the abolishment of the institution of the caliphate by Atatürk in 1924 evoked anger and recrimination, concrete initiatives to restore it proved unproductive. One reason was the political rivalries among the various regional dynasties (the Egyptian king, the Saudi ruler, and the Hashemite king), who all designated themselves as worthy of the title of caliph. But pragmatic religious reasons were also at work. An assembly of high-ranking ʿulamaʾ in Cairo in 1926 reluctantly but realistically concluded that the caliphate, the symbol of the classical

Islamic polity, was truly dead and could not be restored.[28] A memorandum that they composed disclosed that the Islamic union of the past had
dissolved:

> The countries and peoples of Islam have been divorced from one another
> in government, administration, and policy; and many of their inhabitants
> have been possessed by a nationalistic agitation that prevents one group
> from accepting the leadership of another, not to speak of submitting to
> being governed by it and permitting it to interfere in its public affairs. In
> these circumstances it is difficult for the caliphate, as defined above, to be
> realized.[29]

Although a few voices in the Islamic spectrum, both ʿulamaʾ and Islamists,
continued to foster the notion of the caliphate, their discourse was essentially utopian and left them on the margins of the Islamic consensus.[30]

The cultural milieu of the ʿulamaʾ, however, in contrast to their political milieu, was far broader and allocated a central position to a shared
moral vision as embedded in the holy texts. This universalistic perception was reinforced by the transnational learning orbit in which Muslim
scholars throughout the Arab-Islamic world functioned, establishing
professional and personal contacts with one another as part of a tradition of travel to enrich their knowledge.[31] The adherence of the ʿulamaʾ
to such a broad corpus allowed them to endorse the notion of a territorial
entity whose ethical content would be guided in the spirit of Islam.

This discourse of defining moral boundaries also dictated the nature
of the interaction between the ʿulamaʾ and national movements. In some
spheres, such as the struggle against colonial rule or efforts to restrain a
tyrannical government, this interaction was largely harmonious. In other
spheres that were potentially threatening to the religious ethos integral
to a truly Muslim society, such as the organic unity between state and
religion and the superiority of the shariʿa in matters of personal status, the
interaction was problematic and resulted in dissent.

A careful reading of the historical record provides ample evidence of
the discourse of the ʿulamaʾ in setting the boundaries of Islam. ʿUlamaʾ
in Egypt, Syria, Palestine, Iraq, Algeria, and Morocco were enlisted to
back the anticolonial struggle. Most of them held religious positions as
muftis, qadis, imams, and *ashraf* and were leaders and members of Sufi
orders. In these capacities they controlled significant communal assets (a
wide network of mosques, madrasas, and charitable associations) along
with moral resources, such as sermons and fatwas that sanctified jihad and

self-sacrifice and turned Islam into a powerful wellspring of resistance. Thus religion could and did function as a facilitating factor in defining national identity and its territorial boundaries. Examples beyond the Sunni orbit include the integral linkage between Shi'ism and Iranian national identity and between Judaism and Jewish national identity. The national idea, however, went beyond territory and anticolonial struggle. It also harbored a political ideology that sought to expand the sovereignty of the state as well as advocating more rational and integrative forms of society. In these realms, conflicts were ignited between political elites and religious spokesmen. The response of the 'ulama', for their part, was to contain nationalist passions and set limitations to them in accordance with the injunctions of Islam.

In writings and fatwas Egyptian 'ulama' challenged the emancipation of non-Muslims from their legally inferior status as "subjected" people required to conform to prescribed socioeconomic regulations (see chapter 6). In Syria the 'ulama' went further, taking steps to nullify the legalized rights of Christians and Jews and excluding them from participation in local councils. In some cases 'ulama' instigated organized attacks against Christians. In promoting their cause, 'ulama' used Islam as an ethnic marker, defining the social and cultural boundaries between Muslims and their non-Muslim neighbors. In the same vein, 'ulama' in Egypt and Syria delegitimized the improved legal status of women and their access to the public sphere. While the legal discourse of some muftis, and especially qadis, better defined and even guaranteed women's rights in matters of marriage, divorce, and the custody of children, its aim was to do so in the context of shari'a law only and not outside it.[32]

The collapse of the Ottoman Empire in the wake of World War I provided a strong impetus to the spread of Arab nationalism as a compelling ideology in the Fertile Crescent. Nevertheless, the role of Islam did not disappear, especially in light of the struggle against the French Mandate in Syria and its termination of King Faisal's rule in 1920. Despite the secular outlook of Syria's political leaders and the absence of religious figures in their ranks, they enlisted the symbolic force of Islam and its religious institutions to recruit the support of the urban masses for the national cause. In the city of Hamah, for example, a group of army officers collaborated with religious figures to form a local party, Hizb Allah (Party of God), in 1925. The choice of the name, one of the leading officers explained, was aimed at recruiting the support of the 'ulama' and arousing Islamic sentiment against the French regime in a city noted for its religious conservatism.[33] Although not deeply involved in actual

participation in the resistance against the French, Syrian ʿulamaʾ did provide "cultural capital" by glorifying the duty of jihad.[34]

Side by side with their moral enlistment in the national struggle,
preachers, legal arbiters, and other ʿulamaʾ worked toward curbing the involvement of the French Mandate in local life. The attempt by the French
to introduce reforms in the extant Islamic-based laws of personal status
encountered effective resistance on the part of the qadis. The religious establishment also put up a stubborn struggle to block French efforts to take
over the administration of the *awqaf*. Ultimately, the French succeeded
in this area, though only after prolonged efforts. Moreover, the Mandate
period of the 1920s and 1930s witnessed the emergence of Islamic welfare
and cultural associations in Damascus, Aleppo, and Hamah involving
large numbers of ʿulamaʾ, with the aim of curtailing the perceived immoral influence of the foreign Western presence. These associations were
to act as an important base for the growth of the Muslim Brotherhood
movement at the beginning of the 1940s.[35]

In Palestine, too, the ʿulamaʾ played a leading role in promoting
a national agenda to counter both the Zionist movement and the British Mandate, under the aegis of the Supreme Muslim Council, founded
in 1922. Under ʿulamaʾ leadership, the council was transformed from a
purely bureaucratic body acting on behalf of the Mandate to supervise the
religious life of Muslims in Palestine into a de facto Islamic government
striving to undermine the very authority of the Mandate. The council's
well-developed infrastructure—together with the charismatic leadership
of the mufti of Jerusalem, Hajj Amin al-Husayni, and his extensive connections with Arab rulers and dignitaries—facilitated its emergence as
the main arena of Palestinian Arab politics.[36]

The council's agenda centered on the sanctification of the territorial
boundaries of Palestine as defined essentially by the colonial administration. Serving this agenda, "Islam was the medium rather than the message," to quote historian Musa Budeiri,[37] in endowing the land of Palestine with an aura of holiness and eternity. The Palestinian liberation
movement was led by a council whose members were mostly ʿulamaʾ,
which ensured a large measure of harmony between religious and national identities, yet this was so only with regard to the political and territorial dimensions.[38] In the social and cultural realms the council discour-
aged reformist or ecumenical tendencies, elevating the political issue of
defending the land as the central and unifying cause. Moreover, due to
the pervasive presence of Islam in Palestinian political life, the incorporation of the Christian Arab population into the Palestinian leadership was

problematic, while secular alternatives such as political parties or unions did not gain momentum during the Mandate period. In seeking to raise Palestinian Muslim consciousness, the council also enforced a strict moral code, including the wearing of the veil and censorship of theaters and other places of entertainment.[39]

The historical literature has emphasized the challenge presented to the Supreme Muslim Council by radical groups with militant agendas, especially by the charismatic Shaykh ʿIzz al-Din al-Qassam in the early 1930s.[40] The Qassamist movement preached and carried out uncompromising jihad against heretics, while blending it with an egalitarian social agenda that opposed control by the urban elite and championed the new middle class, the workers, and the peasants. This movement remained essentially dissident, however, and failed to weaken the political or communal status of the council. Moreover, al-Qassam himself was a religious scholar, which meant that ʿulamaʾ were key players in Palestinian public life at least until the end of the 1930s.

The situation in the semitribal areas of the Arab Middle East (such as the Arabian Peninsula and North Africa) revealed a similar discourse that incorporated religio-ethnic boundaries in contending with the national impetus. In these regions, which were comparatively less exposed to the forces of modernization and Westernization, the ʿulamaʾ exerted a greater influence on the nature of local nationalism in light of their historically stronger authority and higher status. They played a key role in the struggle for independence and were integral in the process of state building, occupying judicial, educational, administrative, and even governmental posts.

Upon the establishment of ʿAbd al-ʿAziz ibn Saʿud dynasty in Saudi Arabia in 1932, the ʿulamaʾ became his ideological associates, serving as the guardians of the Wahhabi ethos and acquiring supervisory and executive authority in various religious areas.[41] In North Africa, following the French occupation, Morocco was the scene of close cooperation between nationalists and ʿulamaʾ, reflected in the co-option of several ʿulamaʾ in the establishment of the Istiqlal (Independence) Party in 1946.[42] This collaboration was linked to the similar urban social origins of the two sectors as well as to the conservative orientation of the nationalist leaders, who sought to preserve the country's social and political structures rather than adopt new Western models. Some ʿulamaʾ perceived the national cause as a vital means for reviving Morocco's past glory; others were motivated by pragmatic and personal considerations, seeking to ensure their communal status in the postwar independent state. The clerical endorsement of the

Istiqlal Party was reinforced by the retention of a religious monarchy that claimed descent from the family of the Prophet and attributes of sanctity.[43] A more secular and socialist orientation was adopted by the Front de Libération Nationale (FLN) in Algeria, although its leaders nevertheless relied heavily on Islamic motifs as a means of enlisting the masses against the French and were anxious to co-opt 'ulama' in their institutions. Their aim was to neutralize the puritanical neo-Wahhabi trend, which opposed the notion of the emancipation of women and demanded the prohibition of immoral manifestations such as alcohol, gambling, and music.[44]

The strategy of enlisting Islam in the cause of independence was also adopted by the nationalist Neo-Dustur Party (New Constitution Party) in Tunisia founded by Habib Bourguiba in 1943; but, in contrast to the situation in Morocco and Algeria, it was estranged from the establishment 'ulama'.[45] As a conservative sector, the 'ulama' expressed concern about the religious reforms promoted by the nationalist movement and their dissatisfaction with some of its leaders who adopted a French lifestyle. The Islamic establishment thus made efforts to curb the interference of the French government in the religious and cultural life of the country.[46]

A SHI'I PERSPECTIVE

In displaying religious assertiveness, Sunni 'ulama' found common ground with their Shi'i counterparts in Iraq and Iran in the early twentieth century. Shi'i 'ulama' in Iraq played an active role in local politics, backed by multifaceted scholarly and patronage networks, especially in the holy cities of Najaf and Karbala, and a growing reservoir of believers as a result of the conversion of Sunni Arab tribes to Shi'ism. Such involvement was intensified following the Young Turk Revolution (1908–14), which sought to reduce the power of the Shi'i clerics in Iraq, and even more so with the British occupation in 1918, which also fostered the entrenchment of secular ideas in the Iraqi entity. The growing politicization of Iraqi Shi'ism, and its interaction with Sunni nationalists to free the country from foreign control, was reflected in the anti-British revolt of 1920, in which Shi'i 'ulama' in the south were a driving force toward the goal of establishing Islamic rule. Their political alliance with the Sunni Arabs in Baghdad, however, deteriorated into antagonism after the suppression of the revolt and the subsequent establishment of a Western-oriented Sunni monarchy under British patronage. Moreover, despite constituting a demographic majority, the entire Shiʿi population found itself marginalized in national politics.[47]

The ʿulamaʾ in Iran were more successful. They had been key players in state politics and had developed their own economic power bases ever since Shiʿism became the state religion under the Safavids in the early sixteenth century. The status of the Shiʿi ʿulamaʾ was reinforced in the eighteenth century with the victory of the Usulis or *mujtahids* (who stressed the use of reason as a source of law) over the Akhbaris, who were followers of the traditions transmitted by the infallible imams. The *mujtahids* were endowed with the legal authority to interpret the law, and the population was obliged to obey their rulings unquestioningly. This development posited the ʿulamaʾ as the de facto agents of the Twelfth (Hidden) Imam during his occultation in regulating the affairs of the community.[48]

In the area of politics, however, the notion that the *mujtahids* should assume the rulership of the country in the absence of the Hidden Imam was shared by only some of the ʿulamaʾ. Others advocated a dual rulership involving both the religious and the state authorities. In practice, many ʿulamaʾ sought accommodation with the shah, recognizing the need for the coercive power of the state to defend the country against infidel invasion and to protect the Shiʿa rite from deviant sects, such as the Sufis and the Babis. Nevertheless, the perception of the status of the *mujtahids* in Shiʿi political doctrine as equal or even superior to that of the state resulted in a growing confrontation between the two sides.[49]

As prominent players on the Iranian political stage, the ʿulamaʾ became the authentic spokesmen of the populace during political and economic upheavals. They also enhanced the harmony between religious and territorial identities. Indeed, the perpetual state of conflict between Iran and its Sunni neighbors—the Ottoman Empire and Afghanistan—turned the Shiʿi faith into a facilitator in enhancing the unique ethnic-territorial nature of the Iranian polity.

The dual role of the ʿulamaʾ as spiritual-cum-national leaders of the community was particularly pronounced in the protest movements against encroaching foreign exploitation as well as against the centralist tendencies of the Qajar dynasty in the late nineteenth and early twentieth centuries. The ʿulamaʾ, responding to pressure by local merchants, led the tobacco revolt in 1891–92 against the monopoly over the production, sale, and export of tobacco throughout Iran granted by the state to a Briton. The ʿulamaʾ provided the moral and communal underpinning for this collaborative move, while the merchants provided the economic infrastructure. A third, smaller element in the coalition was the Western-ized liberals.[50] The revolt spread through large parts of the country and eventually resulted in the revocation of the contentious license. This groundbreaking display of political power was to serve as a prologue to the constitutional revolution of 1905–11.

Government steps to restrain the political power of the clerical sector in Iran were the main cause of the outbreak of the revolution. The tri-partite coalition of ʿulamaʾ, merchants, and liberals that had formed dur-ing the tobacco revolt—and especially the alliance between the ʿulamaʾ and the liberals—coalesced even further around the common cause of a constitution. Their demands resulted in a violent confrontation with the regime.[51]

The liberals' goal was the establishment of a representative govern-ment based on Western principles. The ʿulamaʾ, by contrast, viewed a con-stitution as a means of defending the faith, implementing the shariʿa, and attaining social justice by restraining the tyrannical power of the mon-archy. They had no desire to reshape the traditional social and political order; all they wanted was to improve its moral attributes.[52] The differ-ences in emphasis between these two camps were blurred by the liberals; anxious to secure the continued support of the ʿulamaʾ, they couched the framework of the proposed constitutional government in ambiguous terms.[53] This ambiguity was best reflected in a comment by Sayyid Mu-hammad Tabatabaʾi, one of the two leading *mujtahid*s of Tehran: "We [the ʿulamaʾ] had no direct experience of constitutionalism. But we heard from those who had seen countries with constitutional regimes that con-stitutionalism conduces to the security and prosperity of a country. So we conceived an enthusiastic interest and made arrangements for establish-ing a constitution in this country."[54]

The establishment of a new representative assembly (*majles*) by an official decree issued by the shah in 1906 marked the pinnacle of the con-stitutional movement's achievement. At the same time, it also signaled its demise: once the delegates began formulating the various articles of the constitution and defining parliamentarianism more precisely, the deep ideological and political divides between the liberals and the ʿulamaʾ surfaced. A major controversy developed over terminology: the liberals advocated the use of the term *majles-e shura-ye melli* (national assembly), while the ʿulamaʾ favored *majles-e shura-ye eslami* (Islamic consultative assembly). Many of the ʿulamaʾ shifted from support to opposition con-cerning the entire issue of constitutional reform. For them, Islam was the sole point of reference for the principles of liberty, equality, and justice championed by the revolution. Accordingly, any Western-oriented constitution was perceived as an expression of anarchism and cultural imperialism.[55]

In treatises written at the time prominent ʿulamaʾ such as Sayyid Faz-lallah Nuri, Muhammad Husayn Tabrizi, and ʿAbd al-Husayn Lari reaf-firmed not only the superiority of Islamic law as the "most complete of all laws" but also the superiority of the *mujtahid*s as its sole authorized inter-preters. Accordingly, human legislation was delegitimized as "infidelity" and parliament as a "house of corruption."[56]

Theological considerations apart, the emphasis on the immutable linkage between the shariʿa and its authentic interpreters also aimed at safeguarding the jurists' supervision of the political process. Only a few ʿulamaʾ supported the adoption of Western concepts as a means of neu-tralizing the tyrannical rule of the shah and promoting social justice. One of them, Sayyid Muhammad Ismaʿil Mahallati, a middle-ranking Persian cleric who resided in the Shiʿi city of Najaf in Iraq, pointed out that hu-man welfare was a universal goal unrelated to a specific religion and there-fore the approval of a constitution did not mean surrendering to the West. Others went a step further and warned that collaboration with the shah against the elected parliament was tantamount to following in the foot-steps of Yazid ibn Muʿawiyya, the Umayyad caliph responsible for the massacre of the Prophet's grandson Husayn and his family in Karbala in 680. Younger clerics, who also tended to support the constitutional cause, shifted the emphasis from the political to the religious sphere, calling for reform in Shiʿi educational institutions, which were viewed as conserva-tive and unsuited to modern times.[57] Such views, although marginal in the ʿulamaʾ community, nevertheless attested to the diversity of Shiʿi po-litical thought.

The anticonstitutional campaign supported by influential ʿulamaʾ played into the hands of the shah. Loath to relinquish any of his authority, he tried to co-opt the ʿulamaʾ as allies by delegitimizing the new political system as incompatible with the shariʿa. Indeed, the ʿulamaʾ eventually denounced the liberal constitutionalists as *murtaddun* (apostates) for their willingness to grant equal civil rights to women and to minorities and demanded that parliamentary legislation be subject to the right of veto by a forum of five senior *mujtahid*s.[58] This demand was accepted by the liberals and was incorporated into the constitution,[59] but the political crisis did not end. Rather, it exacerbated domestic anarchy and ultimately facilitated the British and Russian invasions of 1911 and the division of Iran into two zones of influence.

The constitutional revolution revealed the strong commitment of the Iranian ʿulamaʾ to promoting a national agenda that would resist foreign encroachment while restraining the powers of the shah. Yet it also exposed their unequivocal dissent when this agenda began to drift toward a secular Western course, perceiving such a development as a threat to the religious underpinnings of society. Notably, the ideological raison d'être of Islamic politics was the establishment of a moral society based on the Qurʾanic imperative to "forbid wrong." This principle positioned the ʿulamaʾ as guardians of the faith and largely dictated their political conduct during the revolution.

A CONCLUDING NOTE

While the Shiʿi ʿulamaʾ retained their independent communal and political assets, the Sunni ʿulamaʾ in the Arabic-speaking countries lost their traditional assets in education, the judiciary, and the *awqaf,* mainly with the collapse of the Ottoman Empire and the formation of nation-states during the post–World War I period.

Nationalism in the Arab Middle East, however, did not follow the radical path taken by Turkey in separating religion from the state; rather, it incorporated Islam into its political discourse, granting the ʿulamaʾ establishment the status of a national institution. As observed by Anthony Smith in his book *The Ethnic Origins of Nations* (1986), the nationalization of religion, whether in Europe (for example, in Poland and in Ireland) or in the Middle East, "inevitably means a new focus for the religious organization and its local priesthoods; they become political weapons and national mobilizers, over and above their traditional role as ethnic repositories and transmitters."[60] Thus ʿulamaʾ in Egypt and elsewhere in the modern Middle East were transformed into national and cultural brokers who also promoted their own religious and sectoral cause.

9 Conclusion

During the course of the nineteenth century Egyptian society was exposed to a new ethical code—secular and Western, with a considerable hedonistic element. How did this exposure affect the ancient theological seminary al-Azhar? Leading historians, including H. A. R. Gibb, Afaf Lufti al-Sayyid-Marsot, Ira Lapidus, P. J. Vatikiotis, Gabriel Baer, and Hava Lazarus-Yafeh, have emphasized al-Azhar's crisis and decline in the process of modernization and institutionalization of the Egyptian state. Other scholars, such as Gilles Kepel, Olivier Roy, Emmanuel Sivan, Martin Kramer, and John Esposito, have tended to minimize the role of al-Azhar in Egypt's social and political life or, conversely, to emphasize the challenge to its legal authority presented by the new intellectuals—modernists and especially Islamists.

The present study suggests a relative rather than total crisis experienced by the institution. Azharis lost their political and economic assets along with their monopoly as scholars, educators, and intellectuals; yet they retained a considerable degree of moral influence in society. At precisely the time that Western historiography defined as the period of discontinuity with the past and the breakdown of the religious establishment (the second half of the nineteenth century), Azhari spokesmen demonstrated communal vitality, including political involvement.

The climax of this activist thrust occurred during the ʿUrabi revolt, an episode that placed al-Azhar in the eye of the storm. The venerable institution constituted a key arena for the confrontation between ʿUrabi's supporters and supporters of the khedive in a struggle for the loyalty of the populace and legitimation by the Ottoman sultan. This development pointed to the political elite's recognition of the important role of al-Azhar in molding the collective consciousness, despite the erosion of the institution's standing and the demotion of the ʿulamaʾ to the status of governmental bureaucrats during the course of the nineteenth century.

The ʿUrabi episode also revealed the segmented character of al-Azhar. Ensconced in the institution were a variety of groups whose ideological support for or opposition to the revolt was intertwined with power struggles over hierarchical positions and judicial supremacy, especially among the Shafiʿi, Maliki, and Hanafi legal schools.

The majority of the senior ʿulamaʾ tended to display a quietist, low-profile stance on political issues and remained loyal to the khedive, viewing him as the legitimate authority and as a bulwark against anarchy and sedition among Muslims. Their voices were drowned out by the religious fervor of the minority, however, whose spokesmen were remote from the modest scholarly and ascetic image portrayed by ʿAli Mubarak in *al-Khitat*.[1] As Azhari scholars, qadis, or Sufi shaykhs, these activists were involved in public life through the fatwas and commentaries they issued, their Sufi influence, or their empathy for the masses. Their moral authority stemmed from a combination of ideological and, even more importantly, sociological factors. They turned Islamic tradition into the main opposition narrative against the khedival regime and the foreign presence. This provided the ʿUrabist cause, which was essentially militaristic, with a popular, proto-national coloration.

Retrospectively, the accusations against the ʿulamaʾ sector leveled in the press at the time—an absence of fervor for their religion and neglecting their holy mission to combat political evil—were baseless.[2] This also holds true for modern historical observations, such as Rifaat A. Dika's contention that "although the ʿUrabi movement was supported by some of the ʿulamaʾ of al-Azhar, such as Muhammad ʿAbduh, al-Azhar and Sufi orders played a marginal role in the ʿUrabi movement."[3]

The pro-ʿUrabi ʿulamaʾ not only granted religious legitimization to the political moves undertaken by the revolutionary officers but were also involved in molding these moves and conveying them to the Egyptian public. Besides the moral resources they had at their disposal, the ʿulamaʾ could also gather support by dint of their social influence and their affinity for the Sufi orders in both the urban and the rural milieus. Their scholarly eminence and the charisma they radiated created power. Harnessing this power to a political agenda was only a short step away.

Not surprisingly, with the reestablishment of the khedive's regime under the patronage of the British, Tawfiq sought to sever the strong affinity between religious erudition and politics, which had worked to his disfavor during the events of the ʿUrabi revolt. Addressing the heads of the ʿulamaʾ in September 1882, he warned: "You are men of letters and not politicians. The first to be guilty again of interfering with politics will be severely punished."[4] His son ʿAbbas Hilmi II, who succeeded him in 1892, followed the same policy, pointing out in 1906 that al-Azhar was an institution for religious instruction and that its residents must deal only with the sciences of Islam and distance themselves from incitement or political deviation. Otherwise they would be expelled.[5] Hilmi's message was delivered fourteen years after the ʿUrabi episode, which shows that the Azharis had not abstained entirely from involvement in national politics. Moreover, the authorities themselves were not strict about enforcing the principle of separation between religion and politics and had no qualms about recruiting ʿulamaʾ to promote their policies and discredit their rivals.

The involvement of Azharis in ʿUrabi politics altered the pale, obedient, reclusive image of the ʿulamaʾ that was dominant in the research about Egypt of the nineteenth century. It also exposed a multifaceted world of Islamic discourse in which an Islamic Ottoman identity existed side by side with an Egyptian identity, protecting both religion and the homeland.

The intensity of the danger threatening Muslim Egypt in the final decades of the nineteenth century dictated the intensity of the Azharis' response, which reached a climax in the fatwa issued in July 1882 deposing Tawfiq. The danger of foreign conquest was also the cause that united the more conservative ʿulamaʾ and their ideological rivals, such as the reformist Islamic trend led by ʿAbduh and ʿAbdallah Nadim and the Westernized intellectuals. Nevertheless, the moment of crisis did not remove or blur the ideological divides between these groups in all that concerned the moral image of society. Struggles swirled over issues such as reforms in Islamic thought and in the Azhar curriculum, the public role of Sufism, and the status of women and religious minorities in society. In these areas the ʿUrabist ʿulamaʾ found more common ground with their adversaries, the pro-khedival ʿulamaʾ, than with liberal reformists.

Significantly, the cultural corpus of the Azharis who joined ʿUrabi (as reflected in their large body of written work) was much more complex and nuanced than indicated in the research literature, which focuses primarily on the personalities of al-Afghani, ʿAbduh, and Nadim. This corpus also illuminates the Islamic ideological aspect of the ʿUrabist episode, which functioned as a catalyst no less important than the political or socio-ethnic aspects emphasized by Alexander Schölch and Juan R. Cole. It also reveals the existence of a well-established "ideological village" in

which Egyptian ʿulamaʾ debated with their colleagues throughout the
Arab-Ottoman domain over theological, judicial, cultural, and political issues, including those impelled by their changing social reality. Al-
Azhar served as a compass and guide in this ideological village—further
evidence of its centrality in the Islamic discourse of the time.

The struggle over the image of Egyptian society continued into the
twentieth century, conducted in a changed historic context. The traditional Islamic political order, which disappeared with the collapse of
the Ottoman Empire, made way for a new Western-style governmental
system. National coalescence under the leadership of the Wafd Party led
to the formulation of a new agenda for the inhabitants of the Nile Valley. Several Azharis were involved in this process. Many more, however,
clung to the principles of the old order and forged an alliance with its undisputed representative, the royal court. Their failed initiative to restore
the institution of the caliphate (annulled by Atatürk in 1924) and to base
it in Egypt forced the ʿulamaʾ to confront three main challengers: the
government, the modernist intellectuals, and the Islamists. This multidimensional struggle resulted in a relative rather than an absolute crisis: it
weakened the status of the ʿulamaʾ but did not turn them into "crippled
players"—in Carly Murphy's contention—in the struggle for Egypt's
soul.[6]

The continued presence of Islam in the Egyptian milieu, in the context of canonical texts, ethoses, rituals, and monuments, guaranteed
its survival in an essentially secular system installed at the height of the
process of modernization and state building. This presence provided the
ʿulamaʾ with an ideological framework that embodied a historical perspective and moral validation, also ensuring their continued presence in
the public sphere. The cultural world with which the ʿulamaʾ were identified thus remained an important component in the cosmic order of society. Another source of support and inspiration for the ʿulamaʾ was the
heroic heritage of al-Azhar as standing in the forefront of the defense of
the faith and its believers against political and social exploitation—for
example, during the French occupation, the British occupation, and to
a lesser degree the 1919 revolution. Notably, the role played by quietist,
accommodating ʿulamaʾ in these events was marginalized in the historic
narrative of the venerable religious institution.[7]

The close identification of al-Azhar as the defender of Islam and Muslims became part of the credo of that venerable institution. In 1949 Mahmoud Abu al-Eyoun, secretary-general of al-Azhar, portrayed this strong
link between Islam and al-Azhar thus:

Al-Azhar's mission is that of Islam which is the propagation of the prophet's call which has been maintained by his followers and which they relentlessly defended and fought for. It is the firm belief of al-Azhar that its duty is to explain to all peoples the right teachings and doctrines of Islam, and to reform the evils of society according to Islamic rules.… Islam was revealed in order to reform communities, so as to raise the standards of humanity and to lift up souls to high levels of dignity and pride.… All Islamic teachings aim at the purification of the soul and at laying the foundation for moral principles. Islam approves of enjoying all that is good and prevents only evil deeds and things. Islam puts an end to tyranny and caprice. It defines the principles of social institutions and legislation, all of which aim for the welfare of humanity and the happiness of society. This is a brief summary of the principles of Islam and al-Azhar's mission.[8]

The Egyptian case can illuminate the status of Sunni ʿulamaʾ in other parts of the urban Middle East in the late nineteenth and early twentieth centuries. ʿUlamaʾ in those regions displayed varied degrees of involvement in politics and interaction with nationalist movements, depending on the specific geopolitical and cultural attributes of their native polity. Yet they held much in common in their impetus to preserve the Islamic image of the community and thereby also reestablished their traditional status as the sole moral authority, which had been eroded under the impact of modernization.

Indeed, the Islamic cause was on the defensive in the face of state building and the reshaping of the collective identity along national lines in the post-Ottoman era. However, the fragility of Arab politics in the context of socioeconomic upheavals entailed a reliance on heightened state loyalty to Islam as a prime source of legitimacy in neutralizing political rivals. The state granted the religious establishment budgets, positions, official *iftaʾ* bodies, and publications. These assets enabled the Sunni ʿulamaʾ to emerge as a pressure group and reclaim their role as guardians of the faith, supported by their designation as the "heirs of the prophets."

Notes

INTRODUCTION

1. David Ohana, *The Promethean Passion: The Intellectual Origins of the Twentieth Century from Rousseau to Foucault;* Anthony D. Smith, *The Ethnic Origins of Nations,* pp. 154–59. The term "metaphysical revolt" is attributed to Albert Camus, who in his essay "The Rebel" (*L'Homme révolté,* 1951) defied God's legitimacy because He condemned humankind to suffering and death. Camus, *The Rebel: An Essay of Man in Revolt,* chapter 2.
2. Robert Towler, "The Social Status of the Anglican Minister"; Paul M. Harrison, "Religious Leadership in America."
3. Harrison, "Religious Leadership in America," p. 974.
4. These religions were defined as having "no collective ritual of worship, no fully developed theology, and no ethical system. They were happy with much of the secular world and had a generally positive attitude to humankind and to the 'self.'" In Bruce's view, they were embodied in the 1990s by the cultic New Age religion, which lacked any attempt to define a canon of acceptable revelations. Steve Bruce, *Religion in the Modern World: From Cathedrals to Cults,* pp. 25–68, 169–95.
5. See, e.g., Stewart Ranson, Alan Bryman, and Bob Hinings, *Clergy, Ministers and Priests,* pp. 1–20.
6. Wan Mohd Nor Wan Daud, *The Concept of Knowledge in Medieval Islam;* Michael Chamberlain, *Knowledge and Social Practice in Medieval Damascus, 1190–1350,* mainly chapters 2 and 4; Jonathan Berkey, "Tradition, Innovation and the Social Construction of Knowledge"; idem, *The Formation of Islam: Religion and Society in the Near East, 600–1880,* pp. 224–30.
7. See Stefan Leder, "Charismatic Scripturalism: The Hanbali Maqdisis of Damascus"; Daniella Talmon-Heller, *Islamic Piety in Medieval Syria: Mosques, Cemeteries and Sermons under the Zangids and Ayyubids, 1146–1260,* pp. 213–24; idem, "ʿIlm, Shafaʿah and Barakah: The Resources of Ayyubid and Early Mamluk ʿUlamaʾ."
8. Berkey, *The Formation of Islam,* pp. 231–47; Spencer Trimingham, *The Sufi Orders in Islam,* pp. 1–30; Alexander Knysh, *Islamic Mysticism: A Short History.*
9. S. N. Eisenstadt (ed.), *Max Weber on Charisma and Institution Building.* See also Clifford Geertz's criticism in *The Interpretation of Cultures: Selected Essays,* pp. 164–65.
10. Aviad Kleinberg, *Flesh Made Word: Saints' Stories and the Western Imagination,* pp. 1–8; also Michael Goodich, "The Politics of Canonization in the Thirteenth Century: Lay and Mendicant Saints"; Pierre Delooz, "Towards a Sociological Study of Canonized Sainthood in the Catholic Church."
11. See Talmon-Heller, "ʿIlm, Shafaʿah and Barakah"; Mark J. Sedgwick, *Islam and Muslims: A Guide to Diverse Experience in a Modern World,* p. 29; Daphna Ephrat, *Spiritual Wayfarers, Leaders in Piety: Sufis and the Dissemination of Islam in Medieval Palestine,* mainly pp. 139–52.

12. See, e.g., Annemarie Schimmel, *Mystical Dimensions of Islam*, pp. 62–77; Esther
    Peskes, "The Wahhabiyya and Sufism in the Eighteenth Century."
13. See Reinhard Schulze, *Islamischer Internationalismus im 20. Jahrhundert*, esp.
    part 1.
14. See, e.g., Hisham Sharabi, *Arab Intellectuals and the West: The Formative Years,
    1875–1914*, pp. 1–52; Dale F. Eickelman and James Piscatori, *Muslim Politics*, p. 131;
    Gudrun Krämer and Sabine Schmidtke, "Introduction: Religious Authorities in
    Muslim Societies: A Critical Overview," pp. 12–13.
15. See, e.g., Gilles Kepel, *The Prophet and Pharaoh*; Emmanuel Sivan, *Radical Islam:
    Medieval Theology and Modern Politics*, pp. 50–56; Hava Lazarus-Yafeh, "The
    Ulama vis-à-vis the Militants," pp. 175–79; Martin Kramer, *Political Islam*.
16. John L. Esposito and John O. Voll, *Makers of Contemporary Islam*, pp. 17–22;
    Olivier Roy, *Globalised Islam: The Search for a New Ummah*, pp. 158–71.
17. Shahrough Akhavi, "Shiʿi Ulama," p. 261.
18. See, e.g., E. Gellner, "Doctor and Saint," pp. 310–11, 325–26; Raphael Danziger,
    *ʿAbd al-Qadir and the Algerians: Resistance to the French and Internal Consolida-
    tion*; E. Evans-Pritchard, *The Sanusi of Cyrenaica*, pp. 1–28; 62–89; P. M. Holt,
    The Mahdist State in the Sudan, 1881–1898; Nehemia Levtzion and John O. Voll,
    "Introduction"; Pessah Shinar, "ʿUlamaʾ, Marabouts and Government: An Over-
    view of Their Relationships in the French Colonial Magrib."
19. See, e.g., Bernard Lewis, *Islam in History*, p. 12; also Ira M. Lapidus, *A History of
    Islamic Societies*, pp. 514–15, 581, 821–22.
20. H. A. R. Gibb and Harold Bowen, *Islamic Society and the West*, vol. 2, pp. 112–13.
21. P. M. Holt, *Egypt and the Fertile Crescent*, pp. 168–70; Lewis, *Islam in History*,
    p. 12, reaffirmed in the second edition of 1993, p. 4; Lapidus, *A History of Islamic
    Societies*, pp. 617–18 (and updated editions of 1995 and 2002); also Sharabi, *Arab
    Intellectuals and the West*, pp. 12–14.
22. Iftikhar Zaman, "Sunni Ulama," p. 259.
23. Esposito and Voll, *Makers of Contemporary Islam*, pp. 14–16; Roy, *Globalised
    Islam*, pp. 158–67. See also Mehran Kamrava, "Introduction: Reformist Islam in
    Comparative Perspective," pp. 3–5.
24. Afaf Lutfi al-Sayyid-Marsot, "The Role of the Ulama in Egypt during the Early
    Nineteenth Century," p. 264; Daniel Crecelius, "Non-ideological Responses
    of the Egyptian Ulama to Modernization," p. 185; Gabriel Baer, "Islamic Politi-
    cal Activity in Modern Egyptian History: A Comparative Analysis," pp. 39–40,
    43–49. See also Haim Shaked, "The Biographies of Ulama in ʿAli Mubarak's
    Khitat as a Source for the History of the Ulama in Nineteenth-Century Egypt."
25. Carly Murphy, *Passion for Islam*, p. 228.
26. Lila Abu-Lughod, "Introduction: Feminist Longings and Postcolonial Condi-
    tions"; Walter Armbrust, *Mass Culture and Modernism in Egypt*, mainly pp. 1–10,
    190–220; Timothy Mitchell, *Colonising Egypt*, pp. 161–79; Gregory Starret, *Put-
    ting Islam to Work: Education, Politics and Religious Transformation in Egypt*,
    mainly pp. 15–18; Benjamin C. Fortna, *Imperial Classroom: Islam, the State, and
    Education in the Late Ottoman Empire*, pp. 93–95.
27. See, e.g., M. Hoexter, S. N. Eisenstadt, and N. Levtzion (eds.), *The Public Sphere
    in Muslim Societies*.

28. See, e.g., Ehud R. Toledano, *Egypt on the Threshold of the Modern Age*, pp. 60–69; Nelly Hanna, *In Praise of Books*.

29. See, e.g., Haim Gerber, *Ottoman Rule in Jerusalem, 1890–1914*, pp. 9–11, 250–61; Jane Hathaway, "Problems of Periodization in Ottoman History"; idem, *The Arab Lands under Ottoman Rule, 1516–1800*, pp. 1–9, chapters 4–5; Suraiya Faroqhi, Bruce McGowan, and Donald Quantaert, *An Economic and Social History of the Ottoman Empire*, vol. 2, pp. 639ff.

30. See, e.g., James P. Piscatori, *Islam in a World of Nation-States*, pp. 47–100; John L. Esposito, *The Islamic Threat: Myth or Reality*, pp. 62–67; Sami Zubaida, *Islam, the People and the State*, pp. 123–29; Haim Gerber, "The Limits of Constructedness: The Case of Middle Eastern Nationalism"; idem, *Remembering and Imagining Palestine: Identity and Nationalism from the Crusades to the Present*, pp. 14–79; idem. "The Muslim Umma and the Formation of Middle Eastern Nationalisms."

31. Anwar Alam, *Religion and State, Egypt, Iran and Saudi Arabia: A Comparative Study*, p. 71. Egyptian writing was also influenced by this approach. Malik Rashwan, in an essay in 1989, asserted that Muhammad ʿAli's regime managed to take the wind out of the sails of Islam—the very same wind that linked religion with the material world. Al-Azhar authorities thus became "religious authorities only." Malik Muhammad Rashwan, *ʿUlamaʾ al-Azhar bayna Bunabart wa-Muhammad ʿAli*, pp. 360–69.

32. Richard T. Antoun, *Muslim Preacher in the Modern World*, pp. 257–62.

33. Malika Zeghal, *Gardiens de l'Islam: Les oulémas d'Al-Azhar dans l'Égypte contemporaine;* idem, "Religion and Politics in Egypt: The Ulema of al-Azhar, Radical Islam and the State, 1952–1994," pp. 378–88; also Shadaab H. Rahemtulla, "Reconceptualizing the Contemporary Ulama: al-Azhar, Lay Islam and the Egyptian State," pp. 84–107.

34. See Meir Hatina, "Historical Legacy and the Challenge of Modernity: The Case of al-Azhar in Egypt."

35. Malika Zeghal, "'The Recentering' of Religious Knowledge and Discourse: The Case of al-Azhar in Twentieth-Century Egypt," pp. 107–30.

36. Muhammad Qasim Zaman, *The Ulama in Contemporary Islam*.

37. Additional insights can be found in Meir Hatina (ed.), *Guardians of Faith in Modern Times: ʿUlamaʾ in the Middle East*.

38. Jürgen Habermas, *The Structural Transformation of the Public Sphere*. For debates about and criticism of Habermas's concept, see Craig J. Calhoun (ed.), *Habermas and the Public Sphere*.

39. Hoexter, Eisenstadt, and Levtzion, *The Public Sphere in Muslim Societies*.

40. Tala Asad, *Genealogies of Religion: Discipline and Reasons of Power in Christianity and Islam*, pp. 202–3.

41. Ami Ayalon, *The Press in the Arab Middle East: A History*, pp. 39–62. The impressive development of the Egyptian press was also acknowledged by the British authorities, who charged that some of the local newspapers were involved in anti-British incitement and were using intellectual terror against those Egyptians who did not share their belligerent stance. See *Reports by His Majesty's Agent and Consul-General on the Finances, Administration and Condition of Egypt and Sudan in 1906*, pp. 8–9.

42. Michael Gasper, "ʿAbdallah al-Nadim, Islamic Reform, and 'Ignorant' Peasants: State-Building in Egypt?" p. 85.

43. On the features of the Egyptian public sphere in the last quarter of the nineteenth century, see, e.g., Juan R. Cole, *Colonialism and Revolution in the Middle East: Social and Cultural Origins of Egypt's ʿUrabi Movement,* chapters 5, 6, 8, 9; F. Robert Hunter, *Egypt under the Khedives, 1805–1879;* Ehud R. Toledano, *State and Society in Mid-Nineteenth-Century Egypt,* pp. 221–30; Ayalon, *The Press in the Arab Middle East: A History,* pp. 167–73; Abbas Kelidar, "The Political Press in Egypt, 1882–1914"; Armando Salvatore, "After the State: Islamic Reform and the Implosion of Shariʿa"; see also Israel Gershoni and James Jankowski, *Confronting Fascism in Egypt: Dictatorship versus Democracy in the 1930s,* pp. 51–55.

44. Michel Foucault, *Power/Knowledge: Selected Interviews and Other Writings, 1972–1977,* pp. 78–108; on Foucault's observation in the Egyptian context, see Mitchell, *Colonising Egypt,* chapters 2–3.

45. See Mitchell, *Colonising Egypt,* p. 82; Lars Bjørneboe, *In Search of the True Political Position of the ʿUlama,* pp. 324–29.

46. Alexander Schölch, *Egypt for the Egyptians: The Socio-political Crisis in Egypt, 1878–1882;* Cole, *Colonialism and Revolution in the Middle East.*

CHAPTER 1

1. ʿAbd al-Rahman Ibn al-Jawzi, *al-ʿIlal al-Mutanahiya fiʾl-ahadith al-wahiya,* vol. 1, pp. 81–82; Muhammad ibn Ismaʿil al-Bukhari, *Sahih al-Bukhari,* vol. 1, p. 37.

2. Abu Hamid al-Ghazali, *Ihyaʾ ʿulum al-din,* vol. 1, pp. 4–13.

3. See Chamberlain, *Knowledge and Social Practice in Medieval Damascus, 1190–1350,* chapter 2; George Maqdisi, *The Rise of Colleges: Institutions of Learning in Islam and the West.*

4. See, e.g., Berkey, *The Formation of Islam,* pp. 216–20; Ira M. Lapidus, "Muslim Cities and Islamic Societies," pp. 49–60; Daphna Ephrat, "Religious Leadership and Associations in the Public Sphere of Seljuk Baghdad," pp. 37–41.

5. Talmon-Heller, "ʿIlm, Shafaʿah and Barakah"; also Chamberlain, *Knowledge and Social Practice in Medieval Damascus,* chapter 4.

6. Miriam Hoexter and Nehemia Levtzion, "Introduction," p. 11.

7. Al-Ghazali, *Ihyaʾ ʿulum al-din,* vol. 1, p. 17; also quoted in Henri Laoust, *La politique de Gazali,* p. 197.

8. See Berkey, *The Formation of Islam,* pp. 124–29; Ira M. Lapidus, "The Separation of State and Religion in the Development of Early Islamic Society."

9. For a general survey of al-Azhar in premodern times, see Bayard Dodge, *al-Azhar: A Millennium of Muslim Learning.*

10. Berkey, *The Formation of Islam,* pp. 203–15.

11. According to C. F. Petry's data, during the later Middle Ages some thirty percent of the Cairene ʿulamaʾ were not native to the city. Petry, *The Civilian Elite of Cairo in the Later Middle Ages,* pp. 37–81.

12. Ibid., pp. 246–69.

13. Hathaway, *The Arab Lands under Ottoman Rule,* pp. 114–37; Bjørneboe, *In Search of the True Political Position of the ʿUlama,* pp. 39–53; Michael Winter, *Egyptian*

Society under Ottoman Rule, 1517–1798, pp. 118–27; Kamal Hamid Mughith, *Misr fi'l-ʿasr al-ʿUthmani 1517–1798,* pp. 163–70.

14. The Islamic historical term "Bilad al-Sham" is tantamount to what was known as "Greater Syria" in early twentieth-century diplomatic and political usage, covering the modern political entities of Syria, Lebanon, Jordan, Israel, and the West Bank of Palestine.

15. Mughith, *Misr fi'l-ʿasr al-ʿUthmani,* pp. 163–68; also Albert Hourani, "The Syrians in Egypt in the Eighteenth and Nineteenth Centuries," pp. 221–22.

16. Gamal El-Din El-Shayyal, "Some Aspects of Intellectual and Social Life in Eighteenth-Century Egypt," in P. M. Holt (ed.), *Political and Social Change in Modern Egypt,* pp. 117–21. A more significant picture of the engagement with rational sciences can be found in the Ottoman scholarly community. According to Khaled El-Rouayheb, the study of disciplines such as logic, dialectics, philosophy, and rational theology continued unabated in the Ottoman Empire in the seventeenth century and even intensified due to the dramatic rise in the number of educational institutions and the influx of scholarly works, and scholars, from Azerbaijan and Persia. El-Rouayheb, "The Myth of 'The Triumph of Fanaticism' in the Seventeenth-Century Ottoman Empire."

17. ʿAli ʿAbd al-Wahid Wafi, *Lamha fi taʾrikh al-Azhar,* pp. 26–31.

18. Martin Hartmann, *The Arabic Press of Egypt,* p. 14.

19. ʿAli Mubarak, *al-Khitat al-tawfiqiyya al-jadida li-Misr al-Qahira,* vol. 4, pp. 36–38; J. Heyworth-Dunne, *An Introduction to the History of Education in Modern Egypt,* pp. 36–42.

20. Nelly Hanna, "Culture in Ottoman Egypt," in M. W. Daly (ed.), vol. 2, pp. 94–100.

21. Al-Hijazi quoted in Mahmud al-Sharqawi, *Misr fi'l-qarn al-thamin ʿashar,* vol. 2, p. 162.

22. Al-Jabarti quoted in ibid., vol. 2, pp. 149–50.

23. Thomas Philipp and Moshe Perlmann (eds.), *ʿAbd al-Rahman al-Jabarti's History of Egypt,* vol. 1, p. 11.

24. Al-Jabarti cited in al-Sharqawi, *Misr fi'l-qarn al-thamin ʿashar,* vol. 2, pp. 142–61. For other polemical intellectuals and their texts, see Nelly Hanna, *In Praise of Books,* pp. 139–71.

25. Philipp and Perlmann, *ʿAbd al-Rahman al-Jabarti's History of Egypt,* vol. 1, p. 11.

26. On al-Jabarti's search for the ideal ʿalim, see Bjørneboe, *In Search of the True Political Position of the ʿUlama,* mainly chapters 2 and 4; Shmuel Moreh, "al-Jabarati's Attitude towards the ʿUlamaʾ of His Time."

27. Hanna, "Culture in Ottoman Egypt," pp. 100–112. In *In Praise of Books* Hanna also explored the intellectual role of middle-ranking writers and thinkers who emerged during the sixteenth to eighteenth centuries and developed a middle-class culture that was not affiliated with the establishment scholarship at al-Azhar and more closely reflected social realities and concerns. The proliferation of trade and commerce had granted them space, resources, and opportunities to express their views.

28. Sulayman Rasad al-Hanafi, *Kanz al-jawhar fi taʾrikh al-Azhar,* pp. 176–84.

29. Mustafa Ramadan, "Riwaq al-Shuwam bi'l-Azhar iban al-ʿasr al-ʿUthmani," pp. 43–46.

30. Al-Hanafi, *Kanz al-jawhar,* pp. 192–96; Mughith, *Misr fi'l-ʿasr al-ʿUthmani,* pp. 176–85; Jane Hathaway, "The Role of the Ulama in Social Protest in Late Eighteenth-Century Cairo," pp. 24–42, 43–86; Winter, *Egyptian Society under Ottoman Rule,* pp. 109–27; also Gabriel Baer, *Egyptian Guilds in Modern Times.* Similar observations are provided by James Grehan with regard to urban protests in Ottoman Damascus: "Street Violence and Social Imagination in Late-Mamluk and Ottoman Damascus (ca. 1500–1800)," pp. 218–19.

31. Al-Sharqawi, *Misr fi'l-qarn al-thamin ʿashar,* vol. 2, pp. 119–26.

32. See Daniel Crecelius and Hamza ʿAbd al-ʿAziz Badr, "An Agreement between the ʿUlamaʾ and the Mamluk Amirs in 1795: A Test of the Accuracy of Two Contemporary Chronicles."

33. Hartmann, *The Arabic Press of Egypt,* pp. 275–305; Trimingham, *The Sufi Orders in Islam,* pp. 185–90.

34. Ibrahim M. Abu-Rabiʿ, *The Mystical Teachings of al-Shadhili,* pp. 1–9; Faruq Ahmad Mustafa, *al-Binaʾ al-ijtimaʿi li'l-tariqa al-Shadhiliyya fi Misr,* pp. 108–21; ʿAbd al-Halim Mahmud, *al-Madrasa al-Shadhiliyya al-haditha,* pp. 125–44.

35. Philipp and Perlmann, *ʿAbd al-Rahman al-Jabarti's History of Egypt,* vol. 2, pp. 173–76; Mughith, *Misr fi'l-ʿasr al-ʿUthmani,* pp. 191–98 (quotation); Mubarak, *al-Khitat,* vol. 9, pp. 95–96; Muhammad Farid Abu Hadid, *Zaʾim Misr al-awwal: al-Sayyid ʿUmar Makram,* pp. 36–50.

36. Al-Sharqawi, *Misr fi'l-qarn al-thamin ʿashar,* vol. 1, p. 162; ʿAbd al-ʿAziz Muhammad al-Shinnawi, "Dawr al-Azhar fi'l-hifaz ʿala al-tabiʿ al-ʿArabi li'l-Misr ibbana al-hukm al-ʿUthmani," pp. 665–67; also ʿAli ʿAbd al-ʿAzim, *Mashyakhat al-Azhar mundhu inshaʾiha hatta al-an,* vol. 1, pp. 15–27.

37. Abu Hadid, *Zaʾim Misr al-awwal,* pp. 36–50.

38. Al-Sayyid-Marsot, "The Role of the Ulama in Egypt," pp. 270–75; Bjørneboe, *In Search of the True Political Position of the ʿUlama,* p. 72; also ʿAbd al-ʿAziz Muhammad al-Shinnawi and Jalal Yahya (eds.), *Wathaʾiq wa-nusus, al-taʾrikh al-hadith wa'l-muʿasir,* pp. 501–10; Samir Girgis, *The Predominance of the Islamic Tradition of Leadership in Egypt during Bonaparte's Expedition.*

39. Ramadan, "Riwaq al-Shuwam bi'l Azhar," pp. 48–58; Muhi al-Din al-Tuʿmi, *al-Nur al-abhar fi tabaqat shuyukh al-jamiʿ al-Azhar,* p. 45; ʿAbd al-Rahim ʿAbd al-Rahim, "ʿAlaqat Bilad al-Sham bi-Misr fi'l-ʿasr al-ʿUthmani 1517–1798"; Samir ʿAbd al-Maqsud Sayyid, *al-Shuwam fi Misr mundhu al-fath al-ʿUthmani hatta awaʾil al-qarn al-tasiʿ ʿashar;* ʿAbdallah Muhammad ʿAzabawi, *al-Shuwam fi Misr fi'l-qarnayn al-thamin ʿashar wa'l-tasiʿ ʿashar.*

CHAPTER 2

1. Mitchell, *Colonising Egypt,* mainly chapters 2–3; Crecelius, "Non-ideological Responses of the Egyptian Ulama to Modernization," p. 180.

2. Frederick De Jong, *Turuq and Turuq-Linked Institutions in Nineteenth-Century Egypt,* pp. 14–20, 33–35, 50–51, 62–64, 125–40; idem, "Opposition to Sufism in Twentieth-Century Egypt (1900–1970): A Preliminary Survey," p. 312 (quotation).

3. See, e.g., Moshe Maʿoz, "The Ulama and the Process of Modernization in Syria during the Mid-Nineteenth Century," pp. 77–88.

4. Philipp and Perlmann (eds.), ʿAbd al-Rahman al-Jabartiʾs History of Egypt, vol. 4, p. 285; also ibid., pp. 256–58; Butrus Abu-Manneh, "Four Letters of Šayh Hasan al-ʿAttar to Šayh Tahir al-Husayni of Jerusalem," pp. 84–85.

5. Lapidus, A History of Islamic Societies, pp. 545–47; Moshe Gammer, Muslim Resistance to the Tsar.

6. Mitchell, Colonising Egypt, pp. 34–62.

7. Rashwan, ʿUlamaʾ al-Azhar, pp. 370–72; Alam, Religion and State, p. 71; Cole, Colonialism and Revolution, p. 36; Bjørneboe, In Search of the True Political Position of the ʿUlama, pp. 324–29.

8. Cole, Colonialism and Revolution, p. 36; Peter Gran, Islamic Roots of Capitalism in Egypt, 1760–1840; Daniel L. Newman, An Imam in Paris: Account of a Stay in France by an Egyptian Cleric, 1826–1831.

9. Bjørneboe, In Search of the True Political Position of the ʿUlama, pp. 326–29.

10. Shaked, "The Biographies of Ulama in ʿAli Mubarak's Khitat"; De Jong, Turuq and Turuq-Linked Institutions, pp. 20–24, 33–35; also Gabriel Baer, Studies in the Social History of Modern Egypt, pp. 95–99.

11. Eisenstadt (ed.), Max Weber on Charisma and Institution Building, pp. xix–xx; see also Berkey, The Formation of Islam, pp. 149–50.

12. Haim Shaked, "The Views of Rifaʿa al-Tahtawi on Religion and the Ulama in State and Society," pp. 284–88; John W. Livingston, "Western Science and Educational Reform in the Thought of Shaykh Rifaʿa al-Tahtawi"; Mubarak, al-Khitat, vol. 4, pp. 13, 28–29 (quotation); also Michael J. Reimer, "Contradiction and Consciousness in ʿAli Mubarak's Description of al-Azhar," pp. 57–64.

13. Dodge, al-Azhar, pp. 114–17; al-Tuʿmi, al-Nur al-abhar, p. 12; Muhibb al-Din al-Khatib, al-Azhar: madih wa-hadiruhu waʾl-haja ila islahihi, pp. 23–24.

14. Al-Hilal 7 (1899–1900): 522–23; ʿAbd al-ʿAzim, Mashyakhat al-Azhar, vol. 1, pp. 27–28; Saʿid Ismaʿil ʿAli, al-Azhar ʿala masrah al-siyasa al-Misriyya, pp. 175–76. Al-Mahdi's predecessor in the office of grand mufti, Ahmad al-Tamimi, was also said to have confronted Ibrahim Pasha (Muhammad ʿAli's eldest son) and was dismissed for refusing to approve matters that in his view deviated from shariʿa law. Ahmad Taymur, Aʿlam al-fikr al-Islami fiʾl-ʿasr al-hadith, p. 64.

15. Edmund Burke III, "Understanding Arab Protest Movements," p. 337.

16. Jakob Skovgaard-Petersen, Defining Islam for the Egyptian State, pp. 51–56; Ayalon, The Press in the Arab Middle East, pp. 138–59.

17. Khaled Fahmy, "An Olfactory Tale of Two Cities: Cairo in the Nineteenth Century," pp. 160–63.

18. For a useful account of al-ʿArusi's reform program, see Indira Falk Gesnik, "Beyond Modernisms: Opposition and Negotiation in the Azhar Reform Debate in Egypt, 1870–1911," pp. 154–60.

19. See, e.g., ʿIllaysh's strict stance on the issue of the hudud (Qurʾanic punishments), such as stoning for adultery and amputation for theft. Muhammad ʿIllaysh, Hidayat al-salik ila al-masalik fi fiqh imam al-aʾiama Malik ʿala al-sharh al-saghir liʾl-ʿalama al-Dardir, vol. 2, pp. 356–60.

20. Al-Maziri cited in Muhammad ʿIllaysh, Fath al-ʿali al-malik fiʾl-fatwa ʿala madhhab al-Imam Malik, vol. 1, pp. 56–57.

21. Mubarak, al-Khitat, vol. 4, pp. 40–41.

22. ʿIllaysh, Fath al-ʿali al-malik, vol. 1, pp. 236–37, 360–63; vol. 2, p. 10.

23. Mubarak, *al-Khitat*, vol. 4, pp. 40–41; vol. 9, pp. 95–96.

24. A well-known story associated with al-ʿIdwi relates to the visit of Sultan ʿAbd al-ʿAziz to Egypt during Ismaʿil's rule. While the most eminent ʿulamaʾ greeted the sultan by bowing and touching the earth and withdrew while keeping their faces toward him, al-ʿIdwi made his entry with head erect and promptly advised the sultan to show piety toward Allah, fear His punishment, and treat His subjects justly. This incident was quoted even by modern Islamists such as Sayyid Qutb as a true model of the religious scholar, whose "spirit is raised above all worldly values, all temporal powers, and all worldly considerations." Zaki Muhammad Mujahid, *al-Aʿlam al-Sharqiyya*, vol. 1, pp. 98–99; ʿAsim al-Dasuqi, *Mujtamaʿ ʿulamaʾ al-Azhar fi Misr 1895–1961*, pp. 42–43; ʿAbd al-ʿAzim, *Mashyakhat al-Azhar*, vol. 1, pp. 27–28; Sayyid Qutb, *Social Justice in Islam*, pp. 195–96.

25. Mubarak, *al-Khitat*, vol. 4, p. 43.

26. Ibid., vol. 4, pp. 41–42; al-Hanafi, *Kanz al-jawhar*, pp. 159–63; Muhammad ibn Muhammad Makhluf, *Shajarat al-nur al-zakiyya fi tabaqat al-Malikiyya*, pp. 383–84; Ilyas Zakhura, *Mirʾat al-ʿasr fi taʾrikh wa-rusum akabir al-rijal bi-Misr*, vol. 1, pp. 196–97; Yusuf Sarkis, *Muʿjam al-matbuʿat al-ʿArabiyya waʾl-muʿarraba*, vol. 7, pp. 1372–74.

27. Mubarak, *al-Khitat*, vol. 4, pp. 32, 38, 41. Wilfrid Scawen Blunt (d. 1922), a foreign observer, scholar, and poet who was involved in Middle Eastern political affairs in the late nineteenth century, attested to the fervor of the Maliki rite. He depicted the Malikis, more than any other Muslims, as representing "the ancient earnestness of the Prophet's companions, [in that] the sword in their hand is ever the sword of God." Blunt, *The Future of Islam*, pp. 72–73.

28. Mubarak, *al-Khitat*, vol. 4, pp. 32, 38, 41; Jacques Berque, *Egypt: Imperialism and Revolution*, pp. 81–82.

29. Mujahid, *al-Aʿlam al-Sharqiyya*, vol. 1, pp. 98–99; al-Dasuqi, *Mujtamaʿ ʿulamaʾ al-Azhar*, pp. 42–43.

30. *Al-Hilal* 7 (1899–1900): 519–23; Taymur, *Aʿlam al-fikr al-Islami*, pp. 50–61; ʿAbd al-ʿAzim, *Mashyakhat al-Azhar*, vol. 1, pp. 243–54; Jurji Zaydan, *Tarajim mashahir al-Sharq fiʾl-qarn al-tasiʿ ʿashar*, vol. 2, pp. 250–55.

31. On the 1872 Azhari educational reforms under al-Mahdi's tenure, see Gesnik, "Beyond Modernisms," pp. 161–66.

32. The number of al-Azhar graduates increased at the start of the twentieth century. In 1901 it had twenty graduates. Wafi, *Lamha fi taʾrikh al-Azhar*, pp. 48–56, 62–85; ʿAbd al-Mutaʿal al-Saʿidi, *Taʾrikh al-islah fiʾl-Azhar*, vol. 1, pp. 3–34.

33. Al-Mahdi was also a member of the Supreme Special Council (al-Majlis al-Khususi al-Aʿla) of the government and thereby, in ʿAbd al-Rahman al-Rafiʿi's depiction, a "de facto state minister," another indication of his influential status. Al-Rafiʿi, *ʿAsr Ismaʿil*, vol. 2, pp. 330–31.

34. Skovgaard-Petersen, *Defining Islam*, pp. 100–103; Rudolph Peters, "Muhammad al-ʿAbbasi al-Mahdi (d. 1897): Grand Mufti of Egypt and his al-Fatawa al-Mahadiyya," pp. 73–78.

35. Mubarak, *al-Khitat*, vol. 4, pp. 40–41.

36. Cole, *Colonialism and Revolution*, pp. 37–38.

37. Al-Hanafi, *Kanz al-jawhar,* pp. 204–5.

38. Notably, the leadership of al-Azhar was in the hands of the Shafiʿis continuously from 1724 to 1870. Mubarak, *al-Khitat,* vol. 4, pp. 36–37; Ahmad ʿIzzat ʿAbd al-Karim, *Taʾrikh al-taʿlim fi ʿasr Muhammad ʿAli,* vol. 1, pp. 810–19; Muhammad Khalil Subhi, *Taʾrikh al-hayat al-niyabiyya fi Misr,* p. 47; Samir Muhammad Taha, *Ahmad ʿUrabi wa-dawruhu fiʾl-hayat al-siyasiya al-Misriyya,* p. 323.

39. Amin Sami, *Taqwim al-Nil,* vols. 2–3, pp. 921–22; also Schölch, *Egypt for the Egyptians,* p. 31.

40. Newman, *An Imam in Paris,* p. 62; Heyworth-Dunne, *An Introduction to the History of Education in Modern Egypt,* pp. 399–405; Chris Eccel, *Egypt, Islam and Social Change,* pp. 23–27; Gilbert Delanoue, *Moralistes et politiques musulmans dans l'Égypte du XIXe siècle, 1798–1882,* vol. 1, pp. 135–36; also Lois A. Aroian, *The Nationalization of Arabic and Islamic Education in Egypt: Dar al-Ulum and al-Azhar.*

41. The educational reform in the 1870s did not produce a complete break with the traditional system of education, however, in favor of a modern and rational model. As shown by Hoda A. Yousef, indigenous modes of thought and education were embraced by reformist scholars and acquired new meanings. In the last two decades of the nineteenth century, against the background of the British occupation and its disinterest in expanding government education, the two systems of education eventually collided. British policy prompted intellectual leaders to be more vocal about the need for widespread education well beyond the limited options offered by al-Azhar. Yousef, "Reassessing Egypt's Dual Systems of Education under Ismaʿil."

42. Al-Rafiʿi, *ʿAsr Ismaʿil,* vol. 2, pp. 216–19; Zayn al-ʿAbidin Najm, *al-Jamʿiyya al-wataniyya al-Misriyya,* pp. 32–33; Schölch, *Egypt for the Egyptians,* pp. 85–93.

43. Tahir al-Tanahi (ed.), *Mudhakkirat Muhammad ʿAbduh,* pp. 48–50.

44. The book that induced the dispute between ʿAbduh and ʿIllaysh was Masʿud ibn ʿUmar Taftazani's *al-ʿAqaʾid al-nasafiyya.* On the Muʿtazila theology, see D. Gimaret, "Muʿtazila."

45. Al-Mahdi's interference on behalf of ʿAbduh was also based on the testimony of ʿAbduh's friends, such as Muhammad Bakhit, who swore that ʿAbduh was a devoted Muslim, observing worship rituals and attending the Friday prayer during his studies. On the ʿIllaysh/ʿAbduh encounter, see al-Hanafi, *Kanz al-jawhar,* pp. 167–69; Wafi, *Lamha fi taʾrikh al-Azhar,* pp. 26–31; Muhammad Rashid Rida, *Taʾrikh al-imam al-shaykh Muhammad ʿAbduh,* vol. 1, pp. 133–35.

46. Rida, *Taʾrikh,* vol. 1, pp. 134–35, 405–11, 511–12; Ahmad Amin, *Zuʿamaʾ al-islah fiʾl-ʿasr al-hadith,* pp. 288–89. Another disciple of ʿAbduh, Osman Amin, was more vigorous, placing ʿIllaysh in a broader perspective as a member of a group of ultraconservative Azharis who antagonized ʿAbduh. The fanaticism of these champions of the past "reached such a pitch that they would accuse all who dared oppose them of error and deviation from the faith.... Their reaction to him [ʿAbduh] would be revealed at the time of his final examinations." Osman Amin, *Muhammad ʿAbduh,* p. 11.

47. Rida, *Taʾrikh,* vol. 1, pp. 134–35, 405–11, 511–12; Amin, *Zuʿamaʾ al-islah,* pp. 288–89.

CHAPTER 3

1. Cole, *Colonialism and Revolution,* pp. 241–45, 268–72. See also Ignaz Goldziher's observation on the relationship between the press and ʿUrabist politics in Robert Simon, *Ignác Goldziher: His Life and Scholarship as Reflected in His Works and Correspondence,* pp. 47–48; Sami ʿAziz, *al-Sihafa al-Misriyya wa-mawqifuha min al-ihtilal al-Inglizi,* pp. 55–61; William R. C. Phelps, "Political Journalism and the ʿUrabi Revolt."

2. ʿAziz, *al-Sihafa al-Misriyya,* p. 55.

3. Simon, *Ignác Goldziher,* p. 47.

4. This chronology of events is provided by Donald M. Reid, "The Urabi Revolution and the British Conquest, 1879–1882."

5. ʿAbd al-Rahman al-Rafiʿi, *al-Thawra al-ʿUrabiyya waʾl-ihtilal al-Injlizi,* pp. 531–38.

6. Latifa Muhammad Salim, *al-Quwwa al-ijtimaʿiyya fiʾl-thawra al-ʿUrabiyya,* pp. 359–68; Hasan Hanafi, "al-Din waʾl-thawra fiʾl-thawra al-ʿUrabiyya"; Salim al-Naqqash, *Misr liʾl-Misriyyin,* vol. 4, pp. 336–41, vol. 5, pp. 150, 194–95.

7. Lord [Evelyn Baring] Cromer, *Modern Egypt,* p. 252.

8. See ibid., pp. 165–66, 222–23. Another strategy that Cromer used to delegitimize the ʿUrabi movement was portraying it as a sectoral revolt by military officers embittered over the conditions of their pay. In one place he admitted, however, that the revolt "partook in some degree of the nature of a *bona fide* national movement." Cromer, *Modern Egypt,* pp. 137–51, 198–200, 251 (quotation).

9. Ahmad ʿUrabi, *Mudhakkirat ʿUrabi: kashf al-sitar ʿan sirr al-asrar fiʾl-nahda al-Misriyya,* vol. 1, pp. 83–84.

10. Some of the ʿUrabist ʿulamaʾ, especially Muhammad Khalil al-Hijrisi, were also involved (through the mediation of Wilfrid Blunt) in persuading the British consul, Edward Malet, to intervene in the disputed matter and press the khedive to dismiss al-Mahdi. Michael D. Berdine, *The Accidental Tourist: Wilfrid Scawen Blunt and the British Invasion of Egypt in 1882,* p. 103.

11. *Al-Hilal* 3 (August 1897–September 1898): 85–86; Edward Malet (Cairo) to Earl Granville (London), September 23, 1881, quoted in *British and Foreign State Papers, 1881–1882* vol. 73, p. 1148; Schölch, *Egypt for the Egyptians,* p. 160.

12. The appointment of al-Bablawi (d. 1905), a lecturer at al-Azhar and at the Husayni Mosque, stemmed largely from his close relationship with al-Barudi. The extent of his involvement in the events of the revolt is unclear, but following its suppression he expected to be arrested and sentenced, like other ʿulamaʾ. Ultimately, however, the khedive refrained from this type of punishment because of his prestige and made do with dismissing him from Dar al-Kutub while allowing him to continue as a preacher at the Husayni Mosque. He later served as *naqib al-ashraf* and shaykh al-Azhar. Ahmad Taymur, *Aʿlam al-fikr al-Islami fiʾl-ʿasr al-hadith,* pp. 64–68.

13. Salim, *al-Quwwa al-ijtimaʿiyya,* pp. 359–62; al-Naqqash, *Misr liʾl-Misriyyin,* vol. 4, pp. 308–10; Taha, *Ahmad ʿUrabi,* p. 323; Saʿid Ismaʿil ʿAli, *al-Azhar ʿala masrah al-siyasa al-Misriyya,* pp. 176–77.

14. Ahmad Rafiʿ al-Tahtawi, *al-Qawl al-ijabi;* Zakhura, *Mirʾat al-ʿasr,* vol. 1, p. 196; also ʿAbd al-ʿAzim, *Mashyakhat al-Azhar,* vol. 1, pp. 257–69.

15. ʿAli, *al-Azhar ʿala masrah al-siyasa al-Misriyya*, p. 184; Mahmud Khafif, *Ahmad ʿUrabi al-zaʿim al-muftarʾa ʿalay*, vol. 2, p. 20.

16. In a fatwa issued by al-Inbabi in 1887, which was also signed by Mufti Muham-mad al-Banna, he did approve the use of modern sciences such as medicine, geometry, chemistry, astronomy, and geography and their inclusion in the Azhari curriculum; but he conditioned his approval solely on the achievement of material aims useful to strengthening the power of the nation, without adopt-ing any philosophical insights that might jeopardize religious tenets. Rashid Rida mentions in his biography of ʿAbduh that ʿAbduh tried to persuade al-Inbabi to introduce Ibn Khaldun's *al-Muqadama* into the al-Azhar curriculum when he returned to Egypt after his exile for his involvement in the ʿUrabi revolt. Al-Inbabi refused, explaining that entrenched Islamic tradition would not allow it. Rida, *Taʾrikh*, vol. 1, p. 426; also ʿAbd al-ʿAzim, *Mashyakhat al-Azhar*, vol. 1, pp. 262–65.

17. Records of al-ʿIdwi's interrogation after the suppression of the uprising show that he was even suspected of receiving a sum of money from agents of Prince ʿAbd al-Halim in Egypt to fund his mosque activities in exchange for advancing the candidacy of the Egyptian prince for the khedivate. A. M. Broadley, *How We Defended Arabi and His Friends*, p. 371.

18. Schölch, *Egypt for the Egyptians*, p. 172.

19. ʿAbd al-Munʿim Ibrahim al-Jumayʿi, "al-Tanafus ʿala khidiwiyya al-Misriyya bayna al-Amir Halim waʾl-Khidiw Tawfiq," pp. 359–72. For a survey of ʿAbd al-Halim's political intrigues, see Jacob M. Landau, *Middle Eastern Themes: Papers in History and Politics*, pp. 19–30.

20. Salim, *al-Quwwa al-ijtimaʿiyya*, pp. 84, 424; idem, "Masaʿi al-Amir Halim waʾl-Khidiw Ismaʿil min ajl ʿarsh Misr athnaa al-thawra al-ʿUrabiyya"; Başbakanlık Arşivi, Yildiz collection, code: Y.PRK.MK, file 2, folder 46, 19/N/1299 [August 4, 1882].

21. See Başbakanlık Arşivi, Yildiz collection, code: Y.PRK.MK, file 1, folder 70, 8/N/1299 [July 24, 1882].

22. Ibid., code: Y.PRK.MK, file 1, folder 59, 29/S/1299 [January 20, 1882]; also code: Y.EE, file 121, folder 24, 7/B/1299 [May 25, 1882].

23. Ibid., code: Y.EE, file 116, folder 5, 05/B/1299 [May 23, 1882]; also Salah ʿIsa, *Hikayat min daftar al-watan*.

24. Ibid., code: Y.EE, file 121, folder 27, 12/B/1299 [May 30, 1882].

25. Ibid., code: Y.EE, file 128, folder 56, 19/B/1299 [June 6, 1882].

26. ʿUrabi, *Mudhakkirat*, vol. 1, pp. 142–43; ʿIsa, *Hikayat min daftar al-watan*, pp. 43–47; Mahmud Salah, *Muhakamat zaʿim*, p. 59; Jacob M. Landau, *The Poli-tics of Pan-Islam: Ideology and Organization*, pp. 321–35, 364–67; Kemal Karpat, *The Politicization of Islam: Reconstructing Identity, State, Faith, and Community in the Late Ottoman State*, pp. 193–95; Thomas Eich, "The Forgotten Salafi—Abu al-Huda as-Sayyadi."

27. Jeddah to Foreign Secretary, August 6, 1879, December 8, 1879, quoted in A. L. P. Burdett (ed.), *Records of the Hijaz, 1798–1925*, vol. 3, pp. 137–46; Jeddah to Foreign Secretary February 8, 1881, quoted in ibid., pp. 727–29; Karpat, *The*

Politicization of Islam, p. 269. See also Başbakanlık Arşivi, Yildiz collection, code: Y.PRK.AZJ, file 9, folder 109, 29/Z/1301 [October 20, 1884].

28. Schölch notes that the sultan's favored candidate was ʿAbd al-Halim, although Selim Deringil's findings show otherwise. Schölch, *Egypt for the Egyptians,* pp. 244, 246–47; Deringil, "The Ottoman Response to the Egyptian Crises of 1881–82," pp. 3–6.

29. Başbakanlık Arşivi, Yildiz collection, code: Y.EE, file 128, folder 27, 7/B/1299 [May 25, 1882]; Earl of Dufferin (Therapia) to Earl Granville (London), October 4, 1881, quoted in *British and Foreign State Papers, 1881–1882,* vol. 73, pp. 1149–50.

30. Salim, *al-Quwwa al-ijtimaʿiyya,* pp. 262–63, 365; PRO, FO78/3448/No. 198.

31. Al-Naqqash, *Misr liʾl-Misriyyin,* vol. 4, pp. 147–48; ʿUrabi, *Mudhakkirat,* vol. 1, pp. 85–90 (quotation).

32. Michaʾil Sharubim, *al-Khafi fi taʾrikh Misr al-qadim waʾl-hadith,* vol. 4, pp. 255–57. The documents referring to Nizami's delegation are cited in *Bibliyughrafiyya li-wathaʾiq al-thawra al-ʿUrabiyya waʾl-waqaʾiʿ al-harbiyya,* p. 19.

33. Başbakanlık Arşivi, Yildiz collection, code: Y.EE, file 116, folder 58, 28/B/1299 [June 15, 1882].

34. Salim, *al-Quwwa al-ijtimaʿiyya,* pp. 362–63; ʿAbd al-Munʿim Ibrahim al-Jumayʿi, "Mawqif al-dawla al-ʿUthmaniyya min al-thawra al-ʿUrabiyya," p. 147; ʿUrabi, *Mudhakkirat,* vol. 1, pp. 126–31; also *Times* (London), June 12, 1882; Wilfrid Scawen Blunt, *Secret History of the English Occupation of Egypt,* p. 250.

35. Başbakanlık Arşivi, Yildiz collection, code: Y.PRK.MYD, file 2, folder 40, 09/Ş/1299 [July 26, 1882]; ibid., code: Y.PRK.MYD,file 2, folder 46, 19/N/1299 [August 4, 1882].

36. Sharubim, *al-Khafi fi taʾrikh Misr,* pp. 258–59; also Earl of Dufferin (Therapia) to Earl Granville (London), July 17, 1882, quoted in David Gillard (ed.), *British Documents on Foreign Affairs,* vol. 9, pp. 117–18. The documents referring to Darwish's delegation are cited in *Bibliyughrafiyya li-wathaʾiq al-thawra al-ʿUrabiyya,* pp. 19–20.

37. Hasan Adali, "Documents Pertaining to the Egyptian Question in the Yildiz Collection of the Başbakanlık Arşivi, Istanbul," p. 53.

38. Asʿad did not hide his bias against Tawfiq as incompetent and as incapable of maintaining his authority, however, which he made sure to convey to the sultan. Salim, *al-Quwwa al-ijtimaʿiyya,* pp. 280–82; Deringil, "The Ottoman Response"; Başbakanlık Arşivi, Yildiz collection, code: Y.EE, file 116, folder 18, 15/B/1299 [June 3, 1882]; Earl of Dufferin (Therapia) to Earl Granville (London), July 17, 1882, quoted in Gillard, *British Documents on Foreign Affairs,* vol. 9, pp. 117–18; also Broadley, *How We Defended Arabi,* pp. 166–68.

39. Adali, "Documents Pertaining to the Egyptian Question," pp. 52–58. In social and cultural terms, too, the Egyptian polity—mainly the court and the elite—remained very much within the Ottoman orbit throughout the nineteenth century. See Toledano, *State and Society in Mid-Nineteenth-Century Egypt,* pp. 21–22, 77–83; also Hanna, *In Praise of Books;* Hathaway, *The Arab Lands under Ottoman Rule,* chapters 4–5.

40. ʿUrabi's pamphlet, quoted in ʿAbd al-Munʿim Ibrahim al-Jumayʿi (ed.), *al-Thawra al-ʿUrabiyya fi daw al-wathaʾiq al-Misriyya,* p. 82.

41. W. C. Cartwright (Alexandria) to Earl Granville (London), July 21, 1882, quoted in Gillard, *British Documents on Foreign Affairs,* vol. 9, pp. 108–9; PRO, FO78/3440, W. C. Cartwright (Alexandria) to Earl Granville (London), August 5, 1882, no. 515; Cole, *Colonialism and Revolution,* p. 239; ʿAbd al-Rahim Mustafa, *Misr waʾl-masʾala al-Misriyya,* pp. 280–81.

42. Al-Shinnawi and Yahya (eds.), *Wathaʾiq wa-nusus,* p. 695.

43. Notably, Mubarak, who headed the mediation delegation, never returned to Cairo and remained with the khedive. Following the suppression of the revolt by the British in September 1882, he joined Sharif Pasha's new government as minister of public works and was awarded a title of honor by Tawfiq. Baer, *Studies in the Social History of Modern Egypt,* pp. 24–25.

44. Al-Jumayʿi, *al-Thawra al-ʿUrabiyya fi daw al-wathaʾiq al-Misriyya,* p. 83; Mahmud al-Sharqawi and ʿAbdallah al-Mishadd, *ʿAli Mubarak hayatahu wa-daʿwtahu wa-aʾtharahu,* pp. 191–95; Amin Saʿid, *Taʾrikh Misr al-siyasi,* pp. 142–44; Ahmad Turbayn, *Taʾrikh al-Sudan al-hadith al-muʿasir,* pp. 192–205; Edward B. Malet (Cairo) to Earl Granville (London), August 22, 1882, quoted in *British and Foreign State Papers, 1882–1883,* vol. 74, pp. 578–79; also Schölch, *Egypt for the Egyptians,* pp. 262–67.

45. See ʿUrabi's telegrams to the governors of the Egyptian provinces, in W. C. Cartwright (Alexandria) to Earl Granville (London), July 21, 1882, quoted in Gillard, *British Documents on Foreign Affairs,* vol. 9, pp. 107–8.

46. Schölch, *Egypt for the Egyptians,* pp. 269–72; Cole, *Colonialism and Revolution,* pp. 245–46.

47. Al-Shinnawi and Yahya (eds.), *Wathaʾiq wa-nusus,* p. 695. Not all the delegates ratified these decisions willingly; but apparently they were in a minority, as the agenda of the assembly was clear to everyone present. See also the interrogation of Ahmad Rifʿat following the suppression of the revolt, in Başbakanlık Arşivi, Yildiz collection, code: Y.EE, file 116, folder 84, 26/Za/1299 [October 9, 1882].

48. Trevor Le Gassick (trans. and ed.), *The Defense Statement of Ahmad ʿUrabi,* pp. 40–43; Salah, *Muhakamat zaʿim,* pp. 64, 66–69; also Başbakanlık Arşivi, Yildiz collection, code: Y.PRK.MK, file 1, folder 69, 13/N/1299 [June 29, 1882].

49. Mubarak, al-*Khitat,* vol. 15, p. 63; Zakhura, *Mirʾat al-ʿasr,* vol. 1, p. 225; Taymur, *Aʿlam al-fikr al-Islami,* pp. 50–61; Zaydan, *Tarajim mashahir al-Sharq,* vol. 2, pp. 250–55.

50. ʿAli, *al-Azhar ʿala masrah al-siyasa al-Misriyya,* pp. 182–187; PRO, FO78/3440/No. 511. A version of this type of fatwa was presented by ʿUrabi in his defense during his trial and appears in Broadley, *How We Defended Arabi,* pp. 175–77. The name of another shaykh, Muhammad al-ʿAshmuni, was also mentioned in issuing the fatwa. Following the suppression of the revolt, al-ʿIdwi and al-Khalfawi, in their interrogations, denied any involvement in composing such a fatwa. See also the testimony of Khalil Kamal, a senior ʿUrabist army officer, in al-Naqqash, *Misr liʾl-Misriyyin,* vol. 7, p. 279.

51. Blunt, *Secret History,* pp. 248–50.

52. ʿIllaysh, *Fath al-ʿali al-malik,* vol. 2, pp. 344–46, 358; idem, *Hidayat al-salik,* vol. 1, p. 245, vol. 2, pp. 253–55. ʿIllaysh's commentaries (*taqrirat*) appear in Muhammad ibn ʿArafah al-Dasuqi, *Hashiyat al-Dasuqi ʿala al-sharh al-kabir,*

vol. 2, pp. 173–74. The quoted hadith appears in Muslim ibn al-Hajjaj al-Qushayri, *Sahih Muslim*, vol. 3, p. 1478.

53. ʿIllaysh, *Fath al-ʿali al-malik*, vol. 1, pp. 387–92; Delanoue, *Moralistes et politiques musulmans*, vol. 1, 164–66; also Khaled Abou El Fadl, *Rebellion and Violence in Islamic Law*, pp. 334–35. ʿAbd al-Qadir surrendered to the French in 1847, was freed after five years of imprisonment in France, lived in Bursa for a while, and eventually settled in Damascus. Under his leadership, Damascus became a center of religious reform. David Commins, *Islamic Reform: Politics and Social Change in Late Ottoman Syria*, pp. 26–30; Itzchak Weismann, A *Taste of Modernity: Sufism, Salafiyya and Arabism in Late Ottoman Damascus*, pp. 193–224.

54. Schölch, *Egypt for the Egyptians*, p. 355, note 16.

55. ʿAbd al-ʿAzim, *Mashyakhat al-Azhar*, vol. 1, p. 247.

56. Notably, al-Bahrawi was among those who testified against ʿUrabi following the supression of the revolt, claiming that during his speech to the second national assembly ʿUrabi defamed the khedive as an infidel. Salah, *Muhakamat zaʿim*, p. 12.

57. Schölch, *Egypt for the Egyptians*, p. 355, note 16.

58. Mubarak, *al-Khitat*, vol. 8, pp. 28–29; Zaydan, *Tarajim mashahir al-Sharq*, vol. 2, pp. 216–17; Muhammad Kamil al-Fiqqi, *al-Azhar wa-atharuhu fiʾl-nahda al-adabiyya al-haditha*, pp. 371–79.

59. See, e.g., ʿAbd al-Hadi Naja al-Abyari, *al-Mawakib al-ʿaliyya*, pp. 55, 121–22.

60. In an effort to refute al-Inbabi's claim of neutrality, Blunt quotes a letter from him at the height of the crisis between the khedive and ʿUrabi over the Anglo-French ultimatum presented in a memorandum in May 1882. In the letter, the shaykh al-Azhar expresses satisfaction with ʿUrabi and states that the army and the nation were united in an effort to uproot the imperialist plot to sow discord in the country as a pretext for intervention. Blunt, *Secret History*, pp. 248–49; also al-Naqqash, *Misr liʾl-Misriyyin*, vol. 7, p. 279.

61. Cole, *Colonialism and Revolution*, p. 245; Salah, *Muhakamat zaʿim*, pp. 10–11.

62. Muhammad ʿAbd al-Munʿim Khafaji, *al-Azhar fi alf ʿam*, vol. 1, pp. 183–88.

63. Quoted in Rudolph Peters, *Islam and Colonialism*, p. 81.

64. ʿUrabi, *Mudhakkirat*, vol. 1, pp. 203–5; al-ʿIdwi quoted in al-Naqqash, *Misr liʾl-Misriyyin*, vol. 7, pp. 271–72.

65. ʿUrabi, *Mudhakkirat*, vol. 1, pp. 203–5; Salim, *al-Quwwa al-ijtimaʿiyya*, pp. 363–68; al-Hanafi, "al-Din waʾl-thawra," pp. 48–51; ʿAbd al-Ghani's interrogation quoted in al-Naqqash, *Misr liʾl-Misriyyin*, vol. 7, pp. 342–43; also Dar al-Wathaʾiq, Mahafazah 8, dossier 53, which contains a collection of sermons delivered in mosques, cited in *Bibliyughrafiyya li-wathaʾiq al-thawra al-ʿUrabiyya*, pp. 206–8.

66. On Fathallah's biography, see al-Tuʿmi, *al-Nur al-abhar*, p. 25.

67. ʿAli, *al-Azhar ʿala masrah al-siyasa al-Misriyya*, pp. 188–90.

68. Ibid., pp. 188–90; Luwis ʿAwad, *Taʾrikh al-fikr al-Misri al-hadith*, vol. 2, pp. 238–39.

69. ʿUrabi, *Mudhakkirat*, vol. 1, pp. 205–10.

70. ʿAziz, *al-Sihafa al-Misriyya*, pp. 53–59; Sami ʿAziz, Khalil Sabat, and Yunan Labib Rizq, *Huriyyat al-sihafa fi Misr 1798–1924*, pp. 82–92.

71. ʿAbd al-Halim Mahmud, *al-Madrasa al-Shadhiliyya al-haditha*, pp. 125–44;

Faruq Ahmad Mustafa, *al-Bina° al-ijtimaʿi liʾl-tariqa al-Shadhiliyya fi Misr,* pp. 108–21; Abu-Rabiʿ, *The Mystical Teachings of al-Shadhili,* pp. 1–9.

72. De Jong, *Turuq and Turuq-Linked Institutions,* pp. 88–89; Julian Johansen, *Sufism and Islamic Reform in Egypt,* pp. 21–23.

73. Blunt, *Secret History,* pp. 123–27; Mubarak, *al-Khitat,* vol. 15, p. 10; al-Rafiʿi, *al-Thawra al-ʿUrabiyya,* p. 531; Muhammad Khalil al-Hijrisi, *al-Jawhar al-nafis ʿala salawat Ibn Idris,* pp. 5–8; Johansen, *Sufism and Islamic Reform in Egypt,* pp. 42–43; Frederick De Jong, "The Sufi Orders in Egypt during the Urabi Insurrection and the British Occupation, 1882–1914," pp. 132–33.

74. Mubarak, *al-Khitat,* vol. 15, pp. 10–11; Sarkis, *Muʿjam al-matbuʿat,* vol. 7, p. 1323.

75. Al-Hijrisi, *al-Jawhar al-nafis,* pp. 5–8; Blunt, *Secret History,* pp. 123–24; Edith Finch, *Wilfrid Scawen Blunt, 1840–1922,* pp. 129–30, 134.

76. Abu ʿUlyanʾs birthplace in Aswan and his grave in Cairo became pilgrimage sites at which an annual *mawlid* was held. Johansen, *Sufism and Islamic Reform in Egypt,* pp. 41–51.

77. Upon the death of ʿAbd al-Latif, his son ʿAbd al-Jawwad built a mosque and a large religious library in his honor. He also organized a memorial ceremony consisting of the reading of verses from the Qurʾan every Friday with the participation of a large number of ʿulamaʾ. Muhammad al-Qayati, *Khulasat al-tahqiq fi afdaliyyat al-siddiq,* pp. 43–46.

78. Mubarak, *al-Khitat,* vol. 14, pp. 95–97; al-Qayati, *Khulasat al-tahqiq,* pp. 46–49.

79. Al-Qayati, *Khulasat al-tahqiq,* pp. 49–51; ʿAbd al-Razzaq al-Bitar, *Hilyat al-bashar fi taʾrikh al-qarn al-thalith ʿashar al-hijri,* vol. 1, pp. 204–5.

80. Salim, *al-Quwwa al-ijtimaʿiyya,* pp. 367–68; Sharubim, *al-Khafi fi taʾrikh Misr,* p. 323; Muhammad al-Qayati, *Nafhat al-basham fi rihlat al-Sham,* pp. 5–9; Ismaʿil Sarhank, *Haqaʾiq al-akhbar ʿan duwal al-bihar,* vol. 2, p. 409; Husayn Fawzi al-Najjar, *Ahmad ʿUrabi Misr liʾl-Misriyyin,* p. 181.

81. PRO, FO881/4727/No. 56, Inclosure 4.

82. De Jong, "The Sufi Orders in Egypt," pp. 132–34, 138.

83. Baer, *Studies in the Social History of Modern Egypt,* pp. 93–101.

84. Ibid., p. 100.

85. Ibid., pp. 99–100.

86. De Jong, "The Sufi Orders in Egypt," p. 134.

CHAPTER 4

1. Al-Qayati, *Nafhat,* pp. 5–9.

2. Ibid., p. 169.

3. Ibid., pp. 7, 35.

4. Piscatori, *Islam in a World of Nation-States,* pp. 40–75; Zubaida, *Islam, the People and the State,* pp. 123–29; Haim Gerber, *Islamic Law and Culture 1600–1840,* pp. 53–56.

5. See, e.g., Landau, *The Politics of Pan-Islam,* pp. 9–72.

6. Gerber, "The Limits of Constructedness," pp. 257–58.

7. Al-Qayati, *Nafhat,* pp. 42–46, 169.

8. ʿIllaysh, *Fath al-ʿali al-malik,* vol. 1, pp. 375–92.

9. Al-Naqqash, *Misr li'l-Misriyyin*, vol. 7, p. 270; see also al-Basri's statement in ibid., p. 344.

10. Ahmad Zakariyya al-Shalaq, *Ru'ya fi tahdith al-fikr al-Misri*; 'Ali, *al-Azhar 'ala masrah al-siyasa al-Misriyya*, pp. 182–87.

11. Al-Shalaq, *Ru'ya*, pp. 23–27; Jurji Zaydan, *Ta'rikh adab al-lugha al-'Arabiyya*, vol. 3, p. 265. On al-Marsafi's literary work, see Ahmad Mandur, "al-Shaykh Husayn al-Marsafi wa'l-wasila al-adabiyya."

12. Husayn al-Marsafi, *Risalat al-kalim al-thaman,* pp. 12–15.

13. Ibid., pp. 16–17, 18–20.

14. Ibid., pp. 24–26.

15. Ibid., p. 31.

16. Zubaida, *Islam, the People and the State,* pp. 151–53; Cole, *Colonialism and Revolution,* pp. 288–89.

17. Blunt, *The Future of Islam,* p. 58; idem, *Egypt: Letters to the Right Hon. W. E. Gladstone M.P. and Others,* pp. 10, 12–14, 19–20, 27–29, 39, 46; also Berdine, *The Accidental Tourist,* pp. 23–24. Blunt himself lost his optimism in the wake of an attempt on his life in western Egypt in 1887 and observed with disappointment that the hopes he had held for the reform movement had vanished, as there was no true basis for reform in Islam. Wilfrid Scawen Blunt, *My Diaries,* p. 276.

18. Salim, *al-Quwwa al-ijtima'iyya,* pp. 265–73; see also Khafaji, *al-Azhar fi alf 'am,* vol. 1, pp. 183–88.

19. Zubaida, *Islam, the People and the State,* pp. 152–62.

20. Cole, *Colonialism and Revolution,* pp. 245–46; Doris Behrens-Abouseif, "The Political Situation of the Copts, 1798–1923," pp. 193–96; PRO, FO881/4716/ No. 762.

21. 'Abd al-Halim 'Amir, "al-Jam'iyya al-Khayriyya al-Islamiyya"; Tariq Bishri, *al-Muslimun wa'l-Aqbat fi itar al-jama'a al-wataniyya,* pp. 46–50; Samir Seikaly, "Coptic Communal Reform: 1860–1914," pp. 247–53.

22. Petry, *The Civilian Elite of Cairo,* p. 80; Louise Marlow, *Hierarchy and Egalitarianism in Islamic Thought.* See also Juan R. Cole, "Printing and Urban Islam in the Mediterranean World 1890–1920," mainly pp. 344–47, 358–59.

23. Behrens-Abouseif, "The Political Situation of the Copts," pp. 193–94.

24. Blunt, *Egypt: Letters,* p. 10; Subhi Labib, "The Copts in Egyptian Society and Politics, 1882–1919," p. 304; PRO, FO78/3444/No. 837; Sharubim, *al-Khafi fi ta'rikh Misr,* vol. 4, pp. 305–7, 323–28.

25. *Al-Hilal* 3 (September 1896–August 1897): 41–48.

26. Behrens-Abouseif, "The Political Situation of the Copts," pp. 139–94; also *Times* (London), January 3, 1882; PRO, FO78/3439/No. 486.

27. 'Urabi, *Mudhakkirat,* vol. 2, pp. 189–94; Gassick, *The Defense Statement of Ahmad 'Urabi,* pp. 42–43.

28. Schölch, *Egypt for the Egyptians.* pp. 284–85.

29. Hartmann, *The Arabic Press of Egypt,* pp. 9–12; Ami Ayalon, "Muslim 'Intruders,' Muslim 'Bigots': The Egyptian–Syrian Press Controversy in Late Nineteenth-Century Cairo"; Thomas Mayer, *The Changing Past: Egyptian Historiography of the Urabi Revolt, 1882–1983,* p. 9.

30. Rudolph Peters, "The Lion of Qasr al-Nil Bridge: The Islamic Prohibition of Images as an Issue in the Urabi Revolt," pp. 217–20.

31. The report submitted after the battle by the commander of the British Navy, Grant Wellesley, noted that ʿUrabi's army was taken by surprise by the British attack and many of the men laid down their arms and surrendered. Caspar F. Goodrich, *Report of the British Naval and Military Operations in Egypt, 1882,* pp. 149–52.

32. This sympathy was recorded by Thabit Pasha in a letter to the head of the khedival *diwan* on September 6, 1882, in which he observed that many notables and ʿulamaʾ in Istanbul were hoping for ʿUrabi's victory against the British. The Ottoman authorities also issued an order to the editors of the Syrian newspapers not to publish reports on the events in Egypt. See Thabit's letter, quoted in al-Jumayʿi, *al-Thawra al-ʿUrabiyya fi daw al-wathaʾiq al-Misriyya,* p. 83; PRO, FO195/1410 Eldridge (Damascus) to Dufferin (London), July 16, 1882, no. 48; ibid., Eldridge (Damascus) to Dufferin (London), July 29, 1882, no. 53; ibid., Mr. Wyndham (Damascus) to Earl Granville (St. Petersburg), September 28, 1881, no. 490.

33. Başbakanlık Arşivi, Yildiz collection, code: Y.EE, file 84, folder 11, 15/B/1299 [June 2, 1882]; ibid., code: Y.EE, file 84, folder 15, 08/N/1299 [June 24, 1882]; also ibid., code: Y.EE, file 116, folder 11, 16/R/1299 [March 7, 1882].

34. Broadley, *How We Defended Arabi,* pp. 166–70 (quotations); Gassick, *The Defense Statement of Ahmad ʿUrabi,* pp. 49–57; also Başbakanlık Arşivi, Yildiz collection, code: Y.EE, file 116, folder 18, 15/B/1299 [June 3, 1882]; code: Y.EE, file 116, folder 51, 13/B/1299 [June 1, 1882].

35. Blunt, *Secret History,* p. 243; Finch, *Wilfrid Scawen Blunt,* pp. 138–39. In a letter to Prime Minister Gladstone as early as December 1881, however, Blunt stated that ʿUrabi's declarations of allegiance to the sultan were only lip service. According to Blunt, animosity toward the Turks was entrenched in the minds of the ʿUrabists, and enlightened Egyptians viewed the Ottoman caliphate as "truly dead." Blunt, *Egypt: Letters,* pp. 14–15.

36. Rudolph Peters, "Islam and the Legitimation of Power: The Mahdi Revolt in the Sudan," pp. 409–20. Ironically, many of the Sudanese ʿulamaʾ who endorsed and participated in the Mahdiyya movement were graduates of al-Azhar, attesting to its scholarly impact on the Sudanese religious landscape. Muhammad Sulayman, *Dawr al-Azhar fiʾl-Sudan,* pp. 60–62, 82–88.

37. See Başbakanlık Arşivi, Yildiz collection, code: Y.A.RES, file 16, folder 42, 16/N/1299 [August 1, 1882].

38. Sarhank, *Haqaʾiq al-Akhbar,* vol. 2, pp. 404–6 (the complete Ottoman text); also ʿAziz, *al-Sihafa al-Misriyya,* pp. 66–68; *al-Ahram,* August 28, 1882.

39. On the legal concept of *baghy,* see Joel L. Kraemer, "Apostates, Rebels and Brigands," pp. 48–59; Abou El Fadl, *Rebellion and Violence in Islamic Law.*

40. Mustafa Sadiq al-Rifaʿi, "al-Azhar waʾl-thawra al-ʿUrabiyya"; also al-Jumayʿi, *al-Thawra al-ʿUrabiyya fi daw al-wathaʾiq al-Misriyya,* p. 87.

41. Başbakanlık Arşivi, Yildiz collection, code: Y.EE, file 116, folder 86, 29/Z/1299 [November 11, 1882].

42. ʿUrabi, *Mudhakkirat,* vol. 2, pp. 17–19.

43. *Times* (London), September 26 and 27 (quotation), October 2, 1882; al-Naqqash, *Misr liʾl-Misriyyin,* vol. 6, pp. 8–12; *Lisan al-Hal,* October 30, 1882.

44. *Al-Ahram,* September 16, 21, and 27, November 8, 1882.

45. *Al-Ahram,* September 29, 1882, February 10, April 6, 1883.

46. *Al-Ahram,* October 15, 1882 (quotations); *Lisan al-Hal,* October 30, 1882.

47. Al-Naqqash, *Misr liʾl-Misriyyin*, vol. 6, p. 13; Taymur, *Aʿlam al-fikr al-Islami*, pp. 58–69; ʿAli, *al-Azhar ʿala masrah al-siyasa al-Misriyya*, pp. 202–3; also Delanoue, *Moralistes et politiques musulmans*, p. 179. According to al-Rafiʿi, al-Mahdi's request to be released from his role was evoked by friction with the khedive. On one occasion the khedive was informed about meetings of a political nature in al-Mahdi's home attended by a group of dignitaries and merchants. The khedive, who was still dealing with the ramifications of the revolt against him, advised al-Mahdi not to get involved with matters outside his jurisdiction. On another occasion al-Mahdi refused to allow one of Tawfiq's retinue to view a certain legal document, whereupon the courtier complained to the khedive that the shaykh had become an obstacle to the governmental administration. Al-Rafiʿi, *ʿAsr Ismaʿil*, vol. 1, pp. 72–74; see also ʿAbd al-ʿAzim, *Mashyakhat al-Azhar*, vol. 1, pp. 248–49. Another explanation given for al-Mahdi's resignation was internal opposition to the 1885 code in al-Azhar. See Gesnik, "Beyond Modernisms," pp. 273–78.

48. ʿAbd al-ʿAzim, *Mashyakhat al-Azhar*, vol. 1, p. 259.

49. De Jong, *Turuq and Turuq-Linked Institutions*, pp. 121–23; *Times* (London), October 19, 1882; Hartmann, *The Arabic Press of Egypt*, p. 102.

50. Mujahid, *al-Aʿlam al-Sharqiyya*, vol. 4, pp. 92–94; al-Fiqqi, *al-Azhar*, pp. 522–30.

51. Mujahid, *al-Aʿlam al-Sharqiyya*, vol. 4, pp. 92–94.

52. Ibid.; ʿUrabi, *Mudhakkirat*, vol. 2, pp. 163–64; *al-Siyasa al-Usbuʿiyya*, December 31, 1927, pp. 9–10. For the response by al-Laythi's family, see *al-Siyasa al-Usbuʿiyya*, January 14, 1928, pp. 10–11, 24.

53. Rida, *Taʾrikh*, vol. 1, p. 955.

54. ʿUrabi, *Mudhakkirat*, vol. 2, pp. 33–34, 163–64 (quotations); also Hanafi, "al-Din waʾl-thawra fiʾl-thawra al-ʿUrabiyya," pp. 48, 58.

55. ʿAbdallah Habib Nawfal, *Kitab tarajim ʿulamaʾ Tarabulus wa-udabaʾuha*, pp. 88–91; ʿUmar Rida Kahhala, *Muʿjam al-muʾallifin*, vol. 2, pp. 198–99; Muhammad Rashid al-Rafiʿi, *Tarajim hayat al-shaykh ʿAbd al-Qadir al-Rafiʿi*, pp. 4–6; Ramadan, "Riwaq al-Shuwam," pp. 23–37.

56. Al-Rafiʿi, *al-Thawra al-ʿUrabiyya*, pp. 102–3. For denials, see al-Rafiʿi, *Tarajim hayat al-shaykh ʿAbd al-Qadir al-Rafiʿi*, pp. 75–76; Ramadan, "Riwaq al-Shuwam," pp. 58–59. Another indication of ʿAbd al-Qadir's nonintervention was his impressive advance in the religious hierarchy and the honors he accrued from Khedive Tawfiq and his son, ʿAbbas Hilmi II, which peaked in his appointment as mufti of Egypt in 1905, although he died several days later.

57. ʿIllyash's interrogation file in Salim, *al-Quwwa al-ijtimaʿiyya*, p. 365.

58. Al-Qayati, *Nafhat*, p. 10; *al-Ahram*, September 21, 1882; Kahhala, *Muʿjam al-muʾallifin*, vol. 3, p. 104.

59. The sensitivity of the issue of abolishing the post, which was described in the Istanbul press as a blow to the Islamic religion, prompted the Egyptian authorities to deny, albeit unconvincingly, that the position was a statutory one and that this was also the case for the other two legal schools — the Shafiʿi and the Hanbali. Al-Naqqash, *Misr liʾl-Misriyyin*, vol. 6, pp. 191–93; al-Hanafi, *Kanz al-jawhar*, pp. 158–59.

60. Al-Naqqash, *Misr liʾl-Misriyyin*, vol. 7, pp. 269–72; also *Bibliyughrafiyya li-wathaʾiq al-thawra al-ʿUrabiyya*, p. 304.

61. Broadley, *How We Defended Arabi*, p. 359.

62. Al-Naqqash, *Misr li'l-Misriyyin*, vol. 7, pp. 337–40; also *Bibliyughrafiyya li-watha'iq al-thawra al-ʿUrabiyya*, p. 304.

63. Al-Naqqash, *Misr li'l-Misriyyin*, vol. 7, pp. 337–40.

64. Ibid., p. 340. See also the interrogations of two other Azharis, Ahmad ʿAbd al-Ghani and Ahmad al-Basri, in ibid., pp. 342–44.

65. Al-Naqqash, *Misr li'l-Misriyyin*, vol. 7, pp. 343–44.

66. According to British documents, ʿAbd al-Rahman ʿIllaysh also was one of the signatories of the fatwa deposing Tawfiq, which was read out at the general assembly in Cairo in July 1882. PRO, FO78/3618/No. 794, Inclosure 59.

67. The list appears in al-Rafiʿi, *al-Thawra al-ʿUrabiyya*, p. 531.

CHAPTER 5

1. See al-Hijrisi's books *al-Jawhar al-nafis* and *Hadha kitab al-qasr al-mashid fi'l-tawhid*.

2. Al-Qayati, *Nafhat*, pp. 8–11, 56.

3. Mahmud, *al-Madrasa al-Shadhiliyya*, pp. 248–53. Al-Qayati provides a slightly different chronology for ʿAbd al-Rahman's personal history. Al-Qayati, *Nafhat*, pp. 57–58.

4. Commins, *Islamic Reform*, p. 31.

5. Al-Qayati, *Nafhat*, p. 57; Rida, *Ta'rikh*, vol. 1, p. 390.

6. *Al-ʿUrwa al-Wuthqa wa'l-thawra al-tahririyya al-kubra*, pp. 366–67.

7. Commins, *Islamic Reform*, pp. 38–40; al-Qayati, *Nafhat*, pp. 198–202.

8. The large body of information in this work has also served local researchers in tracing social change in the Fertile Crescent during the nineteenth century. See, e.g., Ahmad Turbayn, *Malamih al-taghyir al-ijtimaʿi fi Bilad al-Sham fi'l-qarn al-tasiʿ ʿashar.*

9. As discussed in chapter 1, students and faculty from Riwaq al-Shuwam played an important role in the al-Azhar community and in some cases were involved in local Egyptian politics — for example, during the French conquest and the ʿUrabi revolt. Several chose to make their home in Egypt permanently and held distinguished posts in the fields of education and the judiciary, including as shaykhs al-Azhar. See Ramadan, "Riwaq al-Shuwam"; Nicola Ziyada, "Lubnaniyyun darasu bi'l-Azhar fi'l-qarn al-tasiʿ ʿashar."

10. Al-Qayati, *Nafhat*; Mujahid, *al-Aʿlam al-Sharqiyya*, vol. 2; Taymur, *Aʿlam al-fikr al-Islami*; ʿAbd al-Rahim, "ʿAlaqat Bilad al-Sham"; al-Fiqqi, *al-Azhar*, pp. 373–74, 376–77; Muhammad Mutiʿ Hafiz and Nizar Abaza, *Ta'rikh ʿulama' Dimashq fi'l qarn al-rabiʿ ʿashar*, vol. 2; Muhammad Jamil al-Shatti, *Aʿyan Dimashq fi'l-qarn al-thalith ʿashar wa-nisf al-qarn al-rabiʿ ʿashar*; ʿAbd al-Hadi Naja al-Abyari, *al-Wasa'il al-adabiyya fi'l-rasa'il al-ahdabiyya*; Bashir Nafiʿ, "Nash'at al-itijahat al-siyasiyya fi Filastin fi awakhir al-ʿahd al-ʿUthmani." See also Rafeq, "The Ulama of Ottoman Jerusalem," pp. 48–49; ʿAdil Manna, "Cultural Relations between Egyptian and Jerusalem ʿUlama' in the Early Nineteenth Century"; Gabriel Baer, "Jerusalem Notables in Ottoman Cairo"; Uri M. Kupferschmidt, "Connections of the Palestinian Ulama with Egypt and Other Parts of the Ottoman Empire," pp. 182–85; Hourani, "The Syrians in Egypt."

11. See Cole, "Printing and Urban Islam"; Mona Abaza, "Changing Images of Three Generations of Azharites in Indonesia," pp. 382–83.

12. Al-Qayati, *Nafhat*, pp. 25–31, 35–41.

13. Ibid., pp. 35–37, 147–50, 157.

14. Ibid., pp. 42–46.

15. Ibid., pp. 31, 52–53.

16. Ibid., pp. 60–88.

17. Ibid., pp. 47–50.

18. Ibid., pp. 14, 51–52.

19. Ibid., pp. 50–52.

20. Ibid., pp. 53–56.

21. Delanoue, *Moralistes et politiques musulmans*, p. 323.

22. See also chapter 6.

23. Al-Qayati, *Nafhat*, pp. 129–36, 140–42.

24. Ibid., pp. 150–51. Al-Qayati's enumeration of forbidden practices in Egypt, such as imbibing alcoholic drinks and using hashish, is supported by Toledano's findings on the leisure-time activities of the lower strata. Toledano argued that the use of hashish as well as tobacco in coffeehouses and drinking alcoholic beverages in taverns (*khammaras*) seem to have been more common in mid-nineteenth-century Egypt than is generally believed. Toledano, *State and Society in Mid-Nineteenth-Century Egypt*, pp. 242–427.

25. Al-Qayati, *Nafhat*, pp. 151–52.

26. Ibid.

27. See, e.g., Livingston, "Western Science and Educational Reform"; Israel Altman, "The Political Thought of Rifaʿah Rafiʿ al-Tahtawi: A Nineteenth-Century Egyptian Reformer."

28. See Kupferschmidt, "Connections of the Palestinian Ulama with Egypt and Other Parts of the Ottoman Empire," pp. 176–89; Mahmoud Yazbak, "Nabulsi Ulama in the Late Ottoman Period, 1864–1914," pp. 78–79; Abdul-Karim Rafeq, "The Ulama of Ottoman Jerusalem (16th–18th Centuries)," pp. 48–49.

29. Al-Shinnawi, "Dawr al-Azhar," p. 686; Ramadan, "Riwaq al-Shuwam," pp. 21–23.

30. *Al-Hilal* 13 (April 1, 1899): 411–12. Al-Azhar's guidance was also sought in distant Southeast Asia, as seen from a question addressed to its scholars in *al-Hilal* 6 (1897–98): 496.

31. See, e.g., Albert Hourani, *Arabic Thought in the Liberal Age, 1798–1939*, pp. 130–60; Sylvia G. Haim, *Arab Nationalism: An Anthology*, pp. 19–24; Bassam Tibi, *Arab Nationalism: A Critical Enquiry*, pp. 78–90; Commins, *Islamic Reform*, pp. 30–32; Eliezer Tauber, *The Arab Movements in World War I*, pp. 23–33.

32. Abaza, "Changing Images," pp. 383–91; Giora Eliraz, *Islam in Indonesia*, pp. 1–25.

33. See, e.g., al-Qayati's descriptions of Sufism in Damascus and Sidon. Al-Qayati, *Nafhat*, pp. 60–66, 112–16, 129–36.

34. See notes 1–3 above.

35. Commins, *Islamic Reform*, pp. 47–48, 110–23; Weismann, *A Taste of Modernity*, pp. 273–304.

36. ʿAbd al-Rahman Sami, *al-Qawl al-haqq fi Bayrut wa-Dimashq.*

37. Ibid., pp. 7–16, 22–24, 32.

38. Ibid., pp. 33–34.

39. Ibid., pp. 31–32, 37–38.

40. Ibid., p. 59.

41. Ibid., pp. 13–14, 33–34, 53, 61–68, 73–78, 100–102, 105.

42. Ibid., p. 73.

43. Ibid., pp. 66–67.

44. Ibid., pp. 31–32.

45. Al-Qayati, *Nafhat,* p. 169.

46. Tufan S. Buzpinar, "The Repercussions of the British Occupation of Egypt on Syria, 1882–1883," pp. 86–87.

47. Al-Qayati, *Nafhat,* p. 42; PRO, FO78/3507/No. 12.

48. Buzpinar, "The Repercussions of the British Occupation," pp. 87–88.

49. See, e.g., *al-Janna,* January 2, April 27, May 18, June 26, and September 11, 1883.

50. Al-Qayati, *Nafhat,* p. 169; al-Bitar, *Hilyat al-bashar,* vol. 1, p. 205.

51. See comments by Mahmud, *al-Madrasa,* pp. 252–53; also see De Jong, *Turuq and Turuq-Linked Institutions,* pp. 173–74.

52. Two of the most prominent European admirers were the Italian writer Enrico Insabato, an enthusiastic advocate of a pro-Islamic Italian policy, and the French philosopher René Guénon, a sharp critic of Western secular modernity. Influenced by ʿAbd al-Rahman, Guénon converted to Islam in 1912 and devoted himself primarily to researching the works of Ibn ʿArabi, the illustrious precursor of Sufism. Meir Hatina, "Where East Meets West: Sufism, Cultural Rapprochement and Politics."

53. Khafif, *Ahmad ʿUrabi,* vol. 2, p. 341.

54. Egyptian writers described ʿUrabi as a "stranger in his own land" upon his return to Egypt. Khafif, *Ahmad ʿUrabi,* vol. 2, pp. 350–52; Hanafi al-Mahlawi, *al-Ayyam al-akhira fi hayat ʿuzamaʾ al-siyasa,* p. 40.

55. Kamil's articles were published in his newspaper, *al-Liwaʾ,* in early June 1901 upon ʿUrabi's return. They are reprinted in Yuwaqim Rizq Murqus (ed.), *Awraq Mustafa Kamil: al-maqalat,* vol. 2, pp. 193–200.

56. Mayer, *The Changing Past,* pp. 5–9.

57. Ibid., pp. 16–17.

58. Amira El-Azhary Sonbol (trans. and ed.), *The Last Khedive of Egypt: Memoirs of Abbas Hilmi II,* pp. 33–52. On the royalist school of Egyptian history, see Anthony Gorman, *Historians, State and Politics in Twentieth-Century Egypt,* pp. 15–22.

59. Shawqi quoted in ʿAbd al-Munʿim Ibrahim al-Gamiʿi in his introduction to *Mudhakkirat al-zaʿim Ahmad ʿUrabi,* vol. 2, p. 70; also Amir ʿUmar Tusun, introduction to *Yawm 11 Yuliyu 1882.*

60. ʿUrabi, *Mudhakkirat,* vol. 2, pp. 193–94. Mahmud Sami al-Barudi also used a religious context to deflect similar accusations. In a *qasida* al-Barudi asserted that his motives were pure and centered on protecting religion and the homeland. This discussion appears in Shawqi Dayf, *al-Barudi: raʾid al-shiʿr al-hadith,* p. 84.

Chapter 6

1. Cole, *Colonialism and Revolution,* pp. 122–32; idem, "Printing and Urban Islam," pp. 351–61; Kelidar, "The Political Press in Egypt," pp. 1–6.
2. See Gesnik, "Beyond Modernisms," pp. 221–26; Gasper, "ʿAbdallah al-Nadim," pp. 86–87.
3. For an ideological and historical profile of the modernist school in Islam, see Hourani, *Arabic Thought in the Liberal Age,* chapters 5–6; Charles C. Adams, *Islam and Modernism in Egypt;* H. A. R. Gibb, *Modern Trends in Islam;* Hava Lazarus-Yafeh, "Three Remarks on Islam and Western Political Values: An Attempt to Re-evaluate the Modernist Movement in Islam."
4. Eickelman and Piscatori, *Muslim Politics,* p. 131.
5. See Gesnik, "Beyond Modernisms," pp. 243–45.
6. On fatwas and their function, see, e.g., Uriel Heyd, "Some Aspects of the Ottoman Fetva"; Muhammad K. Masud, Brinkley Messick, and David S. Powers, "Muftis, Fatwas and Islamic Legal Interpretation."
7. Judith E. Tucker, *In the House of the Law: Gender and Islamic Law in Ottoman Syria and Palestine,* pp. 20–22; Heyd, "Some Aspects of the Ottoman Fetva," p. 56; Haim Gerber, *State, Society and Law in Islam: Ottoman Law in Comparative Perspective,* pp. 79–112.
8. Wael B. Hallaq, "Was the Gate of Ijtihad Closed?"; idem, "From Fatwas to Furuʿ: Growth and Change in Islamic Substantive Law"; Norman Calder, "al-Nawawi's Typology of Muftis and Its Significance for a General Theory of Islamic Law," pp. 155–62.
9. Gerber, *Islamic Law and Culture,* pp. 4–5; Wael B. Hallaq, "Iftaʾ and Ijtihad in Sunni Legal Theory: A Development Account"; Skovgaard-Petersen, *Defining Islam,* pp. 6–10. On the role of muftis and fatwas in Bedouin society, see, e.g., Aharon Layish, "The Fatwa as an Instrument of Accommodation."
10. Gerber, *State, Society and Law in Islam,* p. 19.
11. See, e.g., Masud, Messick, and Powers, "Muftis," pp. 26–31; Jakob Skovgaard-Petersen, "Fatwas in Print."
12. Al-Mahdi's fatwas were published in a shortened version by his disciple Shaykh ʿAbd al-Rahman al-Suwaysi, titled *Mukhtasar al-fatawa al-Mahdiyya.* See also Hans-Georg Ebert, "'Die letzte Krankheit': Mohammad al-ʿAbbasi al-Mahdi (gest. 1897) und die Reform der ägyptischen Rechtsordnung," pp. 315–51.
13. Al-Suwaysi, *Mukhtasar,* p. 3.
14. See Gimaret, "Muʿtazila"; R. C. Martin, M. R. Woodward, and D. S. Atmaja, *Defenders of Reason in Islam: Muʿtazilism from Medieval School to Modern Times,* pp. 128–41; Gibb, *Modern Trends in Islam,* pp. 53–54.
15. Tucker, *In the House of the Law,* p. 11.
16. ʿIllaysh, *Fath al-ʿali al-malik,* vol. 1, pp. 52–53.
17. Al-Qayati, *Khulasat al-tahqiq,* pp. 3, 39. Al-Qayati's criticism was also directed at the Shiʿis, who defamed the three most revered *sahaba* (Abu Bakr, ʿUmar, and ʿUthman) for usurping ʿAli's right to the caliphate. Ibid.
18. ʿIllaysh, *Fath al-ʿali al-malik,* vol. 1, pp. 89–104, 108–11. See also al-Bukhari, *Sahih al-Bukhari,* vol. 5, p. 2384.

19. Knut S. Vikor, *Sufi and Scholar on the Desert Edge,* pp. 247–50.

20. ʿIllaysh, *Fath al-ʿali al-malik,* vol. 1, pp. 89–104, 108–11; also Vikor, *Sufi and Scholar,* pp. 250–57; John Ralph Willis, "The Fatwas of Condemnation."

21. ʿIllaysh, *Fath al-ʿali al-malik,* vol. 1, pp. 60–61; also Abu Zakariyya Muhyi al-Din al-Nawawi, *Kitab al-majmuʿ, sharh al-muhadhdhab liʾl-Shirazi.*

22. ʿIllaysh, *Fath al-ʿali al-malik,* vol. 2, p. 355.

23. Ibid., vol. 1, pp. 79, 86–87.

24. Ibid., vol. 1, pp. 57–58, 88; also Delanoue, *Moralistes et politiques musulmans,* vol. 1, pp. 154–55.

25. See Aharon Layish, "The Sudanese Mahdi's Legal Methodology and Its Sufi Inspiration."

26. Muhammad Ibrahim Abu Salim, *Manshurat al-Mahdiyya,* pp. 328–29; idem, *al-Haraka al-fikriyya fiʾl-Mahdiyya.*

27. Peters, "Muhammad al-ʿAbbasi al-Mahdi," pp. 76–82. See also Muhammad al-ʿAbbasi al-Mahdi, *al-Fatawa al-Mahdiyya fiʾl-waqaʾiʿ al-Misriyya,* vol. 2, pp. 27–28.

28. Peters, "Muhammad al-ʿAbbasi al-Mahdi," pp. 76–82.

29. C. E. Bosworth, "The Concept of Dhimma in Early Islam"; Antoine Fattal, *Le statut légal des non-musulmans en pays d'Islams;* A. S. Tritton, *The Caliphs and Their Non-Muslim Subjects;* Mark R. Cohen, *Under Crescent and Cross: The Jews in the Middle East,* pp. 52–74; Yohanan Friedman, *Tolerance and Coercion in Islam.* For an extensive Muslim legal source on the issue of non-Muslims, see Shams al-Din Muhammad ibn Qayyim al-Jawziyya, *Ahkam ahl al-dhimma.*

30. See Hugh Goddard, *A History of Christian-Muslim Relations,* pp. 19–49; Hava Lazarus-Yafeh, *Intertwined Worlds: Medieval Islam and Bible Criticism.*

31. S. D. Goitein, *A Mediterranean Society,* vol. 1, pp. 273–311; Cl. Cahen, "Dhimma."

32. See, e.g., Benjamin Braude and Bernard Lewis, "Introduction," pp. 1, 10–26; Kemal Karpat, "The Ottoman Ethnic and Confessional Legacy in the Middle East"; Amnon Cohen, *Jewish Life under Islam: Jerusalem in the Sixteenth Century,* especially chapters 6 and 7; idem, *Palestine in the 18th Century.* The relatively fair-minded Ottoman attitude contrasted with the more problematic situation of non-Muslims in Iran as well as in the Maghreb. Religious repression in Iran stemmed from the growing power of the ʿulamaʾ, especially under the Qajar dynasty in the eighteenth century, when the ʿulamaʾ in effect personified the authority of the Shiʿite imams by providing both religious and political leadership for the community. With the legal foundations of the *dhimma* institution originally established in Sunni Islam, the Shiʿite ʿulamaʾ tended to display a more restrictive stance toward non-Muslims as yet another expression of defiance of Sunna legal authority. Jews and Christians were viewed not only as infidels but also as impure (*anjas*), a theological classification that had practical implications for Muslim social and commercial interaction with them. A restrictive stance toward non-Muslims was also evident in the Maghreb, in Yemen, and in other areas on the fringes of the Muslim world, where Islam was less normative and less adherent to classical theological injunctions due to the dominant tribal element in society. The ʿulamaʾ exercised considerable influence there, stemming from their intimate relations with local dynasties and the religious services

they provided to the tribes. See Nikki R. Keddie, "The Roots of Ulama's Power in Modern Iran," pp. 211–29; Vanessa Martin, *Islam and Modernism*, pp. 11–35; V. Basch Moreen, "Risala-yi Sawaʿiq al-Yahud (The Treatise Lightning Bolts against the Jews) by Muhammad Baqir b. Muhammad Taqi al-Majlisi (d. 1699)"; Laurence D. Loeb, "Dhimmi Status and Jewish Roles in Iranian Society."

33. ʿAbd al-Majid quoted in Stanford J. Shaw, *The Jews of the Ottoman Empire and the Turkish Republic*, p. 156. See also Butrus Abu-Manneh, *Studies on Islam and the Ottoman Empire in the 19th Century*, pp. 181–85.

34. Shaw, *The Jews of the Ottoman Empire*, pp. 155–57.

35. See, e.g., al-Marsafi, *Risalat al-kalim al-thaman*, pp. 4–79; ʿAli, *al-Azhar ʿala masrah al-siyasa al-Misriyya*, pp. 188–90; Hourani, *Arabic Thought in the Liberal Age*, pp. 130–60; Muhammad ʿAbduh, *al-Taʿassub*.

36. P. J. Vatikiotis, "Muhammad ʿAbduh and the Quest for a Muslim Humanism," pp. 115–16; Oussama Arabi, *Studies in Modern Islamic Law and Jurisprudence*, pp. 19–38.

37. Rida, *Taʾrikh*, vol. 1, pp. 819–29.

38. For the texts of the fatwas, see Muhammad ʿAbduh, *al-Fatawa fiʾl-tajdid waʾl-islah al-dini*, pp. 20–21. On the issue of eating animals slain by non-Muslims, see Ibn Qayyim al-Jawziyya, *Ahkam*, vol. 1, pp. 249–56; ʿAbd al-Rahman al-Jaziri, *Kitab al-fiqh ʿala al-madhahib al-arbaʿa*, vol. 1, pp. 722–31; also ʿIllaysh, *Fath al-ʿali al-malik*, vol. 1, pp. 193–96; idem, *Hidayat al-salik*, vol. 1, pp. 214–15; Skovgaard-Petersen, *Defining Islam*, pp. 123–26.

39. Salah al-Din al-Munajjid and Yusuf Khuri (eds.), *Fatawa al-Imam Muhammad Rashid Rida*, vol. 1, pp. 79–81, 127–28.

40. In the case of Jewish slaughterers, the name "Ezra" was cited in the blessing; in the case of Christians, "Jesus." See also Sura 9:30. Aside from sanctifying the unity of Allah, slaughtering meat in the name of Allah is meant to focus on the intention to take a life not thoughtlessly but solemnly, for food, with the permission of Allah. Other food-related restrictions include the prohibition against eating dead animals, blood, and the flesh of swine.

41. Rida, *Taʾrikh*, vol. 1, pp. 586–87, 646–47, 668–716.

42. *Al-Manar* 1 (1898–99): 504–15; al-Munajjid and Khuri, *Fatawa*, vol. 1, pp. 81–83, 99–103, 128–29. See also Ibn Qayyim al-Jawziyya, *Ahkam*, vol. 1, pp. 200–206.

43. Rida based his argument regarding wills on the Qurʾanic verse "O believers, the testimony between you when any of you is visited by death, at the bequeathing, shall be two men of equity among you; or two others from another folk, if you are journeying in the land and the affliction of death befalls you" (5:106). This verse, Rida argued, is more specific and was written later than the less-detailed one: "Call in to witness two men of equity from among yourselves" (65:2) and therefore takes precedence. Al-Munajjid and Khuri, *Fatawa*, vol. 1, pp. 323–29.

44. Rida, *Taʾrikh*, vol. 1, pp. 648–66; also Ibn Qayyim al-Jawziyya, *Ahkam*, vol. 1, pp. 208–36.

45. Rida, *Taʾrikh*, vol. 1, pp. 672–74, 704–8. See also Skovgaard-Petersen, "Fatwas in Print," p. 83.

46. On the concept of *maslaha* in the modernist discourse, see Aharon Layish, "The Contribution of the Modernists to the Secularization of Islamic Law," pp. 266–67.

47. See notes 124–26 below.

48. See Rudolph Peters, "Religious Attitudes towards Modernization in the Ottoman Empire."

49. ʿIllaysh, *Fath al-ʿali al-malik,* vol. 1, pp. 392–93.

50. Ibid., vol. 1, pp. 158–59, vol. 2, p. 235; ʿIllaysh, *Hidayat al-salik,* vol. 1, pp. 256–60.

51. ʿIllaysh, *Fath al-ʿali al-malik,* vol. 1, pp. 158–59; also vol. 2, p. 348.

52. Al-Dardir quoted in Yusuf al-Qaradawi, *Ghayr al-Muslimin fiʾl-mujtamaʿ al-Islami,* p. 65. See also Ahmad ibn Muhammad al-Dardir, *al-Sharh al-saghir,* vol. 2, pp. 182–90.

53. See, e.g., al-Qayati, *Nafhat,* pp. 18–20, 31, 50–52, 141–42.

54. Ibid., pp. 93, 98–99.

55. In this remark al-Qayati was referring to Shaykh Yusuf ibn al-ʿAsir (d. 1889) of Sidon, who educated many pupils from the Christian community of Beirut, although they denied that his works had any influence on their literary writing. Al-Qayati, *Nafhat,* pp. 18–20.

56. Al-Mahdi, *al-Fatawa al-Mahdiyya,* vol. 2, pp. 32–33, vol. 3, pp. 269–70, 377.

57. Ibid., vol. 5, pp. 307–9. See also Ibn Qayyim al-Jawziyya, *Ahkam,* vol. 2, pp. 725, 737–44.

58. ʿAbd al-Hadi Naja al-Abyari, *al-Mawakib al-ʿaliyya,* pp. 110–11.

59. Edward Ingram (ed.), *Eastern Questions in the Nineteenth Century: Collected Essays,* vol. 2, pp. 123–24.

60. Al-Abyari, *al-Mawakib al-ʿaliyya,* p. 110.

61. For this and similar rulings, see ʿIllaysh, *Fath al-ʿali al-malik,* vol. 2, pp. 358–59.

62. Ibid., pp. 54–55.

63. Al-Suwaysi, *Mukhtasar,* p. 9; also Kraemer, "Apostates, Rebels and Brigands," pp. 43–44.

64. Al-Mahdi, *al-Fatawa al-Mahdiyya,* vol. 2, pp. 18, 20, 26–27. In accordance with the Hanafi ruling, al-Mahdi sanctioned the right of inheritance of the man's Muslim children, but only with regard to property acquired before their father's apostasy. Any property acquired afterward belonged to the state to be dispensed for welfare purposes, he ruled. In contrast, the Shafiʿi and the Maliki schools ruled that the state alone has the right to the property of an apostate, since he has become an enemy of Islam and of Muslims. The Hanbali school, for its part, argued that the apostate's heirs belonged to the faith to which he converted. See Jumʿa Muhammad Barraj, *Ahkam al-mirath fiʾl-shariʿa al-Islamiyya,* pp. 237–46.

65. Al-Mahdi, *al-Fatawa al-Mahdiyya,* vol. 5, pp. 300–303, 306–7.

66. On both affairs, see C. Vivian (Cairo) to Earl of Derby (London), January 18, 1878, PRO, FO78/2853/No. 11; Malet (Cairo) to Earl of Granville (London), January 15, 1883, FO78/3552/No. 12; Malet (Cairo) to Earl of Granville (London), June 12, 1883, FO78/3555/No. 230; draft written by Malet (Cairo), June 22, 1883, FO78/3555/No. 150; Malet (Cairo) to Earl of Granville (London), July 2, 1883, FO78/3555/No. 281.

67. See, e.g., *Majmuʿat rasaʾil al-imam al-shahid Hasan al-Banna,* pp. 69–70, 127–28; Muhammad al-Ghazali, *al-Taʿassub waʾl-tasamuh bayna al-Masihiyya waʾl-Islam,* pp. 35–42; Richard P. Mitchell, *The Society of the Muslim Brothers,* p. 249; Bayly

Winder, "Islam as the State Religion — A Muslim Brotherhood View in Syria," pp. 221–23.

68. On the woman's issue in Egypt at the beginning of the twentieth century, see, e.g., Ron Shaham, *Family and the Courts in Modern Egypt*, pp. 2–10; Beth Baron, *The Women's Awakening in Egypt: Culture, Society and the Press*, chapter 1; idem, *Egypt as a Woman: Nationalism, Gender and Politics*, pp. 17–39.

69. On Amin's biography, see Noëlle Baladi, *L'Émancipation de la femme en Égypte*.

70. On the debate over women's status, see also Juan R. Cole, "Feminism, Class, and Islam in Turn-of-the-Century Egypt," pp. 387–407.

71. On the national struggle and the activity of the Egyptian women's movement, see, e.g., Thomas Philipp, "Feminism and Nationalist Politics in Egypt"; Margot Badran, *Feminists, Islam and Nation: Gender and the Making of Modern Egypt*.

72. ʿIllaysh, *Fath al-ʿali al-malik*, vol. 2, pp. 54, 58.

73. ʿIllaysh, *Hidayat al-salik*, vol. 2, p. 259.

74. Ibid.; also Ron Shaham, "Women as Expert Witnesses in Pre-Modern Islamic Courts."

75. ʿIllaysh, *Fath al-ʿali al-malik*, vol. 2, p. 106.

76. Al-Suwaysi, *Mukhtasar*, p. 13. Notably, the justifications for divorce in judicial proceedings initiated by the wife (husband's illness, nonpayment of support, husband's prolonged absence, or injury that he caused her) are not recognized by the Hanafi legal school, to which al-Mahdi belonged, although they are recognized by the other schools, especially the Maliki.

77. Ibid., pp. 6–7.

78. *Al-Manar* 2 (1899): 332–34.

79. *Makarim al-Akhlaq al-Islamiyya* 23 (November 23, 1900): 356–57.

80. Ibid., pp. 353–58; *Makarim al-Akhlaq al-Islamiyya* 4 (February 15, 1900): 49–55.

81. *Makarim al-Akhlaq al-Islamiyya* 3 (February 1, 1900): 35–36; *Makarim al-Akhlaq al-Islamiyya* 15 (July 13, 1900): 132–35.

82. *Makarim al-Akhlaq al-Islamiyya* 23 (November 23, 1900): 358–59.

83. For general literature on the cultural and historic aspects of Sufism, see, e.g., Schimmel, *Mystical Dimensions of Islam;* Berkey, *The Formation of Islam,* pp. 231–47; Trimingham, *The Sufi Orders in Islam;* Marshall G. S. Hodgson, *The Venture of Islam,* vol. 1, pp. 392–409; Julian Baldick, *Mystical Islam: An Introduction to Sufism,* pp. 13–85; John O. Voll, "Sufi Orders"; Mark J. Sedgwick, *Sufism: The Essentials.*

84. Examples of such jurists are Ibn al-Jawzi (d. 1201), Ibn Taymiyya (d. 1328), and Ibn Qayyim al-Jawziyya (d. 1350).

85. Muhammad Umar Memon, *Ibn Taymiyya's Struggle against Popular Religion,* pp. 24–87; George Makdisi, "The Hanbali School and Sufism"; Christopher S. Taylor, *In the Vicinity of the Righteous: Ziyara and the Veneration of Muslim Saints in Late Medieval Egypt,* pp. 168–218; Josef Van Ess, "Sufism and Its Opponents"; Esther Peskes, "The Wahhabiyya and Sufism in the Eighteenth Century." On contemporary Wahhabi resentment of Sufism, see, e.g., Qasim al-Rifaʿi (ed.), *Fatawa Islamiyya,* vol. 1, pp. 161–67; vol. 4, pp. 271–73.

86. De Jong, *Turuq and Turuq-Linked Institutions,* pp. 20–95. This analysis is less relevant to Sufism in the peripheral, mainly tribal areas of the Muslim world, which were only loosely linked to a central authority and to modernist develop-

ments. See, e.g., Voll, "Sufi Orders," pp. 112–13; Levtzion and Voll, "Introduction"; Gellner, "Doctor and Saint," pp. 310–11, 325–26; Evans-Pritchard, *The Sanusi of Cyrenaica*, pp. 1–28, 62–89; P. M. Holt, *The Mahdist State in the Sudan, 1881–1898*; Elizabeth Sirriyeh, *Sufis and Anti-Sufis*, pp. 29–42.

87. Elbert E. Farman, *Egypt and Its Betrayal*, pp. 58, 60–61; John Gadsby, *My Wanderings: Being Travels in the East*, pp. 276–77, 287–88; Alfred J. Butler, *Court Life in Egypt*, pp. 219–24, 249–53, 262, 296–97; Lucie Duff Gordon, *Letters from Egypt, 1862–1869*, pp. 268–69; Consul E. T. Rogers (Cairo) to Earl Granville (London), September 24, 1873, quoted in Gillard, *British Documents on Foreign Affairs*, vol. 8, pp. 381–82; Edward Malet (Cairo) to Robert Salisbury (London), February 25, 1880, PRO, FO78/3141/No. 90; Edward Malet, *Egypt 1879–1883*, pp. 51–52.

88. Gadsby, *My Wanderings*, p. 276. This account and other Western observations, according to Edward Said in his critical essay *Orientalism*, were hardly historical or anthropological surveys. Rather, he held, they were closely bound to European colonialism and reflected its anxieties and prejudices. Edward W. Said, *Orientalism*, pp. 157–97; idem, *Culture and Imperialism*, pp. xi–xiii.

89. Muhammad ʿAbduh, *Risalat al-tawhid*, pp. 152–56; Sirriyeh, *Sufis and Anti-Sufis*, chapters 3–5; Johansen, *Sufism and Islamic Reform in Egypt*, pp. 11–31; Commins, *Islamic Reform*, pp. 24–26, 34–88.

90. The anti-Sufi polemic of the reformists was deeply influenced by the teaching of Shaykh Jamal al-Din al-Afghani (d. 1897), who lived in Egypt in 1871–79. Sirriyeh, *Sufis and Anti-Sufis*, pp. 68–74, 86–102; al-Marsafi, *Risalat al-kalim al-thaman*, pp. 16–38; ʿAbdallah Nadim, in *al-Ustadh*, April 11, 1893, pp. 786–91; April 25, 1893, pp. 828–43; Rida, *Taʾrikh*, vol. 1, pp. 109–30; *al-Manar* 1 (1898–99): 93–101, 813–16, 823–28, 924–26 (quotation). See also Johansen, *Sufism and Islamic Reform in Egypt*, pp. 16–21, 30; De Jong, "Opposition to Sufism in Twentieth-Century Egypt," pp. 310–11, 312–14.

91. See Gasper, "ʿAbdallah al-Nadim," pp. 77–84; Samuli Schielke, "Hegemonic Encounters: Criticism of Saints-Day Festivals and the Formation of Modern Islam in Late 19th and Early 20th Century Egypt."

92. ʿAbduh's articles published in *al-Waqaʾiʿ al-Misriyya* in 1880–81 appeared in Rida, *Taʾrikh*, vol. 2, pp. 136–42. In later treatises, however, ʿAbduh adopted a stricter stance toward miracles attributed to Sufi saints. He argued that they detract from the unity of Allah by encouraging the masses to worship other human beings believed to be intercessors with the divine. Therefore a Muslim who denies such miracles does not violate the principles of faith. ʿAbduh, *Risalat al-tawhid*, pp. 152–56, 204–6.

93. Rida, *Taʾrikh*, vol. 2, pp. 138, 141.

94. Ibid., p. 138.

95. Ibid., pp. 133–36.

96. Ibid., pp. 141–42; ʿAbduh, *Risalat al-tawhid*, pp. 178–79. See also Michael Cook, *Commanding Right and Forbidding Wrong in Islamic Thought*.

97. ʿIllaysh, *Fath al-ʿali al-malik*, vol. 1, pp. 44–45.

98. Ibid., vol. 1, pp. 44–45.

99. Ibid., vol. 1, pp. 12–14, 93–94; idem, *Taqrib al-ʿaqaʾid al-sanniyya biʾl-adilla al-Qurʾaniyya*, p. 3.

100. ʿIllaysh, *Fath al-ʿali al-malik,* vol. 1, pp. 18–21, 29–30, 37–38. ʿIllaysh's colleagues Hasan al-ʿIdwi and ʿAbd al-Hadi Naja al-Abyari devoted entire books to these issues. Hasan al-ʿIdwi, *Mashariq al-anwar fi fawz ahl al-iʿtibar;* al-Abyari, *Ahwal al-ruh.*

101. ʿIllaysh, *Fath al-ʿali al-malik,* vol. 1, p. 96; also ʿIllaysh's books *Taqrib al-ʿaqaʾid,* pp. 11–12, 18, and *Idah ibdaʾ hikmat al-hakim fi bayan bismilla al-rahman al-rahim,* pp. 44–45.

102. ʿIllaysh was referring to someone who says that Allah can be seen in a dream in the form of a male. This relies on the hadith "I saw my lord in the form of a lad." ʿIllaysh, *Fath al-ʿali al-malik,* vol. 1, pp. 44–46.

103. Ibid., vol. 1, pp. 5–8, 39–40, 208–9.

104. Ibid., vol. 1, pp. 207–8.

105. Ibid., vol. 1, p. 45; vol. 2, pp. 335–37. A main source for ʿIllaysh's ruling was *al-Madkhal,* written by the Cairene Maliki jurist Muhammad Ibn al-Hajj (d. 1336).

106. ʿAbd al-Rahman's fatwa, written in 1900, is found in Oriental Collections, Leiden University Library, Leiden, no. 14, 431/VI.

107. Al-ʿIdwi, *Mashariq al-anwar,* pp. 88–196; idem, *al-Nafahat al-Shadhiliyya fi sharh al-burda al-busiriyya,* vol. 2, pp. 4, 59–71; Muhammad al-Qayati, *Wasilat al-wusul fiʾl-fiqh waʾl-tawhid waʾl-usul,* pp. 6, 19–21; ʿAbd al-Hadi Naja al-Abyari, *Suʿud al-matali fima tadammanahu al-alghaz fi ism hadrat wali Misr min al-ʿulum al-lawamiʿ,* p. 67; idem, *Fann al-tasawwuf,* especially pp. 1–17; al-Hijrisi, *Hadha kitab al-qasr al-mashid fiʾl-tawhid,* pp. 2–3. See also al-Ghazali, *Ihyaʾ ʿulum al-din,* vol. 5, note 1, p. 6; Taylor, *In the Vicinity of the Righteous,* pp. 63–79.

108. Al-ʿIdwi, *al-Nafahat al-Shadhiliyya,* vol. 2, pp. 75–118; al-Hijrisi, *Hadha kitab al-qasr al-mashid,* pp. 58–63.

109. Shams al-Din al-Inbabi, *Taqrirat sharifa wa-tadqiqat munifa,* p. 31.

110. Rida, *Taʾrikh,* vol. 2, pp. 133f., 136–42.

111. Ibid., vol. 2, pp. 133–34; al-Mahdi, *al-Fatawa al-Mahdiyya,* vol. 2, p. 27. On the position of the Hanafi legal school (to which al-Mahdi belonged) regarding raised voices and singing in mosques, see al-Jaziri, *Kitab al-fiqh ʿala al-madhahib al-arbaʿa,* vol. 1, pp. 286, 289.

112. Rida, *Taʾrikh,* vol. 2, pp. 134ff.

113. De Jong, *Turuq and Turuq-Linked Institutions,* pp. 97–101; Johansen, *Sufism and Islamic Reform in Egypt,* pp. 20–23.

114. *Al-Manar* 1 (1898–99): 924–26.

115. Nadim, in *al-Ustadh,* April 11, 1893, pp. 786–91; April 25, 1893, pp. 828–43.

116. Rida, *Taʾrikh,* vol. 1, pp. 109–15; *al-Manar* 1 (1898–99): 93–101, 813–16, 823–28, 924ff.; al-Munajjid and Khuri, *Fatawa,* vol. 1, pp. 75–79, 93ff.; vol. 2, pp. 765ff.; vol. 3, pp. 864ff.; vol. 4, pp. 1468–82, 1592–95, 1906ff. See also Albert Hourani, *The Emergence of the Modern Middle East,* pp. 90–102.

117. Muhammad Tawfiq al-Bakri, *al-Mustaqbal liʾl-Islam,* pp. 14–19; Johansen, *Sufism and Islamic Reform in Egypt,* pp. 26–29.

118. Nadim, in *al-Ustadh,* April 11, 1893, p. 789; April 25, 1893, pp. 840–43.

119. Rida, *Taʾrikh,* vol. 2, pp. 128ff.; *al-Manar* 1 (1898–99): 99ff. But Rida's frustration with the poor results of the reformist agenda eventually resulted in his radicalization. Inspired by the teaching of Ibn Taymiyya and the Wahhabis, he demanded

the establishment of an Islamic state that would enforce the shariʿa, including the *hudud* (Qurʾanic punishments). Any ruler who denied this obligation, Rida argued, should be overthrown. Al-Munajjid and Khuri, *Fatawa,* vol. 4, p. 1478; vol. 6, pp. 2204ff.

120. ʿUmar ʿAli Hasan, *al-Sufiyya waʾl-siyasa fi Misr,* pp. 97–98. See also Frederick DeJong, "Aspects of the Political Involvement of Sufi Orders in Twentieth-Century Egypt, 1907–1970 — An Exploratory Stock-taking," pp. 183–90, 193–96.

121. H. A. R. Gibb and Michael Gilsenan argued that the Sufi orders in early twentieth-century Egypt became peripheral for the middle classes in light of modernization and the rise of new social elements. Both scholars, however, pointed to the sustained influence of the orders among the common people in the towns and villages, as reflected, inter alia, by the ongoing popularity of the cult of saints. In resisting demands for religious reform, Sufi shaykhs found common ground with Azharis, who were also struggling to retain their communal influence in the face of the challenges of modernity. Gibb, *Modern Trends in Islam,* pp. 53–54; M. D. Gilsenan, "Some Factors in the Decline of the Sufi Orders in Modern Egypt"; idem, *Saint and Sufi in Modern Egypt,* pp. 188–207.

122. Islamic tradition, in stressing the importance of the duty of forbidding wrong, used the Qurʾanic threat of turning Muslims who neglect this duty into apes and pigs in the next world, as was the case for the Children of Israel. See, e.g., Uri Rubin, *Between Bible and Qurʾan,* pp. 226–30; Cook, *Commanding Right and Forbidding Wrong.* Also ʿIllaysh, *Hidayat al-salik,* vol. 1, p. 245.

123. Al-Ghazali, *Ihyaʾ ʿulum al-din,* vol. 2, p. 391. For his extensive discussion of this imperative, see ibid., pp. 393–453. See also Taqi al-Din ibn Taymiyya, *al-Hisba.*

124. Al-Ghazali, *Ihyaʾ ʿulum al-din,* vol. 2, pp. 401–2.

125. Cook, *Commanding Right and Forbidding Wrong,* pp. 330–33, 457–58, 523–30. See also Ibrahim Dasuqi al-Shahawi, *al-Hisba fiʾl-Islam,* pp. 46–48; ʿAbd al-Qadir ʿAwda, *al-Tashriʿ al-jinaʾi al-Islami,* vol. 1, pp. 496–97; ʿAli bin Hasan al-Qarni, *al-Hisba fiʾl-madi waʾl-hadir,* pp. 86–88.

126. Thus, for example, the preservation of the legal ideal of the *dhimma* institution in fatwas and other writings in a growing literate community and in the context of anticolonial and anti-Zionist struggle kept the issue of religious minorities on the Egyptian agenda. It also provided the more radical elements in the religious spectrum, mainly the Muslim Brotherhood, with a political handle to attack existing regimes for "deviating from Islam." Similarly, Azhari dissent on the gender issue helped preserve some of the social perceptions of women's roles vis-à-vis men both at home and in the public arena during the first half of the century. A facilitating factor was the legal recognition granted to Islamic law as the arbiter of personal and marital matters, which played into the hands of some qadis in obstructing a more advanced and liberal reform of family life. Still, other qadis applied the reforms in practice or endorsed them fully. Shaham, *Family and the Courts in Modern Egypt,* especially pp. 2–18, 230–36.

127. Lewis, *Islam in History,* p. 12; see also a similar observation by Baer in *Studies in the Social History of Modern Egypt,* pp. 216–20.

128. Smith, *The Ethnic Origins of Nations,* pp. 157–61. A similar rivalry between the guardians of tradition and the reformist-secular wing occurred in Shiʿite Iran as

well, especially during and after the Constitutional Revolution of 1906–11. The entrenched status of the Shiʿite clerics in the Iranian polity, however, weakened the position of their ideological adversaries. Thus, for example, the legal status of religious minorities was only slightly improved during the revolution in comparison to their traditionally inferior status under Shiʿite law. Daniel Tsadik, "The Legal Status of Religious Minorities: Imami Shiʿi Law and Iran's Constitutional Revolution," pp. 405–8.

CHAPTER 7

1. Cromer, *Modern Egypt,* pp. 555–89; idem, "The Government of Subjected Races"; Lawrence Dundas Zetland, *Lord Cromer,* pp. 10, 61–62, 345–55.
2. Muhammad al-Ahmadi al-Zawahiri, *al-Siyasa waʾl-Azhar,* pp. 17–18.
3. Adams, *Islam and Modernism in Egypt,* pp. 68–103.
4. Rida, *Taʾrikh,* vol. 1, pp. 405–11, 425–27, 509–12.
5. On the Umma Party and its platform, see Walid Kazziha, "The Jarida Group and Egyptian Politics."
6. Gasper, "ʿAbdallah al-Nadim," p. 87.
7. According to data provided by Rifaat A. Dika, al-Azhar's total budget in 1892 was £E 3,378, rising to £E 10,388 in 1896 and £E 52,370 in 1911. Rifaat A. Dika, "Islamic Traditions in Modern Politics: The Case of al-Azhar," pp. 120–22.
8. This also included the publishing of fatwas—for example, in *al-Hilal* 6 (1897–98): 496, 552.
9. Crecilius, "Non-ideological Responses of the Egyptian Ulama to Modernization," pp. 184–86.
10. Muhammad al-Ahmadi al-Zawahiri, *al-ʿIlm waʾl-ʿulamaʾ wa-nizam al-taʿlim,* pp. 9–10.
11. See, e.g., Muhammad Rajab al-Bayumi, *Mawaqif taʾrikhiyya li-ʿulamaʾ al-Islam.* An extract from this work appeared in *Majallat al-Azhar* 27 (1937): 171–77, 218–25.
12. Ron Shaham, "Western Scholars on the Role of the ʿUlamaʾ in the Adaptation of the Shariʿa to Modernity: A Critical Review."
13. Crecelius, "Non-ideological Responses of the Egyptian Ulama to Modernization," pp. 185, 190–91; idem, *The Ulama and the State in Modern Egypt,* p. 304.
14. *Makarim al-Akhlaq al-Islamiyya* 1/15 (July 28, 1900): 225–30; 1/20 (October 9, 1900): 314–19.
15. *Makarim al-Akhlaq al-Islamiyya* 1/20 (October 9, 1900): 305–11; *al-Islam* 10/7 (April 1912): 181–88; *al-Islam* 11/2 (February 1913): 46–48.
16. *Makarim al-Akhlaq al-Islamiyya* 1/1 (January 2, 1900): 5–6.
17. *Makarim al-Akhlaq al-Islamiyya* 1/2 (January 14, 1900): 20–22; 1/6 (March 16, 1900): 81–86; 1/15 (July 28, 1900): 235–37, see also 1/5 (March 2, 1900): 68–69.
18. *Makarim al-Akhlaq al-Islamiyya* 1/5 (March 2, 1900): 74–80.
19. Ibid., pp. 65–69.
20. *Makarim al-Akhlaq al-Islamiyya* 1/1 (January 2, 1900): 11; 1/11 (May 30, 1900): 174; also 1/14 (July 13, 1900): 209–16.
21. *Makarim al-Akhlaq al-Islamiyya* 1/1 (January 2, 1900): 7–8; 1/12 (May 13, 1900): 186.

22. *Makarim al-Akhlaq al-Islamiyya* 1/3 (February 1, 1900): 33–41; 1/4 (February 15, 1900): 60–62; 1/7 (April 1, 1990): 97–102.

23. *Makarim al-Akhlaq al-Islamiyya* 1/11 (May 30, 1900): 173.

24. *Makarim al-Akhlaq al-Islamiyya* 1/13 (June 30, 1900): 206–8; 1/22 (November 8, 1900): 344–51.

25. An exception was making dolls for girls, to accustom them to domestic skills and the raising of children. *Makarim al-Akhlaq al-Islamiyya* 1/22 (November 8, 1900): 344–50; 1/23 (November 23, 1900): 365–68.

26. *Makarim al-Akhlaq al-Islamiyya* 1/3 (February 1, 1900): 47–48; 1/16 (August 11, 1900): 248–49. The paper's owner, the Society for Islamic Values, took concrete actions to nurture the character of believers. The spectrum of means for reeducation that the society promoted was broad, ranging from preaching, holding revival conclaves, and organizing philanthropic activity to sending *daʿwa* (preaching) delegations to locations throughout the country. See *Makarim al-Akhlaq al-Islamiyya* 1/2 (January 14, 1900): 31–32; 1/6 (March 16, 1990): 88–91; 1/9 (April 30, 1900): 137–39; 1/10 (May 14, 1900): 145–47, 155–60; 1/11 (May 30, 1900): 175–79; 1/15 (July 28, l900): 237–38.

27. *Makarim al-Akhlaq al-Islamiyya* 1/5 (March 2, 1900): 72.

28. *Makarim al-Akhlaq al-Islamiyya* 1/1 (January 2, 1900): 7–9, 11–12, 47–48; 1/4 (February 15, 1900): 56–57; 1/5 (March 2, 1900): 72–73.

29. *Al-Islam* 10/9 (June 1912): 233–41; 1/10 (July 1912): 257–58; 11/1 (January 1913): 2–9.

30. *Al-Islam* 10/2 (November 1911): 47–48, 79–85; 10/4 (February 1912): 103–7; 10/6 (April 1912): 156–58; 10/8 (May 1912): 199–201; 10/9 (June 1912): 241–46; 10/10 (July 1912): 268–72; 10/11 (July 1912): 299–302; 11/1 (January 1913): 9–10; 11/2 (February 1913): 40–42; 11/5 (May 1913): 138–41; 11/9 (October 1913): 242–43.

31. *Al-Islam* 11/3 (March 1913): 70.

32. *Al-Islam* 11/2 (February 1913): 46–48; also 11/4 (April 1913): 116–22; 11/5 (May 1913): 142–44, 149–58.

33. *Al-Islam* 10/7 (April 1912): 185–88; 11/9 (October 1913): 228.

34. *Al-Islam* 10/1 (October 1911): 22.

35. Ibid., pp. 3–6; *al-Islam* 10/10 (July 1912): 285–86; 11/3 (March 1913): 65–69, 86–87; 11/5 (May 1913): 159–62; 11/9 (September 1913): 213–16.

36. *Al-Islam* 10/7 (April 1912): 171–81.

37. Ibid., p. 6; *al-Islam* 10/7 (April 1912): 20–25; 11/9 (October 1913): 219–23.

38. *Al-Islam* 11/1 (January 1913): 13–30, 36–38.

39. On the 1919 revolt and its aftermath, see Israel Gershoni and James Jankowski, *Egypt, Islam and the Arabs,* pp. 40–54; also Reinhard Schulze, "Kolonisierung und Widerstand: die ägyptischen Bauernrevolten von 1919."

40. Burke, "Understanding Arab Protest Movements," p. 337.

41. ʿAbd al-Rahman al-Rafiʿi, *Thawrat sanat 1919,* pp. 429–30.

42. Hasan al-Banna, *Mudhakkirat al-daʿwa waʾl-daʿiya,* pp. 36–39; Sayyid Qutb, *Tifl min al-qarya,* pp. 150–51.

43. On al-Azhar and the 1919 revolt, see Crecelius, *The Ulama and the State in Modern Egypt,* pp. 256–65; al-Rafiʿi, *Thawrat sanat 1919,* pp. 86, 228–31, 417, 429–34; Reinhard Schulze, *Die Rebellion der ägyptischen Fallahin, 1919,* pp. 139–68; idem, "Colonization and Resistance: The Egyptian Peasant Rebellion, 1919," pp. 189–91;

Majallat al-Azhar 27 (1956–57):. 396–400; *Khamsuna ʿaman ʿala thawrat 1919*, pp. 188–90, 194, 208, 210, 227, 229, 257.

44. Al-Rafiʿi, *Thawrat sanat 1919*, pp. 74–79; Lamʿi al-Mutiʿi, *Mawsuʿat hadha al-rajul min Misr*, pp. 491–96; Mukhlis al-Siyadi, *al-Azhar wa-mashariʿ tatwirihi 1872–1970*, pp. 70–71.

45. This tradition of integrating religious scholarship, Sufism, and national politics continued to guide the Qayati family. Mustafa's brother ʿAbd al-Jawwad held the post of supervisor of Sufi orders in Minya, reporting to the Bakri family. His son Ahmad was elected to parliament in 1938. The Qayatiyya order itself continued to function: it was cited in a 1980 list of Sufi orders. Mustafa, *al-Binaʾ al-ijtimaʿi liʾl-tariqa al-Shadhiliyya fi Misr*, pp. 310–12; De Jong, *Turuq and Turuq-Linked Institutions*, pp. 161–63; Subhi, *Taʾrikh al-hayat al-niyabiyya fi Misr*, pp. 103–35, 303; Mujahid, *al-Aʿlam al-Sharqiyya*, vol. 2, pp. 187–88.

46. Al-Mutiʿi, *Mawsuʿat hadha al-rajul min Misr*, pp. 34–37.

47. See, e.g., M. Cheetham (Cairo) to Earl Curzon (London), March 19, 1919, PRO, FO407/184/No. 93; M. Cheetham (Cairo) to Earl Curzon (London), March 22, 1919, FO407/184/No. 151; E. Allenby (Cairo) to Earl Curzon (London), June 1, 1919, FO407/184/No. 384.

48. The petition is cited in al-Rafiʿi, *Thawrat sanat 1919*, pp. 429–30.

49. For the full version of this program, see *al-Manar* 29 (1928–29): 325–35 . Also Francine Costet-Tardieu, *Un réformiste à l'Université al-Azhar: Oeuvre et pensée de Mustafâ al-Marâghî (1881–1945)*.

50. Crecelius, *The Ulama and the State in Modern Egypt*, pp. 234–48.

51. ʿIllaysh's essays were published in *al-Akhbar* and appeared in al-Saʿidi, *Taʾrikh al-islah fiʾl-Azhar*, vol. 1, pp. 190–200.

52. Al-Saʿidi, *Taʾrikh al-islah fiʾl-Azhar*, vol. 1, pp. 190–200. The controversy over reform in al-Azhar was widely covered in *al-Manar*, whose editor, Rashid Rida, made no effort to hide his aversion to those ʿulamaʾ who championed the "freeze," such as Muhammad Hamza ʿIllaysh. *Al-Manar* 29 (1928–29), pp. 542–48.

53. See Ibrahim M. Abu-Rabiʿ, "al-Azhar Sufism in Modern Egypt: The Sufi Thought."

54. See P. J. Vatikiotis, "Religion and State in Egypt," pp. 119–23.

55. See e.g., Martin Kramer, *Islam Assembled*, pp. 86–105.

56. On Egypt's democratic climate in the interwar period, see Gershoni and Jankowski, *Confronting Fascism in Egypt*; Ayalon, *The Press in the Arab Middle East*, pp. 51–62.

57. ʿAli ʿAbd al-Raziq, *al-Islam wa-usul al-hukm*.

58. Meir Hatina, *Identity Politics in the Middle East: Liberal Thought and Islamic Challenge in Egypt*, pp. 16–19; ʿAbd al-Raziq quoted in *al-Hilal* 37 (1928–29): 21–22 (November 1, 1928).

59. Taha Hussein, *The Days*, pp. 47–52. See also Sayyid Qutb's personal account of the status of Azharis in the countryside, *Tifl min al-qarya*, pp. 50–53, 131–32.

60. Arthur Jeffery, "The Suppressed Qurʾan Commentary of Muhammad Abu Zaid"; Ami Ayalon, *Egypt's Quest for Cultural Orientation*, pp. 7–8.

61. *Majallat al-Azhar* 5 (1936): 411–17.

62. See, e.g., Crecelius, "Non-ideological Responses of the Egyptian Ulama to Modernization," pp. 199–204; Muhammad ʿImara, *al-Islam wa-usul al-hukm li-ʿAli ʿAbd al-Raziq*, pp. 91–92 (quotation).

63. Notably, in 1928 al-Azhar's budget was £E 282,672, while by 1948 it had risen to £E 909,702. During the same period the number of Azhari students rose from 11,157 to 18,582. Mahmoud Abu al-Eyoun, *al-Azhar: A Short Historical Survey,* pp. 84–85, 133–34.

64. For a list of the religious institutes affiliated with al-Azhar in the 1940s, see ibid., p. 79; also al-Hanafi, *Kanz al-jawhar,* pp. 207–9.

65. See, e.g., *Majallat al-Azhar* 97 (May 13, 1935): 76–77.

66. Ayalon, *The Press in the Arab Middle East,* pp. 171–73; *Majallat al-Azhar* 18 (1946): 93.

67. Heather J. Shareky, "Empire and Muslim Conversion: Historical Reflections on Christian Missions in Egypt," pp. 46–48.

68. *Majallat al-Azhar* 26 (January 15, 1955): 545–48; 28 (October 6, 1956): 272–79; see also Abu al-Eyoun, *al-Azhar,* pp. 143–44.

69. Notably, some Azharis did display an affinity with the Salafi political and activist orientation. On the Salafi-Azhari encounter in the interwar period, see Rainer Brunner, "Education, Politics, and the Struggle for Intellectual Leadership: al-Azhar between 1927–1945," pp. 125–31.

70. *Al-Manar* 30 (1929): 507–8.

71. On the effendi nature of the Brotherhood, see Israel Gershoni and James Jankowski, *Redefining the Egyptian Nation, 1930–1945,* pp. 79–100.

72. Crecelius, *The Ulama and the State in Modern Egypt,* pp. 256–72, 290–328; al-Zawahiri, *al-Siyasa wa'l-Azhar,* pp. 33–47, 60–77, 91–94.

73. Al-Sa'idi, *Ta'rikh al-islah fi'l-Azhar,* vol. 1, pp. 90–99.

74. Mitchell, *The Society of the Muslim Brothers,* pp. 211–14 (quotation); Abu-Rabi', "al-Azhar Sufism in Modern Egypt," p. 211.

75. Some Azhari shaykhs also participated in the Brotherhood's endeavor to reformulate nationalism in more Islamic terms. Gershoni and Jankowski, *Redefining the Egyptian Nation,* p. 79; Muhammad 'Abd al-'Aziz Da'ud, *al-Jam'iyyat al-Islamiyya fi Misr wa-dawruha fi nashr al-da'wa al-Islamiyya,* pp. 111–12; Brynjar Lia, *The Society of the Muslim Brothers in Egypt,* pp. 224–27.

76. Donald M. Reid, *Cairo University and the Making of Modern Egypt,* pp. 155–56.

77. Hatina, *Identity Politics in the Middle East,* pp. 22–24.

78. See, e.g., Hussein, *The Days,* especially pp. 66–102; Sayyid Qutb, *A Child from the Village;* Mahmud Taymur, "Wali Allah."

79. Gibb, *Modern Trends in Islam,* pp. 51–53; Gilsenan, "Some Factors in the Decline of the Sufi Orders in Modern Egypt"; idem, *Saint and Sufi in Modern Egypt,* pp. 188–207.

80. Morroe Berger, *Islam in Egypt Today: Social and Political Aspects of Popular Religion,* pp. 73–76; Hasan, *al-Sufiyya wa'l-siyasa fi Misr,* pp. 97–102. Sufism also attained support and backing from al-Azhar circles. This trend was reinforced during 'Abd al-Halim Mahmud's term as shaykh al-Azhar, 1973–78. Mahmud was a prominent follower of the Shadhiliyya order. See also Mahmud, *al-Madrasa al-Shadhiliyya al-haditha;* idem, *Fatawa al-Imam 'Abd al-Halim Mahmud,* vol. 1, pp. 133–34, 273–74, 368–69; vol. 2, pp. 327–407.

81. Hamid Ansari, *Egypt: The Stalled Society,* pp. 211–30.

82. Johansen, *Sufism and Islamic Reform in Egypt,* 3–26; Berger, *Islam in Egypt Today,* pp. 62–72; Daniel Crecelius, "al-Azhar in Revolution"; P. J. Vatikiotis, "Islam and

the Foreign Policy of Egypt," pp. 121–57; Valerie J. Hoffman, *Sufism: Mystics and Saints in Modern Egypt*, pp. 13–16; also Majda ʿAli Salih Rabiʿ, *al-Dawr al-siyasi liʾl-Azhar 1952–1981*, pp. 122–58; Hasan, *al-Sufiyya waʾl-siyasa fi Misr*, pp. 100–102.

83. Mahmud Shaltut, *al-Islam ʿaqida wa-shariʿa*, pp. 398–99. On Shaltut's biography, see Wolf-Dieter Lemke, *Mahmud Šaltut (1893–1963) und die Reform der Azhar.*

84. Dika, "Islamic Traditions in Modern Politics," pp. 129–32; Donald M. Reid, "al-Azhar," in John L. Esposito (ed.), *The Oxford Encyclopedia of the Modern Islamic World*, p. 170.

85. Figures taken from Crecelius, *The Ulama and the State in Modern Egypt*, p. 402. See also *Islamic Heritage in the URA*, pp. 3–16.

86. James Jankowski, "Arab Nationalism in Nasserism and Egyptian State Policy, 1952–1958," pp. 155–57.

87. Ibid., pp. 155–56.

88. Rifʿat Sayyid Ahmad, *Thawrat al-jiniral, qissat Jamal ʿAbd al-Nasir kamila*, pp. 678–79, 681–84; Riyad Ahmad Jawwad, *Fatawa al-Azhar fi wujub al-jihad wa-tahrim al-taʿamul maʿ al-kiyan al-sahyuni*, pp. 49–84.

89. Fauzi M. Najjar, "Egypt's Laws of Personal Status," pp. 320–21.

90. Shaltut, *al-Islam ʿaqida wa-shariʿa*, pp. 23, 153.

91. Hatina, "Historical Legacy and the Challenge of Modernity," pp. 60–62.

92. This position was reinforced in the postrevolutionary era under Anwar Sadat (1970–81) and Husni Mubarak (1981–). The religious resurgence in both its aspects—communal and militant—that swept the Middle East from the early 1970s onward signified a disillusionment with the Western liberal and social-ist models that were adopted. This sense of disillusionment was aptly expressed by the Egyptian author Yusuf al-Qaʿid, who wrote: "Our ambitions were greater than our possibilities. We stepped forward but we found no ground under-neath us; we lifted our heads to touch the clouds and the sky disappeared above us" (Hatina, "Historical Legacy and the Challenge of Modernity," pp. 62–63). Within this context, political Islam in Egypt moved from the periphery to the political center, whereas al-Azhar's position was enhanced by the government in order to counter the Islamist challenge. See, e.g., Zeghal, "Religion and Politics in Egypt," pp. 378–88; Ayalon, *Egypt's Quest for Cultural Orientation*, pp. 13–42; Tamir Mustafa, "Conflict and Cooperation between the State and Religious Institutions in Contemporary Egypt."

CHAPTER 8

1. İsmail Kara, "Turban and Fez: Ulema as Opposition"; Amit Bein, "ʿUlemaʾ and Political Activism in the Late Ottoman Empire: The Political Career of Şeyhülis-lâm Mustafa Sabri Efendi (1869–1954)."

2. See, e.g., Hafiz and Abaza, *Taʾrikh ʿulamaʾ Dimashq*, vol. 1; ʿAbd al-Rahim, "ʿAlaqat Bilad al-Sham bi-Misr"; Mujahid, *al-Aʿlam al-Sharqiyya*, vol. 4: al-Qayati, *Nafhat*, pp. 23–30, 35–41, 60–80, 84–91, 94–107, 109–28; Rafeq, "The Ulama of Ottoman Jerusalem"; Commins, *Islamic Reform*, pp. 7–9; ʿAdil Manna, *Aʿlam Filastin fi awakhir al-ʿahd al-ʿUthmani;* John O. Voll, "Old ʿUlamaʾ Families and Ottoman Influence in Eighteenth-Century Damascus"; Éric Geoffroy, *Le soufisme en Égypte et en Syrie;* Dick Douwes, *The Ottomans in Syria*, pp. 70–75, 79–83.

3. Albert Hourani, "Ottoman Reform and the Politics of Notables."

4. Moshe Maʿoz, "The Ulama and the Process of Modernization in Syria during the Mid-Nineteenth Century"; idem, *Ottoman Reform in Syria and Palestine, 1840–1861;* Ruth Roded, "Tradition and Change in Syria during the Last Decades of Ottoman Rule: The Urban Elite of Damascus, Aleppo, Homs and Hama, 1876–1918," pp. 184–236. Roded points out that some of the old ʿulamaʾ families in Damascus did decline. See also Linda S. Schilcher, *Families in Politics: Damascus Factions and Estates of the Eighteenth and Nineteenth Centuries,* pp. 115–222; Yazbak, "Nabulsi Ulama"; Elizabeth Sirriyeh, "Whatever Happened to the Banu Jamaʿa? The Tale of a Scholarly Family in Ottoman Syria"; Jakob Skovgaard-Petersen, "Levantine State Muftis," pp. 276–79.

5. Maʿoz, *Ottoman Reform,* pp. 95–98.

6. Yet, despite growing missionary activity in Syria and the anxiety it created in the Islamic scholarly community, the phenomenon of conversion from Islam to Christianity was rare and never became a mass movement. This was a further indication of the entrenchment of Islam in society. Goddard, *A History of Christian-Muslim Relations,* pp. 123–36.

7. On the role of ʿulamaʾ in intercommunal strife in Syria, see Maʿoz, "The Ulama and the Process of Modernization in Syria," pp. 82–88; idem, "Communal Conflicts in Ottoman Syria during the Reform Era: The Role of Political and Economic Factors"; Bruce Masters, *Christians and Jews in the Ottoman Arab World: The Roots of Sectarianism,* pp. 37–40.

8. See, e.g., Maʿoz, "The Ulama and the Process of Modernization in Syria," pp. 82–83; Bruce Masters, "The Ottoman Empire's Caravan City," pp. 69–72.

9. Quoted in Bat Yeʾor, *The Dhimmi: Jews and Christian under Islam,* pp. 246–47; Maʿoz, "The Ulama and the Process of Modernization in Syria," pp. 86–87. See also Masters, *Christians and Jews in the Ottoman Arab World,* pp. 145–51.

10. Al-Bitar, *Hilyat al-bashar,* vol. 3, pp. 1134–35 (quotation); ʿAbd al-Raʾuf Sannu, *al-Nazaʿat al-kiyaniyya al-Islamiyya fiʾl-dawla al-ʿUthmaniyya 1877–1881,* p. 184. Notably, an organized reaction to the Hatt-ı Hümayun also took place in Istanbul, the Ottoman capital itself, as mentioned by Butrus Abu-Manneh. It was led by ʿulamaʾ and Sufi shaykhs mainly from the Naqshbandiyya-Mujaddidiyya order and its most prominent branch, the Khalidiyya. Abu-Manneh, *Studies on Islam,* pp. 125–29.

11. Bat Yeʾor, *The Dhimmi,* pp. 201, 245.

12. Moshe Maʿoz, "Muslim Ethnic Communities in Nineteenth-Century Syria and Palestine: Trends of Conflict and Integration," pp. 305–7. Al-Bitar also noted the banishment of the Shafiʿi mufti of Damascus, ʿUmar al-ʿAmri, to Cyprus following his involvement in anti-Christian riots. Al-Bitar, *Hilyat al-bashar,* vol. 2, p. 1135.

13. Maʿoz, *Ottoman Reform,* p. 247.

14. On the thinking of al-Afghani and ʿAbduh and their impact on the Salafiyya in Syria, see Hourani, *Arabic Thought in the Liberal Age,* pp. 103–60; Commins, *Islamic Reform,* pp. 30–32.

15. Nevertheless, the Salafis shared their adversaries' stance in upholding the authority of the ʿulamaʾ in the face of the Westernized secular intelligentsia that challenged it. Commins, *Islamic Reform,* pp. 65–78, 142; Weismann, *A Taste of Modernity,* pp. 273–304.

16. See, e.g., Commins, *Islamic Reform,* pp. 80–82; al-Munajjid and Khuri, *Fatawa,* vol. 2, pp. 765–67, vol. 3, pp. 864–65, 1118–19, vol. 4, p. 1483; ʿAbd al-Hamid al-Zahrawi, "al-Fiqh waʾl-tasawwuf."

17. For the Salafis' social and intellectual profile, see, e.g., Commins, *Islamic Reform,* pp. 34–48, 65–88; Hourani, *Arabic Thought in the Liberal Age,* pp. 222–34; Joseph H. Escovitz, "He Was the Muhammad ʿAbduh of Syria: A Study of Tahir al-Jazaʾiri and His Influence."

18. Commins, *Islamic Reform,* pp. 34–48, 104–15.

19. See David Commins, "Wahhabis, Sufis and Salafis in Early Twentieth Century Damascus," pp. 231–40.

20. Al-Qayati, *Nafhat,* pp. 23–30, 35–41, 60–80, 84–91, 94–107, 109–28; Mujahid, *al-Aʿlam al-Sharqiyya,* vol. 2; Ziyada, "Lubnaniyyun darasu biʾl-Azhar"; Ramadan, "Riwaq al-Shuwam."

21. Commins, *Islamic Reform,* pp. 107–23.

22. On the emergence of Pan-Arabism, see, e.g., Ernest Dawn, "The Rise of Arabism in Syria"; Philip S. Khoury, *Urban Notables and Arab Nationalism,* pp. 53–74; Rashid Khalidi, "Ottomanism and Arabism in Syria before 1914."

23. Eliezer Tauber, *The Emergence of the Arab Movements;* idem, "Rashid Rida as a Pan-Arabist before World War I."

24. Tauber, *The Emergence of the Arab Movements,* pp. 297–300.

25. See, e.g., Khoury, *Urban Notables,* pp. 70–74.

26. Nafiʿ, "Nashʾat al-itijahat al-siyasiyya fi Filastin"; also Muhammad al-Bakir and Muhammad Kurd ʿAli, *al-Baʿtha al-ʿilmiyya ila dar al-khilafa al-Islamiyya.*

27. For more broadly debated discussions of religion and nationalism in the Middle Eastern context, see Piscatori, *Islam in a World of Nation-States,* pp. 40–75; Haim Gerber, "The Muslim Umma and the Formation of Middle Eastern Nationalisms," pp. 209–11; Esposito, *The Islamic Threat,* pp. 62–67; Israel Gershoni and James Jankowski, "Introduction"; Bernard Lewis, *The Middle East and the West,* pp. 70–94; Elie Kedourie, "Introduction," in idem, *Nationalism in Asia and Africa,* pp. 28–31, 69–70; idem, *Democracy and Arab Political Culture,* pp. 1–11; P. J. Vatikiotis, *Islam and the State,* pp. 35–43.

28. Kramer, *Islam Assembled,* pp. 86–105; Donald E. Smith, *Religion, Politics and Social Change in the Third World,* pp. 61–64.

29. Smith, *Religion, Politics and Social Change in the Third World,* pp. 63–64.

30. Such was the case with the Islamic Liberation Party that emerged in Jordan in the 1950s and put forward a pan-Islamic vision. Shua Taji-Farouki, *A Fundamental Quest: Hizb al-Tahrir and the Search for the Islamic Caliphate.*

31. For a historical survey of this international scholarship network, see Joan E. Gilbert, "Institutionalization of Muslim Scholarship and Professionalization of the ʿUlamaʾ in Medieval Damascus," pp. 107–11.

32. Tucker, *In the House of the Law;* Amira El-Azhary Sonbol, "Introduction." Notably, several nationalist reformist circles in Cairo, as well as the Salafis in Syria, also displayed social conservatism and favored limiting women's freedoms. See, e.g., Philipp, "Feminism and Nationalist Politics in Egypt"; Badran, *Feminists, Islam and Nation;* Commins, *Islamic Reform,* pp. 82–83.

33. Michael Provence, "A Nationalist Rebellion without Nationalists? Popular Mobilizations in Mandatory Syria, 1925–1926," pp. 686–87.

34. See Skovgaard-Petersen, "Levantine State Muftis," pp. 281–82.

35. David Commins, "Syria," p. 158; also Philip S. Khoury, *Syria and the French Mandate,* pp. 57–63; Mustafa al-Siba'i, *'Alam wa-amal,* pp. 58–59.

36. See Yehoshu'a Porat, *The Palestinian-Arab National Movement, 1918–1929.* The British attempted to rectify this situation and eventually managed to restore a certain degree of supervision over the council's activity in 1937, while al-Husayni was forced to leave Palestine.

37. Musa Budeiri, "The Palestinian Tensions between Nationalist and Religious Identities," pp. 195–98.

38. See Gerber, *Remembering and Imagining Palestine,* chapters 4–6.

39. Uri M. Kupferschmidt, *The Supreme Muslim Council,* pp. 221–55.

40. See, e.g., Beverley Milton-Edwards, *Islamic Politics in Palestine,* pp. 10–23.

41. See, e.g., Ayman al-Yassini, *Religion and State in the Kingdom of Saudi Arabia,* mainly chapters 2, 3, 4; Joseph Kechichian, "The Role of the Ulama in the Politics of an Islamic State: The Case of Saudi Arabia."

42. Prior to the formation of the Istiqlal Party, some of these 'ulama' were members of a secret anticolonial organization established in 1930, called the Zawiya (Religious Brotherhood).

43. See Henry Munson, *Religion and Power in Morocco,* pp. 83–87; Dale F. Eickelman, *Knowledge and Power in Morocco;* Daniel Zisenwine, "'Ulama', Tribalism and the National Struggle in Morocco, 1944–1956," pp. 195–210.

44. Indeed, the FLN succeeded in absorbing the Association of Algerian Muslim Ulama (AUMA) in 1957, thus enhancing the religious aura of the nationalist struggle for independence. The AUMA, established in 1931 by reformist scholars led by Abdelhamid Ben Badis, campaigned against immoral conduct in society and lobbied for the equal status of Algerians with the French and for the declaration of Arabic as an official language. These activities had a negative effect on relations with the French authorities, leading to growing hostility.

45. The conservative 'ulama' were also challenged by their reformist Salafi colleagues, who urged them to broaden the horizons of Islamic thought in order to regain the dignity of the Muslims. See, e.g., I. William Zartman (ed.), *Man, State and Society in the Contemporary Maghrib,* pp. 151–58.

46. Notably, the Tunisian national movement's reformist agenda was clearly in evidence in the early years following independence in 1956 when Bourguiba's regime aimed to restrict the influence of Islam in civic and political life and take control of the religious educational system, without, however, adopting a radical antireligious policy. In light of the eroded power of the 'ulama', along with the religious revival of the 1970s and thereafter, the nonestablishment Islamist alternative gained support and challenged the existing order. See Norma Salem, *Habib Bourguiba, Islam and the Creation of Tunisia.* For a historical overview of 'ulama'-nationalist relations in the Maghreb, see Shinar, "'Ulama', Marabouts and Government."

47. On the 1920 revolt in Iraq and its ramifications for Shi'ite politics, see Yitzhak Nakash, *The Shi'is of Iraq,* pp. 42–72; also Meir Litvak, *Shi'i Scholars of Nineteenth-Century Iraq: The Ulama of Najaf and Karbala'.*

48. The Hidden Imam was Muhammad ibn Hasan al-'Askari, who is said to have gone into occultation (*ghayaba*) in 872 in order to return on the Day of Judgment

to establish the kingdom of justice. See Moojan Momen, *An Introduction to Shiʿi Islam,* pp. 161–71.

49. On Shiʿite political thought and ʿulamaʾ power in premodern Iran, see, e.g., Martin, *Islam and Modernism,* pp. 11–35; Nikki R. Keddie, "The Roots of Ulamaʾs Power in Modern Iran"; Abdul-Hadi Hairi, "The Legitimacy of the Early Qajar Rule as Viewed by the Shiʿi Religious Leaders."

50. On the tobacco revolt and the ʿulamaʾ, see Nikki R. Keddie, *Religion and Rebellion in Iran: The Tobacco Protest of 1891–1892,* pp. 35–113.

51. Martin, *Islam and Modernism,* pp. 51–85.

52. For the divergent perceptions of constitutionalism by the ʿulamaʾ and secular liberals, see Said Amir Arjomand, "The Ulamaʾs Opposition to Parliamentarianism, 1907–1909"; Janet Afary, *The Iranian Constitutional Revolution, 1906–1911,* pp. 89–115.

53. Arjomand, "The Ulamaʾs Opposition," pp. 177–84.

54. Tabatabaʾi quoted in Hamid Algar, "Religious Forces in Twentieth-Century Iran," p. 733.

55. Afary, *The Iranian Constitutional Revolution,* pp. 98–107.

56. Ghulam Husayn Zargariʾnizhad, *Rasaʾil-i mashrutiyyat,* pp. 47–54; Husayn Abadiyan, *Mabani-i nazari-i hukumat-i mashruta va-mashruʿa,* pp. 28–29, 49–52, 168–69; Hamid Dabashi, "Two Clerical Tracts on Constitutionalism."

57. Zargariʾnizhad, *Rasaʾil-i mashrutiyyat,* pp. 81–90; see also Abdul-Hadi Hairi, *Shiʿism and Constitutionalism in Iran,* pp. 100–103; Said Amir Arjomand, "Ideological Revolution in Shiʿism," pp. 180–84.

58. Afary, *The Iranian Constitutional Revolution,* pp. 108–15.

59. This later became a structural component of Ayatollah Ruhollah Khomeini's concept of *velayat-e faqih* (rule of jurisprudence).

60. Smith, *The Ethnic Origins of Nations,* pp. 159–60.

Chapter 9

1. This approach reflected a certain bias on Mubarak's part. Known for his close relationship with the khedival family, Mubarak did not disguise his aversion to the leaders of the uprising. In his view, they were motivated by narrow interests, defied legitimate authority, and disrupted public order. Not surprisingly, even prominent leaders of the movement such as ʿUrabi, ʿAbduh, and Nadim received no mention at all in *al-Khitat.* See, e.g., Mubarak's biographical sketches of ʿIllaysh, al-ʿIdwi, al-Khalfawi, al-Qalamawi, al-ʿAzzazi, and the Qayati brothers. Mubarak, *al-Khitat,* vol. 4, p. 41; vol. 8, p. 73; vol. 9, pp. 55–58, 96; vol. 14, pp. 95–97, 113–14; vol. 15, p. 63.

2. These accusations are quoted in Cromer, *Modern Egypt,* p. 165; and Dodge, *al-Azhar,* pp. 121–22.

3. Dika, "Islamic Traditions in Modern Politics," pp. 148–49.

4. Tawfiq quoted in the *Times* (London), September 27, 1882.

5. ʿAbbas Hilmi II quoted in Rida, *Taʾrikh,* vol. 1, pp. 513–14.

6. Murphy, *Passion for Islam,* p. 228.

7. Al-Bayumi, *Mawaqif taʾrikhiyya li-ʿulamaʾ al-Islam,* pp. 143–48.

8. Abu al-Eyoun, *al-Azhar,* pp. 143–44.

Bibliography

PUBLIC ARCHIVES

Başbakanlık Arşivi (Prime Minister Archives), Yildiz collection, Istanbul.
Oriental Collections, Leiden University Library, Leiden.
Public Record Office Series (PRO), Foreign Office Archives (FO/78, FO/195, FO/881), London.
Public Record Office Series (PRO), Oriental and Indian Office, London.
St. Antony's College, Dickson Papers, Oxford.

PUBLISHED ARCHIVAL DOCUMENTS

Bibliyughrafiyya li-watha'iq al-thawra al-ʿUrabiyya wa'l-waqa'iʿ al-harbiyya. Cairo: al-Hay'a al-Misriyya al-ʿAmma li'l-Kitab, 1981.
British and Foreign State Papers. Vol. 73–74. London: Ridgway, 1977.
Gillard, David (ed.). *British Documents on Foreign Affairs.* Part 1, Series B, the Near and Middle East, 1856–1914. 20 vols. Frederick, Md.: University Publications of America, 1984–85.
Al-Jumayʿi, ʿAbd al-Munʿim Ibrahim (ed.). *al-Thawra al-ʿUrabiyya fi daw al-watha'iq al-Misriyya.* Cairo: Markaz al-Dirasat al-Siyasiyya wa'l-Istratijiyya bi'l-Ahram, 1982.

NEWSPAPERS AND PERIODICALS

Al-Ahram (Cairo)
Haqa'iq al-Akhbar (Damascus)
Al-Hilal (Cairo)
Al-Islam (Cairo)
Al-Janna (Beirut)
Lisan al-Hal (Beirut)
Majallat al-Azhar (Cairo)
Makarim al-Akhlaq al-Islamiyya (Cairo)
Al-Manar (Cairo)
Al-Siyasa al-Usbuʿiyya (Cairo)
Times (London)
Al-Ustadh (Alexandria)
Al-Watha'iq al-Misriyya (Cairo)

BOOKS AND ARTICLES IN ARABIC

Abadiyan, Husayn. *Mabani-i nazari-i hukumat-i mashruta va-mashruʿa.* Tehran: Nashr-i Nay, 1995.
ʿAbd al-ʿAzim, ʿAli. *Mashyakhat al-Azhar mundhu insha'iha hatta al-an.* 2 vols. Cairo: al-Hay'a al-ʿAmma li-Shuhun al-Matabiʿ al-Amiriyya, 1987.

215

ʿAbd al-Karim, Ahmad ʿIzzat. *Taʾrikh al-taʿlim fi ʿasr Muhammad ʿAli*. 3 vols. Cairo: Matbaʿat al-Nasr, 1945.

ʿAbd al-Rahim, ʿAbd al-Rahim. "ʿAlaqat Bilad al-Sham bi-Misr fiʾl-ʿasr al-ʿUthmani 1517–1798." In *al-Muʾtamar al-duwali al-thani li-taʾrikh Bilad al-Sham 1517–1939*, vol. 1, pp. 275–92. 2 vols. Damascus: Jamaʿat Dimashq, 1978.

ʿAbd al-Raziq, ʿAli. *al-Islam wa-usul al-hukm*. New ed. Beirut: Dar Maktabat al-Hayat, 1966.

ʿAbduh, Muhammad. *al-Taʿassub*. Cairo: Matbaʿat al-Manar, 1930.

———. *Risalat al-tawhid*. New ed. Cairo: Dar al-Manar, 1953.

———. *al-Fatawa fiʾl-tajdid waʾl-islah al-dini*. Susa: Dar al-Maʿarif, 1989.

Abu Hadid, Muhammad Farid. *Zaʾim Misr al-awwal: al-Sayyid ʿUmar Makram*. Cairo: Dar al-Hilal, 1997.

Abu Salim, Muhammad Ibrahim. *Manshurat al-Mahdiyya*. Beirut: Dar al-Jil, 1979.

———. *al-Haraka al-fikriyya fiʾl-Mahdiyya*. 3rd ed. Khartum: Dar Jamaʿat al-Khartum, 1989.

Al-Abyari, ʿAbd al-Hadi Naja. *Suʿud al-mataliʿ fima tadammanahu al-alghaz fi ism had-rat wali Misr min al-ʿulum al-lawamiʿ*. Cairo, Bulaq: al-Matabaʿa al-Khidiwiyya, 1866.

———. *al-Wasaʾil al-adabiyya fiʾl-rasaʾil al-ahdabiyya*. Cairo: Matbaʿat al-Watan, 1883–84.

———. *Ahwal al-ruh*. Cairo: Matbaʿat al-Khayriyya, 1886.

———. *al-Mawakib al-ʿaliyya*. Cairo: Matbaʿat al-Khayriyya, 1886–87.

———. *Fann al-tasawwuf*. French translation by M. Arnaud. Algiers: Adolphe Jourdan, 1888.

Ahmad, Rifʿat Sayyid. *Thawrat al-jiniral, qissat Jamal ʿAbd al-Nasir kamila*. Cairo: Dar al-Huda, 1993.

ʿAli, Saʿid Ismaʿil. *al-Azhar ʿala masrah al-siyasa al-Misriyya*. Cairo: Dar al-Thaqafa, 1974.

Amin, Ahmad. *Zuʿamaʾ al-islah fiʾl-ʿasr al-hadith*. Cairo: Maktabat al-Nahda al-Misriyya, 1948.

ʿAmir, ʿAbd al-Halim. "al-Jamʿiyya al-Khayriyya al-Islamiyya." *al-Majalla al-Taʾrikhiyya al-Misriyya* 38 (1991–95): 419–23.

ʿAwad, Luwis. *Taʾrikh al-fikr al-Misri al-hadith*. 2 vols. Cairo: al-Hayʾa al-Misriyya al-ʿAmma liʾl-Kitab, 1980.

ʿAwda, ʿAbd al-Qadir. *al-Tashriʿ al-jinaʾi al-Islami*. 3rd ed. 2 vols. Cairo: Maktabat Dar al-ʿUruba, 1963.

ʿAzabawi, ʿAbdallah Muhammad. *al-Shuwam fi Misr fiʾl-qarnayn al-thamin ʿashar waʾl-tasiʿ ʿashar*. Cairo: Dar al-Nahda al-ʿArabiyya, 1986.

ʿAziz, Sami. *al-Sihafa al-Misriyya wa-mawqifuha min al-ihtilal al-Inglizi*. Cairo: Dar al-Katib al-ʿArabi, 1968.

ʿAziz, Sami, Khalil Sabat, and Yunan Labib Rizq. *Huriyyat al-sihafa fi Misr 1798–1924*. Cairo: Maktabat al-Waʿy al-ʿArabi, 1972.

Al-Bakir, Muhammad, and Muhammad Kurd ʿAli. *al-Baʿtha al-ʿilmiyya ila dar al-khilafa al-Islamiyya*. Beirut: Matbaʿat Yusuf Sadir, 1916.

Al-Bakri, Muhammad Tawfiq. *al-Mustaqbal liʾl-Islam*. 2nd ed. Cairo: Matbaʿat al-Manar, 1906.

Al-Banna, Hasan. *Mudhakkirat al-daʿwa waʾl-daʿiya*. Cairo: al-Zaharaʾ liʾl-Aʿlam al-ʿArabi, 1990.

Barraj, Jumʿa Muhammad. *Ahkam al-mirath fiʾl-shariʿa al-Islamiyya*. Amman: Dar al-Fikr, 1981.

Al-Bayumi, Muhammad Rajab. *Mawaqif taʾrikhiyya li-ʿulamaʾ al-Islam*. Cairo: Dar al-Hilal, 1884.

Bishri, Tariq. *al-Muslimun waʾl-Aqbat fi itar al-jamaʿa al-wataniyya*. Cairo: al-Hayʾa al-Misriyya al-ʿAmma liʾl-Kitab, 1980.

Al-Bitar, ʿAbd al-Razzaq. *Hilyat al-bashar fi taʾrikh al-qarn al-thalith ʿashar al-hijri*. 3 vols. Damascus: Matbuʿat al-Majmaʿ al-ʿIlmi al-ʿArabi, 1961–63.

Al-Bukhari, Muhammad ibn Ismaʿil. *Sahih al-Bukhari*. 3rd ed. 5 vols. Beirut: Dar Ibn Kathir, 1987.

Al-Dardir, Ahmad ibn Muhammad. *al-Sharh al-saghir*. 2nd ed. 2 vols. Cairo: Matbaʿat al-Midan, 1963.

Al-Dasuqi, ʿAsim. *Mujtamaʿ ʿUlamaʾ al-Azhar fi Misr 1895–1961*. Cairo: Dar al-Thaqafa al-Jadida, 1980.

Al-Dasuqi, Muhammad ibn ʿArafah. *Hashiyat al-Dasuqi ʿala al-sharh al-kabir*. 4 vols. Cairo: Dar Ihyaʾ al-Kutub al-ʿArabiyya, n.d.

Daʾud, Muhammad ʿAbd al-ʿAziz. *al-Jamʿiyyat al-Islamiyya fi Misr wa-dawruha fi nashr al-daʿwa al-Islamiyya*. Cairo: al-Zahraʾ liʾl-Iʿlam al-ʿArabi, 1992.

Dayf, Shawqi. *al-Barudi: raʾid al-shiʿr al-hadith*. Cairo: Dar al-Maʿarif, 1964.

Al-Fiqqi, Muhammad Kamil. *al-Azhar wa-atharuhu fiʾl-nahda al-adabiyya al-haditha*. 2nd ed. Cairo: Maktabat Nahdat Misr, 1960.

Al-Gamiʿi, ʿAbd al-Munʿim Ibrahim. *Mudhakkirat al-zaʿim Ahmad ʿUrabi*. 2 vols. Cairo: Dar al-Kutub, 2005.

Al-Ghazali, Abu Hamid. *Ihyaʾ ʿulum al-din*. 5 vols. Cairo: Muʾassasat al-Halabi, 1967.

Al-Ghazali, Muhammad. *al-Taʿassub waʾl-tasamuh bayna al-Masihiyya waʾl-Islam*. Cairo: Dar al-Kutub al-ʿArabi, n.d.

Hafiz, Muhammad Mutiʿ, and Nizar Abaza. *Taʾrikh ʿulamaʾ Dimashq fiʾl-qarn al-rabiʿ ʿashar*. 3 vols. Damascus: Dar al-Fikr, 1986–91.

Hamza ʿAbd al-ʿAziz Badr, and Muhammad Husam al-Din Ismaʿil (eds.). *Dirasat fi taʾrikh Misr al-iqtisadi waʾl-ijtimaʿi*. Cairo: Dar al-ʾAfaq al-ʿArabiyya, 1996.

Hanafi, Hasan. "al-Din waʾl-thawra fiʾl-thawra al-ʿUrabiyya." In *al-Thawra al-ʿUrabiyya miʾat ʿam*, pp. 34–77. Cairo: Dar al-Mawaqif al-ʿArabi, 1981.

Al-Hanafi, Sulayman Rasad. *Kanz al-jawhar fi taʾrikh al-Azhar*. Cairo: n.p., 1903.

Hasan, ʿUmar ʿAli. *al-Sufiyya waʾl-siyasa fi Misr*. Cairo: Markaz al-Mahrusa, 1997.

Al-Hijrisi, Muhammad Khalil. *al-Jawhar al-nafis ʿala salawat Ibn Idris*. Bulaq: al-Matbaʿa al-Miriyya, 1893.

———. *Hadha kitab al-qasr al-mashid fiʾl-tawhid*. Cairo: al-Matbaʿa al-ʿIlmiyya, 1896–97.

Ibn al-Hajj, Muhammad. *al-Madkhal*. 4 vols. Cairo: Mustafa al-Babi al-Halabi wa-Awladu, 1960.

Ibn al-Jawzi, ʿAbd al-Rahman. *al-ʿIlal al-Mutanahiya fiʾl-ahadith al-wahiya*. 2 vols. Beirut: Dar al-Kutub al-ʿIlmiyya, 1982–83.

Ibn Qayyim al-Jawziyya, Shams al-Din Muhammad. *Ahkam ahl al-dhimma*. 2 vols. Damascus: Matbaʿat Jamiʿat Dimashq, 1961.

Ibn Taymiyya, Taqi al-Din. *al-Hisba*. Cairo: Matbuʿat al-Shaʿb, 1976.

Al-ʿIdwi, Hasan. *al-Nafahat al-Shadhiliyya fi sharh al-burda al-busiriyya*. 2 vols. Cairo: al-Matbaʿa al-ʿAmira, 1879.

———. *Mashariq al-anwar fi fawz ahl al-iʿtibar*. Cairo: al-Matbaʿa al-ʿAmira al-Sharafiyya, 1886.

ʿIllaysh, Muhammad. *Hidayat al-salik ila al-masalik fi fiqh imam al-aʾiama Malik ʿala al-sharh al-saghir liʾl-ʿalama al-Dardir*. 2 vols. Cairo: Matbaʿat al-Wahhabiyya, 1869.

———. *Idah ibdaʾ hikmat al-hakim fi bayan bismilla al-rahman al-rahim*. Cairo: Matbaʿat al- Wahhabiyya, 1878.

———. *Fath al-ʿali al-malik fiʾl-fatwa ʿala madhhab al-Imam Malik*. 2 vols. Beirut: Dar al-Maʿarifa, 1975 [1883].

———. *Taqrib al-ʿaqaʾid al-sanniyya biʾl-adilla al-Qurʾaniyya*. New ed. Cairo: Dar al-Basaʾir, 2005.

ʿImara, Muhammad. *al-Islam wa-usul al-hukm li-ʿAli ʿAbd al-Raziq*. Beirut: al-Muʾassasa al-ʿArabiyya liʾl-Dirasat waʾl-Nashr, 1972.

Al-Inbabi, Shams al-Din. *Taqrirat sharifa wa-tadqiqat munifa*. Cairo: n.p., n.d.

ʿIsa, Salah. *Hikayat min daftar al-watan*. Cairo: Jaridat al-Ahali, 1992.

Jawwad, Riyad Ahmad, *Fatawa al-Azhar fi wujub al-jihad wa-tahrim al-taʿamul maʿ al-kiyan al-sahyuni*. Cairo: Markaz Yafa liʾl-Dirasat waʾl-Abhath, 1998.

Al-Jaziri, ʿAbd al-Rahman. *Kitab al-fiqh ʿala al-madhahib al-arbaʿa*. 4 vols. Cairo: al-Maktaba al-Tijariyya al-Kubra, n.d.

Al-Jumayʿi, ʿAbd al-Munʿim Ibrahim. "Mawqif al-dawla al-ʿUthmaniyya min al-thawra al-ʿUrabiyya." *al-Majalla al-Taʾrikhiyya al-Misriyya* 26 (1979): 141–55.

———. "al-Tanafus ʿala al-khidiwiyya al-Misriyya bayna al-Amir Halim waʾl-Khidiw Tawfiq." *al-Majalla al-Taʾrikhiyya al-Misriyya* 28–29 (1981–82): 359–72.

Kahhala, ʿUmar Rida. *Muʿjam al-muʾallifin*. 5 vols. Beirut: Muʾassasat al-Risala, 1993.

Khafaji, Muhammad ʿAbd al-Munʿim. *al-Azhar fi alf ʿam*. 2nd ed. 3 vols. Beirut: ʿAlam al-Kutub, 1987–88.

Khafif, Mahmud. *Ahmad ʿUrabi al-zaʿim al-muftaraʾa ʿalay*. 2 vols. Cairo: Dar al-Hilal, 1971.

Khamsuna ʿaman ʿala thawrat 1919. Cairo: Muaʾssasat al-Ahram, 1959.

Al-Khatib, Muhibb al-Din. *al-Azhar: madih wa-hadiruhu waʾl-haja ila islahihi*. Cairo: al-Matbaʿa al-Salafiyya, 1926.

Al-Mahdi, Muhammad al-ʿAbbasi. *al-Fatawa al-Mahdiyya fiʾl-waqaʾiʿ al-Misriyya*. 7 vols. Cairo: Matbaʿat al-Azhariyya, 1887.

Al-Mahlawi, Hanafi. *al-Ayyam al-akhira fi hayat ʿuzamaʾ al-siyasa*. Cairo: Nahdat Misr, 1998.

Mahmud, ʿAbd al-Halim. *al-Madrasa al-Shadhiliyya al-haditha*. Cairo: Dar al-Kutub al-Haditha, 1968.

———. *Fatawa al-Imam ʿAbd al-Halim Mahmud*. 4th ed. 2 vols. Cairo: Dar al-Maʿarif, 1994–96.

Majmuʿat rasaʾil al-imam al-shahid Hasan al-Banna. Beirut: al-Muʾassasa al-Islamiyya, 1982.

Makhluf, Muhammad ibn Muhammad. *Shajarat al-nur al-zakiyya fi tabaqat al-Malikiyya*. Beirut: Dar al-Kitab al-ʿArabi, 1980.

Mandur, Ahmad. "al-Shaykh Husayn al-Marsafi wa'l-wasila al-adabiyya." *Sijill al-Thaqafa al-Rafi'a* 29 (May 1959): 35–41.

Manna, 'Adil. *A'lam Filastin fi awakhir al-'ahd al-'Uthmani*. Jerusalem: Jam'iyat al-Dirasat al-'Arabiyya, 1986.

Al-Marsafi, Husayn. *Risalat al-kalim al-thaman*. Cairo: Matba'at al-Jumhur, 1903.

Mubarak, 'Ali. *al-Khitat al-tawfiqiyya al-jadida li-Misr al-Qahira*. 20 vols. Cairo, Bulaq: Dar al-Kutub, 1885–89.

Mughith, Kamal Hamid. *Misr fi'l-'asr al-'Uthmani 1517–1798*. Cairo: Markaz al-Dirasat wa'l-Ma'lumat al-Qanuniyya li-Huquq al-Insan, 1997.

Mujahid, Zaki Muhammad. *al-A'lam al-Sharqiyya*. 4 vols. Cairo: al-Matba'a al-Misriyya al-Haditha, 1949–50.

Al-Munajjid, Salah al-Din, and Yusuf Khuri (eds.). *Fatawa al-Imam Muhammad Rashid Rida*. 6 vols. Beirut: Dar al-Kitab al-Jadid, 1970.

Murqus, Yuwaqim Rizq (ed.). *Awraq Mustafa Kamil: al-maqalat*. 2 vols. Cairo: al Hay'a al-Misriyya al-'Amma li'l-Kitab, 1992.

Mustafa, 'Abd al-Rahim. *Misr wa'l-mas'ala al-Misriyya*. Cairo: Dar al-Ma'arif, 1965.

Mustafa, Faruq Ahmad. *al-Bina' al-ijtima'i li'l-tariqa al-Shadhiliyya fi Misr*. Alexandria: al-Hay'a al-Misriyya al-'Amma li'l-Kitab, 1980.

Al-Muti'i, Lam'i. *Mawsu'at hadha al-rajul min Misr*. Cairo: Dar al-Shuruq, 1997.

Nafi', Bashir. "Nash'at al-itijahat al-siyasiyya fi Filastin fi awakhir al-'ahd al-'Uthmani." *Qira'at Siyasiyya* (Winter 1995): 27–56.

Al-Najjar, Husayn Fawzi. *Ahmad 'Urabi Misr li'l-Misriyyin*. Cairo: al-Hay'a al-Misriyya al-'Amma li'l-Kitab, 1992.

Najm, Zayn al-'Abidin. *al-Jam'iyya al-wataniyya al-Misriyya*. Cairo: al-Hay'a al-Misriyya al-'Amma li'l-Kitab, 1987.

Al-Naqqash, Salim. *Misr li'l-Misriyyin*. 7 vols. Cairo: al-Hay'a al-Misriyya li'l-Kitab, 1997.

Al-Nawawi, Abu Zakariyya Muhyi al-Din. *Kitab al-majmu', sharh al-muhadhdhab li'l-Shirazi*. Cairo: al-Matba'a al-'Arabiyya, 1925.

Nawfal, 'Abdallah Habib. *Kitab tarajim 'ulama' Tarabulus wa-udaba'uha*. Tripoli: Matba'at al-Khadara, 1929.

Al-Qaradawi, Yusuf. *Ghayr al-Muslimin fi'l-mujtama' al-Islami*. 2nd ed. Beirut: Mu'assasat al-Risala, 1983.

Al-Qarni, 'Ali bin Hasan. *al-Hisba fi'l-madi wa'l-hadir*. Riyadh: Maktabat al-Rushd, 1994.

Al-Qayati, Muhammad. *Wasilat al-wusul fi'l-fiqh wa'l-tawhid wa'l-usul*. Cairo: Matba'at al-Khayriyya, 1888.

———. *Khulasat al-tahqiq fi afdaliyyat al-siddiq*. Cairo: Matba'at al-Islam, 1895.

———. *Nafhat al-basham fi rihlat al-Sham*. Beirut: Dar al-Ra'id al-'Arabi, 1981 [1901].

Al-Qushayri, Muslim ibn al-Hajjaj. *Sahih Muslim*. 5 vols. Beirut: Dar Ihya' al-Turath al-'Arabi, n.d.

Qutb, Sayyid. *Tifl min al-qarya*. Jeddah: al-Dar al-Su'udiyya li'l-Nashr, 1945.

Rabi', Majda 'Ali Salih. *al-Dawr al-siyasi li'l-Azhar 1952–1981*. Cairo: Markaz al-Buhuth wa'l-Dirasat al-Siyasiyya, 1992.

Al-Rafi'i, 'Abd al-Rahman. *al-Thawra al-'Urabiyya wa'l-ihtilal al-Injlizi*. 3rd ed. Cairo: al-Dar al-Qawmiyya li'l-Tiba'a wa'l-Nashr, 1966.

———. ʿAsr Ismaʿil. 3rd ed. 2 vols. Cairo: Dar al-Maʿarif, 1982.

———. Thawrat sanat 1919. 4th ed. Cairo: Dar al-Maʿarif, 1987.

Al-Rafiʿi, Muhammad Rashid. Tarajim hayat al-shaykh ʿAbd al-Qadir al-Rafiʿi. Cairo: Dar al-Naqd, 1906.

Ramadan, Mustafa. "Riwaq al-Shuwam biʾl-Azhar iban al-ʿasr al-ʿUthmani." In al-Muʾtamar al-duwali al-thani li-taʾrikh Bilad al-Sham 1517–1939, vol. 1, pp. 17–97. 2 vols. Damascus: Jamiʿat Dimashq, 1978.

Rashwan, Malik Muhammad. ʿUlamaʾ al-Azhar bayna Bunabart wa-Muhammad ʿAli. Cairo: Matbaʿat al-Amana, 1989.

Rida, Muhammad Rashid. Taʾrikh al-imam al-shaykh Muhammad ʿAbduh. 3 vols. Cairo: Matbaʿat al-Manar, 1931.

Al-Rifaʿi, Mustafa Sadiq. "al-Azhar waʾl-thawra al-ʿUrabiyya." Majallat al-Azhar 24 (May 14, 1953): 970–74.

Al-Rifaʿi, Qasim (ed.). Fatawa Islamiyya. 4 vols. Beirut: Dar al-Qalam, 1988.

Saʿid, Amin. Taʾrikh Misr al-siyasi. Cairo: Dar al-Kutub al-Misriyya, 1959.

Al-Saʿidi, ʿAbd al-Mutaʿal. Taʾrikh al-islah fiʾl-Azhar. 2 vols. Cairo: Matbaʿat al-Iʿtimad, 1943.

Salah, Mahmud. Muhakamat zaʿim. Cairo: Madbuli al-Saghir, 1996.

Salim, Latifa Muhammad. al-Quwwa al-ijtimaʿiyya fiʾl-thawra al-ʿUrabiyya. Cairo: al-Hayʾa al-Misriyya al-ʿAmma liʾl-Kitab, 1981.

———. "Masaʿi al-Amir Halim waʾl-Khidiw Ismaʿil min ajl ʿarsh Misr athnaa al-thawra al-ʿUrabiyya." al-Majalla al-Taʾrikhiyya al-Misriyya 30–31 (1983–84): 415–31.

Sami, ʿAbd al-Rahman. al-Qawl al-haqq fi Bayrut wa-Dimashq. New ed. Beirut: Dar al-Raʾid al-ʿArabi, 1981.

Sami, Amin. Taqwim al-Nil. 4 vols. Cairo: Matbaʿat Dar al-Kutub al-Misriyya, 1936.

Sannu, ʿAbd al-Raʾuf. al-Nazaʿat al-kiyaniyya al-Islamiyya fiʾl-dawla al-ʿUthmaniyya 1877–1881. Beirut: Bisan, 1998.

Sarhank, Ismaʿil. Haqaʾiq al-Akhbar ʿan duwal al-bihar. 3 vols. Cairo: al-Matbaʿa al-Amiriyya, n.d. [1894 or 1895–1923].

Sarkis, Yusuf. Muʿjam al-matbuʿat al-ʿArabiyya waʾl-muʿarraba. 7 vols. Cairo: Matbaʿat Sarkis, 1928–30.

Sayyid, Samir ʿAbd al-Maqsud. al-Shuwam fi Misr mundhu al-fath al-ʿUthmani hatta awaʾil al-qarn al-tasiʿ ʿashar. Cairo: al-Hayʾa al-Misriyya liʾl-Kitab, 2003.

Al-Shahawi, Ibrahim Dasuqi. al-Hisba fiʾl-Islam. Cairo: Maktabat Dar al-ʿUruba, 1962.

Al-Shalaq, Ahmad Zakariyya. Ruʾya fi tahdith al-fikr al-Misri. Cairo: al-Hayʾa al-Misriyya al-ʿAmma liʾl-Kitab, 1984.

Shaltut, Mahmud. al-Islam ʿaqida wa-shariʿa. 3rd ed. Cairo: Dar al-Qalam, 1966.

Al-Sharqawi, Mahmud. Misr fiʾl-qarn al-thamin ʿashar. 3 vols. Cairo: Maktabat al-Anjilu al-Misriyya, 1957.

Al-Sharqawi, Mahmud, and ʿAbdallah al-Mishadd. ʿAli Mubarak hayatahu wa-daʿwtahu wa-aʾtharahu. Cairo: Maktabat al-Anjilu al-Misriyya, 1962.

Sharubim, Michaʾil. al-Khafi fi taʾrikh Misr al-qadim waʾl-hadith. 4 vols. Cairo: al-Matabʿa al-Kubra al-Amiryya, 1900.

Al-Shatti, Muhammad Jamil. Aʿyan Dimashq fiʾl-qarn al-thalith ʿashar wa-nisf al-qarn al-rabiʿ ʿashar. Damascus: Dar al-Bishʾar, 1994.

Al-Shinnawi, ʿAbd al-ʿAziz Muhammad. "Dawr al-Azhar fiʾl-hifaz ʿala al-tabiʿ al-ʿArabi liʾl-Misr ibbana al-hukm al-ʿUthmani." In *Abhath al-nadwa al-duwaliyya li-taʾrikh al-Qahira*, vol. 2, pp. 665–725. 3 vols. Cairo: Dar al-Kutub, 1971.

Al-Shinnawi, ʿAbd al-ʿAziz Muhammad, and Jalal Yahya (eds.). *Wathaʾiq wa-nusus, al-taʾrikh al-hadith waʾl-muʿasir*. Alexandria: Dar al-Maʿarif, 1969.

Al-Sibaʿi, Mustafa. *Alam wa-amal*. Beirut: Dar al-Waraq, 2000.

Al-Siyadi, Mukhlis. *al-Azhar wa-mashariʿ tatwirihi 1872–1970*. Beirut: Dar al-Rashid, 1992.

Subhi, Muhammad Khalil. *Taʾrikh al-hayat al-niyabiyya fi Misr*. Cairo: Dar al-Kutub al-Misriyya, 1939.

Sulayman, Muhammad. *Dawr al-Azhar fiʾl-Sudan*. Cairo: al-Hayʾa al-Misriyya al-ʿAmma liʾl-Kitab, 1985.

Al-Suwaysi, ʿAbd al-Rahman. *Mukhtasar al-fatawa al-Mahdiyya*. 2 vols. Cairo: Matbaʿat al-Muʾayyid, 1900/1901.

Taftazani, Masʿud ibn ʿUmar. *al-ʿAqaʾid al-nasafiyya*. Cairo: al-Maktaba al-Azhariyya liʾl-Turath, 2000.

Taha, Samir Muhammad. *Ahmad ʿUrabi wa-dawruhu fiʾl-hayat al-siyasiya al-Misriyya*. Cairo: al-Hayʾa al-Misriyya al-ʿAmma liʾl-Kitab, 1986.

Al-Tahtawi, Ahmad Rafiʿ. *al-Qawl al-ijabi*. Cairo: Matbaʿat al-ʿAmira, 1896.

Taymur, Ahmad. *Aʿlam al-fikr al-Islami fiʾl-ʿasr al-hadith*. Cairo: Lajnat Nashr al-Muʾallafat al-Taymuriya, 1967.

Taymur, Mahmud. "Wali ʿAllah." In idem, *Shifa ghaliza wa-qisas ukhraʾ*, pp. 103–25. Cairo: n.p., 1946.

Al-Tuʿmi, Muhi al-Din. *al-Nur al-abhar fi tabaqat shuyukh al-jamiʿ al-Azhar*. Beirut: Dar al-Jil, 1992.

Turbayn, Ahmad. *Malamih al-taghyir al-ijtimaʿi fi Bilad al-Sham fiʾl-qarn al-tasiʿ ʿashar*. Beirut: Maʿhad al-Inmaʾ al-ʿArabi, 1982.

———. *Taʾrikh al-Sudan al-hadith al-muʿasir*. Beirut: Muaʾssat al-Risala, 1994.

Tusun, Amir ʿUmar. *Yawm 11 Yuliyu 1882*. Alexandria: Matbaʿat Salah al-Din, 1934.

ʿUrabi, Ahmad. *Mudhakkirat ʿUrabi: kashf al-sitar ʿan sirr al-asrar fiʾl-nahda al-Misriyya*. 2 vols. Cairo: Dar al-Hilal, 1953.

Al-ʿUrwa al-Wuthqa waʾl-thawra al-tahririyya al-kubra. Cairo: Dar al-ʿArab, 1958.

Wafi, ʿAli ʿAbd al-Wahid. *Lamha fi taʾrikh al-Azhar*. Cairo: Matbaʿat al-Futuh, 1936.

Al-Zahrawi, ʿAbd al-Hamid. "al-Fiqh waʾl-tasawwuf." In ʿAbdallah Nabhan (ed.), *ʿAbd al-Hamid al-Zahrawi: al-aʾmal al-kamila*, vol. 1, pp. 289–308. 2 vols. Damascus: Wizarat al-Thaqafa, 1995.

Zakhura, Ilyas. *Mirʾat al-ʿasr fi taʾrikh wa-rusum akabir al-rijal bi-Misr*. 3 vols. Cairo: al-Matbaʿa al-ʿUmumiyya, 1897.

Zargariʾnizhad, Ghulam Husayn. *Rasaʾil-i mashrutiyyat*. Tehran: Kavir, 1995.

Al-Zawahiri, Muhammad al-Ahmadi. *al-ʿIlm waʾl-ʿulamaʾ wa-nizam al-taʿlim*. Cairo: al-Matbaʿa al-ʿUmumiyya, 1904.

———. *al-Siyasa waʾl-Azhar*. Cairo: Matbaʿat al-Iʿtimad, 1945.

Zaydan, Jurji. *Taʾrikh adab al-lugha al-ʿArabiyya*. 4 vols. Cairo: Dar al-Hilal, 1957.

———. *Tarajim mashahir al-Sharq fiʾl-qarn al-tasiʿ ʿashar*. 2 vols. Beirut: Dar Maktabat al-Hayat, 1970.

Ziyada, Nicola. "Lubnaniyyun darasu biʾl-Azhar fiʾl-qarn al-tasiʿ ʿashar." In *al-Muʾtamar al-duwali al-thani li-taʾrikh Bilad al-Sham 1517–1939*, vol. 2, pp. 171–87. 2 vols. Damascus: Jamaʿat Dimashq, 1978.

BOOKS AND ARTICLES IN OTHER LANGUAGES

Abaza, Mona. "Changing Images of Three Generations of Azharites in Indonesia." In Bryan S. Turner (ed.), *Islam: Critical Concepts in Sociology*, vol. 4, pp. 382–418. 4 vols. New York: Routledge, 2003.

Abou El Fadl, Khaled. *Rebellion and Violence in Islamic Law*. Cambridge: Cambridge University Press, 2001.

Abu al-Eyoun, Mahmoud. *al-Azhar: A Short Historical Survey*. Cairo: al-Azhar Press, 1949.

Abu-Lughod, Lila. "Introduction: Feminist Longings and Postcolonial Conditions." In idem (ed.), *Remaking Women: Feminism and Modernity in the Middle East*, pp. 3–32. Princeton, N.J.: Princeton University Press, 1998.

Abu-Manneh, Butrus. *Studies on Islam and the Ottoman Empire in the 19th Century, 1826–1876*. Istanbul: Isis Press, 2001.

———. "Four Letters of Šayh Hasan al-ʿAttar to Šayh Tahir al-Husayni of Jerusalem." *Arabica* 50/1 (January 2003): 79–95.

Abu-Rabiʿ, Ibrahim M. "al-Azhar Sufism in Modern Egypt: The Sufi Thought." *Islamic Quarterly* 32 (1988): 207–35.

———. *The Mystical Teachings of al-Shadhili*. Albany: State University of New York Press, 1993.

Adali, Hasan. "Documents Pertaining to the Egyptian Question in the Yildiz Collection of the Başbakanlık Arşivi, Istanbul." In P. M. Holt, *Political and Social Change in Modern Egypt*, pp. 52–58. Oxford: Oxford University Press, 1968.

Adams, Charles C. *Islam and Modernism in Egypt*. 2nd ed. New York: Russell and Russell, 1968.

Afary, Janet. *The Iranian Constitutional Revolution, 1906–1911*. New York: Columbia University Press, 1996.

Ajami, Fuad. *The Dream Palace of the Arabs*. New York: Vintage Books, 1999.

Akhavi, Shahrough. "Shiʿi Ulama." In John L. Esposito (ed.), *The Oxford Encyclopedia of the Modern Islamic World*, vol. 4, pp. 261–65. 4 vols. New York: Oxford University Press, 1995.

Alam, Anwar. *Religion and State, Egypt, Iran and Saudi Arabia: A Comparative Study*. Delhi: Gyan Sagar Publications, 1998.

Algar, Hamid. "Religious Forces in Twentieth-Century Iran." In Peter Avery et al. (eds.), *The Cambridge History of Iran*, vol. 7, pp. 732–64. 7 vols. Cambridge: Cambridge University Press, 1991.

Altman, Israel. "The Political Thought of Rifaʿah Rafiʿ al-Tahtawi: A Nineteenth-Century Egyptian Reformer." Ph.D. dissertation. Los Angeles: University of California, 1976.

Amin, Osman. *Muhammad ʿAbduh*. Trans. Charles Wendell. Washington, D.C.: American Council of Learned Societies, 1953.

Ansari, Hamid. *Egypt: The Stalled Society*. Albany: State University of New York Press, 1986.

Antoun, Richard T. *Muslim Preacher in the Modern World*. Princeton, N.J.: Princeton University Press, 1989.

Arabi, Oussama. *Studies in Modern Islamic Law and Jurisprudence.* The Hague: Kluwer
    Law International, 2001.
Arjomand, Said Amir. "The Ulama's Opposition to Parliamentarianism, 1907–1909."
    Middle Eastern Studies 7 (April 1981): 174–90.
———. "Ideological Revolution in Shiʿism." In idem, *Authority and Political Culture in
    Shiʿism*, pp. 179–209. Albany: State University of New York Press, 1988.
Armbrust, Walter. *Mass Culture and Modernism in Egypt.* Cambridge: Cambridge Uni-
    versity Press, 1996.
Aroian, Lois A. *The Nationalization of Arabic and Islamic Education in Egypt: Dar al-
    Ulum and al-Azhar.* Cairo Papers in Social Science, vol. 6, monograph 4. Cairo:
    American University in Cairo Press, 1983.
Asad, Tala. *Genealogies of Religion: Discipline and Reasons of Power in Christianity and
    Islam.* Baltimore: Johns Hopkins University Press, 1993.
Ayalon, Ami. *The Press in the Arab Middle East: A History.* Oxford: Oxford University
    Press, 1995.
———. *Egypt's Quest for Cultural Orientation.* Tel Aviv: Moshe Dayan Center, 1999.
———. "Muslim 'Intruders,' Muslim 'Bigots': The Egyptian–Syrian Press Controversy in
    Late Nineteenth-Century Cairo." In Tudor Parfitt and Yulia Egorova (eds.), *Jews,
    Muslims, and Mass Media: Mediating the "Other,"* pp. 15–30. New York: Routledge-
    Curzon, 2005.
Badran, Margot. *Feminists, Islam and Nation: Gender and the Making of Modern Egypt.*
    Princeton, N.J.: Princeton University Press, 1995.
Baer, Gabriel. *Egyptian Guilds in Modern Times.* Jerusalem: Israel Oriental Society,
    1964.
———. *Studies in the Social History of Modern Egypt.* Chicago: University of Chicago
    Press, 1969.
———. "Islamic Political Activity in Modern Egyptian History: A Comparative Analy-
    sis." In G. R. Warburg and U. Kupferschmidt (eds.), *Islam, Nationalism and Radi-
    calism in Egypt and the Sudan*, pp. 33–54. New York: Praeger, 1983.
———. "Jerusalem Notables in Ottoman Cairo." In Amnon Cohen and Gabriel Baer
    (eds.), *Egypt and Palestine: A Millennium of Association*, pp. 167–75. New York:
    St. Martin's Press, 1984.
Baladi, Noëlle. *L'Émancipation de la femme en Égypte.* Nantes: Éditions Amalthée, 2005.
Baldick, Julian. *Mystical Islam: An Introduction to Sufism.* London: I. B. Tauris, 1989.
Baron, Beth. *The Women's Awakening in Egypt: Culture, Society and the Press.* New
    Haven: Yale University Press, 1998.
———. *Egypt as a Woman: Nationalism, Gender and Politics.* Berkeley: University of
    California Press, 2003.
Bat Yeʾor. *The Dhimmi: Jews and Christians under Islam.* Rutherford: Fairleigh Dickin-
    son University Press, 1985.
Behrens-Abouseif, Doris. "The Political Situation of the Copts, 1798–1923." In Benjamin
    Braude and Bernard Lewis (eds.), *Christians and Jews in the Ottoman Empire*, vol. 2,
    pp. 185–205. 2 vols. New York: Holmes and Meier, 1982,
Bein, Amit. "ʿUlamaʾ and Political Activism in the Late Ottoman Empire: The Politi-
    cal Career of Şeyhülislâm Mustafa Sabri Efendi (1869–1954)." In Meir Hatina

(ed.), *Guardians of Faith in Modern Times: ʿUlamaʾ in the Middle East*, pp. 65–90. Leiden: Brill, 2008.

Berdine, Michael D. *The Accidental Tourist: Wilfrid Scawen Blunt and the British Invasion of Egypt in 1882*. New York: Routledge, 2005.

Berger, Morroe. *Islam in Egypt Today: Social and Political Aspects of Popular Religion*. Cambridge: Cambridge University Press, 1970.

Berkey, Jonathan. "Tradition, Innovation and the Social Construction of Knowledge." *Past and Present* 146 (1995): 38–65.

———. *The Formation of Islam: Religion and Society in the Near East, 600–1880*. Cambridge: Cambridge University Press, 2003.

Berque, Jacques. *Egypt: Imperialism and Revolution*. London: Faber and Faber, 1972.

Bjørneboe, Lars. *In Search of the True Political Position of the ʿUlama*. Langelandsgade: Aarhus University Press, 2007.

Blunt, Wilfrid Scawen. *Egypt: Letters to the Right Hon. W. E. Gladstone M.P. and Others*. London: Kegan Paul, Trench, 1882.

———. *My Diaries*. New York: Alfred A. Knopf, 1922.

———. *Secret History of the English Occupation of Egypt*. New York: Alfred A. Knopf, 1922.

———. *The Future of Islam*. New ed. London: RoutledgeCurzon, 2002.

Bosworth, C. E. "The Concept of Dhimma in Early Islam." In Benjamin Braude and Bernard Lewis (eds.), *Christians and Jews in the Ottoman Empire*, vol. 1, pp. 37–51. 2 vols. New York: Holmes and Meier Publishers, 1982.

Braude, Benjamin, and Bernard Lewis. "Introduction." In idem (eds.), *Christians and Jews in the Ottoman Empire*, vol. 1, pp. 1–36. 2 vols. New York: Holmes and Meier Publishers, 1982.

Broadley, A. M. *How We Defended Arabi and His Friends*. London: Chapman and Hall, 1884.

Bruce, Steve. *Religion in the Modern World: From Cathedrals to Cults*. Oxford: Oxford University Press, 1996.

Brunner, Rainer. "Education, Politics, and the Struggle for Intellectual Leadership: al-Azhar between 1927–1945." In Meir Hatina (ed.), *Guardians of Faith in Modern Times: ʿUlamaʾ in the Middle East*, pp. 109–40. Leiden: Brill, 2008.

Budeiri, Musa. "The Palestinian Tensions between Nationalist and Religious Identities." In Israel Gershoni and James Jankowski (eds.), *Rethinking Nationalism*, pp. 191–206. New York: Columbia University Press, 1997.

Burdett, A. L. P. (ed.). *Records of the Hijaz, 1798–1925*. 8 vols. London: Archive Editions, 1996.

Burke, Edmund, III. "Understanding Arab Protest Movements." *Arab Studies Quarterly* 8 (Fall 1986): 333–45.

Butler, Alfred J. *Court Life in Egypt*. London: Chapman and Hall, 1887.

Buzpinar, Tufan S. "The Repercussions of the British Occupation of Egypt on Syria, 1882–1883." *Middle Eastern Studies* 36/1 (January 2000): 82–91.

Cahen, Cl. "Dhimma." In *Encyclopedia of Islam*, Vol. 2, pp. 228–30. Leiden: Brill, 1965.

Calder, Norman. "al-Nawawi's Typology of Muftis and Its Significance for a General Theory of Islamic Law." *Islamic Law and Society* 3/2 (1996): 137–64.

Calhoun, Craig J. (ed.). *Habermas and the Public Sphere*. Cambridge, Mass.: MIT Press, 1992.

Camus, Albert. *The Rebel: An Essay of Man in Revolt*. New York: Vintage Books, 1991.

Chamberlain, Michael. *Knowledge and Social Practice in Medieval Damascus, 1190–1350*. Cambridge: Cambridge University Press, 1994.

Cohen, Amnon. *Palestine in the 18th Century*. Jerusalem: Magnes Press, 1973.

———. *Jewish Life under Islam: Jerusalem in the Sixteenth Century*. Cambridge, Mass.: Harvard University Press, 1984.

Cohen, Mark R. *Under Crescent and Cross: The Jews in the Middle East*. Princeton, N.J.: Princeton University Press, 1994.

Cole, Juan R. "Feminism, Class, and Islam in Turn-of-the-Century Egypt." *International Journal of Middle East Studies* 13/1 (1981): 387–407.

———. *Colonialism and Revolution in the Middle East: Social and Cultural Origins of Egypt's ʿUrabi Movement*. Princeton, N.J.: Princeton University Press, 1993.

———. "Printing and Urban Islam in the Mediterranean World, 1890–1920." In Leila Tarazi Fawaz and C. A. Bayly (eds.), *Modernity and Culture: From the Mediterranean to the Indian Ocean*, pp. 344–64. New York: Columbia University Press, 2002.

Commins, David. *Islamic Reform: Politics and Social Change in Late Ottoman Syria*. New York: Oxford University Press, 1990.

———. "Syria." In John Esposito (ed.), *The Oxford Encyclopedia of the Modern Islamic World*, vol. 4, pp. 156–60. 4 vols. New York: Oxford University Press, 1995.

———. "Wahhabis, Sufis and Salafis in Early Twentieth Century Damascus." In Meir Hatina (ed.), *Guardians of Faith in Modern Times: ʿUlamaʾ in the Middle East*, pp. 231–46. Leiden: Brill, 2008.

Cook, Michael. *Commanding Right and Forbidding Wrong in Islamic Thought*. Cambridge: Cambridge University Press, 2000.

Costet-Tardieu, Francine. *Un réformiste à l'Université al-Azhar: Oeuvre et pensée de Mustafâ al-Marâghî (1881–1945)*. Paris: Karthala, 2005.

Crecelius, Daniel. "al-Azhar in Revolution." *Middle East Journal* 20 (Winter 1966): 34–49.

———. "Non-ideological Responses of the Egyptian Ulama to Modernization." In Nikki R. Keddie (ed.). *Scholars, Saints and Sufis*, pp. 167–209. Berkeley: University of California Press, 1972.

———. *The Ulama and the State in Modern Egypt*. Ann Arbor: University Microfilms International, 1978 [1968].

Crecelius, Daniel, and Hamza ʿAbd al-ʿAziz Badr. "An Agreement between the ʿUlamaʾ and the Mamluk Amirs in 1795: A Test of the Accuracy of Two Contemporary Chronicles." In D. Crecelius and et al. (eds.), *Dirasat fi taʾrikh Misr al-iqtisadi waʾl-ijtimaʿi*, pp. 9–21. Cairo: Dar al-Afaq al-ʿArabiyya, 1996.

Cromer, Lord [Evelyn Baring]. *Modern Egypt*. London: Macmillan, 1911.

———. "The Government of Subjected Races." In idem, *Political and Literary Essays, 1908–1913*, pp. 3–53. London: Macmillan, 1913.

Dabashi, Hamid. "Two Clerical Tracts on Constitutionalism." In Said Amir Arjomand (ed.), *Authority and Political Culture in Shiʿism*, pp. 354–68. Albany: State University of New York Press, 1988.

Danziger, Raphael. *ʿAbd al-Qadir and the Algerians: Resistance to the French and Internal Consolidation*. New York: Holmes and Meier Publishers, 1977.

Dawn, Ernest. "The Rise of Arabism in Syria." In idem, *From Ottomanism to Arabism*, pp. 148–79. Urbana: University of Illinois Press, 1973.

De Jong, Frederick. *Turuq and Turuq-Linked Institutions in Nineteenth-Century Egypt.* Leiden: Brill, 1978.

———. "Aspects of the Political Involvement of Sufi Orders in Twentieth-Century Egypt, 1907–1970—An Exploratory Stock-taking." In G. R. Warburg and U. Kupferschmidt (eds.), *Islam, Nationalism and Radicalism in Egypt and the Sudan*, pp. 54–73. New York: Praeger, 1983.

———. "The Sufi Orders in Egypt during the Urabi Insurrection and the British Occupation, 1882–1914." *Journal of the American Research Center in Egypt* 21 (1984): 131–39.

———. "Opposition to Sufism in Twentieth-Century Egypt (1900–1970): A Preliminary Survey." In F. De Jong and Bernd Radtke (eds.), *Islamic Mysticism Contested*, pp. 310–23. Leiden: Brill, 1999.

Delanoue, Gilbert. *Moralistes et politiques musulmans dans l'Égypte du XIXe siècle, 1798–1882.* 2 vols. Cairo: Institut Français d'Archéologie Orientale du Caire, 1982.

Delooz, Pierre. "Towards a Sociological Study of Canonized Sainthood in the Catholic Church." In Stephen Wilson (ed.), *Saints and Their Cults*, pp. 189–216. Cambridge: Cambridge University Press, 1985.

Deringil, Selim. "The Ottoman Response to the Egyptian Crises of 1881–82." *Middle Eastern Studies* 24/1 (January 1988): 3–24.

Dika, Rifaat A. "Islamic Traditions in Modern Politics: The Case of al-Azhar." Ph.D. dissertation. Detroit: Wayne State University, 1990.

Dodge, Bayard. *al-Azhar: A Millennium of Muslim Learning.* Washington, D.C.: Middle East Institute, 1961.

Douwes, Dick. *The Ottomans in Syria.* London: I. B. Tauris, 2000.

Duff Gordon, Lucie. *Letters from Egypt, 1862–1869.* New ed. London: Virago, 1997.

Ebert, Hans-Georg. "'Die letzte Krankheit': Mohammad al-ʿAbbasi al-Mahdi (gest. 1897) und die Reform der ägyptischen Rechtsordnung." *Der Islam* 81 (2004): 303–51.

Eccel, Chris. *Egypt, Islam and Social Change.* Berlin: Klaus Schwartz, 1984.

Eich, Thomas. "The Forgotten Salafi—Abu al-Huda as-Sayyadi." *Die Welt des Islams* 43 (2003): 61–87.

Eickelman, Dale F. *Knowledge and Power in Morocco.* Princeton, N.J.: Princeton University Press, 1985.

Eickelman, Dale F., and James Piscatori. *Muslim Politics.* Princeton, N.J.: Princeton University Press, 1996.

Eisenstadt, S. N. (ed.). *Max Weber on Charisma and Institution Building.* Chicago: University of Chicago Press, 1968.

Eliraz, Giora. *Islam in Indonesia.* Brighton: Sussex, 2004.

Ephrat, Daphna. "Religious Leadership and Associations in the Public Sphere of Seljuk Baghdad." In M. Hoexter, S. N. Eisenstadt, and N. Levtzion (eds.), *The Public Sphere in Muslim Societies*, pp. 31–48. Albany: State University of New York Press, 2002.

———. *Spiritual Wayfarers, Leaders in Piety: Sufis and the Dissemination of Islam in Medieval Palestine.* Cambridge, Mass.: Harvard Center for Middle Eastern Studies, 2008.

Escovitz, Joseph H. "He Was the Muhammad ʿAbduh of Syria: A Study of Tahir al-Jazaʾiri and His Influence." *International Journal of Middle East Studies* 18 (1986): 293–310.

Esposito, John L. *The Islamic Threat: Myth or Reality*. 2nd ed. New York: Oxford University Press, 1995.

——— (ed.). *The Oxford Encyclopedia of the Modern Islamic World*. 4 vols. New York: Oxford University Press, 1995.

Esposito, John L., and John O. Voll. *Makers of Contemporary Islam*. Oxford: Oxford University Press, 2001.

Evans-Pritchard, E. *The Sanusi of Cyrenaica*. 2nd ed. Oxford: Oxford University Press, 1968.

Fahmy, Khaled. "An Olfactory Tale of Two Cities: Cairo in the Nineteenth Century." In Jill Edwards (ed.), *Historians in Cairo*, pp. 155–88. Cairo: American University in Cairo Press, 2002.

Farman, Elbert E. *Egypt and Its Betrayal*. New York: Grafton Press, 1908.

Faroqhi, Suraiya, Bruce McGowan, and Donald Quantaert. *An Economic and Social History of the Ottoman Empire*. 2 vols. Cambridge: Cambridge University Press, 1994.

Fattal, Antoine. *Le statut légal des non-musulmans en pays d'Islams*. Beirut: Imprimerie Catholique, 1958.

Finch, Edith. *Wilfrid Scawen Blunt, 1840–1922*. London: Jonathan Cape, 1938.

Fortna, Benjamin C. *Imperial Classroom: Islam, the State, and Education in the Late Ottoman Empire*. Oxford: Oxford University Press, 2002.

Foucault, Michel. *Power/Knowledge: Selected Interviews and Other Writings, 1972–1977*. Ed. and trans. Colin Gordon. New York: Pantheon, 1980.

Friedman, Yohanan. *Tolerance and Coercion in Islam*. Oxford: Oxford University Press, 2003.

Gadsby, John. *My Wanderings: Being Travels in the East*. London: A. Gadsby, 1875.

Gammer, Moshe. *Muslim Resistance to the Tsar*. London: Frank Cass, 1994.

Gasper, Michael. "ʿAbdallah al-Nadim, Islamic Reform, and 'Ignorant' Peasants: State-Building in Egypt?" In Armando Salvatore (ed.), *Muslim Traditions and Modern Techniques of Power*, pp. 75–92. Münster: Lit Verlag, 2001.

Gassick, Trevor Le (trans. and ed.). *The Defense Statement of Ahmad ʿUrabi*. Cairo: American University in Cairo Press, 1982.

Geertz, Clifford. *The Interpretation of Cultures: Selected Essays*. New York: Basic Books, 1973.

Gellner, E. "Doctor and Saint." In Nikki R. Keddie (ed.), *Scholars, Saints and Sufis*, pp. 307–26. Berkeley: University of California Press, 1972.

Geoffroy, Éric. *Le soufisme en Égypte et en Syrie*. Damascus: Institut Français d'Études Arabes de Damas, 1995.

Gerber, Haim. *Ottoman Rule in Jerusalem, 1890–1914*. Berlin: Klaus Schwarz Verlag, 1985.

———. *State, Society and Law in Islam: Ottoman Law in Comparative Perspective*. Albany: State University of New York Press, 1994.

———. *Islamic Law and Culture, 1600–1840*. Leiden: Brill, 1999.

———. "The Limits of Constructedness: The Case of Middle Eastern Nationalism." *Nations and Nationalism* 10 (2004): 251–68.

———. "The Muslim Umma and the Formation of Middle Eastern Nationalisms." In

Athena S. Leoussi and Steven Grosby (eds.), *Nationalism and Ethnosymbolism: History, Culture and Ethnicity in the Formation of Nations*, pp. 209–20. Edinburgh: Edinburgh University Press, 2007.

———. *Remembering and Imagining Palestine: Identity and Nationalism from the Crusades to the Present*. New York: Palgrave Macmillan, 2008.

Gershoni, Israel, and James Jankowski, *Egypt, Islam and the Arabs*. Cambridge: Cambridge University Press, 1986.

———. *Redefining the Egyptian Nation, 1930–1945*. Cambridge: Cambridge University Press, 1995.

———. "Introduction." In idem (eds.), *Rethinking Nationalism in the Arab Middle East*, pp. ix–xxvi. New York: Columbia University Press, 1997.

———. *Confronting Fascism in Egypt: Dictatorship versus Democracy in the 1930s*. Palo Alto: Stanford University Press, 2010.

Gesnik, Indira Falk. "Beyond Modernisms: Opposition and Negotiation in the Azhar Reform Debate in Egypt, 1870–1911." Ph.D. dissertation. Washington University, St. Louis, 2000.

Gibb, H. A. R. *Modern Trends in Islam*. Chicago: University of Chicago Press, 1967.

Gibb, H. A. R., and Harold Bowen. *Islamic Society and the West*. 2 vols. London: Oxford University Press, 1957.

Gilbert, Joan E. "Institutionalization of Muslim Scholarship and Professionalization of the ʿUlamaʾ in Medieval Damascus." *Studia Islamica* 32 (1980): 105–34.

Gilsenan, M. D. "Some Factors in the Decline of the Sufi Orders in Modern Egypt." *Muslim World* 57 (January 1967): 11–18.

———. *Saint and Sufi in Modern Egypt*. Oxford: Oxford University Press, 1973.

Gimaret, D. "Muʿtazila." In *Encyclopedia of Islam*, Vol. 7, pp. 783–93. Leiden: Brill, 1993.

Girgis, Samir. *The Predominance of the Islamic Tradition of Leadership in Egypt during Bonaparte's Expedition*. Bern: Herbert Lang, 1975.

Goddard, Hugh. *A History of Christian-Muslim Relations*. Chicago: New Amsterdam Books, 2000.

Goitein, S. D. *A Mediterranean Society*. 2 vols. Berkeley: University of California Press, 1971.

Goodich, Michael. "The Politics of Canonization in the Thirteenth Century: Lay and Mendicant Saints." In Stephen Wilson (ed.), *Saints and Their Cults*, pp. 169–87. Cambridge: Cambridge University Press, 1985.

Goodrich, Caspar F. *Report of the British Naval and Military Operations in Egypt, 1882*. Washington, D.C.: Government Printing Office, 1885.

Gorman, Anthony. *Historians, State and Politics in Twentieth-Century Egypt*. London: RoutledgeCurzon, 2003.

Gran, Peter. *Islamic Roots of Capitalism in Egypt, 1760–1840*. New ed. Syracuse: Syracuse University Press, 1998.

Grehan, James. "Street Violence and Social Imagination in Late-Mamluk and Ottoman Damascus (ca. 1500–1800)." *International Journal of Middle East Studies* 35/2 (2003): 215–36.

Habermas, Jürgen. *The Structural Transformation of the Public Sphere*. Trans. Thomas Burger. Cambridge, Mass.: MIT Press, 1989.

Haim, Sylvia G. *Arab Nationalism: An Anthology*. Berkeley: University of California Press, 1962.

Hairi, Abdul-Hadi. *Shi'ism and Constitutionalism in Iran*. Leiden: Brill, 1977.

————. "The Legitimacy of the Early Qajar Rule as Viewed by the Shi'i Religious Leaders." *Middle Eastern Studies* 24 (July 1988): 271–86.

Hallaq, Wael B. "Was the Gate of Ijtihad Closed?" *International Journal of Middle East Studies* 16 (1984): 3–41.

————. "From Fatwas to Furu': Growth and Change in Islamic Substantive Law." *Islamic Law Studies* 1 (1994): 29–65.

————. "Ifta' and Ijtihad in Sunni Legal Theory: A Development Account." In Muhammad K. Masud, Brinkley Messick, and David S. Powers (eds.), *Islamic Legal Interpretation: Muftis and Their Fatwas*, pp. 33–43. Cambridge, Mass.: Harvard University Press, 1996.

Hanna, Nelly. "Culture in Ottoman Egypt." In M. W. Daly (ed.), *The Cambridge History of Egypt*, vol. 2, pp. 87–112. 2 vols. Cambridge: Cambridge University Press, 1998.

————. *In Praise of Books*. Syracuse: Syracuse University Press, 2003.

Harrison, Paul M. "Religious Leadership in America." In Donald R. Cutler (ed.), *The Religious Situation, 1968–1969*, vol. 2, pp. 957–77. 2 vols. Boston: Beacon Press, 1968–69.

Hartmann, Martin. *The Arabic Press of Egypt*. London: Luzaq, 1899.

Hathaway, Jane. "The Role of the Ulama in Social Protest in Late Eighteenth-Century Cairo." M.A. thesis. Austin: University of Texas, 1986.

————. "Problems of Periodization in Ottoman History." *Turkish Studies Association Bulletin* 20/2 (1996): 25–31.

————. *The Arab Lands under Ottoman Rule, 1516–1800*. Harlow: Longman, 2008.

Hatina, Meir. "Historical Legacy and the Challenge of Modernity: The Case of al-Azhar in Egypt." *Muslim World* 93 (January 2003): 51–68.

————. *Identity Politics in the Middle East: Liberal Thought and Islamic Challenge in Egypt*. London: I. B. Tauris, 2007.

————. "Where East Meets West: Sufism, Cultural Rapprochement and Politics." *International Journal of Middle East Studies* 39/3 (August 2007): 389–409.

———— (ed.). *Guardians of Faith in Modern Times: 'Ulama' in the Middle East*. Leiden: Brill, 2008.

Heyd, Uriel. "Some Aspects of the Ottoman Fetva." *Bulletin of the School of Oriental and African Studies* 32 (1969): 35–56.

Heyworth-Dunne, J. *An Introduction to the History of Education in Modern Egypt*. 2nd ed. London: Frank Cass, 1968.

Hodgson, Marshall G. S. *The Venture of Islam*. 3 vols. Chicago: University of Chicago Press, 1974.

Hoexter, M., S. N. Eisenstadt, and N. Levtzion (eds.). *The Public Sphere in Muslim Societies*. Albany: State University of New York Press, 2002.

Hoexter, Miriam, and Nehemia Levtzion. "Introduction." In M. Hoexter, S. N. Eisenstadt, and N. Levtzion (eds.), *The Public Sphere in Muslim Societies*, pp. 9–16. Albany: State University of New York Press, 2002.

Hoffman, Valerie J. *Sufism: Mystics and Saints in Modern Egypt*. Columbia: University of South Carolina Press, 1995.

Holt, P. M. *Egypt and the Fertile Crescent*. Ithaca: Cornell University Press, 1966.

————. *The Mahdist State in the Sudan, 1881–1898*. 2nd ed. Oxford: Oxford University Press, 1970.

Hourani, Albert. "Ottoman Reform and the Politics of Notables." In William R. Polk
    and Richard L. Chambers (eds.), *Beginnings of Modernization in the Middle East*,
    pp. 41–68. Chicago: University of Chicago Press, 1968.
———. "The Syrians in Egypt in the Eighteenth and Nineteenth Centuries." In *Colloque
    internationale sur l'histoire du Caire*, pp. 221–33. Cairo: Ministry of Culture of the
    Arab Republic of Egypt, 1972.
———. *The Emergence of the Modern Middle East*. Oxford: Macmillan Press, 1981.
———. *Arabic Thought in the Liberal Age, 1798–1939*. 3rd ed. Cambridge: Cambridge
    University Press, 1983.
Hunter, F. Robert. *Egypt under the Khedives, 1805–1879*. Pittsburgh: University of Pitts-
    burgh Press, 1984.
Hussein, Taha. *The Days*. Cairo: American University in Cairo Press, 1997.
Ingram, Edward (ed.). *Eastern Questions in the Nineteenth Century: Collected Essays*.
    2 vols. London: Frank Cass, 1993.
Islamic Heritage in the URA. Cairo: n.p., n.d.
Jankowski, James. "Arab Nationalism in Nasserism and Egyptian State Policy, 1952–1958."
    In Israel Gershoni and James Jankowski (eds.), *Rethinking Nationalism in the Arab
    Middle East*, pp. 150–68. New York: Columbia University Press, 1997.
Jeffery, Arthur. "The Suppressed Qurʾan Commentary of Muhammad Abu Zaid." *Der
    Islam* 20 (1932): 301–8.
Johansen, Julian. *Sufism and Islamic Reform in Egypt*. Oxford: Clarendon Press, 1996.
Kamrava, Mehran. "Introduction: Reformist Islam in Comparative Perspective." In
    idem (ed.), *The New Voices of Islam*, pp. 1–27. London: I. B. Tauris, 2006.
Kara, İsmail. "Turban and Fez: Ulema as Opposition." In Elisabeth Özdalga (ed.), *Late
    Ottoman Society: The Intellectual Legacy*, pp. 162–200. London: RoutledgeCurzon,
    2005.
Karpat, Kemal. "The Ottoman Ethnic and Confessional Legacy in the Middle East." In
    Milton J. Esman and Itamar Rabinovich (eds.), *Ethnicity, Pluralism, and the State
    in the Middle East*, pp. 35–53. Ithaca: Cornell University Press, 1988.
———. *The Politicization of Islam: Reconstructing Identity, State, Faith, and Community
    in the Late Ottoman State*. Oxford: Oxford University Press, 2001.
Kazziha, Walid. "The Jarida Group and Egyptian Politics." *Middle Eastern Studies* 13/3
    (October 1977): 373–85.
Kechichian, Joseph. "The Role of the Ulama in the Politics of an Islamic State: The Case
    of Saudi Arabia." *International Journal of Middle East Studies* 17 (1985): 37–50.
Keddie, Nikki R. *Religion and Rebellion in Iran: The Tobacco Protest of 1891–1892*. Lon-
    don: Frank Cass, 1966.
———. "The Roots of Ulama's Power in Modern Iran." In idem (ed.), *Scholars, Saints
    and Sufis*, pp. 211–30. Berkeley: University of California Press, 1972.
Kedourie, Elie. "Introduction." In idem, *Nationalism in Asia and Africa*, pp. 1–152. New
    York: World Publishing Co., 1970.
———. *Democracy and Arab Political Culture*. 2nd ed. London: Frank Cass, 1994.
Kelidar, Abbas. "The Political Press in Egypt, 1882–1914." In Charles Tripp (ed.), *Con-
    temporary Egypt: Through Egyptian Eyes*, pp. 1–21. London: Routledge, 1993.
Kepel, Gilles. *The Prophet and Pharaoh*. London: Al-Saqi Books, 1985.
Khalidi, Rashid. "Ottomanism and Arabism in Syria before 1914." In R. Khalidi et al.

(eds.), *The Origins of Arab Nationalism*, pp. 50–69. New York: Columbia University Press, 1991.

Khoury, Philip S. *Urban Notables and Arab Nationalism*. Cambridge: Cambridge University Press, 1983.

——. *Syria and the French Mandate*. Princeton, N.J.: Princeton University Press, 1987.

Kleinberg, Aviad. *Flesh Made Word: Saints' Stories and the Western Imagination*. Cambridge, Mass.: Belknap Press of Harvard University Press, 2008.

Knysh, Alexander. *Islamic Mysticism: A Short History*. Leiden: Brill, 2000.

Kraemer, Joel L. "Apostates, Rebels and Brigands." *Israel Oriental Studies* 10 (1980): 34–73.

Krämer, Gudrun, and Sabine Schmidtke. "Introduction: Religious Authorities in Muslim Societies: A Critical Overview." In idem (eds.), *Speaking for Islam: Religious Authorities in Muslim Societies*, pp. 1–14. Leiden: Brill, 2006.

Kramer, Martin. *Political Islam*. Beverly Hills, Calif.: Sage Publications, 1980.

——. *Islam Assembled*. New York: Columbia University Press, 1986.

Kupferschmidt, Uri M. "Connections of the Palestinian Ulama with Egypt and Other Parts of the Ottoman Empire." In Amnon Cohen and Gabriel Baer (eds.), *Egypt and Palestine: A Millennium of Association*, pp. 167–89. New York: St. Martin's Press, 1984.

——. *The Supreme Muslim Council*. Leiden: Brill, 1987.

Labib, Subhi. "The Copts in Egyptian Society and Politics, 1882–1919." In G. R. Warburg and U. Kupferschmidt (eds.), *Islam, Nationalism and Radicalism in Egypt and the Sudan*, pp. 301–20. New York: Praeger, 1983.

Landau, Jacob M. *Middle Eastern Themes: Papers in History and Politics*. London: Frank Cass, 1973.

——. *The Politics of Pan-Islam: Ideology and Organization*. Oxford: Clarendon Press, 1994.

Laoust, Henri. *La politique de Gazali*. Paris: P. Geuthner, 1970.

Lapidus, Ira M. "Muslim Cities and Islamic Societies." In idem (ed.), *Middle Eastern Cities*, pp. 47–79. Berkeley: University of California Press, 1969.

——. "The Separation of State and Religion in the Development of Early Islamic Society." *International Journal of Middle East Studies* 6 (1975): 363–85.

——. *A History of Islamic Societies*. New York: Cambridge University Press, 1988.

Layish, Aharon. "The Contribution of the Modernists to the Secularization of Islamic Law." *Middle Eastern Studies* 14/3 (1978): 263–77.

——. "The Fatwa as an Instrument of Accommodation." In Muhammad K. Masud, Brinkley Messick, and David S. Powers (eds.), *Islamic Legal Interpretation*, pp. 270–77. Cambridge, Mass.: Harvard University Press, 1996.

——. "The Sudanese Mahdi's Legal Methodology and Its Sufi Inspiration." *Jerusalem Studies in Arabic and Islam* 33 (2007): 279–308.

Lazarus-Yafeh, Hava. "Three Remarks on Islam and Western Political Values: An Attempt to Re-evaluate the Modernist Movement in Islam." *Israel Oriental Studies* 10 (1980): 187–94.

——. *Intertwined Worlds: Medieval Islam and Bible Criticism*. Princeton, N.J: Princeton University Press, 1992.

———. "The Ulama vis-à-vis the Militants." In Shimon Shamir (ed.), *Egypt from Monar-chy to Republic*, pp. 173–80. Boulder: Westview Press, 1995.

Leder, Stefan. "Charismatic Scripturalism: The Hanbali Maqdisis of Damascus." *Der Islam* 74 (1997): 279–304.

Lemke, Wolf-Dieter. *Mahmud Šaltut (1893–1963) und die Reform der Azhar*. Frankfurt am Main: P. D. Lang, 1980.

Levtzion, Nehemia, and John O. Voll. "Introduction." In idem (eds.), *Eighteenth-Century Renewal and Reform in Islam*, pp. 3–20. Syracuse: Syracuse University Press, 1987.

Lewis, Bernard. *The Middle East and the West*. New York: Harper Torchbooks, 1964.

———. *Islam in History*. London: Alcove Press, 1973.

Lia, Brynjar. *The Society of the Muslim Brothers in Egypt*. London: Ithaca Press, 1998.

Litvak, Meir. *Shiʿi Scholars of Nineteenth-Century Iraq: The Ulama of Najaf and Karbalaʾ*. Cambridge: Cambridge University Press, 1998.

Livingston, John W. "Western Science and Educational Reform in the Thought of Shaykh Rifaʿa al-Tahtawi." *International Journal of Middle East Studies* 28/4 (1996): 543–64.

Loeb, Laurence D. "Dhimmi Status and Jewish Roles in Iranian Society." In S. Deshen and W. P. Zenner (eds.), *Jews among Muslims: Communities in the Precolonial Middle East*, pp. 247–60. Houndmills: Macmillan Press, Ltd., 1996.

Makdisi, George. "The Hanbali School and Sufism." *Humaniora Islamica* 2 (1974): 61–72.

Malet, Edward. *Egypt 1879–1883*. London: John Murray, 1909.

Manna, ʿAdil. "Cultural Relations between Egyptian and Jerusalem ʿUlamaʾ in the Early Nineteenth Century." *Asian and African Studies* 17 (1983): 139–52.

Maʿoz, Moshe. *Ottoman Reform in Syria and Palestine, 1840–1861*. Oxford: Oxford University Press, 1968.

———. "The Ulama and the Process of Modernization in Syria during the Mid-Nineteenth Century." *Asian and African Studies* 7 (1971): 77–88.

———. "Communal Conflicts in Ottoman Syria during the Reform Era: The Role of Political and Economic Factors." In Benjamin Braude and Bernard Lewis (eds.), *Christians and Jews in the Ottoman Empire*, vol. 2, pp. 91–101. 2 vols. New York: Holmes and Meier, 1982.

———. "Muslim Ethnic Communities in Nineteenth-Century Syria and Palestine: Trends of Conflict and Integration." *Asian and African Studies* 19 (1985): 283–307.

Maqdisi, George. *The Rise of Colleges: Institutions of Learning in Islam and the West*. Edinburgh: Edinburgh University Press, 1981.

Marlow, Louise. *Hierarchy and Egalitarianism in Islamic Thought*. Cambridge: Cambridge University Press, 1997.

Martin, R. C., M. R. Woodward, and D. S. Atmaja. *Defenders of Reason in Islam: Muʿtazilism from Medieval School to Modern Times*. Oxford: Oxford University Press, 1997.

Martin, Vanessa. *Islam and Modernism*. Syracuse: Syracuse University Press, 1989.

Masters, Bruce. "The Ottoman Empire's Caravan City." In Edhem Elden, Daniel Goff-man, and Bruce Masters (eds.), *The Ottoman City between East and West: Aleppo, Izmir, Istanbul*, pp. 17–78. Cambridge: Cambridge University Press, 1999.

———. *Christians and Jews in the Ottoman Arab World: The Roots of Sectarianism*. Cambridge: Cambridge University Press, 2001.

Masud, Muhammad K., Brinkley Messick, and David S. Powers. "Muftis, Fatwas and Islamic Legal Interpretation." In idem (eds.), *Islamic Legal Interpretation*, pp. 3–32. Cambridge, Mass.: Harvard University Press, 1996.

Mayer, Thomas. *The Changing Past: Egyptian Historiography of the Urabi Revolt, 1882–1983*. Gainesville: University of Florida Press, 1988.

Memon, Muhammad Umar. *Ibn Taymiyya's Struggle against Popular Religion*. The Hague: Mouton, 1976.

Milton-Edwards, Beverley. *Islamic Politics in Palestine*. London: I. B. Tauris, 1996.

Mitchell, Richard P. *The Society of the Muslim Brothers*. New ed. New York: Oxford University Press, 1993.

Mitchell, Timothy. *Colonising Egypt*. Cambridge: Cambridge University Press, 1988.

Mohd Nor Wan Daud, Wan. *The Concept of Knowledge in Medieval Islam*. London: Mansell, 1989.

Momen, Moojan. *An Introduction to Shiʿi Islam*. New Haven: Yale University Press, 1985.

Moreen, V. Basch. "Risala-yi Sawaʿiq al-Yahud (The Treatise Lightning Bolts against the Jews) by Muhammad Baqir b. Muhammad Taqi al-Majlisi (d. 1699)." *Die Welt des Islams* 32 (1992): 177–95.

Moreh, Shmuel. "al-Jabarti's Attitude towards the ʿUlamaʾ of His Time." In Meir Hatina (ed.), *Guardians of Faith in Modern Times: ʿUlamaʾ in the Middle East*, pp. 47–63. Leiden: Brill, 2008.

Munson, Henry. *Religion and Power in Morocco*. New Haven: Yale University Press, 1993.

Murphy, Carly. *Passion for Islam*. New York: Scribner, 2002.

Mustafa, Tamir. "Conflict and Cooperation between the State and Religious Institutions in Contemporary Egypt." *International Journal of Middle East Studies* 32 (2000): 3–22.

Najjar, Fauzi M. "Egypt's Laws of Personal Status." *Arab Studies Quarterly* 10/3 (Summer 1988): 319–44.

Nakash, Yitzhak. *The Shiʿis of Iraq*. 2nd ed. Princeton, N.J.: Princeton University Press, 1994.

Newman, Daniel L. *An Imam in Paris: Account of a Stay in France by an Egyptian Cleric, 1826–1831*. London: Saqi Books, 2004.

Ohana, David. *The Promethean Passion: The Intellectual Origins of the Twentieth Century from Rousseau to Foucault* (Hebrew). Jerusalem: Bialik Institute, 2000.

Peskes, Esther. "The Wahhabiyya and Sufism in the Eighteenth Century." In F. De Jong and Bernd Radtke (eds.), *Islamic Mysticism Contested*, pp. 145–61. Leiden: Brill, 1999.

Peters, Rudolph. *Islam and Colonialism*. The Hague: Mouton Publishers, 1979.

———. "Islam and the Legitimation of Power: The Mahdi Revolt in the Sudan." *Zeitschrift der Morgenländischen Gesellschaft*, supplement 5: 409–20. 21. Deutscher Orientalistentag, 24. bis 29 Marz 1980, Ausgewählte Vorträge.

———. "Religious Attitudes towards Modernization in the Ottoman Empire." *Die Welt des Islams* 26 (1986): 76–105.

———. "Muhammad al-ʿAbbasi al-Mahdi (d. 1897): Grand Mufti of Egypt and His al-Fatawa al-Mahadiyya." *Islamic Law and Society* 1/1 (1994): 66–82.

———. "The Lion of Qasr al-Nil Bridge: The Islamic Prohibition of Images as an Issue in the Urabi Revolt." In Muhammad K. Masud, Brinkley Messick, and David S. Powers (eds.), *Islamic Legal Interpretation*, pp. 214–20. Cambridge, Mass.: Harvard University Press, 1996.

Petry, C. F. *The Civilian Elite of Cairo in the Later Middle Ages.* Princeton, N.J.: Princeton University Press, 1981.

Phelps, William R. C. "Political Journalism and the ʿUrabi Revolt." Ph.D. dissertation. Ann Arbor: University of Michigan, 1978.

Philipp, Thomas. "Feminism and Nationalist Politics in Egypt." In Lois Beck and Nikki Keddie (eds.), *Women in the Muslim World*, pp. 277–94. Cambridge: Cambridge University Press, 1978.

Philipp, Thomas, and Moshe Perlmann (eds.), ʿAbd al-Rahman al-Jabarti's History of *Egypt*. 4 vols. Stuttgart: Franz Steiner Verlag, 1994.

Piscatori, James P. *Islam in a World of Nation-States.* Cambridge: Cambridge University Press, 1986.

Porat, Yehoshuʿa. *The Palestinian-Arab National Movement, 1918–1929.* London: Frank Cass, 1974.

Provence, Michael. "A Nationalist Rebellion without Nationalists? Popular Mobilizations in Mandatory Syria, 1925–1926." In Nadine Méouchy and Peter Sluglett (eds.), *The British and French Mandates in Comparative Perspectives*, pp. 673–92. Leiden: Brill, 2004.

Qutb, Sayyid. *Social Justice in Islam*. Trans. John B. Hardie. Oneonte, N.Y.: Islamic Publications International, 2000.

———. *A Child from the Village*. Trans. and ed. with an introduction by John Calvert and William Shepard. Syracuse: Syracuse University Press, 2004.

Rafeq, Abdul-Karim. "The Ulama of Ottoman Jerusalem (16th–18th Centuries)." In Sylvia Aduld and Robert Hillenbrand (eds.), *Ottoman Jerusalem: The Living City, 1517–1917*, pp. 45–53. Jerusalem: Altajir World of Islam Trust, 2000.

Rahemtulla, Shadaab H. "Reconceptualizing the Contemporary Ulama: al-Azhar, Lay Islam and the Egyptian State." M.A. thesis. Burnaby, Simon Fraser University, 2007.

Ranson, Stewart, Alan Bryman, and Bob Hinings. *Clergy, Ministers and Priests.* London: Routledge, 1977.

Reid, Donald M. *Cairo University and the Making of Modern Egypt.* Cambridge: Cambridge University Press, 1990.

———. "Al-Azhar." In John L. Esposito (ed.), *The Oxford Encyclopedia of the Modern Islamic World*, vol. 1, pp. 168–71, 4 vols. New York: Oxford University Press, 1995.

———. "The Urabi Revolution and the British Conquest, 1879–1882." In M. W. Daly (ed.), *The Cambridge History of Egypt*, vol. 2, pp. 217–38. 2 vols. Cambridge: Cambridge University Press, 1998.

Reimer, Michael J. "Contradiction and Consciousness in ʿAli Mubarak's Description of al-Azhar." *International Journal of Middle East Studies* 29/1 (1997): 53–69.

Reports by His Majesty's Agent and Consul-General on the Finances, Administration and Condition of Egypt and Sudan in 1906. London: Harrison and Sons, 1907.

Roded, Ruth. "Tradition and Change in Syria during the Last Decades of Ottoman Rule: The Urban Elite of Damascus, Aleppo, Homs and Hama, 1876–1918." Ph.D. dissertation. University of Denver, 1984.

El-Rouayheb, Khaled. "The Myth of 'The Triumph of Fanaticism' in the Seventeenth-Century Ottoman Empire." *Die Welt des Islams* 48 (2008): 196–221.

Roy, Olivier. *Globalised Islam: The Search for a New Ummah*. London: Hurst, 2002.

Rubin, Uri. *Between Bible and Qurʾan*. Princeton, N.J: Darwin Press, 1999.

Said, Edward W. *Orientalism*. New York: Pantheon Books, 1979.

———. *Culture and Imperialism*. New York: Knopf, 1994.

Salem, Norma. *Habib Bourguiba, Islam and the Creation of Tunisia*. London: Croom Helm, 1984.

Salvatore, Armando. "After the State: Islamic Reform and the Implosion of Shariʿa." In idem (ed.), *Muslim Traditions and Modern Techniques of Power*, pp. 123–40. Münster: Lit Verlag, 2001.

Al-Sayyid-Marsot, Afaf Lutfi. "The Role of the Ulama in Egypt during the Early Nineteenth Century." In P. M. Holt (ed.), *Political and Social Change in Modern Egypt*, pp. 264–80. London: Oxford University Press, 1968.

Schielke, Samuli. "Hegemonic Encounters: Criticism of Saints-Day Festivals and the Formation of Modern Islam in Late 19th and Early 20th Century Egypt." *Die Welt des Islams* 47/3–4 (2007): 318–55.

Schilcher, Linda S. *Families in Politics: Damascus Factions and Estates of the Eighteenth and Nineteenth Centuries*. Stuttgart: Franz Steiner Verlag/Wiesbaden: Gambii, 1985.

Schimmel, Annemarie. *Mystical Dimensions of Islam*. Chapel Hill: University of North Carolina Press, 1975.

Schölch, Alexander. *Egypt for the Egyptians: The Socio-political Crisis in Egypt, 1878–1882*. London: Ithaca Press, 1981.

Schulze, Reinhard. *Die Rebellion der ägyptischen Fallahin, 1919*. Berlin: Baalbek Verlag, 1981.

———. *Islamischer Internationalismus im 20. Jahrhundert*. Leiden: Brill, 1990.

———. "Colonization and Resistance: The Egyptian Peasant Rebellion, 1919." In Ferhad Kazem and John Waterbury (eds.), *Peasants and Politics in the Modern Middle East*, pp. 171–202. Miami: Florida International University Press, 1991.

———. "Kolonisierung und Widerstand: die ägyptischen Bauernrevolten von 1919." In Alexander Schölch and Helmut Mejcher (eds.), *Die ägyptische Gesellschaft im 20. Jahrhundert*, pp. 11–54. Hamburg: Deutsches Orient-Institut, 1992.

Sedgwick, Mark J. *Sufism: The Essentials*. Cairo: American University in Cairo Press, 2000.

———. *Islam and Muslims: A Guide to Diverse Experience in a Modern World*. Boston: Intercultural Press, 2006.

Seikaly, Samir. "Coptic Communal Reform: 1860–1914." *Middle Eastern Studies* 6 (October 1970): 247–75.

Shaham, Ron. *Family and the Courts in Modern Egypt*. Leiden: Brill, 1997.

———. "Women as Expert Witnesses in Pre-Modern Islamic Courts." In idem (ed.), *Law, Custom, and Statute in the Muslim World*, pp. 41–65. Leiden: Brill, 2007.

———. "Western Scholars on the Role of the ʿUlamaʾ in the Adaptation of the Shariʿa to Modernity: A Critical Review." In Meir Hatina (ed.), *Guardians of Faith in Modern Times: ʿUlamaʾ in the Middle East*, pp. 171–92. Leiden: Brill, 2008.

Shaked, Haim. "The Views of Rifaʿa al-Tahtawi on Religion and the Ulama in State and Society." *Hamizrah Hehadash* (Hebrew) 16/3–4 (1966): 271–91.

———. "The Biographies of Ulama in ʿAli Mubarak's Khitat as a Source for the History of the Ulama in Nineteenth-Century Egypt." *Asian and African Studies* 7 (special issue, 1971): 41–76.

Sharabi, Hisham. *Arab Intellectuals and the West: The Formative Years, 1875–1914*. Baltimore: Johns Hopkins Press, 1970.

Sharkey, Heather J. "Empire and Muslim Conversion: Historical Reflections on Christian Missions in Egypt." *Islam and Christian-Muslim Relations* 16 (January 2005): 43–60.

Shaw, Stanford J. *The Jews of the Ottoman Empire and the Turkish Republic*. New York: New York University Press, 1991.

El-Shayyal, Gamal El-Din. "Some Aspects of Intellectual and Social Life in Eighteenth-Century Egypt." In P. M. Holt (ed.), *Political and Social Change in Modern Egypt*, pp. 117–32. London: Oxford University Press, 1968.

Shinar, Pessah. "ʿUlamaʾ, Marabouts and Government: An Overview of Their Relationships in the French Colonial Magrib." *Israel Oriental Studies* 10 (1980): 211–29.

Simon, Robert. *Ignác Goldziher: His Life and Scholarship as Reflected in His Works and Correspondence*. Leiden: Brill, 1986.

Sirriyeh, Elizabeth. *Sufis and Anti-Sufis*. Richmond, Surrey: Curzon, 1999.

———. "Whatever Happened to the Banu Jamaʿa? The Tale of a Scholarly Family in Ottoman Syria." *British Journal of Middle Eastern Studies* 28/1 (May 2001): 55–65.

Sivan, Emmanuel. *Radical Islam: Medieval Theology and Modern Politics*. New Haven: Yale University Press, 1990.

Skovgaard-Petersen, Jakob. *Defining Islam for the Egyptian State*. Leiden: Brill, 1997.

———. "Fatwas in Print." *Culture and History* 16 (1997): 73–88.

———. "Levantine State Muftis." In Elisabeth Özdalga (ed.), *Late Ottoman Society: The Intellectual Legacy*, pp. 274–88. London: RoutledgeCurzon, 2004.

Smith, Anthony D. *The Ethnic Origins of Nations*. Oxford: Blackwell, 1986.

Smith, Donald E. *Religion, Politics and Social Change in the Third World*. New York: Free Press, 1971.

Sonbol, Amira El-Azhary. "Introduction." In idem (ed.), *Women, the Family, and Divorce Laws in Islamic History*, pp. 1–20. Syracuse: Syracuse University Press, 1996.

——— (trans. and ed.). *The Last Khedive of Egypt: Memoirs of Abbas Hilmi II*. London: Ithaca, 1998.

Starret, Gregory. *Putting Islam to Work: Education, Politics and Religious Transformation in Egypt*. Berkeley: University of California Press, 1998.

Taji-Farouki, Shua. *A Fundamental Quest: Hizb al-Tahrir and the Search for the Islamic Caliphate*. London: Grey Seal, 1996.

Talmon-Heller, Daniella. *Islamic Piety in Medieval Syria: Mosques, Cemeteries and Sermons under the Zangids and Ayyubids, 1146–1260*. Leiden: Brill, 2008.

———. "ʿIlm, Shafaʿah and Barakah: The Resources of Ayyubid and Early Mamluk ʿUlamaʾ." *Mamluk Studies Review* 13/2 (2009): 23–45.

Tauber, Eliezer. "Rashid Rida as a Pan-Arabist before World War I." *Muslim World* 79/2 (1989): 102–12.

———. *The Arab Movements in World War I*. London: Frank Cass, 1993.

———. *The Emergence of the Arab Movements*. London: Frank Cass, 1993.

Taylor, Christopher S. *In the Vicinity of the Righteous: Ziyara and the Veneration of Muslim Saints in Late Medieval Egypt*. Leiden: Brill, 1999.

Tibi, Bassam. *Arab Nationalism: A Critical Enquiry*. New York: St. Martin's Press, 1981.

Toledano, Ehud R. *State and Society in Mid-Nineteenth-Century Egypt*. Cambridge: Cambridge University Press, 1990.

———. *Egypt on the Threshold of the Modern Age* (Hebrew). Tel Aviv: Ministry of Defense, 1996.

Towler, Robert. "The Social Status of the Anglican Minister." In R. Robertson (ed.), *Sociology of Religion*, pp. 443–50. Harmondsworth: Penguin Books, 1969.

Trimingham, Spencer. *The Sufi Orders in Islam*. New ed. Oxford: Oxford University Press, 1998.

Tritton, A. S. *The Caliphs and Their Non-Muslim Subjects*. London: Frank Cass, 1970 [1930].

Tsadik, Daniel. "The Legal Status of Religious Minorities: Imami Shiʿi Law and Iran's Constitutional Revolution." *Islamic Law and Society* 10 (2003): 376–408.

Tucker, Judith E. *In the House of the Law: Gender and Islamic Law in Ottoman Syria and Palestine*. Berkeley: University of California Press, 1998.

Van Ess, Josef. "Sufism and Its Opponents." In F. De Jong and Bernd Radtke (eds.), *Islamic Mysticism Contested*, pp. 22–44. Leiden: Brill, 1999.

Vatikiotis, P. J. "Muhammad ʿAbduh and the Quest for a Muslim Humanism." *Islamic Culture* 31 (1957): 109–26.

———. "Islam and the Foreign Policy of Egypt." In J. Harris Proctor (ed.), *Islam and International Relations*, pp. 121–57. New York: F. A. Praeger, 1965.

———. *Islam and the State*. New York: Croom Helm, 1987.

———. "Religion and State in Egypt." In idem, *The Middle East: from the End of Empire to the End of the Cold War*, pp. 117–31. London: Routledge, 1997.

Vikor, Knut S. *Sufi and Scholar on the Desert Edge*. Evanston: Northwestern University Press, 1995.

Voll, John O. "Old ʿUlamaʾ Families and Ottoman Influence in Eighteenth-Century Damascus." *American Journal of Arabic Studies* 3 (1975): 48–59.

———. "Sufi Orders." In John L. Esposito (ed.), *The Oxford Encyclopedia of the Modern Islamic World*, vol. 4, pp. 109–17. 4 vols. New York: Oxford University Press, 1995.

Weismann, Itzchak. *A Taste of Modernity: Sufism, Salafiyya and Arabism in Late Ottoman Damascus*. Leiden: Brill, 2001.

Willis, John Ralph. "The Fatwas of Condemnation." In Muhammad K. Masud, Brinkley Messick, and David S. Powers (eds.), *Islamic Legal Interpretation*, pp. 153–61. Cambridge, Mass.: Harvard University Press, 1996.

Winder, Bayly. "Islam as the State Religion—A Muslim Brotherhood View in Syria." *Muslim World* 44 (1954): 215–26.

Winter, Michael. *Egyptian Society under Ottoman Rule, 1517–1798*. London: Routledge, 1992.

al-Yassini, Ayman. *Religion and State in the Kingdom of Saudi Arabia*. Boulder: Westview Press, 1985.

Yazbak, Mahmoud. "Nabulsi Ulama in the Late Ottoman Period, 1864–1914." *International Journal of Middle East Studies* 29 (1997): 71–91.

Yousef, Hoda A. "Reassessing Egypt's Dual Systems of Education under Ismaʿil." *International Journal of Middle East Studies* 40/1 (February 2008): 109–30.

Zaman, Iftikhar. "Sunni Ulama." In John L. Esposito (ed.), *The Oxford Encyclopedia of the Modern Islamic World*, vol. 4, pp. 258–61. 4 vols. New York: Oxford University Press, 1995.

Zaman, Muhammad Qasim. *The Ulama in Contemporary Islam*. Princeton, N.J.: Princeton University Press, 2002.

Zartman, I. William (ed.). *Man, State and Society in the Contemporary Maghrib*. New York: Praeger, 1972.

Zeghal, Malika. *Gardiens de l'Islam: Les oulémas d'Al-Azhar dans l'Égypte contemporaine*. Paris: Presses de la Fondation Nationale des Sciences Politiques, 1996.

———. "Religion and Politics in Egypt: The Ulema of al-Azhar, Radical Islam and the State, 1952–1994." *International Journal of Middle East Studies* 31 (August 1999): 371–99.

———. "'The Recentering' of Religious Knowledge and Discourse: The Case of al-Azhar in Twentieth-Century Egypt." In Robert W. Hefner and Muhammad Qasim Zaman (eds.), *Schooling Islam: The Culture and Politics of Modern Muslim Education*, pp. 107–30. Princeton, N.J.: Princeton University Press, 2007.

Zetland, Lawrence Dundas. *Lord Cromer*. London: Hodder and Stoughton, 1932.

Zisenwine, Daniel. "ʿUlamaʾ, Tribalism and the National Struggle in Morocco, 1944–1956." In Meir Hatina (ed.), *Guardians of Faith in Modern Times: ʿUlamaʾ in the Middle East*, pp. 195–210. Leiden: Brill, 2008.

Zubaida, Sami. *Islam, the People and the State*. London: Routledge, 1989.

Index